THE LATINO NINETEENTH CENTURY

AMERICA AND THE LONG 19TH CENTURY

General Editors: David Kazanjian, Elizabeth McHenry, and Priscilla Wald

The Latino Nineteenth Century

Edited by
Rodrigo Lazo and Jesse Alemán

NEW YORK UNIVERSITY PRESS
New York

NEW YORK UNIVERSITY PRESS
New York
www.nyupress.org

© 2016 by New York University
All rights reserved

References to Internet websites (URLs) were accurate at the time of writing.
Neither the author nor New York University Press is responsible for URLs that may have
expired or changed since the manuscript was prepared.

ISBN: 978-1-4798-9683-7 (hardback)
ISBN: 978-1-4798-5587-2 (paperback)

For Library of Congress Cataloging-in-Publication data, please contact the Library of
Congress.

New York University Press books are printed on acid-free paper, and their binding materials
are chosen for strength and durability. We strive to use environmentally responsible suppli-
ers and materials to the greatest extent possible in publishing our books.

Manufactured in the United States of America

10 9 8 7 6 5 4 3 2 1

Also available as an ebook

CONTENTS

PREFACE

JESSE ALEMÁN

Although the chapters in this collection present a lot of new material, the book isn't so much a revision of literary history per se as it's a return to the circuits of texts, print cultures, artists, and intellectuals that constitute in real and imaginary ways the Latino nineteenth century. Initially, the volume emerged as a direct response to nineteenth-century American literary studies, which, as early as Stanley Williams's *The Spanish Background of American Literature*, gestures toward but never quite grasps what we're calling the Latino nineteenth century. The gesture implies an understanding that there's always been a greater context for American literature—the contiguous Americas, shared revolutionary histories, the Spanish language, and, more recently, rapidly changing population demographics. But American literary studies rarely reaches the Latino nineteenth century because American literature tends to uphold an English-only mentality, extending the laws of the land to the layout of literary history.

The following collection of chapters, however, situates "U.S. Latino/a" as a central literary, historical, and analytical category to foreground the significance and significant presence of Latino/a writers, texts, and readers in nineteenth-century American culture. Until now, many of the Latino/a texts and the lives of those who wrote and read them have suffered the same fate as Manuel Torres, who, as Emily Garcia poignantly explains in her chapter, remains buried in obscurity in the graveyard of Philadelphia's St. Mary's Catholic Church. In this grim light, the book inherits from Latin American studies and the Recovering the U.S. Hispanic Literary Heritage Project an understanding of the rich, complicated, and complementary histories that connect, divide, and redraw the Americas across literary, linguistic, national, and racial borders, where the term *Latino* is not, as some might assume, an anachronism but a marker of nineteenth-century transnationality that the following chapters excavate.

The Latino Nineteenth Century begins with an insistence on the legibility of Spanish-language texts that were written over—buried, if you will—by the logic and practice of an English-only approach to American literary history. Silly, naïve, and racist as he might be, Herman Melville's Amasa Delano has one up on most scholars of nineteenth-century American literature: He knows Spanish. So no matter how culturally critical nineteenth-century American literary studies can be, and there's been some canon-busting work out there, American literature, as a curriculum and field of study, often reproduces the national imaginary's impulse to subsume difference into a homogenizing narrative about Anglophone America—its young romanticism, free-floating racial guilt, horrifying civil war, and refortification just in time for the reality of modernity, all in English. Yet the writers, writings, and people who populate the Latino/a nineteenth century inhabited a Hispanophone world. Theirs is a world of Spanish-language print culture, circuits, readerships, and routes that, while not at all surprising for nineteenth-century America, prove more difficult to decipher and narrate in the largely Anglophone literary history of the United States. For us, this is the first intervention of the Latino/a nineteenth century: Our work insists on reading Spanish-language texts. No progressive, revisionist project for nineteenth-century American literary studies can get around this issue of language. We need as much fluency as silly Amasa to converse with nineteenth-century America, and even then, we still might misread its cues.

The second intervention is related to the first: The Latino/a nineteenth century is not the same tradition, movement, or aesthetic as the one emerging from New England, even if there are some historical overlaps, textual confluences, and authorial connections. Rather, the Latino/a nineteenth century displaces the center of American literary history across the United States, from Florida to Philadelphia, New York to New Mexico, and Texas to California; it also dispossesses American literature from the United States entirely, traversing Mexico, Cuba, Argentina, Chile, and Guatemala, for example, with an errant spirit traceable sometimes only through the print culture it left behind. So, if the book's first intervention is one of language, the second is one of geography to insist that, especially with the industrial innovations that circulated people, paper, and print with surprising ease, it is a deliberate Anglocentric ideological gesture to continue to fancy New England as the center of American literature and print culture. It was, to be sure, a site of literary culture, but as it turns out, so were New Orleans, Philadelphia, Key West, and Santa Fe, to name a few locales within the United States that circulated Spanish-language writings to Latino/a readers. Add Cuba, Chile, Argentina, Guatemala, and Mexico to the list, and the persistence of New England in nineteenth-century American literary studies begins to look strategically provincial.

The fugitive nature of the Latino nineteenth century is all the more reason to track it textually, geographically, biographically, and historically, for only a combination of gestures can map the movement of bodies, lives, texts, and communities that struggled to survive in the belly of the beast. We present some of those survivors here and look forward to finding more to come.

ACKNOWLEDGMENTS

We begin by thanking the contributors to the volume. Their intellectual energy, insight, and enthusiasm made it possible for this project to develop from a conversation into a collection of chapters. The idea of a book emerged from a panel at the first conference sponsored by C19: The Society of Nineteenth-Century Americanists at Penn State in 2010. While the session was lively and well attended, the presenters walked away thinking that U.S. nineteenth-century studies had little interest in the concerns of Latino studies. Nevertheless, C19 continued to be an important venue for conversation and hosted "Latino Nineteenth Century" panels at its next two conferences, in 2012 and 2014. Kirsten Silva Gruesz and José Aranda were there from the start and helped us conceptualize the collection. The new Latina/o Studies Association conference also hosted sessions related to this project at its first gathering in Chicago in 2014, and some of our contributors joined us after that important meeting.

We thank the School of Humanities at the University of California, Irvine, and particularly former Dean Vicki Ruiz for hosting a workshop that allowed some of the contributors to bring first drafts of papers and share them in a seminar discussion. Cristina Rodriguez helped to organize the workshop. The UC Irvine Humanities Commons provided a publication support grant. At the University of New Mexico, we're grateful for the unfettered access to the Leon Howard Memorial Library, where we holed up for a long weekend to work among Howard's books, and we appreciate the colleagues in the English Department's American Literary Studies group for their sustained commitment to redefine the field.

Our editor at New York University Press, Eric Zinner, offered encouragement from the project's earliest moment. He has been a consistent supporter of this book and Latino studies as a field. We also thank Karen Roybal and Alicia Nadkarni for assistance with the preparation and submission of the manuscript. Sections of Chapter 12 appeared in different form in *Exile and Revolution: José D. Poyo, Key West, and Cuban Independence* by Gerald E. Poyo (Gainesville: University Press of Florida, 2014): 168–84, and are reprinted with the permission of the University Press of Florida.

We thank our friends, colleagues, and families for their ongoing support. In New Mexico, thanks to Daniel Worden, Marissa Greenberg, and Randall Gann for fortifying friendships, and Melina Vizcaíno-Alemán for her tenacious, fierce love. In Irvine, thanks to the Department of English for its ongoing support and to Arlene Keizer, Lilith Mahmud, and Erika Hayasaki for being "Suspicious Minds"; much love to Amy DePaul, Gabriel Lazo, and Francisco Lazo.

Introduction

Historical Latinidades and Archival Encounters

RODRIGO LAZO

On January 9, 1878, Ramón de Contador y Muñiz brought in the new year in San Francisco with the thirty-third issue of his newspaper *El Eco de la Raza Latina*. Proposing shared interests among populations in the United States, Latin America, and Spain, Contador described his paper as "el organo de los intereses materiales y morales de España y los españoles en particular, y de toda la raza latina en general" or in his own English description "the organ of the moral, political and commercial interests of all the latine race." (Fluent in French, Contador inserted the Francophone feminine *latine*.) Like many other Spanish-language newspapers in the nineteenth-century United States, *El Eco de la Raza Latina* included news from Europe and the Americas, advertisements for local Spanish-speaking businesses, and literary offerings: a selection from the novelist Benito Pérez Galdós's *Episodios nacionales* and Contador's own translation of Victor Hugo's *Histoire d'un crime*. And also like so many other Spanish-language newspapers in U.S. history, *El Eco de la Raza Latina* remains today as a fragment. Only the solitary issue of 1878 is at the UC Berkeley libraries.

The texts of the Latino nineteenth century come to us in pieces. And yet despite fragmented remains, archival holdings register the views and aspirations of people who share (or at least engage with) concerns related to bilingualism, social formation, and political organization. In the case of Contador's paper, a commonality is presented under the banner of a "Latin" people who can read his Spanish-language paper. Among the topics covered are some that are still relevant in the Spanish-language media almost 140 years later: a census of "Spanish" populations, methods for learning the English language, and the latest news from Mexico, Ecuador, and Colombia.

Contador's use of the term *la raza Latina* provides a lexical antecedent to the present-day Latino/Latina, and thus it introduces continuity and difference—continuity in the sense that some nineteenth-century populations first adopted the term *Latino/Latina* in reference to themselves but difference because this usage was clearly influenced by a genealogical claim to European connections associated with a broad geographic and historical sense of "Latin." In the nineteenth century, the words *Latino* and *Latina* appeared throughout the Americas not only to name América Latina but also to posit a people, *"la raza Latina,"* with the latter claiming a European antecedent that was Catholic and went back to Rome. Contador adopts a hemispheric and transatlantic usage as he seeks to circulate his newspaper in the "United States, Cuba, Spain, Mexico, Central and South America," searching for readers in various countries. Arturo Ardao, Mónica Quijada, and Walter Mignolo are among scholars who have studied the idea of Latin America, which emerged as a pan-Latin formation with a Eurocentric bent that connected *criollos* in the Americas to France.[1] Most important, the notion of Latin America was used in contradistinction to an Anglo-Saxon America, the latter represented by the United States. In his *América Latina y la latinidad*, Ardao traced the term not only to various intellectuals from Latin America (most prominently José María Torres Caicedo and his poem "Las dos Américas") but also to the French intellectual Michel Chevalier, who sought to build an alliance between Mexico and France as part of "Latin" people.[2] The Spanish *raza*, closer in its historical usage to *lineage* than to the twentieth-century English *race*, was marshaled to argue for the achievements of a people going back to Roman greatness. Chevalier, for one, positioned Mexico as a site where the greatness of a Latin (French-inflected) Catholicism could respond to the Protestant North.[3]

The prominence of France in the notion of *"la raza Latina"* explains a curious excursus in a letter by María Amparo Ruiz de Burton, whose novels are an important dimension of the Latino nineteenth century. In 1869, Ruiz de Burton invokes *"la raza Latina"* in a passage excoriating the United States and Manifest Destiny: "La historia no miente y la historia nos dice cuan gloriosa ha sido la carrera de la raza Latina" (History does not lie and history tells us how glorious has been the development of *la raza Latina*). But Ruiz de Burton clarified, only *la raza Latina* under a government in conjunction with its people. As if influenced by Chevalier himself, she positions France as a superior example: "De las naciones Latinas, ¿cuál es la única que progresa? La Francia. . . . ¿Por qué? porque es la única que adoptando todos los adelantes del siglo. . . . en ideas y materialmente—ha conservado un gobierno que es el único capaz de manejar a los franceses" (Of all the Latin nations which is the only one that progresses? France. . . . Why? Because it is the only one that by adopting all of the advances of the century . . . in ideas and materially—has maintained a government that is the only one capable of leading the French).[4] (Given this type of French turn, it is not surprising that the Chilean migrant to California Vincente Pérez Rosales sometimes identified as French, as Juan Poblete tells us in his contribution to this collection.) Ruiz de Burton's class-inflected Francophilia differs from Contador y Muñiz's commercially viable grouping in *El Eco de la Raza Latina*. And yet both make necessary a historical interpretation of the term.

Latino/a is not an anachronism in the nineteenth century, either in usage or in its communal longings, even if *la raza Latina* can introduce celebrations of France and Rome that are at odds with contemporary implications of the term. Contador's paper shows us how Spanish-speaking populations established linguistic and cultural connections, in this case mediated by print culture, while Ruiz de Burton reminds us of the sociopolitical complications of assuming the form of those connections. The unexpected historical contexts informing various types of Latino affiliation are a major concern of the articles in *The Latino Nineteenth Century*. This collection registers Latino aspirations at various points in the century while engaging with partial, sometimes fragmented, and regularly dispersed textual remains. We seek to open research into writing and textual production that may move us in unexpected directions and to new archival sites. In doing so, the chapters are in dialogue with the contemporary concerns of Latino studies and respond to the limitations of nationalist U.S. literature and regionalist Latin American studies.

The relationship of the nineteenth century (and other centuries) to Latino studies is vexed by the field's own history—its emergence in response to civil rights movements of the late twentieth century. Because Latino studies is often focused on the past fifty years, historically minded scholars raise questions about the effects of deploying contemporary investments in other centuries. Some years ago, Quentin Skinner, writing about the history of ideas, described the challenges of historical vision driven by a preconceived paradigm: "The perpetual danger, in our attempts to enlarge our historical understanding, is thus that our expectations about what someone must be saying or doing will themselves determine that we understand the agent to be doing something which he would not—or even could not—himself have accepted as an account of what he *was* doing."[5] As Skinner describes it, the anachronistic assumptions of the present (a contemporary "understanding" of the past) would drive the interpretation of historical actions and texts.[6] But that assumes a stable present-day epistemology. In the case of Latino studies, that would require a denotative sense of the term *Latino* that is deployed across time as an analytical starting point. But is there such an understanding? *Latino* is a word that is used to signify an identity, a concept, an ethnic label, a demographic category, and an opportunity for debate. Its use today sets off a tension between a pan-national umbrella and specific national designations, such as Puerto Rican and Chicano/a.[7]

This naming instability stretches into the nineteenth century, as "*la raza Latina*" shows, so that it is possible to consider *Latino* in a longer historical span of time, a *longue durée* signaling the difficulty of naming a population with common elements while conjuring a dispersal of experiences and meanings. In both English and Spanish publications of the nineteenth century, as scholars in this collection and elsewhere have also noted, the range of words used to describe people included *Hispano-americanos, Americanos,* Spanish, Spanish American, and creoles, as well as a variety of nation-specific designations, sometimes in combination (e.g., Cuban Spaniard). In relation to these usages, Raúl Coronado has written, "The difficulty is in tracking the shift in discursive formations that allowed individuals to identify in various ways, from Spanish American to Latino, an issue linked with the question of whether nation, race, or both serve as the ontological basis of identity."[8] And yet it is possible to approach this challenge historically and in relation to the textual remains that are available. *Spanish American* was commonly used in the 1810s and 1820s in the U.S. Northeast, while *Latino/a* as an adjective begins circulating in the late 1830s in various parts of the Americas. As a result of migration from the southern Americas to the United States and the U.S. acquisition of territories, sometimes ethnic identification was linked to bilingual negotiations. Ruiz de Burton, whose work again proves instructive, deploys one of the most curious terms early in her novel *The Squatter and the Don* (1885). Speaking of laws enacted after the U.S.–Mexico War that would dispossess Mexican Californians of their land and effectively nullify provisions in the Treaty of Guadalupe Hidalgo, Clarence Darrell says, "I only wish I could wipe out those stains on our national honor by repealing at once laws so discreditable to us. Yes, the more so, as they bear directly upon the most defenseless, the most powerless of our citizens—the orphaned Spano-Americans."[9] Darrell's *Spano-Americans* emphasizes that the population in California had become part of the U.S. nation, even as he seeks an adjectival form that would recognize a cultural difference from Anglo America. Although an awkward Anglicization of *Hispano*, *Spano-Americans* is no more a misnomer than any other term circulating at the time. Instead, it registers the difficulty of naming difference that changes over the century. Today some critics prefer the use of *Latino* to signal "how frail a word is / when faced with the thing it names," to quote the poetry of Julia Álvarez, while others use *Latina/o* to specify a gendered reference more directly. Still others, especially in the blogosphere, opt for the gender-neutral *Latin@*.[10]

Chapters in *The Latino Nineteenth Century* complicate assumptions about fixed terminology, modifying terms and showing how texts and conditions can help us rethink the historical dimensions of *Latino*. What are the material conditions, spatial trajectories, hemispheric movements, and forms of colonization and war that influence texts of the Latino nineteenth century? And how are the textual remains connected to people who struggled to build communities, organize political movements, fight in wars, make their way through a new and sometimes hostile country, and publish their writing?

Trans-American contexts at times demand that the term *Latino* be used with modifiers and in light of specific historical conditions. Kirsten Silva Gruesz opens the collection by introducing the notion of an "errant Latino," which she develops through a reading of José Irisarri's novel *El cristiano errante* (The Errant Christian, 1847). Gruesz's approach is to read the nineteenth century against a set of present-day expectations regarding immigrants and their assumed trajectories. She argues that today the redemptive belief in immigration as an historical dimension of the United States and the exclusionary conception of undocumented people as lawbreakers and intruders both rely on an assumption of intention on the part of the immigrant. But what if we conceive of an errant subject as one who is not tied to a particular nation-state but rather moves in and with contingency, seeking a new and alternative way to grapple with the legacy of colonial domination and neoimperialism in the Americas? Such contingent readings are important for all of this collection's chapters, whose range of study turns to texts by a diplomat from Spain, a Chilean Forty-Niner, Argentine travelers, and a pair of brothers who fought in the U.S. Civil War and Cuba's Ten Years War.

Robert McKee Irwin also responds with a geographic challenge to the use of *Latino* as a U.S.-based identity category. Introducing the term *Almost Latino*, Irwin raises questions about those migrating people whose movement to the United States is truncated or made impossible. What happens to those who go back or are deported before they can claim or negate a U.S.-based ethnic label? What about those who undertake migrations but never make it and thus end up somewhere between Latin America and the United States? Irwin's *Almost Latino* raises important questions about the relationship of U.S. Latinidades to Latin American beginnings, while also reminding us of the importance of epistemological limitations. In another approach to these types of questions, Jesse Alemán returns to *trans-American* as a term for the two Cuban-born U.S. citizens in his chapter, describing them as "hemispheric citizens whose sense of belonging traversed the Americas rather than being bound by its national borders."

Modifiers such as *errant* and *almost*, as well as a notion of *"la raza Latina"* and hemispheric subjectivity, present spatial conceptions of Latinidades that cross the Americas. Because of its geographic reach, work on Latino writing must consider historical conditions across various countries and be done in at least two languages. But Spanish-language materials are at odds with Anglophone conceptions of nineteenth-century U.S. literature. Many practitioners of American (U.S.) literature have not taken seriously the historical concerns of Latino studies, in part because such a move would involve the reorganization of what Donald Pease called a field-Imaginary, in other words the field's "fundamental syntax—its tacit assumptions, convictions, primal words, and the charged relations binding them together."[11] While Latino literature written in the United States after the 1960s is predominantly in English, the archival remains of texts written prior to 1900 are mostly in Spanish (with notable exceptions to both). As Raúl Coronado argues in his contribution to this collection, U.S. literary history has proven resistant to the revisionary strains of Latino studies in part because of the demands of working across languages, literary traditions, and historical contexts. The tendency in academic study to split the Americas into North/South or Spanish/English or U.S. American/Latin American is a hindrance to considering texts that cross those divisions in their contents or print culture histories.

The nineteenth century marks the establishment of nation-states in the Americas and the invigoration of nationalistic thinking, but it also presents for Latino America numerous cases in which intellectuals and writers are on the move. As such, the analytical framework should expand to encompass multiple traditions and nations, even multiple colonial legacies. Just as an Anglophone world has to contend with England, so does the explication of Hispanophone texts of the United States necessarily need to engage Spain and its colonial legacy. In Coronado's chapter, these methodological considerations lead to a reading of a pamphlet published by Valentín de Foronda, a wealthy nobleman from Spain who served as that country's general counsel in Philadelphia from 1801 to 1807. Foronda's presence emphasizes the weight of colonial legacy on early Latino writing.

Because texts written in Spanish do not necessarily fit into Anglophone literary categories, the Latino nineteenth century is at odds with forms of U.S. literary history driven by the canonical desires of U.S. American literature and the fetishization of major writers. The ongoing consideration of the "great American novel," even when approached with some skepticism, continues to be an Anglophone undertaking.[12] Over the past four decades, scholars trying to build a more comprehensive version of U.S. literature have sought to expand its texts and articulate minority dimensions within it, seeking writings by people from various ethnic groups and making overtures toward new geographies of interpretation, including the conceptions of hemispheric American studies. Multilingual America has been an important consideration for scholars such as Susan Gillman, Werner Sollors, Marc Shell, Anna Brickhouse, and Ralph Bauer. At the same time, a nationalist wing of U.S. literature continues to foster extraordinary interest in the usual suspects, writers associated with the so-called American Renaissance and its Anglophone heirs. The construction of U.S. literature has always been influenced by a sense that its major authors were following an Anglophone tradition of writing. In other words, F. O. Matthiessen's Renaissance was American as a westward continuation of the English Renaissance. This is not to say that everyone accepted the New England–centric focus of the American Renaissance. Nevertheless, Walden Pond and the Old Manse continue to exert an influential pull. In contrast to the centripedal force of national U.S. literature, a Latino nineteenth century calls for engagement with hemispheric geographies, a variety of textual production, and multiple archival sites.

This collection's challenge to late-twentieth-century field-epistemology is also important for Latin American studies, which has had a vexed relationship with Latino studies. A version of Latin American studies that refuses to engage with the United States as an important site of migration overlooks the historical role of figures who moved in and out of cities such as Philadelphia, New York, New Orleans, and San Francisco. *The Latino Nineteenth Century* presents the U.S. trajectories of diplomats, travelers, migrants, and residents of colonized spaces who might otherwise be situated in Latin American studies and even written as national figures. In her contribution, Carmen Lamas questions the effect on scholarship of the presumed separation of U.S. Latino and Latin American studies. What if we were to consider subjects along a "Latino continuum," she asks? In a suggestive interpretation of writing and translation work by the Cuban revolutionary, lawyer, and writer Raimundo Cabrera (1852–1923), Lamas challenges scholars to delve into the Latin American studies archive to locate figures whose residency, even temporary, in the United States help us uncover unknown sites of the Latino nineteenth century. Carrie Tirado Bramen also reads from the South, drawing on the writing of Argentines who held diplomatic posts and traveled in the late-nineteenth-century United States. This writing, Bramen argues, "reverses the dominant gaze by showing the United States as the cultural 'other'" and thus allows for a critical response both to U.S. and Argentine forms of exceptionalism. Both Bramen and Lamas discuss people who were in the United States for only a brief period and yet produced writing and translations that engage with important dimensions of the Latino nineteenth century. Although the diplomats in Bramen's chapter are Argentine, their writing unsettles the organization of knowledge along a U.S./Latin American opposition and suggests the need for ongoing consideration of movement in American spatial conceptions.

The sense of a Latino continuum reminds us of the ongoing need to excavate archival sites in search of a multiplicity of texts: diaries, newspaper clippings, and letters. It is no surprise that many of our contributors have been involved with the Recovering the U.S. Hispanic Literary Heritage Project, which since its inception in 1992 has been an archival undertaking. Nicolás Kanellos's monumental work establishing the Project deployed *recovery* as a term that included the locating of texts that had not been seen for decades or even centuries and also collecting, indexing, and republishing them.[13] Kanellos's contribution to this collection, a return to the work of the Afro–Puerto Rican printer and biographer Sotero Figueroa, whose trajectories brought him into contact with José Martí and Arturo Schomburg in New York, exemplifies the work done by the project over the past twenty-five years. Recovery scholars have turned to archival sites, including at times personal collections, in order to paint a panorama of Hispanic literary heritage. The Recovery Project and Arte Público Press have made available to contemporary readers the anonymous novel *Jicoténcal* (Philadelphia, 1826), the poetry collection *El laúd del desterrado* (New York, 1858), and the immigrant novel *Lucas Guevara* (New York, 1914), among other books, and have also published several volumes of articles by scholars whose criticism engaged with the newly recovered publications and introduced still other texts that were not always available to a wide readership.[14] In turn, the Project has sought to build an archive. At first institutionalized in its home at the University of Houston, parts of that archive are now available through the sale to libraries of a database run by the company EBSCO.[15] An archive introduces a series of problems related to occlusion, partial recuperation, and a fiction of knowledge, as Agnes Lugo-Ortiz has pointed out in her discussion of *Herencia: The Anthology of Hispanic Literature of the United States*.[16] But archives in various forms are also sites of potential for the ongoing emergence of the Latino nineteenth century.

Scholars working in the historical dimensions of Latino studies are faced with an archive that is dispersed, multilingual, and incomplete.

This material raises questions about the notion of an archive (singular) versus archives that are not always and not easily accessible. National archives established to represent a nation-state either forget certain people or frame mobile subjects in relation to a national lens, sometimes cutting out experiences in various countries. An archive is a problem more than a place. As I have argued elsewhere, turns in archive theory have shown the ontological impossibility of the archive, affected by the slippage of a defining category and the contradictions it attempts to contain. Instead, certain forms of scholarship call for a turn to "migrant archives" that are not widely available and break away from a standard language and official stories.[17]

Archival encounters—their imperatives, possibilities, and limitations—are an important dimension of the Latino nineteenth century, a periodization that calls for a reconsideration of what counts as an archive. The traditional repository of information may not be the only place to find texts and contexts, and that calls for venturing beyond the building as a repository of documents. For Emily García, one such archival site is St. Mary's Church in Philadelphia, which displays a plaque celebrating the contributions of Manuel Torres, an early exile to what was then the newly founded United States. Settling in Philadelphia and becoming a parishioner of that church in the first decades of the century, Torres engaged with republican government as it was emerging in his new country and fostered a conversation with independence movements in Latin America, prompting the newspaper editor William Duane to call Torres "the Franklin of the southern world." The plaque shows how the search in new sites alters what can function as an archive and why it is important to bring it forward. While the plaque celebrates Torres, he is largely forgotten, even in St. Mary's Church today. At the time of his death in 1822, he was widely known in the United States, and newspapers across the country celebrated his appointment as the first ambassador from a new South American country, received by a U.S. president, James Monroe. A month after that meeting, Torres died, and his funeral procession included an armed infantry corps and four separate bands of instruments and was estimated to have drawn 20,000 people in Philadelphia.[18] The recovery of Torres challenges a tendency in U.S. society to exclude or forget certain cultural and political resonances, particularly those that emerge from immigrant communities whose populations are not easily integrated into an Anglo or a black/ white conception of the nation.

The archives of the Latino nineteenth century sometimes point to pieces and partial information rather than a book with a glossy cover. In José Aranda's chapter, the metaphor of a collision speaks to the contradictory effect created when scholars go into archives with particular expectations. What if newly located information challenges such an expectation? Because archives operate under an organizing term, most noticeably the *national* archives of a particular nation-state, they foster certain commitments and even ideologies. What are we to make of the textual remains that are at odds or even challenge the archival designation *Hispanic* or a more particular term such as *Chicano/a*? For Aranda, archival holdings point to the need to remake the nineteenth century in relation to not only whom we study but also what we read. He writes, "[T]he multi-regional presence of the Spanish language press in this period alone makes evident how far the field of nineteenth century studies still needs to expand and revise just to incorporate only one aspect of a Latino nineteenth century." As we have seen with the newspaper *El Eco de la Raza Latina*, these periodicals are sometimes available in pieces.[19] John Alba Cutler calls the remains of short fiction in the periodical press a "fugitive archive," and the errancy Gruesz associates with migration might also be a way to consider newspapers.

The importance of the periodical press and the challenges of recovering it are an inspiration for ongoing research across the Americas. Newspapers, for example, added an important component to Gruesz's *Ambassadors of Culture* (2002), an influential book-length study that shifted a focus from specific Chicano or Cuban dimensions and adopted "a nongenealogical view of Latino identity grounded in a larger web of transamerican perceptions and contacts."[20] If anything, the nineteenth-century U.S. Spanish-language press crosses national groups and nations so as to create proto-Latino alliances. Contributors to *The Latino Nineteenth Century* turn to newspapers for information but also read the papers themselves as exhibiting a material condition of Latinidad in a country that has not always preserved its Spanish-language materials. Cutler recovers two important stories and traces their appearances in the Spanish-language periodical press across different parts of the United States and the Americas. "[T]he short story's literary genealogies are distinct in Spanish and English," he writes, recognizing difference in both social content and literary form and bringing forward a hemispheric approach. Cutler's article suggests that what Meredith McGill has called a "culture of reprinting" stretches into the Spanish-language periodical press and should be considered across the Americas.

Materials pulled out of archives create a variety of hermeneutic difficulties and possibilities. This prompts Coronado to propose that we consider Latino "textualities" rather than emphasize generic categories and literary forms that may not be relevant. Sometimes the documents come as unsigned pamphlets or articles and cannot be so easily placed in a container, even if that container takes the form of academic institutions: field formation, books, centers of research. The documents of a Latino past point as much to multiplicity and flight as they do to something that we might call heritage. In other words, they point away from a central holding and toward movement.

The Latino nineteenth century opens to textual multiplicity as opposed to prescriptive points that define text or identity in the historical period. Here "multiplicity" is not so much numerical, not solely a reference to a large number of discrete objects, but rather a reference to degrees of difference. A numerical multiplicity would imply division among a set of units. Instead, "textual multiplicity" points to many kinds and many qualities, not always quantifiable because they point to interior states and degrees of representation. Gilles Deleuze associates this type of multiplicity with succession, heterogeneity, and difference in kind, "a *virtual and continuous* multiplicity that cannot be reduced to numbers."[21] Textual multiplicity emerges in the range of conditions presented by the texts. And this multiplicity engages with lived experiences in various sites.

One of the goals of the collection is to consider the relationship of textual remains to the lived experiences of the people who make up the Latino nineteenth century. In some articles, the emphasis is not on textuality per se but on how sources such as the periodical press allow us to recuperate historical circumstances and the agency of the people involved. Gerald Poyo, for example, offers a meticulously researched reconstruction of Cuban exile politics in late-nineteenth-century Key West that depicts the importance of U.S. legislative and governmental positions to transnational community formations. Even as they organized to oppose Spanish colonialism on the home island, Cubans were very active in local politics, church groups, baseball leagues, and local businesses. "The ease with which Cubans became United States citizens to defend their local social and economic interests betrayed an adamant rejection of Spanish nationality," Poyo writes. In other words, despite a vision that kept its eyes on Cuba (and thus could be seen as one example of a series of hemispheric concerns), the local site was tremendously important in this community. Poyo's article is also a reminder of the on-going need for narrative history in the recovery of the Latino nineteenth century.

Even as they organized politically and elected some of their own to office, Cubans in Key West also faced discrimination and even threats of lynching, thus facing manifestations of racism in a period that saw the emergence of legally sanctioned segregation. Latino experiences with race and racism throughout the century are affected not only by histori-cal conditions and geographic location but also by a particular person's skin tone and class position. In U.S. Latino history, some figures are con-sidered white and/or elite in their home countries, which in his response Ralph Bauer points out is a colonial effect that placed *criollos* in Span-ish America toward the top of a hierarchy that denigrated indigenous populations and slaves. But once *criollos* enter the United States, they must confront a different racial taxonomy inspired by an Anglo/Latin opposition that reads a racial distinction into culture and appearance. In the most pernicious cases, this distinction is marshaled in support of a presumed Anglo American nation-state that would exclude Lati-nos. In his contribution, Juan Poblete focuses on the writings of Vicente Pérez Rosales—a politician, merchant, and miner—to show how Chil-eans and other economic migrants in California in the wake of the war against Mexico were racialized into a single category in opposition to an Anglo American notion of citizenship. For Poblete, the racism and dis-criminatory structural effect of this treatment among Gold Rush min-ers is an early indication of "the category of the illegal alien that would have such a long, constitutive, and productive history in the state to this day." Reading history into the present and vice versa, Poblete empha-sizes the structural effects of a U.S.-based Latinizing process that draws in many countries and people in contradistinction to an imagined U.S. white citizenry. What becomes clear is that local racial formations such as those that emerged in California in 1849 are not isolated but rather intertwined with an economic network that sometimes flows back into other parts of the Americas. Poblete also turns the question of racial national formation on Pérez Rosales's Chile, because Pérez returns to his country and promotes German immigration as a way to build what he conceives as an industrious national population. Like Bramen, Poblete also interprets the U.S.-based experience of writer/travelers in relation to their home countries.

Those who move from one part of the Americas to another grapple with racial formations in more than one place, even as they face the discursive and juridical demands of presumed connections between race (or color) and national belonging. Marissa K. López returns to Ruiz de Burton's *The Squatter and the Don* to argue that the novel complicates a notion of a white and healthy national U.S. subject that does not include populations of Mexican descent after the U.S.–Mexico War. Looking at the role of trains and railroads in the novel and their relationship to bodies, López proposes that a Latino dismodern negates a hierarchy of health that would separate Anglo Americans from a putatively unhealthy or disabled Mexican subjectivity. Instead of a binary opposition, Ruiz de Burton's novel offers what López calls "a series of faulty bodies" that are at odds with a notion of an idealized and perfect white national subject. López is among contributors to the collection who navigate the contours of racial formation and remind us that the Latino nineteenth century complicates black/white readings of the history of U.S. racism. That is not to say that racism against blacks was not an important concern in the Latino nineteenth century.

How did Latino subjects respond to conditions for blacks in the United States, especially considering that many countries in the Americas had their own histories of slavery and black/white racism? Laura Lomas confronts that question directly by turning to late-nineteenth-century urban contexts that called for engagement with racism against blacks. Lomas reads Francisco Gonzalo "Pachín" Marín, of Puerto Rico, alongside José Martí and the labor organizer Lucy Eldine Gonzalez Parsons. In a suggestive contribution, Lomas argues that a class- and race-conscious Latinidad emerged in the late 1800s, particularly in relation to Afro-Latino labor politics with connections to the Caribbean. She writes that this Latinidad called for "an end to a quotidian experience of

discrimination, disdain and exclusion on the basis of nonnative pronunciation in English, bias against a 'swarthy' or 'half-breed' appearance,
or stereotypes about how Latin American countries and their peoples
should relate to the country and people of the United States." Lomas
brings forward the anarchist and labor politics experienced by Martí
and Pachín Marín in New York, so that the urban experience becomes
an important dimension of how these figures considered racial discrimination and their notions of Latinidad. Moving beyond the oft-cited essay
"Our America," one of the neocanonical pieces of the Latino nineteenth
century, Lomas argues that "anti-racism became conjoined to class critique through Martí's attentive observation of Lucy Parsons' oratory and
through his close association with Afro-Latino/a collaborators."

While this collection does not dwell on major figures, Martí and Ruiz
de Burton continue to raise crucial questions for the Latino nineteenth
century. Their importance is not only the result solely of literary production but of the types of questions they raise: What are the economic
and class dimensions of hierarchies along racial lines? How does gender
enter forms of discrimination, particularly as majority cultures in the
United States encounter and engage with women from countries such
as Mexico? How does movement throughout the Americas complicate
national affiliations and historical conceptions?

Among Martí's collaborators in New York was Sotero Figueroa, whose
work took him from Puerto Rico to New York and on to Cuba after 1898.
As a printer and newspaper editor, Figueroa participated in the late-
century debates about war and race that stretched from the United States
to the Caribbean. Kanellos reconsiders Figueroa's biographical writing,
which was itself an attempt to recover the contributions of blacks in the
Caribbean and ranged from Toussaint L'Ouverture to a local educator in
Puerto Rico. Figueroa's biographical pieces were no less than a revisionary attempt to write back into history subjects who had been excluded
by structures of domination in their racist societies. Kanellos situates
Figueroa as a precursor to but also contemporary of Schomburg, whose
archival work has become important to African American history and
literature.

The different experiences of intellectuals in late-century New York
and those in early Philadelphia remind us that the nineteenth century
is a domain that is unwieldy and expansive. The collection offers the

contours of textual changes over the century. Given the difficulty of cutting off historical conditions at a particular date, it is no surprise that scholars often speak of a long nineteenth century. Not so much a period—which is usually associated with a mode (romanticism or realism), an intellectual movement (transcendentalism or *modernismo*), or a major writer (the age of Whitman or of Martí)—the nineteenth century marks a duration that allows for a variety of voices that emerge in tandem with a series of historical events. *The Latino Nineteenth Century* offers the contours of changes in textual production over the decades. In the early "Spanish American" decades before 1830, texts are produced in conjunction with Latin America's wars of independence and attendant hemispheric and transatlantic networks of migration and publication. (For scholars working in U.S.-based American studies, the various wars of independence in the Americas suggest the limitations of using the term "the early Republic.") In the mid–nineteenth century, which brings on the U.S.–Mexico War and the threats of Manifest Destiny, newspapers and other periodicals become a dominant mode of publication and communication for Latino intellectuals. And in the latter part of the century, a growing body of literary texts and periodicals engage with the growing influence of the U.S. empire, which culminates in U.S. intervention in Cuba's war for independence.

The Latino Nineteenth Century seeks new geographical and historical trajectories that can alter a nation-based approach to defining important historical moments. In Jesse Alemán's article, the experiences of the brothers Adolfo and Frederic Cavada open a reconsideration of the relationship between the U.S. Civil War and Cuba's Ten Years War. Having fought in both conflicts, the Cavadas lived through subjective experiences in two countries and two languages, leading Alemán to position them as trans-American subjects. How does the timeline of Ten Years War, 1868–78, add another dimension to what is widely considered in nineteenth-century American literature a milestone and dividing line: 1865? How does the ongoing U.S. intervention in the Caribbean after the Civil War complicate the nationalist racial frame of "Reconstruction"? For decades, scholars in U.S. literary studies have organized survey courses around the 1865 break. But many a Civil War general's autobiography begins in Mexico.[22] The Latino nineteenth century offers other important points: 1826 (the Congress of Panama organized by Simón

Bolívar), 1848 (The Treaty of Guadalupe Hidalgo), 1849 (the California Gold Rush), 1856 (the filibustering of Nicaragua), and 1868 (the outbreak of revolts in Puerto Rico and Cuba).

Rather than offer a hemispheric mapping of a field that combines the United States with the many territories of Latin America, our contributors approach hemispheric movements as discrete historical manifestations. That is to say, the hemisphere is too vast to function as an alternative map for Latino America, but hemispheric movements offer a tremendously important analytical potential for Latino/a studies. Movements here refer not only to geographic relocations but also to political alliances and changes in perspective. Like Pérez Rosales, many of the Latino/a writers and intellectuals who moved in and out of the United States in the nineteenth century often grappled with comparative national imaginaries that they conceived or adopted through experiences of economic migration and travel. In some cases, these figures retained a vexed relationship to the United States and did not identify themselves in relation to U.S.-based categories of identity or citizenship.

Latino studies as a field is nurtured by demographic changes in the United States in the past forty years, and thus it is inclined toward contemporary considerations, sometimes of an excessively sociological bent. But it also prompts a historical approach that emphasizes the contingency of textual remains and challenges the previously separate spheres of U.S. American studies and Latin American studies. *The Latino Nineteenth Century* complicates the study of America on both sides of the North–South divide by presenting textual multiplicity and how those texts register the experiences of people seeking new ways to make sense of the changes they have encountered and conceive of communal affiliation. The elements that come up in our chapters, including a varied and dispersed textual record, discrete historical conditions, and shifts in language, make the Latino nineteenth century a multiplicity of the uncommon.

NOTES

1 Arturo Ardao, *Génesis de la idea y el nombre de América Latina* (Caracas: Centro de Estudios Latinoamericanos Rómulo Gallegos, 1980); Mónica Quijada, "Sobre el Origen y Difusión del Nombre 'América Latina,'" *Revista de Indias* 43 #214 (1998): 595–616; Walter Mignolo, *The Idea of Latin America* (Malden, Mass.: Blackwell, 2005).

2 Arturo Ardao, *América latina y la latinidad* (Mexico: Universidad Nacional Autónoma, 1993).

3 Chevalier circulated his work decades before the French invasion of Mexico and installation of the Emperor Maximilian in 1864. See, for example, Michel Chevalier, *Mexico: Before and After the Conquest* (Philadelphia: Carey and Hart, 1846), 90–91.

4 María Amparo Ruiz de Burton, *Conflicts of Interest: The Letters of María Amparo Ruiz de Burton*, ed. Rosaura Sánchez and Beatrice Pita (Houston: Arte Público, 2001), 301. Unless otherwise noted, translations are mine. Ellipses are in the copies of the original letters at the Huntington Library.

5 Quentin Skinner, "Meaning and Understanding in the History of Ideas," *History and Theory* 8:1 (1969), 6.

6 This "danger" differs significantly from Walter Benjamin's use of the same word in his "Theses on the Philosophy of History," in which the danger is a threat to the historian: "that of becoming a tool of the ruling classes," a point he makes after dismissing the importance of articulating the past "the way it really was." Walter Benjamin, "Theses on the Philosophy of History," *Illuminations*, ed. Hannah Arendt (New York: Schocken Books, 1968), 255.

7 Frances Aparicio and Suzanne Bost remind us that "Identity terminology is particularly tricky in Latino/a studies," in that the terms raise questions of location in the Americas, racial mixing, immigration status, and national affiliation. "The central lesson to draw from this terminological friction is that all of these identity terms are contested, sometimes fluid, and always relational." Suzanne Bost and Frances Aparicio, *The Routledge Companion to Latino/a Literature* (New York: Routledge, 2012), 1–2.

8 Raúl Coronado, *A World Not to Come: A History of Latino Writing and Print Culture* (Cambridge and London: Harvard University Press, 2013), 29.

9 María Amparo Ruiz de Burton, *The Squatter and the Don* (Houston: Arte Público, 1997), 97. Later in the book, Darrell's interlocutor, Don Mariano Alamar, adopts the same phrase: "we, *the natives* of California, the Spano-Americans" (162).

10 Julia Álvarez, "Bilingual Sestina," in *The Other Side/El Otro Lado* (New York: Plume, 1995), 4. For a discussion of how the term *Latino* emerges as a "site of permanent political contestation" rather than a descriptor, see Cristina Beltrán, *The Trouble with Unity: Latino Politics and the Creation of Identity* (New York: Oxford University Press, 2010), 8–9.

11 Donald Pease, "National Identities, Postmodern Artifacts, and Postnational Narratives," in *National Identities and Post-Americanist Narratives*, ed. Donald Pease (Durham, N.C.: Duke University Press, 1994), 1.

12 Lawrence Buell, *The Dream of the Great American Novel* (Cambridge, Mass.: Belknap Press of Harvard University Press, 2014).

13 *Recovery* also implies restoration and the regaining of a better condition. Ramón Gutiérrez and Genaro Padilla called for the sustained study of Hispanic literary heritage in order to "document its regional and national diversity, to

view from various perspectives and angles the matrix of power in which it
was created, and to celebrate its hybridity, its intertextuality and its polyvocal-
ity." These goals of recovery work are still with us. See Gutiérrez and Padilla,
Introduction to *Recovering the U.S. Hispanic Literary Heritage* (Houston: Arte
Público, 1993), 21.

14 The first of the seven volumes was edited by Gutiérrez and Genaro Padilla in
1993, the seventh edited by Gerald E. Poyo and Tomás Ybarra-Frausto in 2009.
The Project has also published *Recovering the U.S. Hispanic Linguistic Heritage*,
ed. Alejandra Balestra, Glenn Martínez, and María Irene Moyna (Houston: Arte
Público, 2008). Many of the contributors to *The Latino Nineteenth Century* have
published articles in those volumes. Some of us met at Recovery Project conferences, and still others have been involved in the Project's Board of Editorial
Advisers.

15 The cost of the EBSCO database, which is sold only to libraries and not individual
researchers, can run into the thousands of dollars. As such, it raises important
questions about the economic effects of digitizing archives.

16 "A partir de esa evidencia, se plantea lo hispánico como un elemento constitutivo
de esta nación, de sus procesos culturales y del orden de la escritura como esfera
privilegiada para la valoración de lo cultural." Agnes Lugo-Ortiz, "La antología y
el archivo: Reflexiones en torno a *Herencia, En otra voz* y los límites de un saber,"
in *Recovering the U.S. Hispanic Literary Heritage*, vol. V, ed. Kenya Dworkin y Mé-
ndez and Agnes Lugo-Ortiz (Houston: Arte Público, 2006), 145. For a discussion
of archival limitations, see 157–58.

17 See my articles "The Invention of America Again: On the Impossibility of an
Archive," *American Literary History* 25.4 (Winter 2013): 751–71, and "Migrant Ar-
chives," in *States of Emergency*, ed. Russ Castronovo and Susan Gillman (Chapel
Hill: University of North Carolina Press, 2009), 36–54.

18 "Funeral of the Colombian Ambassador," *Aurora General Advertiser*, 18 July 1822;
"The Franklin of South America (From the New York Evening Post)," *Aurora
General Advertiser*, 24 July 1822.

19 For an overview of the periodical press, see Nicolás Kanellos with Helvetia Martell, eds., *Hispanic Periodicals in the United States, Origins to 1960* (Houston: Arte
Público, 2000).

20 Kirsten Silva Gruesz, *Ambassadors of Culture: The Transamerican Origins of
Latino Writing* (Princeton and Oxford: Princeton University Press, 2002), xii.

21 Gilles Deleuze, *Bergsonism* (New York: Zone Books, 1988), 38. For Latino studies,
historical "textual multiplicity" points to the importance of moving beyond the
dialectic of self and other. "We are told that the Self is one (thesis)," writes Deleuze, "and it is multiple (antithesis), then it is the unity of the multiple (synthe-
sis)" (44). Rather than work with a binary opposition between Anglo and Latino
or even along oppositions between groups from different countries, the multiplicity of the Latino nineteenth century shows slippages in categories.

22 I thank Ian Litwin for pointing this out.

1

The Errant Latino

Irisarri, Central Americanness, and Migration's Intention

KIRSTEN SILVA GRUESZ

To what purpose came we into the Wilderness? . . . [to] dwell
in a place of our own, *that we might move no more.*
—Samuel Danforth, "A Brief Recognition of New-Englands
Errand into the Wilderness," 1670 (emphasis in original)

Vida errante y de gitano, de expatriado de la gran patria
americana. [The errant, gypsy life of an expatriate from the
great American *patria.*]
—Self-description by Antonio José de Irisarri, 1863

Fui migrante y me hospedaron. [I was a migrant, and you
took me in.]
—Idiosyncratic translation of Matthew 25:35 by human
rights activist Father Alejandro Solalinde, featured on the
website of his mission for migrants in Ixtepec, Oaxaca

Recalling a long-ago journey through the Guatemalan highlands, the
narrator of Antonio José de Irisarri's *El cristiano errante* (*The Errant
Christian*, 1847) describes his compulsion to linger at the seven Maya-
K'iche' villages along the way. "He found those Indians hard-working,
intelligent, agile, alert, well-formed, robust, dedicated to agriculture,
commerce, and the arts" and praises their homes, their products, and
their public works, including aqueducts and ingenious hydraulics that
irrigated productive fields "whose yields were held in common." He concluded that the *indios* of Los Altos "seemed to him more intelligent than
the *mestizos, zambos,* and Spaniards of the other parts of America, for

they were infinitely more skilled master builders." Ignorant of indigenous lifeways prior to this journey, the young Creole "found in all of these villages a life, an activity, a surge of civilizing energy that he did not expect to find, nor would he find again among larger populations in Peru, Chile, Argentina, Bolivia, Ecuador, or Colombia"—some of the places in which he would later live during his long, peripatetic life.[1] Irisarri depicts the highlands Maya-K'iche'—apparently so isolated from the currents of Enlightenment thought that were animating revolutionary movements throughout the hemisphere—as having arrived, on their own, at the practical goals of those movements: functional self-governance, a fair justice system, free trade, peace. Reflecting on that visit from the vantage point of middle age, some forty years later, the narrator allows the point to sink in: America bloodied and nearly destroyed itself in order to achieve a harmonious social state that had already been attained by the very people those movements had most excluded.

The title of *El cristiano errante* echoes that of one of the most globally popular novels of the day, Eugène Sue's *Le juif errant*, known in Spanish as *El judío errante*. Rather than follow the usual English translation of Sue's title as "The *Wandering* Jew," I want to revive the antiquated term *errant* as a way of linking a nineteenth-century text to contemporary U.S. discourses about migrancy. Errancy suggests wandering without a goal, without intention; the epiphany of Irisarri's protagonist is the more powerful because he stumbled upon it while on his way to somewhere else. Yet even defenders of immigrant rights disavow such accidents, emphasizing intentionality of movement when they cast undocumented persons as determined, long-suffering pilgrims in search of a better life. Establishing sympathy for their cause depends on linking these groups to a longer national narrative of such pilgrimage. Stories about the accidental or reluctant migrant, the wanderer blown off course, the person at the end of his or her chances are less adaptable to the inevitably moralizing affect of sympathy.[2] In this chapter, then, I want to use Irisarri—his "*vida errante*" and his errantly titled novel—to trouble the way such purposefulness can be used not only to embrace or demonize migrants but also to establish someone's place within a narrative of national and ethnic belonging.

Irisarri appears as a founding father in cultural histories of Guatemala, Chile, Colombia, Ecuador, and even Curaçao. Yet no scholar has tried to position him similarly within U.S. (Latino) American literary history, despite the fact that he spent his final eighteen years in the United States—a longer period than José Martí—and published numerous books, pamphlets, and newspaper articles there. Irisarri demonstrated no desire to become a U.S. citizen, and he did not leave any obvious signs of a Latino or Central American–American identity.[3] Instead, he makes a case for an ethics of identification that embraces *non*purposefulness and pushes against genealogy as a form of common sense.

Although *El cristiano errante* did not appear in book form in the United States (as did a later novel, a collection of poetry, and various nonfiction works), new archival evidence indicates that Irisarri published it serially in a New Orleans newspaper in 1851. This previously unremarked phase of Irisarri's wanderings places him at the ground zero of fanatical schemes for the expansion of a Southern slaveholding empire: the financial and military launching-place for various filibustering expeditions and development and colonization companies aimed all across the Central American isthmus. As he joined forces with two seasoned local editors, Eusebio José Gómez and Victoriano Alemán, to publish *La Unión* in Spanish and English, Irisarri's earlier admiration for the United States hardened into the critical anti-imperialist stance it would take for the remainder of his life. The discovery of this New Orleans edition of *El cristiano errante*, I argue, shifts this text outside its minor place in the developmental history of the Latin American novel and into the complex transnational history that yokes together the United States with Central America through the subjects who move between them, in ways that are often marked by state violence. Although the novel itself does not describe the lives of Spanish-speaking and Latino people then living in the United States, its serial incarnation in this periodical context links them *as readers* to the vision of a regional, community-based defense of Central America's sovereignty—even though Irisarri continued his lifelong opposition to the federation of those small nations into a single state.

The Mayan territory through which Irisarri had traveled in 1806 now encompasses a second border between Latin America and the United States: a dark shadow and foreshadowing of the *frontera* that runs along and beyond the Río Grande. Along the railroad line that Irisarri correctly guessed would be built toward the end of the nineteenth century to link

Guatemala with Chiapas, undocumented migrants undergo violent abjectification by the Mexican state (and by the organized crime cartels it tolerates), which has mimicked and exaggerated the tactics of those state agencies that patrol the U.S.–Mexico border. The emerging discipline of Latino studies, loosely assembled from the planks of Chicano/a, Puerto Rican, and Cuban American studies, has just begun to conceptualize the growing presence of Central American–Americans within the Latino bloc: sometimes successfully resisting the affect of sympathetic pity, sometimes not. U.S. American studies, too, needs to consider the implications of this GuateMexican border zone that lies well outside, but is still *of*, the United States. I want to ask how errancy and nonintentionality might provide not only a different *ethos* of migration and movement rights, but a different *mythos* as well. How might errancy talk back to that foundational trope of American studies, the Puritan *errand* into the wilderness and its self-justifying "escape to freedom"?

A Peripatetic Textual History

El cristiano errante, though introduced in its Prologue as something other than a factual history, correlates broadly with events and landscapes in Irisarri's own itinerary; thus, a logical place to begin is with a sketch of the author's life. Unlike critics who have plumbed the resemblances between Irisarri and the protagonist (Romualdo de Villapedrosa from "Nueva Babilonia"), I am less interested in classifying its ratio of fiction to autobiography than in charting the spaces in which it was received. The author's name and reputation do matter, as we retrace this novel's movement along what Robert Darnton calls the communications circuit—but so do the other nodes of that circuit. Irisarri sometimes functions as his own editor and publicist and at other times is linked financially to political patrons; his reviewers and readers are mostly, though not always, caught up in those webs of partisan affiliation as well. The point along the circuit that matters most here is that of *preservation and survival*: how a stateless author and his digressive text were first neglected, then posthumously inserted into narratives of national tradition. The marginality of this novel, moreover, was compounded by the extreme degree to which its existence depended upon that most fragile of material formats, the newspaper.[4]

It is for his work in establishing newspapers wherever he went—the Johnny Appleseed of the nineteenth-century Latin American press— that Antonio José de Irisarri is mostly remembered. Born in 1786 to a wealthy family in Guatemala City, Irisarri traveled to Mexico City at age twenty to sort out the financial affairs of his deceased father, a merchant who had taken the daring step of trading in Philadelphia and Baltimore against the inconsistent decrees of the Spanish crown.[5] After collecting family debts in Callao, Lima, and Valparaíso, Irisarri married and settled in Santiago de Chile, agitating on behalf of independence in the seminal monthly he founded in 1813 and attaching himself to Bernardo O'Higgins.[6] Dispatched to London as ambassador to England and France, he brokered a controversial million-pound loan and befriended Andrés Bello, whose interest in philology—and whose defense of the Spanish spoken in the New World—he would later imitate. Returning to Guatemala in 1826, this nonmilitary man found himself named defense minister and thrust into a war against the Liberal Francisco Morazán, whose followers were trying to hold together the disintegrating Federal Republic of Central America. Morazán defeated him in—of all places— Los Altos and threw him into a Salvadoran prison for eleven months; Irisarri escaped in 1830.[7] Finally returning to Chile to see the grown children he had known only as babies, Irisarri again embroiled himself in controversial government service: In 1837, he was accused of treason for having negotiated a treaty that would have ended the War of the Confederation with a concession of Chilean defeat. He never returned there, nor did he collect on the commissions and personal loan payments he claimed he was owed by four newly independent republics. The vast fortune he had inherited and received from his wife's family would dwindle to $81 by the time of his death, in a rented room in Brooklyn, in 1868.[8]

In his early forties Irisarri began his life over, returning to the journalistic role he had adopted in Chile, starting newspapers in Ecuador, Guatemala, Nueva Granada, Venezuela, and Trinidad and leveraging his trademark style—by turns bitingly eloquent and hilariously satirical—to ridicule the ideas of the opposition party. Of course, when the party that was underwriting the paper's publication fell out of power, there would be an urgent need to move on. *El cristiano errante* came into being during one of these new beginnings. Irisarri arrived in Bogotá in 1846 with a commendation to Tomás Cipriano Mosquera, then in his first term as president of Nueva Granada. A major anti-Mosquera newspaper was titled *Libertad y Orden*, so as a first counter-punch, Irisarri titled his new weekly *Nosotros: Orden y Libertad*. A rival journalist wrote that the editorial voice in *Nosotros* was so distinctive and quirky that "no-one from nowhere" could have written it: Surely the new writer in town must be *El judío errante*, the Wandering Jew. The intended insult was clear: Rather than speaking for "us," for the Colombian public, Irisarri's new paper spoke from the perspective of a suspect, stateless being. Turning the slur on its head, Irisarri immediately changed the name of his weekly to *El cristiano errante*.[9]

Because *El cristiano errante*, the "novel that resembles a history," began serialization in the newspaper *El cristiano errante* shortly after this episode, Irisarri had probably written much of it before setting foot in Bogotá. The journalistic mudslinging, so typical of its period, seems to have lent the novel both a title and a key trope: that of the wanderer whose constant movement allows him to compare one place to another and thus to see beyond the narrow prejudices and petty loyalties of located identities (as the fictive name of his birthplace, "New Babylon," suggests). Being errant does not make him noncommittal, though: The many digressions in the narrative muse about what the pan-American republics had wanted to be, how those ideals were corrupted, and what they still might become. The comparison of Irisarri's Romualdo to Ahasuerus, the *juif errant* of popular European fantasy, was thus apt. The wild narrative that Sue had scaffolded around this figure had no time to waste on mere anti-Semitism; his Ahasuerus was held up as a prophet, an ageless time traveler who observed the corruption of the world around him (associated mostly with the Jesuit order that was Sue's particular target). Sue's sensational novel had been a global publishing phenomenon in 1844–45, keeping readers on edge awaiting the next installment, and imitators—including some in Spain, where popular fiction had barely taken hold—sprang up immediately. The ten-volume bound version of *Le juif errant* remained a bestseller even as the *entregas* of Irisarri's *Cristiano errante* appeared, from August 1846 to March 1847.[10]

The story of Romualdo's extraordinary journey through the continental revolutions was projected to cover seven volumes: If completed, it would have been nearly as prolix as Sue's book. But as with that novel, the more significant material context has to do with *El cristiano erran-*

te's seriality, which establishes a particularly intense relationship among individuals within the readership who expectantly await the next installment together. Serial readers of *El cristiano errante* would be better equipped to associate the novel's narrator with a contemporary editorial voice. Those readers might also recognize the "errant Christian" as a model for a particular kind of literary ambition, the ambition of the independent man of letters: When the novel ends, Romualdo is still only twenty-one and has discovered his vocation as a writer, though not as one whose words could change the political world. So only by association with the newspaper *El cristiano errante* could the novel *El cristiano errante* take the shape, in a reader's judgment, of a *Künstlerroman*. In the Prologue, Irisarri calls out his "shiftless readers" as consumers of newspapers, "spending your time reading the day's papers, and the harangues of our agitators": These, he says, are even worse fodder than the chivalric romances that Cervantes had mocked. He goes on to say to this newspaper addict, "you may as well occupy yourself with something that might do you some good"—that is, to accompany the narrator back in time to the early Independence period by following Romualdo's adventures.[11]

The book format usually has a distinct advantage when it comes to survival, the final phase in Darnton's communications circuit. Although the printer of the weekly *El cristiano errante*, José Ayarza's Imprenta de Espinosa, issued a codex version in late 1847, fewer than a hundred copies were printed. Nineteenth-century literary historians referenced the novel, but few seem to have read it until its recovery by a prominent Chilean historian, Guillermo Feliú Cruz, who published a new edition in 1929. Working with Irisarri's descendants, who granted him access to private family papers, Feliú Cruz attempted to give Irisarri the triumphant return to Chile he had never had, by recognizing him as a national founding father.[12] Not to be outdone, from the 1950s onward the Ministry of Public Education in Guatemala began reissuing Irisarri's literary works, along with dozens of his political essays and diplomatic letters. Amilcar Echeverría's Introduction to the 1960 Guatemalan edition of *El cristiano errante* acknowledged Feliú Cruz's work while wresting the label of foundational national writer back from the Chileans, comparing Irisarri to his celebrated contemporary Juan José Millás (Salomé Jil), who created the iconic character of "Juan Chapín." Now reconstructed as a book object, *El cristiano errante* was dutifully acknowledged in micro-

and macro-histories of Spanish American literature, with critics poking away at problems of classification (was it more of a novel, or an autobiography? what to make of Irisarri's theory of the interrelationship between *historia* and *novela*, roughly truth and fiction, in the Prologue?). Lost in these recoveries was the mobile, successive quality of the original serial publication and the spaces in which it had first circulated: maps of reception centered not in Chile or Guatemala but in New Granada and in the southern United States.

Bogotá, Humboldt's "Athens of South America," was a print-culture capital despite its relative isolation and the necessity of moving printed objects by slow nineteenth-century transportation. It was also one of the places where Bolívar's legacy and the right to claim it was hotly contested in the 1840s. *El cristiano errante* does not mention O'Higgins or the revolutionary leaders Irisarri had actually known in Chile, but it does meditate on the dream of the continental unity of América, on the failure of putting Enlightenment political theory into practice there.[13] Following up the "*novela que parece historia*" with an unrepentant "*historia*," Irisarri then let it be known in Colombia that he had completed his magnum opus: a meticulously researched exposé of the plot to assassinate Antonio José de Sucre, Bolívar's political heir, in 1830. Titled *La defensa de la historia: Crítica del asesinato cometido contra la persona del Mariscal de Ayacucho* (The Defense of History: An Exposé of the Assassination Committed against the Marshall of Ayacucho), it named as conspirators in Sucre's murder various former revolutionaries who were still in power. Irisarri's life was threatened. Again he left the country, completing his passage through the three nations into which the Bolivarian republic of Gran Colombia had shattered: first Ecuador, then New Granada, and then Venezuela, where he also failed to convince terrified printers to release his Sucre book. It was finally published in Curaçao in 1849, and the new paper Irisarri started there, *El Revisor: Periódico político y literario*, tried to make it notorious, reprinting evidence about the assassination to bolster Irisarri's claims. The threats continued, and so did the long march northward.

In October 1849, Irisarri arrived in the United States, whose people he had once described admiringly as "our brothers."[14] He was able, by January of the following year, to launch a New York incarnation of *El Revisor*, which added material more relevant to its new target audi-

ence: reporting on the conflicts between the thousands of gold-seekers
streaming across Colombian territory and local Panamanians. According to a contemporary source, Irisarri tried to market the weekly to the
Spanish-language teachers in the city as a fount of well-crafted material
from which pupils could learn good style.[15] But apparently the students
enrolled in Spanish schools were more interested in getting along in
California than in quoting Cervantes; El Revisor failed in May 1850. In a
despairing letter to his wife that summer, Irisarri wrote,

> Estoy muy mal por ahora, de resulta del mal éxito que he tenido con mi
> última empresa, por lo cual me he retirado de Nueva York al campo . . .
> todo llegue a faltar . . . hace doce años ando así, haciendo pruebas sobre
> pruebas; teniendo tiempo en tiempo algunas muy lisonjeras esperanzas,
> y luego viniéndolas convertidas en humo.

> I'm doing very poorly now as a result of the lack of success I had with
> my last enterprise, so I've left New York for the country. . . . everything I
> do fails. . . . for the past twelve years it's gone this way for me, trying one
> thing and another, having some very flattering hopes and then, time after
> time, seeing them go up in smoke.[16]

Somewhere around this time, in a move that has escaped notice
until now, Irisarri went south to join forces with the two most
successful editors of a Spanish-language newspaper in the nation:
Louisiana-born Eusebio José Gómez and the Spanish-born Victoriano Alemán, who over the previous four years had built La Patria
of New Orleans into an internationally known periodical that now
appeared three times a week and printed and sold other materials
in its own bookstore. Gómez and Alemán, as it happened, were also
avid about serial fiction: Not only did they sell Sue's Wandering Jew
in Spanish at the store, they rushed to translate installments of his
latest novel in La Patria. They had serialized an original "mysteries
of the city" novel set in Havana and Gómez's own Un matrimonio
como hay muchos: Novela que parece historia (A Marriage Like
Many Others: A Novel That Resembles History), arguably the first
novel by a U.S. Latino.[17] When Gómez, Alemán, and Irisarri banded
together, after negotiations we can only speculate about, one of the

first issues of their new triweekly carried the initial installment of *El cristiano errante: Novela que tiene mucho de historia, Publicada en 1847 por Don Antonio José de Irisarri, y corregida después por él mismo.*[18]

Why does this forgotten New Orleans context matter? As with the serialized Bogotá edition, readers in Louisiana, Cuba, Texas, Mexico, and elsewhere along *La Unión*'s considerable sales circuit were directly implicated as newspaper readers by the narrating voice, which they understood to be coming from a journalist as well as a novelist. The paper identified Irisarri as someone worth listening to *not* on the basis of his participation in world-shaping events—as someone who had personally known O'Higgins, Sucre, and Bello—but through his editorial experience in the United States. The masthead of the first issue credentials Gómez and Alemán as "Late of La Patria," and Irisarri as "Late of El Revisor, New York." The mission statement affirms that *La Unión* will "defend the Spanish race from the frequent and unjust attacks to which it is often exposed in this country"; a small English section was added "in view of how little justice has been done by the Anglo-American press" to Spanish and Spanish America.[19] Readers of this New Orleans edition of *El cristiano errante*, wherever they may have lived, were bombarded with the problem of whether the United States supported or held back the freedoms of the rest of America. On the other pages of the newspaper, they were reminded of the way that the recent U.S. acquisition of half of Mexico's territory had radically changed the rules of engagement in the hemisphere: Yucatán and Cuba seemed likely to become states, and with the hordes of gold-seekers heading to California, the isthmian crossing points of Panama, Nicaragua, and Tehuantepec were now seen as spaces that needed to be brought under U.S. control—and not only by southerners seeking to expand their slaveholding empire in Central America and the Caribbean.

Editorially, Gómez and Alemán preached Latin American sovereignty and decried the "piracy" of filibustering expeditions like that of Narciso López in Cuba. But they had to tread carefully, because New Orleanians were among the major investors in development schemes in the isthmus, as well as major traders with Havana and Veracruz. A "Prognostication about the Year 1851" that appeared in the first issue of *La Unión* (and recalls Irisarri's style) reveals the contexts in which these readers were immersed. The editors can only guess about the year to come:

... si la república francesa continuará siendo república; si la unión americana se rompe en este año o en el otro; si el canal de Tehuantepec llega
a ser canal y no se queda en proyecto; si el otro canal de Nicaragua se
queda en especulación de agiotistas y en motivo de contestaciones entre
Inglaterra y los EU, y si el otro canal de Panamá se queda, como nosotros
creemos, reducido a un camino de hierro. Cosas más fáciles que estas se
han emprendido y han sido abandonado. Lo que no se abandonará es
el protectorado de los Mosquitos por Inglaterra, ni los proyectos de los
anexionistas en los Estados Unidos.

... whether the French Republic will continue to be a republic; whether
the American Union will rupture this year or the next; whether the Tehuantepec Canal will become a canal or remain on the drawing board;
whether the other canal through Nicaragua will become anything more
than the speculation of money-changers and the cause of disputes between England and the U.S.; and whether the other canal through Panama will—as we believe—be reduced to a railroad. Simpler things than
this have been undertaken and abandoned. What will not be abandoned
is the English protectorate of the Kingdom of Mosquitia, and the schemes
of annexationists in the United States.

But the editors could not have foreseen what 1851 had in store for *La
Unión* itself. That August a crowd of pro-expansionist southerners,
incensed by the paper's pleasure about the guilty verdict against Narciso
López's collaborators, stormed the printing office, wrecked the equipment and stock, and shot at Alemán, who jumped across the roofs of
the *Vieux-Carré* and ran for his life with a broken leg, while the angry
mob went on to destroy other "Spanish-owned" businesses. As Joanna
Brooks has written, "books, like people, have life chances."[20] What were
the chances that cartons of copies of Gómez's 1848 novel, and some of
Irisarri's as well, were burned that night? If they had survived and been
preserved closer to their birthplace, how might the literary history of the
"Latin American" novel, or the "Southern" novel, have evolved differently? Irisarri escaped, but we hear no more of him for six years, when
he resurfaces in New York. Here we confront the problem of fragility and
politicized selectivity that, according to Rodrigo Lazo, characterizes the
"migrant archive" of U.S. Latinos: None of the relevant Latin American

state archives have gathered his traces from the early 1850s, perhaps because they are scarce, but more likely because, during that period especially, he belonged to no national tradition.[21] Serially expelled, he was truly *un errante*, a stateless person from everywhere and nowhere in América.

Finally, in 1857, Irisarri was named plenipotentiary minister (chief ambassador) of Guatemala to the United States by Rafael Carrera, the Conservative *mestizo* president who had returned to power on the backs of the many rural Mayans to whom he allowed a limited autonomy. Shortly after, Irisarri took on the same position for El Salvador, even during a brief renewal of war between the neighboring nations, living in Brooklyn and traveling to Washington when necessary. It is this diplomatic position that cleared the way for the twentieth-century celebration of Irisarri as a *Guatemalan* founding father, despite the fact that he spent very little of his adult life there. In his diplomatic correspondence and his letters there is a presciently Martí-like voice, speaking out against filibusterism, land grabs, colonization schemes, and anything Irisarri saw as an outgrowth of the Monroe Doctrine. He became assimilable as a good Central American, in other words, by becoming properly anti-American. But the timing of his forgotten association with *La Unión* suggests that he acquired this deep and lasting suspicion of U.S. intentions in Central America under the tutelage of Gómez and Alemán, two younger colleagues who had intimate knowledge of the engine of southern expansionism's financing, as well as the roots of popular sentiment in favor of it. New Orleans was the belly of that beast.

Reading Errantly: The Scene from Los Altos

Let us now return to the episode in Los Altos, which occurs in the seventh and eighth chapters of *El cristiano errante*. As is the case throughout the novel, Romualdo tests what he has read against what he actually observes. Earlier, his first effort to reach Mexico City from Guatemala City by sea had been interrupted by an English pirate who proved—against expectations—to be generous and good company; when he attempts the journey again, overland this time, he is rather comically masquerading as a postal carrier.[22] This guise is figuratively apt, for the naïve hero is weighed down from too much reading. His source for information about the Highlands had been the seventeenth-century English Catholic convert Thomas Gage's famous *New Survey of the West Indies*. What he sees, of course, contradicts Gage's account at most every turn: The neat fields of maize and productive textile industries he finds among the Maya-K'iche' identify them, in his view, as a forward-moving society rather than one that exists in a primitive, backward state. (Contrast this with John Lloyd Stephens's widely read dismissal of Los Altos: "here the people had no character and nothing in which we took any interest, except their backs.")[23] The *alcalde* system fascinated Irisarri as an example of functional local democracy, but the *alcalde*'s authority unfortunately did not extend beyond the contact zone between the Mayan world and that of the Spanish and *ladinos*. Irisarri also admired their traditional justice system: "those villages had somehow hit upon the principle in English jurisprudence, that a man could only be tried by his peers, which gives the person on trial the best guarantee against pettiness and rivalry." But the Mayans suffered under a colonial system, and then a national one, which made no such provision. Spanish justice "never failed to be fatal to Indians when Spaniards were the defendants" in complaints they brought.[24]

The voyage Irisarri draws on for this episode took place in 1806, but this retrospective telling is also informed by his ignominious 1828 military defeat in the same region. Returning to Guatemala after two decades away, he had missed the first episodes of significant Mayan resistance to the new political order of nationhood. Irisarri digresses temporally from the story of Romualdo here into a discussion of the 1820 Mayan uprising in San Miguel Totonicapán led by Lucas Aguilar and Atanasio Tzul.[25] Although he had not witnessed that uprising, he judges that it was not only legitimate but also logically consistent with the Enlightenment principles of the independence movements. He anticipates a reader's protest with a barrage of rhetorical questions, asking:

> ¿Si los indios eran o no eran ciudadanos como los otros? ¿Si la igualdad era cosa tratándose de indios y otra cosa de las demás castas? ¿Si los indios por ser más antiguos en el país deben tener menos derechos que los que lo poblaron más recientemente, y si era justo que porque una cuarta parte de ciudadanos querían una cosa, las otras tres cuartas partes debiesen querer lo mismo? (176–77)

Whether the Indians are not citizens like everyone else? Whether equality was one thing with Indians, and another with other castes? Whether the Indians, by virtue of having been in this country longer, should have fewer rights than those who populated it more recently, and whether it was just that if one-quarter of the citizens [meaning *criollos* and *ladinos*] wanted one thing, the other three-quarters should want the same?

In the same passage, Irisarri refutes the rhetoric of progress that drove so many forms of exclusion in the nineteenth-century Americas on the grounds that nonwhites were not yet ready for democracy in action. Tzul had been chosen by a vote, but the government refused to recognize the choice as legitimate self-determination. "The only kind of progress I recognize is that of natural reason, which is sufficient to convince me that what we are calling 'politics' is no more than acting against one's principles, committing the most obvious contradictions." Guatemala's government had done no better than the United States with "their" Indians, with their shamefully enslaved Africans. "No one in the world can have any reason, no pretext of Enlightenment nor of civilization and progress, to oppose the will of the majority of a people," he concludes, noting that Totonicapán had not yet lost "the hope of recovering their nationality."[26]

Rather than represent the Highlands Maya as the least assimilable to a modern, secular political order, Irisarri casts them as typical of the *fracaso* of independence. They had tested Enlightenment principles of sovereignty and self-rule, only to be thwarted by the naked, unchecked self-interest of others:

En el comercio, en la política, en todas las transacciones humanas, hasta en las domésticas, hallamos esta especie de guerra que nos hacemos los mortales mientras vivimos; guerra, como en todas las guerras, en que cada cual hace a otro el mal que puede, buscando su propia ventaja; en que todas las celadas, todos ardides, todos engaños, todo egoísmo, toda hostilidad para el pobre prójimo. Examinemos bien nuestro modo de proceder en esta sociedad que llamamos humana, y que no debíamos llamar sino leonina, porque cada uno de nosotros queremos ser el león en ella, y sacar por nuestro individuo toda la ventaja, sin dejar ninguno al socio. (88–89)

In commerce, in politics, in all human relations even in the domestic realm, we find this sort of warfare that we mortals wage while we are alive; a war, like all wars, in which each one does the evil that he can to another, seeking his own advantage; in which we find all jealousies, all passions, all deceptions, all egoism, all hostility toward the next person. Let us carefully examine our way of carrying on in this society that we call human, and which we might better call leonine, for each one of us seeks to be a lion in it, and to take everything for our individual gain without leaving anything for our fellow.

Irisarri refers consistently, if sometimes hopelessly, to this Lockean principle of civil society as a group of fellows or *socios*—a term that might also be translated as "business associate"—setting aside their individual brute interests in the name of securing greater advantage for all.[27] When he emphasizes the economic industriousness of the highlanders (national independence, he reports sadly, ruined the great textile trade of Quetzaltenango), it is to show them as better, or at least less hypocritical, *socios* than those who waged near-perpetual warfare in the name of peace and freedom.

It is worth speculating on how this passage of the novel—and the many others that make glancing comparisons with the United States— might have played differently to the 1851 readers of *El cristiano errante* in *La Unión*. Among them would have been Cuban slaveholders, investors in Central American and Mexican development schemes that required the displacement of indigenous villages, and readers who, whatever their position on slavery, were accustomed to figuring *all* "Indians," whether in the Yucatán or in Texas, as dangerously uncivilized. What *would* have struck an affirmative chord with New Orleans readers is Irisarri's language of animal rapaciousness and self-interest applied to political affairs. *La Patria/La Unión* had decried the U.S. war with Mexico, as well as the filibusters that war helped to spawn, as a bloodthirsty seizure of the sovereign rights of others, a betrayal of the rules of fellowship among nations. In his diplomatic and personal writing after the New Orleans period, Irisarri identified a host of threats to Central American sovereignty—whether from the U.S. nation-state or from its citizens, like William Walker—as versions of the same animal greed that betrayed the rational desire among *socios* to maintain the social compact. Even his official letters rarely pull punches. An 1856 protest to the U.S. secretary of state about the puppet ambassador of the Walker government in Nicaragua complains about the jingoistic press that has promoted the idea that Manifest Destiny extends to Central America, Mexico, and Cuba, believing "anything that is, or might be, beneficial to the United States is just and fair, even if it did damage and harm to the rest of the world." Although some right-thinking *yanquis* don't support filibustering, he writes, "these just men have not been able to triumph over the party that wants to annex Spanish America to the U.S. by force and re-establish slavery in it."[28]

The violations arising from the Monroe Doctrine are a constant theme in Irisarri's writing in the later 1850s and 1860s, even in private letters: That pronouncement "is and has been the basis of North American filibustering," and even those who might have once supported its noble-sounding fraternal ideal now recognize it as a "disgrace."[29] Irisarri became a kind of pan–Central American figure during this period, instrumental in the negotiations over the site of a future trans-isthmian canal; in Latin American protests over the British presence in Belize and Mosquitia; in the rejection of the Lincoln administration's rumored plan to send emancipated blacks to Central America; and most powerfully in the defeat of Walker, which came about through what Irisarri biographer Carlos Garcia-Bauer memorializes as a singular moment of "solidarity among the nations of the isthmus, and Central American brotherhood."[30] But ideals invite ironies. Having gone to prison for opposing a united Central American *state*, Irisarri gained a place in posterity for advancing the greatest practical success of the Central American *idea*.

Errant, into the Wilderness

When Irisarri died in 1868, his body was buried in Brooklyn's Calvary Cemetery. After the filiopietistic revival of interest in creating a Guatemalan national tradition in the mid–twentieth century, his remains were exhumed and reburied with pomp in Guatemala City in 1971. A set of second-tier state honors, the "Orden de Antonio José de Irisarri," was created—the medals of ribbons and gilt that he wore for his old-age portrait but mocked in his writings.[31] Thus repatriated to their "proper" national ground, Irisarri's bones raise the question of identity he had

evaded when he described his own life as "errant," as that of "an expatriate from the great American *patria*."³² While he vigorously defended
the sovereignty of peoples, he never had anything good to say about
national borders. He lamented that independence had brought with it a
new order of absurd exclusions: Where once there was liberty of movement, now there was "damned nationality"; "back when there were no
American nations, all men of this America were brothers."³³ The figure of Irisarri still slips the noose of national memory, despite the best
efforts of Chilean historiographers who have reviled or defended him,
despite the lavish decorations of a Guatemala he declined to return to in
his old age. Architect of the boldest Pan-American solidarity plan to be
drafted between the days of Bolívar and of Martí, he may belong—like
them—everywhere and nowhere, a (Central-) American (-American)
Ahasuerus.³⁴

What is the antecedent, though, to the repatriation of bones? What
does it mean for a body to be "patriated," to belong to a place? The suggestion that Irisarri and his U.S.-published works might be understood
within the framework of *Latino*—as part of a narrative we could tell
about the Central American–American past in the United States—will
surely raise objections that he never sought citizenship (so far as we
know); that his views about *los yanquis* during his final eighteen years
were largely negative; or that his diplomatic status placed him in a special limbo, neither exile nor immigrant. Yet Irisarri arrived in New York
as he had in Quito, in Bogotá, in Caracas, in Curaçao: in flight from certain danger and in search of new opportunities. For the first six years in
New York and New Orleans, prior to those diplomatic appointments, his
status was no different from that of any other migrant, trying to make
what living he could from the skills he had. By reading backward from
the end of his story—the repatriation of his bones and his figural rein-
carnation as a medal of honor—Irisarri could be inserted into a Guatemalan genealogy of culture. But what might happen if we let go of this
preoccupation with the *telos* and consider persons, works, and circuits
of communication *in their moment*?

Nicolás Kanellos classifies U.S. Latinos and their texts as belonging
to one of three categories: the "native" (whose community predates U.S.
borders), the "immigrant," and the "exile."³⁵ Yet the last two of these
categories can be difficult to disentangle, for they require a judgment

about intentionality and carry an implicit *telos*: Exiles intend to return to their homeland, and if they do, they are not Latinos but something else. Immigrants may or may not intend to assimilate, but if they remain here at their deaths, they have become Latino by default. These retrospective categorizations about individuals become the foundation for histories that trace the "roots" of specific communities—the Puerto Rican *colonia* in New York, for instance—and in so doing celebrate the success of those who initially, intentionally, planted themselves there. As Robert McKee Irwin points out elsewhere in this volume, these narratives must leave out the stories of failure—of getting turned back at the border, shipwrecked en route, or, as in the case of the Hispanophone community of New Orleans in 1851, burned, beaten, and run out of town. It's worth questioning the celebration of communal root-setting and successful genealogical reproduction by recalling these "failed Latinos," but it is also important to challenge the way discourses of migration and assimilation rely heavily on moral judgments about what the subject *intended* to do. In closing, I want to offer Irisarri's term *errant* as a way of focusing on the undecidability of movement's present tense: a way of resisting the narrative structures that impose categories of belonging retrospectively, based upon their endings.

Intentionality scaffolds positions on both sides of contemporary debates about (im)migration. A stated intention to cross the border no matter what, or to overstay a visa illegally, will be taken by some as a sign of criminality, by others as a sign of a healthy, vigorous desire to remake oneself that has ample precedent in U.S. immigration history. Both views may be traced to a particular national myth of purposefulness that has also lent a key trope to U.S. American studies. In the 1670 Election Sermon of John Danforth that I cite among my epigraphs, the sermon that famously provided Perry Miller with the foundational trope of the Puritan (then-American) Errand into the Wilderness, the preacher searches for clues about the meaning of the colony's trials. He asks, "To what purpose came we into this place, and what expectation drew us hither?" The answer: God "planted us" and "made us dwell in a place of our own, that we may move no more" after their exile from England and Holland. However disillusioned the colonists may have become when they saw that no one across the Atlantic cared much about their experiment ("left alone with America," as Perry Miller memorably put it), Danforth finds redemption in affirming their *purposeful* decision to stay where they had been planted, to "move no more." The virtue attached to purposefulness here highlights an important philological distinction between the seventeenth-century English *errand* and the nineteenth-century English *errant*, on the one hand, and the Spanish *errante* on the other—a distinction that may be able to illuminate some of the unfulfilled claims that remain for Latino studies to make upon U.S. American studies.[36]

While in English usage the noun *errand*, derived from Saxon-Germanic roots, is consistently linked to a sense of mission and purpose (as in Danforth's sermon), the verb *to err* and its relations are Latinate, from a plethora of spoken Romance forms that evolved from *errare*, to stray, and *iterare*, to travel. The English *knight-errant*, in contrast, is a back-formation from the French *errant* that entered the language during the vogue of chivalric romance (and its burlesque, in the form of Don Quixote, although in Spanish the knight-errant is a *caballero andante*, not *errante*). The knight-errant—like the Wandering Jew, another late-medieval literary figure—represents the opposite of the purposeful mission, wandering from place to place with a clear set of values but without a specific goal (cf. *erratic*). Like an installment of a serial novel whose end is not yet known to a reader, each episode along the errant wanderer's itinerary may be appreciated in its present-ness; it need not be judged by the *telos* of how the journey or the life will ultimately end. The philosophical tradition that runs from Levinas and Blanchot through Derrida finds a particular resonance in the term *errancy* and its association with such nonpurposefulness. The poetic or prophetic word that hopes to make itself heard through the dead shell of language's conventions must get to the truth waywardly, from the margins: For Blanchot, "this is an essentially errant word, for it is always cast out of itself."[37]

An errant wandering, then, is different from a pilgrimage or a mission. It must be apprehended in the temporality of its moment. Irisarri's own presence in the United States was not a long-planned act of asylum-seeking, but the best among imperfect choices to be made at the time. Could this alternate *telos* help explain the lack of ready ways, in our culture, to think about immigrants who are anything less than fully committed to a happy-ending vision of their acceptance into the Promised Land? For many individuals who have been, now are, and will in the future be understood as U.S. Latinos, the act of migration has been less than wholly purposeful, less than fully chosen. Nor do we know what the ultimate status of many persons of Latin American origin now residing in the United States will turn out to be, given the many potential versions of "paths to citizenship" being proposed at the time of this writing—that "path" being yet another secularization of a Puritan type, the narrow path to righteousness. For the transmigrant, for the deportee, it may lead backward. Perhaps *errancy*—not as a synonym for a mistake, but as a name for a movement that has no idea where it is ultimately headed—captures more of the experience of undocumented people and their relationship to this inscrutable future than the more neutral "migrancy."[38]

If Danforth's Errand into the Wilderness intervenes in a moment of present crisis to project a clear path from past to future that the colony could follow, then Miller's reanimation of the figure in the mid–twentieth century also tried to intimate what the destiny of a nation—newly become the dominant global power—might be. Amy Kaplan influentially argued in 1993 that Miller's reading of Puritan exceptionalism sought to isolate the United States as an object of study from the complicating entanglements of empire and urged scholars to trace the webs of U.S. political and economic power, especially outside its borders. Toward the end of the essay, she points to transnational Chicano and transnational border studies as one intellectual space where these entanglements could be made visible.[39] Some two decades later, the place of Latino studies within post-imperial "American" scholarship is still far from central. The field may have shed much of its former Anglocentrism, but has it left behind its attachment to Puritan purposefulness, to the privileged "errand" of becoming-American? Is it possible to adopt an ethical stance toward the migrant that does not judge according to intentions, to the imputed purity or criminality of her ultimate purpose?

Neither critical lens of the Kaplan and Pease moment—empire/colonialism—quite captures the present-day complexity of the regime of surveillance and control over the bodies of the 12 million undocumented persons now living in the United States, a regime that Alicia Schmidt Camacho identifies as the "assault on migrant personhood." And beyond those 12 million are others who might join or resist that flow, who fall under heavy yet indirect U.S. influence through the state's financial pressure upon partner governments: Mexico, for example, has adopted many of the most brutal tactics of ICE and its predecessors to police its southern border with Guatemala, the principal funnel for tens of thousands annually of Salvadorans, Guatemalans, Hondurans, and migrants from elsewhere around the globe.[40] This route—crisscrossed by Irisarri several times—is now one of the most violent and dangerous international borders in the world; the railway he foresaw being built along the coast is now visually associated, in recent filmic and textual exposés, with the precarious lives of the mostly Central American migrants who ride northward on the tops of its trains. Yet, as Claudia Milian reminds us, we must exercise caution lest this space of crisis, too, be pressed into the service of another sentimentalized racial hierarchy that figures Central Americans as "guileless rustic beings who supply 'us' with unusual underdeveloped things."[41]

Father Alejandro Solalinde, the Mexican activist whose longtime service to migrants in Oaxaca has earned him both multiple death threats and Mexico's 2012 Human Rights Medal, powerfully deflects this tendency with his concept of *el migromo humano*. The desire for movement is, he says, an essential part of our species-being in the twenty-first century; and like the human genome, the "migrome" is a puzzle we are just learning how to read, to map, and to interpret. In a beautiful example of categorical inversion, the migrant is transformed from the most abject of souls—*no one from nowhere*—into the exemplary member of the species. Our identity comes not from where we land but from the way we move. On the website of his mission, *Hermanos en el Camino* (Brothers Along the Road), Solalinde recasts the language of Matthew 25:35—the injunction to feed the hungry and give shelter to the homeless—with an idiosyncratic translation: "Fui migrante, y me hospedaron."[42] From an errant Latino perspective, the "American" story would uncouple itself from the ends it has long been attached to. It would stop reading migrant narratives through a predetermined *telos*. It would stop caring whether the migrant has intention or not, whether he ultimately takes root or moves on to another place. It would take him in no matter what.

NOTES

1 All citations are from Irisarri, *El cristiano errante: Novela que parece historia*, ed. R. Amilcar Echeverría B. (Guatemala City: Ministerio de Educación Pública, 1960). "Encontró aquellos indios laboriosos, inteligentes, ágiles, despiertos, bien

formados, robustos, aplicados a la agricultura, al comercio, a las artes" 128; "cuyos beneficios eran comunes" 129; "le parecían más inteligentes que los mestizos, zambos y españoles de las otras partes, pues ellos eran infinitamente más hábiles alarifes que los maestros de la arquitectura que había visto en la América meridional" 132; "Halló en todos aquellos partes una vida, una actividad, un movimiento de civilización, que no esperaba hallar, ni encontró después en otras mayores poblaciones del Perú, de Chile, de las provincias argentinas, de Bolivia, del Ecuador y de la Nueva Granada" 127–28.

2 Intentionality is, of course, also at the root of criminalized discourse about "illegals": the notion that one has intentionally broken the law. There is a considerable bibliography on the problem of sympathy as a false politics, with sentimental abolitionism at its root; see Lauren Berlant, ed., *Compassion: The Culture and Politics of an Emotion* (New York: Routledge, 2004). It would be important to discuss affect theory with regard to recent bursts of liberal sympathy toward Latino migrants.

3 Arturo Arias embraces the "stutter" of the term *Central-American-American*, arguing that its very awkwardness demonstrates the inability of mainstream Latin American and Latino scholarship to account for U.S. populations of Salvadoran, Guatemalan, Honduran, Nicaraguan, Costa Rican, and Panamanian descent. See his "Central-American-Americans: Invisibility, Power, and Representation in the U.S. Latino World," *Latino Studies* 1:1, 168–87 (2003).

4 The amended model of the communications circuit endorsed by Darnton (and adaptable to different moments in the social history of books) runs from author and text to publisher/printer/paper-maker/binder; to distributor/smuggler; to agent/bookseller; to reviewer/critic/censor; to reading public(s) who buy, exchange, or pirate a text; and finally to the spaces of preservation and survival: libraries, archives, and other spaces that lead later readers to assign value to the text according to its connection to others collected in the same site. See Darnton, "'What Is the History of Books?,' Revisited," *Modern Intellectual History* 4 (2007): 495–508.

5 John Browning, *Vida e ideología de Antonio José de Irisarri* (Guatemala City: Ed. Universitaria, 1986), 10.

6 His paper *El Semanario Republicano*, like those of his ally Camilo Henríquez, disseminated revolutionary ideas; later newspapers included *La Aurora de Chile, El Monitor Araucano*, and *El Duende de Santiago* (1818). While in London in 1820, he founded *El censor americano*, on which his friend Bello collaborated.

7 Morazán, a fierce defender of the Federal Republic of Central America, was not well received by the church-backed oligarchy in Guatemala, which had historically dominated the region. Historians of Central America remain strongly divided about Morazán's "liberal" legacy.

8 The bibliography on Irisarri's political life is extensive but largely partisan, especially in Chile. In contrast to Guillermo Feliú Cruz's mostly positive assessments of Irisarri, Chilean historiography tends to depict him as a contradictory figure

who planted Enlightenment political theory in Chile but ultimately betrayed his revolutionary commitments. Following the negative assessments of Benjamin Vicuña Mackenna and Ricardo Donoso, the conservative Chilean historian Claudio Véliz has decried the million-pound loan that Irisarri negotiated in London as unnecessary, attacked Irisarri's intentions as venal, and argued that the resulting international debt crisis led to O'Higgins's downfall and to the subsequent war between Chile and Peru. See Véliz, "The Irisari Loan," *Boletín de Estudios Latinoamericanos y del Caribe* 23 (December 1977), 3–15. The controversy over Irisarri's actions with the English loan was compounded by the Treaty of Paucarpata: Irisarri's defenders point out that the treaty attempted to save the remnants of an army that had been resoundingly crushed in Peru. But the Chilean public, previously uncommitted to the war, angrily repudiated the treaty's terms. The state then reinforced the navy and army and eventually defeated the combined Peru–Bolivia forces, dissolving their confederation to Chile's great strategic advantage. Browning's research is the most neutral and the most thorough and includes documents either not consulted by, or ignored by, Donoso that contradict his characterization of Irisarri as a self-interested traitor.

9 On the novel's birth and the later-excised pirate episode, see John D. Browning, "*El Cristiano Errante* de Antonio Jose de Irisarri: su genesis, su acogida y sus 'Paginas Perdidas,'" *Revista Iberoamericana* 36, no. 73 (1970), 613–27. While his youthful writing was full of revolutionary citations of Rousseau, Locke, and Paine, his political ideology evolved: He was later willing to entertain constitutional monarchy, as were Bolívar and Bello. He was moderately anticlerical with liberal social views—a strong advocate of deregulated finances and free trade. He was mostly associated with Conservative politicians (with notable exceptions like Mosquera), although it would be a mistake to assume that either *Liberal* or *Conservative* represents a consistent political position during this period. (For instance, the four newspapers Irisarri founded during his seven years in Ecuador were underwritten by Juan José Flores and supported by his former enemy, the Liberal Vicente Rocafuerte—whose rebellion against Flores in 1845 sent Irisarri on to Nueva Granada, the very nation from which Ecuador had broken away.)

Nor should we overstate Irisarri's attachment to the term *Christian*, which he uses as a careless synonym for *person*. He described himself as a "primitive Christian" who tried to follow the self-abnegation of Jesus (Browning, *Vida* 181), as well as a lowercase *liberal*, which he defines as "tolerance of differing opinions, and the strict observance of the principles that uphold social liberalism" rather than advance one's personal agenda (Browning, *Vida* 152; translation mine).

10 See Lou Charnon-Deutsch, "Of Jews and Jesuits in the Nineteenth-Century French and Spanish Feuilleton," *Comparative Literature Studies* 46: 4 (2009), 589–617. On serial publication and periodicity, see Patricia Okker's Introduction to *Transnationalism and American Serial Fiction* (New York: Routledge, 2011).

11 "Ocupándote tú en leer los periódicos del día, y las arengas de nuestros tribunos"; "ocúpate en algo que te traiga algún provecho" (Irisarri 2). "Tribuno" revives the Roman sense of the speaker/writer who defends the rights of the people—that is, the modern journalist.

12 The rare 1847 Bogotá edition, which scholars fruitlessly hunted for as late as the 1980s, can now be accessed electronically on the website of the Biblioteca Nacional de Colombia; it contains charmingly mock-archaic chapter titles that are missing from the Guatemalan edition. Feliú Cruz's restorative work took place during a fertile period in Chilean revolutionary historiography, when educational reformists aimed to instill cultural nationalism in a much broader swath of the country's middle and working classes. The publication of *El cristiano errante* by the national university press may be seen as a kind of re-adoption into Chilean cultural genealogy: Irisarri's son Hermógenes also became a politician and minor poet; his daughter married an important Chilean landscape painter; and a great-great-granddaughter served in the Bachelet cabinet. But see note 8 on the later backlash from Donoso and his followers who challenged his loyalty to Chile. Another twist to these national dramas of filiopietism is that Irisarri fathered at least one child outside marriage, a son who became rector of a university in Cartagena and founded a college in Panama named in Irisarri's honor (García Bauer 32).

13 The hero of Irisarri's other novel, *Historia del perínclito Epaminondas de Cauca* (*History of the Incomparable Epaminondas of Cauca*) (New York, 1863), was modeled on Bolívar's tutor, Simón Rodríguez. Among Irisarri's other extant fictional works are three short stories using the univocal constraint: "*Amar hasta fracasar*," using *a* as the only vowel; "*Pepe, el de Jerez*," using *e*, and "*Los mozos gordos*," using *o*. This constraint had been a minor fad among some seventeenth-century writers in Spain, preceding the Oulipians of the twentieth (García Bauer 65–70). These interests in history and in language converge in his other major publication from this period, *Cuestiones filológicas* (New York, 1865).

14 See Browning, *Vida* 205–15 on the transformation of his youthful admiration for Paine and Franklin, and for the liberal immigration policy of the United States, which he believed to be responsible for its greater success with the democratic experiment despite slavery, which he condemned. As late as the 1830s, he wrote that he would be a populist democrat if he lived in the United States (205). Only after the U.S.–Mexico War, which he decried in his Bogotá paper, does his criticism of the expansionism and interventionism encouraged by the Monroe Doctrine begin.

15 The historian Ames McGuinness traced a single extant copy of the New York *El Revisor*, which is not catalogued anywhere in the United States, to an archive in Panama and transcribed three articles about Panama from it (personal communication). There is also one issue in the Biblioteca Nacional de Colombia. J. M. Torres Caicedo interviewed Irisarri for his *Ensayos biográficos y de crítica literaria sobre los principales poetas y literatos hispano-americanos* (Paris, 1863) and pro-

vides the detail about Irisarri's marketing strategy for Spanish-language learners (1: 217).

16 Family letter quoted in Browning, *Vida* 200.

17 None of Irisarri's biographers mentions anything about New Orleans: Because he began and ended his time in the United States in New York, they seem to have simply assumed that he never left the city; this letter's reference to going to "the country" already puts this into question. His name appears in the New Orleans City Directory for 1851 next to the address of the print shop/bookstore: "Irisarri, I. A. [*sic*], firm Aleman, Gomez & Irisarri." On the importance of *La Patria/La Unión* in transnational print culture, and on Gómez's own serial novel, see my article "Tracking the First Latino Novel" in Okker, *op. cit.*, 36–63. Gómez's subtitle, "Novela que parece historia," is strikingly similar to Irisarri's "Novela que tiene mucho de historia," and although of course this play between *novel* and *history* runs rampant in the first century and a half of the novel as a form, it raises the possibility that Gómez had perhaps read one of the Bogotá versions of *Cristiano*, discovered Irisarri was in the United States, and subsequently invited him to collaborate on the newspaper. Gómez had himself started a paper in New York City in 1845, but it failed financially; an editorial in *La Patria*'s final issue before the name change (December 31, 1850) boasts of how Spanish print culture has thrived in New Orleans, in contrast.

18 *La Unión*, January 8, 1851, 1. I have not yet attempted a line-by-line comparison of the Bogotá serial or codex versions next to the New Orleans version to see what was "corrected." The serialization was completed in May 1851.

19 "[D]efender la raza hispanoamericana de los frecuentes e injustos ataques a que suele verse expuesta en este país"; "en vis a la poca justicia que se ha hecho por la prensa anglo-americana." *La Unión*, January 3, 1851, 2.

20 "The Unfortunates: What the Life Spans of Early Black Books Tell Us About Book History," in *Early African-American Print Culture*, eds. Jordan Stein and Lara Cohen (Philadelphia: University of Pennsylvania Press, 2012), 42.

21 Lazo, "Migrant Archives," in Russ Castronovo and Susan Gillman, eds., *States of Emergency* (Chapel Hill: University of North Carolina Press, 2009), 37–54. There may be much more evidence about Irisarri's life between 1849 and 1857 in the family papers held by Irisarri's descendants in Santiago de Chile: As Lazo points out, such private archives illustrate gaps about what the state does not deem worth collecting. I thank Alejandra Díaz Balart in Buenos Aires, who found out about my research on *La Patria* on the Internet, for copies of her ancestor Victoriano Alemán's letters describing his dramatic flight from the New Orleans mob in August 1851; her family also holds the only complete copy of the 1850 run of *La Patria*, of which only a few numbers exist in the United States. The only consistent run, from 1846–47, 1849, and 1851, is preserved at the Historic New Orleans Collection: On the original leather bindings, the spines were stamped "V. Aleman."

22 The most convincing literary reading of *Cristiano* is that of Jorge Shan Chem, who describes it as most strongly resembling the digressive, mixed travel-and-satirical-

commentary character of eighteenth-century writing. See *"El cristiano errante: entre la encrucijada discursiva y el desencanto utópico,"* *Filología y Lingüística* 30: 1 (2004): 61–73; and in particular, on Irisarri's refutation of Buffon and dePauw on the supposed inferiority of the New World, 66–67. Fernando Unzueta closes his *La imaginación histórica y el romance nacional en Hispanoamérica* (Lima: Latinoamericana Editores, 1996) with a chapter on *Cristiano*, which he reads as staunchly conservative in its rejection of progressive narratives. While the scientific and philosophical digressions take Irisarri's novel too far from the hero's journey at times to label it as "picaresque," in other respects its homage to Cervantes is obvious: The Prologue (which contains the phrase *"de cuyo nombre no quiero acordarme"* in the very first sentence) meditates on the distinction between truth and fiction; Don Quixote's status as a *"cristiano viejo"* informs the type of the "errante Christian"; and Romualdo makes two sallies on his journey.

23 Stephens, *Incidents of Travel in Central America, Chiapas, and the Yucatan* (1841), qtd. in Stephen Benz, *Guatemalan Journey* (Austin: University of Texas Press, 1996), 113–14. Benz's volume surveys the range of misapprehensions of indigenous Guatemalans, from dismissive views like Stephens's to the still-powerful tendency to romanticize and exoticize them.

24 "[S]e hallaban en aquellos pueblos, sin saber cómo, el principio de la jurisprudencia inglesa de no ser juzgado el hombre sino por sus iguales, lo que debía dar a los juzgados la mejor de las garantías contra el espíritu de rivalidad y de prevención," "no dejaba las más veces de ser fatal a los indios cuando eran españoles los demandados," 139–40.

25 This was one of several efforts by heavily indigenous regions to break away from the early Central American states. The anti-Tzul historiography of Irisarri's time argued that the uprising had not been supported by most Mayans in Los Altos and was instead a despotic power grab by the briefly crowned "King Lucas." Over the course of the nineteenth century, Mayan political organizations became increasingly stratified into elite and peasant classes in exchange for limited sovereignty. See Greg Grandin, *The Blood of Guatemala* (Durham, N.C.: Duke University Press, 2000), 54–81. I am certainly not arguing that Irisarri does, or could, speak from a Mayan perspective here. However, his rejection of most of his contemporaries' ideas about primitivism and progress sets him apart from those liberal thinkers, including Martí, who urged Indian assimilation.

26 "Ni tengo cuenta con otros progresos, que las de la razón natural y esta me basta para hacerme conocer que lo que estamos llamando política no es sino obrar contra los principios, cometiendo las más evidentes contradicciones." "Lo que los angloamericanos hicieron con ellos y con los descendientes de africanos, de no considerarlos sino como harina de otro costal, o como el salvado de la harina" (177). "Nadie en el mundo puede tener razón ninguna, ni alegar pretextos de luces del siglo, ni de progreso de civilización, para oponerse a la voluntad de la mayoría de un pueblo" (178). "Los indios [de Totonicapán] no pierdan la esperanza de recobrar su nacionalidad" (174).

27 See Chen Sham 4 and Browning 69 for further discussion of the *socio* as the ideal citizen, and society modeled as a commercial enterprise.

28 ". . . es justo y equitativo todo lo que es, o puede ser provechoso a los Estados-Unidos, aunque sea en daño y perjuicio del mundo entero." ". . . estos hombres justos no han podido triunfar del partido que quiere hacer por fuerza la anexación de la América Española a los EU para que vuelva a establecerse en aquellos paises la esclavitud" (Carlos García Bauer, *Antonio José de Irisarri, diplomático de América: Su actuación en los Estados Unidos; la colonización negra y la invasión filibustera* [Guatemala City: Imprenta Universidad de San Carlos, 1970], 48). Irisarri was at the time awaiting recognition, which he eventually received, as the legitimate U.S. ambassador for the loyalist Nicaraguan government. His vigorous work against U.S. state support for Walker, and his facilitation of the cooperative military efforts among the often-warring states of Guatemala, El Salvador, Honduras, and Costa Rica to oust Walker between 1856 and 1860, is detailed in this volume.

29 Letter dated May 15, 1865, in Enrique del Cid Fernández, ed., *Epistolario inédito de Antonio José de Irisarri, 1857–1868*, (Guatemala City: Ed. del Ejército, 1966), 155. The letter expresses a concern that because the Civil War has ended, the United States will take up its former expansionism again and make all of Latin America "una colonia de los Estados Unidos": "si como yo creo, de esta vez viniese a tierra la fatal doctrina, yo tendría la gloria de haber sido el primero en combatirla" (if the fatal doctrine does come to this, as I believe, I would have the glory of being the first one to have fought against it). For other writing about the Monroe Doctrine as a rationale for unchecked expansion, see Cid Fernández 60, 64, 185, 200–1, 220–21.

30 Irisarri, he says, offers "una hermosa demostración de comprensión y de grandeza civica, de solidaridad entre los países del istmo y de hermandad centroamericana" (*Diplomático*, 125).

31 The recipients of the "Orden de Antonio José de Irisarri" span quite an ideological gamut: from a novelist who was denounced by the Left for not speaking out against the repressive government of the 1970s, to longtime diplomats, to human rights lawyers. The vision of returning the bones, of course, raises the spectre of the indigenous genocide and civil violence of the 1980s and contemporary debates about the spaces of its memorialization.

32 Qtd. in Echeverría, "Introducción" to *El cristiano errante* (Guatemala, 1960), 1.

33 "Maldita nacionalidad," "Cuando no había naciones americanos, todos hombres de esta América éramos hermanos": qtd. in Browning 130. He is recalling here the trauma of being detained at the border during his return to Central America in the 1820s, when he was briefly defense minister of Guatemala: While the Irisarri family home had been in Guatemala City, their *hacienda* was in Sonsonte, now located in El Salvador. Salvadoran independence had been a movement against centuries of dominance by Guatemalan governors, as well as against Spanish colonial rule.

34 U.S. historians have neglected Irisarri's central role in designing the "Confederación de los Estados Hispanoamericanos" in 1856. It explicitly excluded the

United States and was thus quite different from the Pan-American Union and the OAS that followed. Although signed by representatives of seven countries, this mutual defense accord was never ratified by all their congresses. See Garcia Bauer, *Antonio José de Irisarri: Insigne escritor y polifacético prócer de la independencia americana* (Guatemala City: Tipografía Nacional, 2002), 57–64.

35 Nicolás Kanellos, Introduction to *Herencia: The Anthology of Hispanic Literature of the United States* (Oxford: Oxford University Press, 2002), 5–29. The division, while perhaps necessary at some level, is problematic in that the category corresponds to the status of the author within one of those three categories, assuming that readers and texts will follow.

36 Samuel Danforth, "A Brief Recognition of New-Englands Errand into the Wilderness: An Online Electronic Text Edition," ed. Paul Royster, 18, http://digitalcommons.unl.edu/libraryscience/35/. My thanks to Jesse Alemán for pointing out the suggestive proximity of Irisarri's title to the foundational *errand* in the wilderness. Intentionality isn't only the intent to start a tradition through genealogy; it's also crucial to the property laws governing land claims in many histories of settler colonialism: to "stake a claim" is to declare an intention to settle for a defined period of time, and the fulfilment of that intention (often by violently evicting others) conveys proper title.

37 Maurice Blanchot, *The Space of Literature*, trans. Ann Smock (Lincoln: University of Nebraska Press, 1989), 51. For the figure of the poet/prophet crying in the wilderness, see Emmanuel Levinas, "The Poet's Vision," in *Proper Names*, trans. Michael Smith (Stanford, Calif.: Stanford University Press, 2007), 127–39. Levinas, Blanchot, and Jacques Derrida embrace errancy as the means through which the imperfect, error-filled vehicle of language can commit itself to a truth that paradoxically lies outside the power of language to express. Usefully for my argument here, poststructuralism challenges the notion of an intentional subject: Language exceeds or subverts intention.

38 My concept of the "errant Latino" owes something to Laura Lomas's notion of the "migrant Latino subject" exemplified by Martí, and for this reason I have drawn some comparisons between Irisarri and Martí throughout. Not every Latino is a migrant, and even the cases most likely to attract white sympathy for immigration reform—undocumented persons brought as children to the United States—may not be best understood through tropes of movement. The nonteleological sense of errancy, I believe, better suits the uncertainties of many individuals who must learn to live without a clear story of their future identities. See Lomas, *Translating Empire: José Martí, Migrant Latino Subjects, and American Modernities* (Durham, N.C.: Duke University Press, 2009).

39 Amy Kaplan, "Left Alone with America: The Absence of Empire in the Study of American Culture," in Kaplan and Donald Pease, *Cultures of US Imperialism* (Durham, N.C.: Duke University Press, 1994); see especially 16–17. For a summary of how Latina scholars Lora Romero and Josie Saldaña-Portillo have responded to Kaplan's glancing reference to Chicano studies here, see Richard T. Rodriguez,

"The Locations of Chicano/a and Latino/a Studies," in John Carlos Rowe, ed. *Concise Companion to American Studies* (Hoboken, N.J.: Wiley, 2010), 201–5.

40 Alicia Schmidt Camacho, "Hailing the Twelve Million: U.S. Immigration Policy, Deportation, and the Imaginary of Lawful Violence," *Social Text* 28:4 (Winter 2010), 1–24, 20. Schmidt Camacho considers the southern Mexican border within the "migratory circuit" linked to the United States: "It is time to create another category of legal subject, to honor the membership of migrants in U.S. society, and to recognize our bonds of community beyond the limited borders of the nation" (19). She argues that a human rights approach to migrancy would reimagine citizenship as the default category by which people are presumed to be deserving of rights.

41 Journalistic books about the journey by train across this "shadow border" widely circulated in the United States include Sonia Nazario's *Enrique's Journey* (2007) and Oscar Martínez's *The Beast* (English translation 2013), complementing Cory Fukunaga's feature film *Sin Nombre* (2009) and Pedro Ultreras's documentary *The Beast* (2011). The revisionist "1848/1898" periodizations offered by post-imperial American studies, which have also been made to serve narratives of early (Mexican/Caribbean) Latino history, don't resonate for Central Americans. Latino studies is scrambling to address the fact that Salvadorans now outnumber Cubans in the United States; see the Summer 2013 special issue of *Latino Studies* co-edited by Arturo Arias and Claudia Milian for a summary of the state of the field. On the "dark-brownness" associated with Central Americans and especially with Guatemalans, see Milian, *Latining America: Black-Brown Passages and the Coloring of Latino/a Studies* (Athens: University of Georgia Press, 2013), 123–50.

42 Lecture at Lozano Long Conference on Central Americans and the Latino Landscape, UT-Austin, February 24, 2012, https://www.utexas.edu/cola/insts/llilas/digital-resources/llilas_av/archive/archived_av.php. Spanish translations of this verse usually give *forastero* or *extranjero* (foreigner/stranger); Solalinde's substitution of *migrant* is clearly directed toward the context.

2

Historicizing Nineteenth-Century Latina/o Textuality

RAÚL CORONADO

Why has the Latina/o nineteenth century proven so recalcitrant to assimilation into the national U.S. canon and, indeed, to historicization? One could easily ask the same of Mexican, Puerto Rican, Cuban, and other Latin American literary traditions, though certainly few have actually made this case. Given that most of those working in the field of nineteenth-century Latina/o literary history—the vast majority of the contributors to this volume, for example—work in English as opposed to Spanish departments, one could assume that the goal is to integrate Latina/o literature into the U.S. canon. However, I submit that it is the conceptual framework of the nation which raises serious problems: To which national literary tradition would nineteenth-century Latina/o writers belong?[1] Literary canons and modern historiography, as we will see, emerged as ways to buttress the spirit of the newly born American nations, hoping to offer them ontological certainty.

In many ways, nation-formation has been the *sine qua non* of modern academic disciplines. The rise of modern history during the late eighteenth century went hand in hand with the rise of modern nations; they sought each other out, as it were, and history provided the nation with its much-desired antiquity.[2] The institutionalization of the study of U.S. literature took place much more recently, during the early twentieth century, and parallels the literary arrival of the United States on the world's stage. Some fifty years prior, in 1879, Henry James may have lamented the dismal literary state of affairs in the United States, but the American scene was quite another by the late 1930s.[3] By then Pound, Fitzgerald, Hemingway, and others had become world-renowned writers providing the United States with that much-yearned-for cultural supremacy which nineteenth-century authors had so desperately desired.

While U.S. literature had finally received European adulation, the story within the U.S. academy was a different one, and the academic study of U.S. literature struggled to establish itself as a distinct field of study until the mid–twentieth century. It was along the lines of Cold War cultural nationalism that it established itself, rising as it did concomitantly with the institutionalization of American studies.[4] U.S. literary historiography came to parallel the grand narrative of Manifest Destiny, establishing itself on the eastern seaboard with the British colonies and, with time, expanding and moving west across the United States.

It is no surprise then that the multicultural movement of the 1980s and '90s received such a strong conservative backlash, re-inscribing as it did those who had long been marginalized or excluded from these grand narratives of history and belonging, for even then one could see that re-inscription could not and would not merely entail some logic of accretion. If these marginalized subjects had been written out of national (literary) histories, the task of writing them back into history would by necessity require a logic other than that of national formation. One can identify this tension in Ramón Saldívar's now classic *Chicano Narrative* (1990). Saldívar is at pains at locating Chicana/o narrative as a component of a national U.S. literature even as he describes it as the "literary productions of a culture at the margin of *both* the Anglo-American and Latin American cultural worlds."[5] Indeed, one may say that national histories could be written on the basis of the very elision of marginalized peoples as subjects from history.[6] The relationship between these subaltern subjects and national narratives is at best an antagonistic one.

Given that the discipline of literary studies arose on the bedrock of the nation itself, how does one write a literary history that falls outside the logic of the nation? How does one work within a discipline that constructed its object of knowledge ("American literature") and its methods along the perimeters of the nation? How does one write a literary history of Latinas/os that transcends and predates national borders? I use *Latina/o* to refer not to identities—few if anyone, in fact, identified as Latina/o in the nineteenth century—but to the manner in which nineteenth-century Spanish American communities in the United States drew from both Hispanic-Catholic and Anglo-Protestant epistemologies to understand the world they inhabited. The question is not restricted to Latina/o literary history alone. The persistent model of nation-formation may account for the still emergent field of nineteenth-century Latina/o historiography writ broadly. Innumerable literary critics and historians have taken nation-time as its periodization, starting with the juridical birth of Mexican Americans giving us the date of 1848 (the conquest and annexation of half of Mexico's territory) or with the 1898 Spanish–American War, which led to the colonization of Puerto Rico, Cuba, the Philippines, and Guam. But how does one think *across* these periods, given that, after all, the Latinas/os living *across* these periods surely did not cast off their subjectivities for new ones, nor did their social formations shift as quickly as the nation was called into being?

The task here is to think against the grain, against the nation as te-leology. If the birth of Latinas/os has been aligned with the foundational dates of 1848 or 1898, I propose that Latina/o history refuse this periodization and think creatively through and with the archive. One strategy of refusing the nation is to look askew at these foundational moments by turning to alternative—minoritized, as it were—documents that yield different narratives of belonging.[7] Rather than center on the fetishized U.S.–Mexico War, literary historians could focus instead on the circulation of ideas before the arrival of the printing press in what is today the Southwest. The first presses begin to enter as early as 1813, but they entered a complex yet completely understudied world dominated by a centuries-old manuscript culture and tradition of declamation. How did these communities engage with ideas, the imagination, and writing, and how did the printing press transform (or not) the uses to which writing had long been put? Historians could also focus on how Latinas/os developed the centuries-long Catholic counter-Reformation concept of the secular. Indeed, it was the Protestant Reformation itself that produced the concept of the secular, cleaving forever the Divine from the temporal world.[8] Rather than write literary histories that enshrine Latina/o resistance to Anglo American conquest and colonization, historians could focus instead on the accidents and reverse formations that led socially complex Latina/o communities to see themselves devolve from elite, Spanish American, Catholic communities of colonizers to increasingly racialized communities that were seen as homogeneous and devoid of sociocultural complexity. Instead of narratives of triumph, historians could focus on moments of failure, of dreams that failed to cohere, and offer contemplative histories of these moments. What would it

mean to write literary histories of Latinas/os that did not lead to the presumed and critically undertheorized goal of assimilating into the canon
of U.S. literary studies or, even, that of any Spanish American nation?

In effect, Latina/o history could develop what the historian Gyan
Prakash has described as "post-foundational" histories. Such histories
seek "to make cultural forms and even historical events contingent . . .
[in order to] write those histories that history and historiography have
excluded."[9] It is precisely the narrative of nation-formation that has occluded and makes opaque the discursive world of nineteenth-century
Latinas/os, a world filled with texts and individuals that held competing, often contradictory, beliefs. If the goal is to think outside the logic
of the nation, then the challenge for Latina/o literary historians is to
write a nonteleological history that does not set out to arrange the literary archive only to reaffirm the long history of Latina/o resistance and
triumph of nationally imagined communities.

Latina/o literary history will have to deconstruct the category of the
literary even as it narrates a new history. We now know that the contemporary definition of *literature* as an autonomous, imaginative, aesthetic
sphere of writing largely independent of other genres of writing only
began to emerge in the nineteenth century. A mutation occurred in the
history of writing in the West (Catholic and Protestant), one originating
with the Reformation and becoming distinct in the eighteenth century
and into the nineteenth. It is during the nineteenth century that the category of the literary, as we know it, emerged as a recognizable genre
distinct from other forms of writing.[10] But embedded in this notion of
the literary was writing as a search for immanence and belonging, for
what Jacques Derrida described as a yearning for a metaphysics of presence. Writing increasingly becomes a means of approximating a sense of
the divine: "God is the name and the element of that which makes possible an absolutely pure and absolutely self-present self-knowledge . . .
[I]t can be *produced as auto-affection*, only through the *voice*: an order
of the signifier by which the subject takes from itself into itself, does not
borrow outside of itself the signifier that it emits and that affects it at the
same time."[11] Rather than merely reflect God's fixed meaning, language
comes to be seen as a self-reflexive, flexible tool of understanding.

Prior to the late eighteenth century, literature had been embedded in an expansive, signifying language related to other knowledge-forms. In writing about the history of the Latin American novel, for example, Roberto González Echevarría argues that the novel "brings us back to the beginnings of writing, looking for an empty present wherein to make a first inscription"; it is a search for the "origin of being."[12] Similar claims have been made of Anglo American literature. Larzer Ziff theorizes this historical transformation as being one of a movement from immanence to representation, "from a common belief that reality resided in a region beneath appearance and beyond manipulation to the belief that it could be constructed and so made identical with appearance."[13] Ziff, too, claims that a shift occurred at the end of the eighteenth century, one in which representation became the dominant mode of understanding the relationship one had with writing in which one used language to construct one's reality. This shift from immanence to representation, from the idea that one spoke or wrote from an immutable, fixed sense of self to one where "there is no assumed real self that is being represented" provided some of the ideological infrastructure that would allow novels and fiction to flourish.[14]

What characterizes the modern definition of literature is its search for what Derrida describes as a metaphysics of presence or what Ziff describes as a search for immanence but with an abiding sense that that search itself is a representation, a self-reflexive attempt to arrive at foundational truth while simultaneously being aware that that truth is but a product of language that could be infinitely peeled back layer after layer. The history of Latina/o literary culture must be situated between these competing histories of American literatures. It becomes clear that this enterprise must be interdisciplinary, weaving between literary and intellectual history, pursuing this yearning for a sense of ontological certainty, for presence across any form of representation.[15]

In tracing the discursive dispersal of writing prior to the consolidation of the literary, literary historians are often at pains to demonstrate that what they are studying eventually *did* yield to the novel or, more broadly, to the literary. But what if it had not or did not? What if writing continued to manifest itself in its undifferentiated form as it had before *qua* literature? Instead of tracing the discursive origins of the literary, what if literary historians turned instead to what Derrida described as a history of grammatology, a discursive history of textuality that did not necessarily yield to the teleological category of the literary, one in which textuality was not reduced to script but inhabited a more capacious world that also included the work of orality and visuality in the making of knowledge?[16]

Rather than a history of Latina/o literary culture, we should describe this enterprise as a history of textuality, a grammatology of sorts, one that does not seek to reduce the plurality of textuality to the fetishized aesthetic polished forms of literature (e.g., the novel, the short story, the poem, the play) but seeks instead to trace the discursive (trans)formations of writing as a mode of searching for immanence. Nineteenth-century Latina/o textuality, then, operated in an undifferentiated field of writing, one that was dominated by oral and visual culture, manuscripts, epistolary forms, revolutionary pamphlets and broadsides, political journalism, memoirs, poetry, histories, and novels that sought to sustain and establish its own sense of presence of being, a desire to achieve transcendence and belonging in the world. What we find in the nineteenth-century Latina/o archive is not a wholesale contestation of U.S. imperialism (though that too does emerge). Rather, we find a yearning for the creation of a new modern world, one that begins in the nineteenth century by imagining an improved transatlantic Hispanic world, continues by seeking to replace that world with Spanish American nations, and concludes the century beaten, baffled, and discombobulated by recalcitrant racial violence and U.S. colonialism.

To pursue this project, let me suggest a three-part methodology. First, as several literary historians have argued, Latina/o literary history must be comparative: We must be familiar with the literary and intellectual histories of the United States, Spanish America, and Spain, because these histories shaped and impacted the lives and thought of nineteenth-century Latinas/os, many of whom traveled throughout the Pacific and Atlantic worlds.[17] Second, in order to track the discursive shifts in textuality, literary historians must engage in interdisciplinary archival research. The Spanish empire was an empire of paper that produced a vast "documentary umbilical cord," as Angel Rama described it.[18] The Spanish and Mexican archives in Texas, New Mexico, and California, for example, produced an extraordinary amount of documentation of nineteenth-century Latina/o life and culture, and so too did the various Spanish diplomats living in Washington, D.C., Philadelphia, and New Orleans, especially in regard to the various movements for independence in Spanish America.[19] Studying these archives, however, will require extensive Spanish-reading skills and familiarity with nineteenth-century manuscripts.

Given that the vast majority of these archival collections remains largely untapped, Latina/o historians of writing should focus on regional histories. As Francisco A. Lomelí proposed: "Concentrating on a single geographical area allows for viewing a complex network of interfacing data that provide a three-dimensional representation of a regional society. The cross-sectional stratification offers a more complete picture of trends, happenings and ideas. It encompasses historical revisionism, cultural anthropology, theories on culture, consciousness of race and class, partisan politics and literary theory."[20] The regional case model should be placed in productive tension with other larger, discursive networks in which the region was embedded. Though nineteenth-century communities in Texas, New Mexico, and California had very little communication with one another, they were embedded in larger discursive worlds. Early-nineteenth-century Spanish Texas, for example, had long been enmeshed with Louisiana, and, from there, with other important routes of trade, with Philadelphia, St. Louis, Florida, Cuba, and Mexico. California, on the other hand, had extensive networks with other port cities on the Pacific coast. Beginning with the Gold Rush, San Francisco, in particular, cultivated a literary-journalistic network that connected communities in Los Angeles, Mexico, and Chile, as other contributors to this volume show.

Yet, in order for the archival research to be efficient, historians of textuality must develop expertise in the historiography of the region and period in which they are working. Doing so will not only allow the grammatologist to better understand the historical context, but these published histories more often than not also contain references to some of the most intriguing of texts in archives. But engaging in this kind of interdisciplinary work will also require a rethinking of the history of writing and its epistemological claims of causality, especially in relation to other branches of history, such as literary, intellectual, cultural, social, and political history. Rather than see these historical subfields in some kind of competition for "truth," we should see them as complementing one another, each emphasizing methods and archives that flesh out our understanding of the past, and we should engage in rigorous, animated interdisciplinary conversations.

By working inductively through primary materials, historians of textuality can then begin to develop alternative histories of imagined communities that transcended, indeed preceded, the nation. Finally, as Lomelí suggested above, historians must develop different, interdisciplinary reading strategies to read both with and against the archive. The idea that the historian merely lines up facts in order to tell a story has long been revealed as a naïve fiction; the historian selects certain facts while ignoring others in order to emplot them into a particular kind of history, whether the historian is aware of this process or not.[21] Theories of formal textual analysis or close reading offer the historian skills to interpret the archive in order to unpack the various discursive significances of a text (whether they be aesthetic, formal, generic, subjective, political, historical, etc.). At a more deductive level, theories or philosophies of history, language, and knowledge will allow the historian to theorize self-consciously the type of history they produce.[22] Historians should engage in extensive discussions regarding the creation of archives, evidence, and disciplinary differences. It may be that historians of Latina/o writing will reveal imagined communities that do not align neatly with the nation and may thus offer new ways of imagining communities of belonging that redress the contemporary aporias of the nation.

If history has served as the nation's right-hand man, how will history have to be rewritten in order to move beyond the nation? National histories have long been emplotted as Romance.[23] What alternatives can take the place of Romantic histories of the coming-into-being of the nation? Because of the ubiquity of histories emplotted as Romances, the genres of tragedy or satire might offer a more capacious interpretive framework for understanding the nineteenth century, a century that began with the optimism and utopian spirit of early-nineteenth-century Spanish American revolutionaries and concluded with the pessimism of a dwindling, increasingly racialized community of Spanish Americans.

It is not that emplotting histories as tragedy will offer a more "accurate" account than emplotting them as Romances; however, given the proliferation of Romantic histories, it may be that we may learn more from the less-told tragic history. Tragic histories would de-emphasize nostalgia in favor of "taking seriously the forces which *oppose* the effort at human redemption."[24] These would be non-nostalgic, meditative histories seeking to understand in depth particular moments in time. Instead of grand narratives of the manifest destiny of U.S. expansion, empire, and colonialism—and, thus, the inevitable incorporation of Spanish American literary expression into U.S. literary studies—Latina/o literary history should, in the words of Kirsten Silva Gruesz, who cites Walter Benjamin, "'blast a specific era out of the homogenous course of history' [263], and in doing so to open up a new kind of experience of the past."[25]

The anthropologist David Scott has contemplated a similar impasse in Romantic postcolonial historiography, and has, too, advocated for the tragic mode: "What then is the sense of the tragic for our postcolonial time? Because tragedy has a more respectful attitude to the contingencies of the past in the present, to the uncanny ways in which its remains come back to usurp our hopes and subvert our ambitions, it demands from us more patience for paradox and more openness to chance than the narrative of anticolonial Romanticism does, confident in its striving and satisfied in its own sufficiency."[26] In a similar vein, then, rather than produce teleologies of Latina/o subject-formation ("we were always there"), the genre of the tragedy would refuse to rush to conclusion—that is, to *end* with the arrival of contemporary Latinas/os. Instead, the emphasis would be on pausing, reflecting, contemplating the discursive formations that weave in and out of Latina/o history, full of its own complexity and contradictions. If the goal is to think outside the logic of the nation, the historian of textuality may indeed become a Foucaultian genealogist producing, in the words of Giorgio Agamben, a "philosophical archaeology": "a science of ruins, a 'ruinology' whose object [of study are the *archai* or origins of] . . . . what could or ought to have been given and perhaps one day might be; for the moment, though, they exist only in the condition of partial objects or ruins."[27] How can this dystopic history at the margins—figuratively and literally—of Spanish America and the United States reveal alternative though perhaps all-too-often closed-off paths to modernity? Rather than write Romantic histories of Latina/o resistance or histories that serve to celebrate the diversification of the U.S. literary canon, we should experiment by writing histories that are more in line with the archive: histories of a world that was not to come. Here I would like to turn to one of the earliest Spanish-language publications from Philadelphia as an example of how one text can open up a new window into our understanding of the past.

The Hispanic world at the turn of the nineteenth century was in turmoil.[28] The elite in Spain, Spanish America, and the Philippines were bitterly aware that the Hispanic monarchy, comprising the kingdoms of the Spanish peninsula and the vice-royalties in America and the Philippines, had long lost its grandeur and global political-economic power. Indeed, the eighteenth-century Spanish monarchy had sought to reform the Hispanic world and did so by implementing the Bourbon reforms. But the reforms, in the eyes of many, worked too slowly and, in the eyes of Spanish Americans, merely sought to colonize Spanish America further. Among the voices of reform, one of the most cherished goals was transforming the top-down logic of mercantile capitalism by embracing Adam Smith's radically new ideas of free-trade capitalism, with its emphasis on allowing those at the local level to determine the flow of goods.

From Philadelphia would emerge some of the earliest Spanish-language imprints that radically advocated for these changes. The first Spanish diplomats to the United States—Carlos Martínez de Irujo, the Marquis de Casa Irujo; and his consul general Valentín de Foronda—embraced these new Enlightenment-inspired political economic theories. Both of these men stand as symbols of the particular stream of Enlightenment thought that entered Spain, a stream that emphasized more the modern discourse of political economy than that of natural rights.[29] French philosophers, such as Condillac and Condorcet, had translated and, in the process, altered the work of English and Scottish philosophers such as John Locke and Adam Smith. And their translations were, in turn, likewise translated and altered by Casa Irujo and Foronda, among others, producing significantly transformed philosophies. In Philadelphia, both men became some of the earliest Hispanic members of the American Philosophical Society, where they both contributed to the early history of Hispanophone publishing in the United States.

In 1803, on the eve of the wars of Spanish American independence that would begin five years later, the American Philosophical Society of Philadelphia published an anonymous Spanish-language document that advocated the separation of Spain from America. *Carta sobre lo que debe hacer un príncipe que tenga colonias a gran distancia (Letter concerning what a prince should do with his colonies held at a great distance)* did not seek so much the independence of America as it did its abandonment, and the letter did so in the name of ensuring the tranquility and well-being of the people. The author sought to improve the Hispanic monarchy and proposed the abandonment of mercantilism in favor of free trade as the best way to do so. As it turns out, this little-known document reveals the fascinating world of Hispanic transatlantic thought and print culture, one that does not necessarily point to a large Spanish-language community in Philadelphia but does reveal how integral Philadelphia was to the circulation of thought in the turn-of-the-nineteenth-century Hispanic world.

The letter is signed only with the initial "F.," yet internal evidence makes it clear that Valentín de Foronda is the author.[30] At fourteen pages, it is a convoluted, curious document, brief as it is, and comprises an eight-page letter prefaced with a one-page note, a three-page postscript, and a two-page appendix. Foronda goes to great lengths to distance himself from the arguments presented, creating elaborate, confusing subterfuges, and well he should have. The Spanish Inquisition had a long history of condemning and imprisoning formerly endeared political ministers for veering from Spain's official doctrine. Years later, Foronda would not be able to escape this fate even as he continued to seek ways to transform Spanish society. For now, however, in 1803, Foronda produced an enchanting document full of displaced authors, intricate dreams, and conversations between an unnamed narrator and other unnamed characters. Most telling, the paper may have been published in 1803, the year of the Louisiana Purchase, but the letter itself is dated March 1, 1800, the year in which Spain secretly signed the Treaty of San Ildefonso, ceding the Louisiana Territory to France.[31]

The essay begins with a prefatory *"Advertencia del Editor"* (Note from the Editor), wherein the anonymous editor claims that "As I like the Spanish language, I try to engage with Spaniards" (Como gusto de la lengua Española, procuro tratar con los Españoles) (2). Here, already, the anonymous editor distances himself from the claims made in the essay by implying that he is not a Spaniard but merely a Hispanophile. The editor continues by describing a conversation he had recently had with an unnamed Spanish friend regarding Spain's colonies: "I praised his Nation's great happiness for possessing the Kingdoms of Mexico and Peru" (le ponderé la gran felicidad de su Nacion que poseia los Reynos de Mexico y el Perú). His Spanish friend disagrees with him, but rather than offer his own criticism, the Spaniard offers a letter "written by [yet] another unnamed friend of mine regarding the problem of the Colonies, in order to add them to those he had written to an imaginary Prince" (que escribio un amigo mio sobre el problema de las Colonias, para añadirla á las que habia escrito á un Principe imaginario). In effect, the essay references the traditional genre of ministerial advice given to monarchs. The editor reads this letter and, finding that its arguments "deserve the attention of Political-Economic Spaniards" (merecen la atencíon de los Economico-Políticos Españoles) decides to "print it" (imprimirla) so that "Political Truths may be discovered, leaving Opinions to struggle amongst themselves" (las Verdades Politicas se descubren dexando á las Opíniones, que luchen entre sí).

Already thrice displaced, the letter's author begins by reflecting on the bitter, frustrated plans developed by "politicos" to develop the imaginary Prince's colonies and protect them from "ambitious Nations" (Nacíones ambiciosas) (3). These plans are full of contradictions and false principles, claims the author: "Some of these cold, amateur dissertators . . . completely forget the first principles of political Economy . . . assuming that the Colonies are nothing but sheep to be kept by their owner in order to cut their wool and drink their milk!" (algunos helados y superficiales dissertadores . . . olvi[dan] enteramente los primeros elementos de la Economía política . . . de suponer las Colonias como una oveja que debe conservar su ámo para cortarle la lána y chuparle la lèche). So many opinions exist, says the author, but "shall I put my mind to print so that my ideas may be distilled into wisdom?" (pondré en prensa mi cerebro para que destíle una porcion de juicio). No, says the author; rather, he resigns himself to recounting a dream he'd had the previous night, believing that this dream may aid in "resolving the problem of the Colonies" (resolv[iendo] el problema de las Colonias).

He dreams that a friend of his (yet another displacement) is a prince and "owner of a vast country that was located between the New World and Asia. All in all, quite similar to our Americas" (dueño de un país inmenso, que se habia encontrado entre el Nuevo mundo, y la Asia en todo, todo, parecido á nuestras Americas) (4). The narrator insists at the outset that this is merely a "philosophical" exercise, refusing to concretize his example, and explicitly states that this prince is not the Spanish king or the imagined land America: "Your Grace must not think that I speak of Spain" (No crea Vm. Que háblo de la España) (7n1). But the narrator abandons the chimera halfway through the essay, writing at last that "I'll assume as well [that your Kingdom] is a Peninsula" (tambien supongo [que su principado] será una Península). He offers a strident critique of mercantilism and embraces Adam Smith's free-trade principles. The narrator draws upon Smith's arguments and makes the case that expansion and wealth should come about only as a result of "negotiation and never by force since even when I sleep [referring to his dream] I'm directed by the maxims of justice and humanity" (negociacion, y jamas por la fuerza; pues aun quando duermo me dirigen las maxîmas de justicia y humanidad) (4). Dreaming that Spain had rid itself of its colonies, the narrator becomes perplexed by all the positive outcomes:

> [M]e confundi al ver, que con el dinero que le producía à Vm. la mitad de la nueva isla pagaba todas sus deudas, que llenaba todo su Principado de camínos, de canales de navegacion, y de regadio, que mandaba construir todos los puentes que necesitan los rios, y hacer las obras que se requieren para evitar las inundaciones; que convertia las tierras cenagofas que no sirven sino de enfermar el ayre, en campos fertiles, y que cubria su Principado de Hospitales, de casas de misericordia y de albergues piadosos para aliviar la miseria pública. (5–6)

I became overwhelmed in seeing that the money produced for Your Grace [the imaginary king] by selling the colonies would pay all of the Kingdom's debts, fill the entirety of his Principality with roads, canals for navigation and irrigation, the construction of bridges, works required to prevent floods, the conversion of swamplands—that serve no purpose but to pollute the air—into fertile fields, and that it would blanket the

Kingdom with Hospitals, houses of mercy and halfway homes in order to alleviate public misery.

Foronda's voice emerges crystal-clear here, echoing the exact same goals he had stated for *Humanidad*, a newspaper he had sought to establish in 1799.[32] Spain needed commerce, not colonies, those "vampires always sucking from the treasury" (Bampiro[s] chupador[es] de los bolsillos), and this required a shift in national priorities: from mercantilism and protected trade to free markets with little governmental interference, and the first step was to rid Spain of its colonies (6).

Mercantilism had focused the monarch's vision on possessing wealth and had thus been the cause of endless wars. The author recalls a French author's analysis (Condorcet's compendium of Adam Smith's *The Wealth of Nations*, which Casa Irujo had translated into Spanish) in which Condorcet delineated how "the real merchant is [not the trader] but the laborer, the manufacturer" (el verdadero comerciante [no es el traficante], és el Labrador, el manufacturero) (9). His dream made him realize how wrong "various governments" (varios Gobiernos) are in understanding their role in promoting commerce, because to them the goal was to control national wealth. The author, instead, argues for a dispersion of economic power, from the hands of the monarch's administrators to those of merchants and manufacturers.

Such a shift, the author declares, would amount to an "unexpected revolution" (inesperada revolucion) that would cause consternation at first, but then tremendous benefits for the common good. The revolution would be a political, economic revolution, a wholesale abandonment of mercantilism with its top-down control of the economy, an inversion in which manufacturers through their individual decisions would shape the economy and well-being of the nation. Like many of his contemporary Spanish ministers, Foronda appears to be cognizant not only of the radical shift in economic priorities but that these changes—from mercantilism to free-trade capitalism—would result in an epistemic revolution, one in which Spain's long-valued virtues of military glory and territorial conquest would be replaced by more modern ones like the well-being of the entire social body, and not just its elite.

This economic line of thinking contains the germs of what will later lead to an actual revolution, the shifting of power from the sovereign to the subjects-*cum*-citizens. The author of the letter in no way gestures toward a *political* revolution and nowhere mentions natural rights or the bourgeois rationale for revolution. There is no mention, for example, of "life, liberty, and property," as John Locke had it; nor is there any trace of Foronda's good friend Thomas Jefferson, who sublimated the materiality of property into the ethereal dream of "pursuing happiness." With that absence of an actual revolution, it is no surprise that political philosophy in its various guises (republican, democratic, constitutional monarchical) is not discussed or debated at length.[33]

Still, notwithstanding the absence of political philosophy, the author of the letter understood the politically radical gesture of using the word *revolution*. On the title page of this document, written in what appears to be contemporary script, someone noted that it had been presented to the American Philosophical Society on February 3, 1804. The pamphlet was printed, then, at the close of the Haitian Revolution (Jean Jacques Dessalines declared Haiti independent on January 1, 1804), and with the bitter memories of the French Revolution (1789–99) and beheading of the Spanish king's cousin Louis XVI still fresh in their minds, elite Hispanic readers must have shuddered at seeing the word *revolution* in print. Still, the word appears rather innocently, politically neutral even. In this sense, Foronda, the diplomat-becoming-bourgeois (he was involved in various business ventures), uses the word capaciously, for all that it can and will signify. He yearns to give it a different Spanish signification that might be devoid, as one of the characters in his document says, of the "the carnage of human blood" (carnicerías de sangre humana) (10). In effect, and not unlike Adam Smith, Foronda yearns for a peaceful economic revolution that would increase public happiness (felicidad pública).

Yet this is all a dream, a man's dream of an imagined prince and an imaginary land in an anonymous letter presented to an anonymous editor. As the author of the anonymous letter notes, "As soon as this unexpected revolution establishes itself, I thought in my dream, Your Grace would become the most envied of all Princes" (Desde el momento, decia en mi sueño, que se verifique ésta inesperada revolucion, sera Vm. el mas envidiado de todos los Principes). With this, the author awakens from his reverie:

[Y] acordandome de todo lo que habia pasado por mi imaginacion, me alegré de haber soñado en la felicidad de los hombres. Qué placer puede equivaler á pensar en disminuir la suma de los males que aflixen á nuestros semejantes? Yo creo que nínguno; así estoy contentisimo de haber pasado una buena noche. (10)

[A]nd remembering everything that had passed through my imagination I was happy to have dreamt of the happiness of mankind. What pleasure can equal the thought of diminishing the amount of evils afflicting our fellow man? I don't think anything can; thus, I am thrilled at having had a good night.

The letter closes, and the author signs it with the initial "F."

The "editor" added an appendix detailing the United States' exports for 1801 as evidence that commerce not only leads to the cessation of wars but also indubitably increases the wealth of nations, an argument lifted from Smith's *Wealth of Nations*. In this appended note—and, thus, formally outside the realm of dreams—and in the very last two sentences of Foronda's document, the optimism of the dream leads to the pessimism of a melancholic reality: "Then Spain is not as happy, as I had thought, for possessing the Americas. Then this dream is applicable to the colonies belonging to this magnanimous and glorious Nation" (Luego la España no es tan felíz, como yo pensaba por poseer las Americas. Luego este sueño es aplicable á las Colonias de esta magnanima y gloriosa Nacíon) (15).

Foronda's melancholy is far from unique.[34] The trope was a dominant one in eighteenth-century Hispanic culture and may be understood as related to the epistemic shift in viewing the world as a fixed, received order—from God—to a world in which humans come to see themselves as actively producing their world. Pessimism, then, becomes the affective manifestation of the disenchantment of the world, with the withering away of God. Foronda says little as to how Spain would go about "ridding" itself of its colonies. He mentions, in passing, the king's "selling" and later "exchanging" the colonies for other territory, but the majority of the essay preoccupies itself with explaining the benefits of free trade over mercantilism. His emphasis throughout, nonetheless, is the development of Spain and the happiness of mankind. It would not be long, however, before his compatriots, this time from Spanish America, would arrive in Philadelphia with plans of their own.

A mere two years later, in May 1808, Napoleon Bonaparte would invade Spain and depose the Spanish king. Overnight, the Hispanic world was transformed forever.[35] Foronda was still in Philadelphia and from there did everything he could to aid his homeland, including consulting with his friend Thomas Jefferson as Foronda prepared his study of a new liberal constitution for Spain. Elsewhere, Spaniards, Filipinos, and Spanish Americans, including those living in what is today the United States, sought ways to bolster transcendental truth: If a Catholic God had created the cosmos and ordained monarchical rule, who or what could possibly replace the supreme political authority of the deposed sovereign? Indeed, what if a Catholic God did not exist?[36] The immediate reaction around the Hispanic globe was one of undying patriotism for their *deseado* (desired) Spanish monarch King Fernando VII. But that reaction quickly though unevenly gave way to outright rebellion, resulting many years later in the independence of the vast part of Spanish America.

The path to reform—both modest and radical—that many Hispanics (again, in Spain, the Americas, and the Philippines) had long sought would come to a screeching halt. The dreams that Foronda had been forced to sublimate, much like those of his global compatriots, would be quashed by conservative Hispanics who viewed any kind of change as a threat to their *patria*. These long-forgotten dreams, vexing as they may have been, are not unrelated from those that Simón Bolívar and José Martí would later dream of in the future. They each, in all their myriad, complicated ways, carry traces of alternative, minoritized Western concepts of sovereignty and rights, of the common good and the *pueblo*, concepts rooted in a Catholic-Hispanic modernity. But this divergent modernity also has its own internally and just as marginalized radically divergent voices, those of indigenous peoples, women, and the non-elite. These were subaltern voices that were not seen, in their own period as now, as comparable to those of the unmarked, ideal, universal subject of knowledge. This, then, is what I have characterized elsewhere as modernity not as a linear narrative but as historical trauma: the forced collapse of the Hispanic world brought about externally by a foreign invader and a search on the part of the Spanish monarch's subjects for new sources of transcendental-political authority. This is why historians now see the initial wars of Spanish American independence during the early nineteenth century as a *global* Hispanic civil war, involving Spain, Spanish America, and the Philippines: It was a war of competing social imaginaries, with various social groups fighting to establish their points of view as authority in the wake of the deposed king and, by extension, religion.[37]

In the years that followed, more Hispanics—revolutionaries from Spain and the Americas—would descend upon Philadelphia, long seen as a liberal bastion for exiled revolutionaries from throughout the Atlantic world. They too would turn to the press and unleashed even more daring dreams.[38] From Philadelphia, they would launch transatlantic literary volleys, aiming them at ports where their compatriot Hispanic revolutionaries were working to make these new social imaginaries a reality: in London, Spain, the Gulf of Mexico and Caribbean, and down along the Atlantic coast and around up the Pacific. From here, we can begin to trace—with no clear origin or conclusion—the blurry outlines of a Latina/o history of writing, one that is full of accidents and reversals, often completely unexpected and unwelcomed, that would transform these peoples and their worlds.

NOTES

1 I use *Spanish American* to refer to people of the former Spanish colonies in the Americas. *Latin American*, on the other hand, refers to people of the former Spanish, Portuguese, and in some cases to the French colonies in the Americas. Leslie Bethell, "Brazil and 'Latin America,'" *Journal of Latin American Studies* 42: 3 (2010): 457.

2 See, for example, Benedict Anderson, *Imagined Communities: Reflections on the Origin and Spread of Nationalism* (New York: Verso, 1991), 192–99; Joyce Oldham Appleby et al., *Telling the Truth about History* (New York: Norton, 1994), 91–125; Enrique Florescano, *Historia de las historias de la nación mexicana* (Mexico City: Taurus, 2002).

3 One only need recall James's memorable litany of cultural forms missing in the United States: "No sovereign, no court, no personal loyalty, no aristocracy, no church, no clergy . . . no literature, no novels, no museums, no pictures." Henry James, *Hawthorne* (Ithaca, N.Y.: Cornell University Press, 1879 [1997]), 34–35. In their absence, James wondered how anything called the "American" imagination could flourish.

4 David R. Shumway, *Creating American Civilization: A Genealogy of American Literature as an Academic Discipline* (Minneapolis: University of Minnesota Press, 1994), 299–319; Claudia Stokes, *Writers in Retrospect: The Rise*

of American Literary History, 1875–1910 (Chapel Hill: University of North
Carolina Press, 2006), 103–37; Elizabeth Renker, The Origins of American
Literature Studies: An Institutional History (New York: Cambridge University
Press, 2007), 23–39.

5 Ramón Saldívar, Chicano Narrative: The Dialectics of Difference (Madison: University of Wisconsin Press, 1990), 4, emphasis added. Luis Leal, however, writing
in 1973, claimed that it was "too idealistic" to claim that Chicana/o literature was a
part of American literature because "for the time being, Chicanos are considered
a group apart." Luis Leal, "Mexican American Literature: A Historical Perspective," Revista Chicano Riqueña 1:1 (Spring 1973): 33.

6 For an analogous argument, see Gyan Prakash, "Writing Post-Orientalist Histories of the Third World: Perspectives from Indian Historiography," Comparative
Studies in Society and History 32: 2 (April 1990), 399.

7 For a similar methodological approach, see Dipesh Chakrabarty, Provincializing
Europe: Postcolonial Thought and Historical Difference (Princeton, N.J.: Princeton
University Press, 2000), 46.

8 See part one, "Absolutism and the Lutheran Reformation," Quentin Skinner, The
Foundations of Modern Political Thought: The Age of the Reformation, vol. 2 (New
York: Cambridge University Press, 1978).

9 Prakash, "Post-Orientalist Histories," 401.

10 Foucault, Order, 42–44, 81–92, 299–300; Michael T. Gilmore, "The Literature of
the Revolutionary and Early National Periods," in Cambridge History of Ameri-
can Literature, ed. Sacvan Bercovitch and Cyrus R. K. Patell, vol. 1 (New York:
Cambridge University Press, 1994), 541; Roberto González Echevarría, Myth and
Archive: A Theory of Latin American Narrative (Durham, N.C.: Duke University
Press, 1998), 1–42; Julio Ramos, Divergent Modernities: Culture and Politics in
Nineteenth-Century Latin America, trans. John D. Blanco (Durham, N.C.: Duke
University Press, 2001), xl–xli.

11 Jacques Derrida, Of Grammatology, trans. Gayatri Chakravorty Spivak (Baltimore:
Johns Hopkins University Press, 1997), 98.

12 González Echevarría, Myth and Archive, 4, 13.

13 Larzer Ziff, Writing in the New Nation: Prose, Print, and Politics in the Early United
States (New Haven, Conn.: Yale University Press, 1991), xi.

14 Ziff, Writing in the New Nation, 77.

15 For the present, I will describe it as literary, even while acknowledging the complex, theoretical question of discipline and subfield formation.

16 Derrida, Of Grammatology, 27–73.

17 These literary histories also offer heuristic models of how literary canons are
produced. María Herrera-Sobek, "Canon Formation and Chicano Literature," in
Recovering the U.S. Hispanic Literary Heritage, ed. Ramón Gutiérrez and Genaro
Padilla, vol. 1 (Houston: Arte Público, 1993).

18 Angel Rama, The Lettered City, trans. John Charles Chasteen (Durham, N.C.:
Duke University Press, 1996), 33.

19 For a brief survey of important archival collections, see Ramón Gutiérrez, "The UCLA Bibliographic Survey of Mexican-American Literary Culture, 1821–1945: An Overview," in Gutiérrez and Padilla, *Recovering*. To this list, I would also add the voluminous Spanish–Mexican governmental archives in Texas, New Mexico, and California. Many states have extensive bibliographic studies on imprints in those states that provide a history of the press in said state along with a bibliography of the imprints, many of which are in Spanish. See, for example, Robert Ernest Cowan, *A Bibliography of the Spanish Press of California, 1833–1845* (San Francisco: s.n., 1919); George L. Harding, "A Census of California Spanish Imprints, 1833–1845," *California Historical Society Quarterly* 12, no. 2 (1933); Henry R. Wagner, "New Mexico Spanish Press," *New Mexico Historical Review* 12 (January 1937); Vito Alessio Robles, *La primera imprenta en las provincias internas de oriente: Texas, Tamaulipas, Nuevo León, y Coahuila* (Mexico City: Antigua Librería Robredo, de José Porrúa e Hijos, 1939); Illinois Historical Records Survey, *Check List of New Mexico Imprints and Publications, 1784–1876: Imprints, 1834–1876; Publications, 1784–1876* (Detroit: Historical Records Survey, 1942); Raymond MacCurdy, *A History and Bibliography of Spanish Language Newspapers and Magazines in Louisiana, 1808–1949* (Albuquerque: University of New Mexico Press, 1951); Raymond R. MacCurdy, "A Tentative Bibliography of the Spanish-Language Press in Louisiana, 1808–1871," *The Americas* 10:3 (1954); Thomas W. Streeter, *Bibliography of Texas, 1795–1845* (Cambridge, Mass.: Harvard University Press, 1955); Herbert Fahey, *Early Printing in California, From its Beginning in the Mexican Territory to Statehood, September 9, 1850* (San Francisco: Book Club of California, 1956); Edward Cleveland Kemble, *A History of California Newspapers, 1846–1858* (Los Gatos, Calif.: Talisman Press, 1962); Doyce B. Nunis, Jr., *Books in Their Chests: Reading Along the Early California Coast* (San Francisco and Berkeley: California Library Association, 1964); Douglas A. McMurtie, "The History of Early Printing in New Mexico, with Bibliography of Known Issues, 1834–1860," *New Mexico Historical Review* (October 1, 1929); John Melton Wallace, *Gaceta to Gazette: A Check List of Texas Newspapers, 1813–1846* (Austin: University of Texas Press, 1966); Florence M. Jumonville, *Bibliography of New Orleans imprints, 1764–1864* (New Orleans: Historic New Orleans Collection, 1989).

20 Francisco A. Lomelí, "Po(l)etics of Reconstructing and/or Appropriating a Literary Past: The Regional Case Model," in Gutiérrez and Padilla, *Recovering*, 233.

21 Hayden V. White, *Metahistory: The Historical Imagination in Nineteenth-Century Europe* (Baltimore: Johns Hopkins University Press, 1973), 1–42.

22 See, for example, Kirsten Silva Gruesz, "*Utopía Latina*: The Ordinary Seaman in Extraordinary Times," *Modern Fiction Studies* 49:1 (Spring 2003); Kirsten Silva Gruesz, "The Once and Future Latino: Notes Toward a Literary History *todavía para llegar*," in *Contemporary US Latino/a Literary*

Criticism, ed. Lyn Di Iorio Sandín and Richard Pérez (New York: Palgrave Macmillan, 2007).

23 In his study of European historiography, Hayden White defines the Romance as "fundamentally a drama of self-identification symbolized by the hero's transcendence of the world of experience, his victory over it, and his final liberation from it. . . . It is a drama of the triumph of good over evil, of virtue over vice, of light over darkness, and of the ultimate transcendence of man over the world in which he was imprisoned by the Fall." White, *Metahistory*, 8–9.

24 White, *Metahistory*, 9.

25 Gruesz, "Utopía Latina," 61.

26 David Scott, *Conscripts of Modernity: The Tragedy of Colonial Enlightenment* (Durham, N.C.: Duke University Press, 2004), 220.

27 Giorgio Agamben, *Signature of All Things: On Method* (New York: Zone Books, 2009), 82.

28 I use *Hispanic* to refer to those people who belonged to and identified with the global Catholic-Spanish monarchy.

29 For an elaboration of this discursive transformation in the Hispanic world, of political economy and reform, including these diplomats, see Coronado, *A World Not to Come: A History of Latino Writing and Print Culture* (Cambridge, Ma.: Harvard University Press, 2013), 101–78.

30 Valentín de Foronda, *Carta sobre lo que debe hacer un principe que tenga colonias a gran distancia* (Philadelphia: American Philosophical Society, 1803), 10, hereafter cited in text. I have not modernized the orthography. The only Spanish members of the Society living in Philadelphia at the time were Casa Irujo and Foronda, and the narrator in the essay admits to having written *Cartas económicas-políticas*, which Foronda had published in 1789 (8).

31 Spain would continue to rule the territory until 1803.

32 Robert Sidney Smith, "Valentín de Foronda: Diplómatico y Economista," *Revista de Economía Política* 10 (1959): 427n8.

33 Foronda, however, would come to develop his own account of a social contract based on liberty, equality, and property. Valentín de Foronda, *Carta sobre el modo que tal vez convendría a las Cortes seguir en el examen de los objetos que conducen a su fin, y dictamen sobre ellos* (Cádiz, Spain: Imprenta de Manuel Ximenez, 1811).

34 Coronado, *A World Not to Come*, 104–6, 136–37, 170–74.

35 Gabriel H. Lovett, *Napoleon and the Birth of Modern Spain*, 2 vols. (New York: New York University Press, 1965); Jaime E. Rodríguez O., *The Independence of Spanish America* (New York: Cambridge University Press, 1998).

36 According to Habermas, Hegel was the first to articulate this dilemma for (Protestant) modernity: how to constitute absolute or transcendental meaning in the wake of reason's critique of religion. Jürgen Habermas, "Hegel's Concept of Modernity," trans. Frederick Lawrence, in *The Philosophical Discourse of Modernity* (Cambridge, Mass.: MIT Press, 1987). The related question is how Catholics shifted from religion to reason as providing the primary basis of transcendental meaning.

37 Rodríguez O., *Spanish America*, 36–74. Coronado, *A World Not to Come*, 26. See also Vicente L. Rafael, "Welcoming What Comes: Sovereignty and Revolution in the Colonial Philippines," *Comparative Studies in Society and History* 52, no. 1 (2010).

38 See Rodrigo J. Lazo, "'La Famosa Filadelfia': The Hemispheric American City and Constitutional Debates," in *Hemispheric American Studies*, ed. Caroline F. Levander and Robert S. Levine (New Brunswick, N.J.: Rutgers University Press, 2008); Coronado, *A World Not to Come*, 139–78.

3

On the Borders of Independence

Manuel Torres and Spanish American Independence in Filadelphia

EMILY GARCÍA

On the façade of St. Mary's, the second Roman Catholic church in Phila-delphia, a large plaque commemorates Manuel Torres and his burial in the church graveyard. The plaque offers the following explanation: "As Minister of the Republic of Colombia he was the first Latin American diplomatic representative in the United States of America. Tribute from the Government of Colombia and from Philadelphia descendants of his friends. July 20, 1926." The plaque takes up a good portion of the right wall of the entrance to the church and is hard to miss even from the sidewalk. I first saw it when I was on my way to speak to a church archi-vist about Torres, who had been a parishioner of St. Mary's in the late eighteenth and early nineteenth centuries. As an early Americanist who studies individuals whom others often know little or nothing about, I was ecstatic to see Torres's name so prominently displayed. It was all the more significant given the relatively little information on Torres I had gathered from librarians at several of the city's research libraries: The plaque seemed to indicate that finally I might gain the deeper knowl-edge of my subject that I was seeking. I was soon to be disappointed: The graveyard map showed no exact location for Torres's grave, and the groundskeeper I spoke to had not heard of him (even after being reminded that Torres was the subject of the plaque on the façade). The archivist, who it turned out kept her office at St. Joseph's Cathedral, also hadn't heard of Torres. I relay this anecdote not to fault the archivists. Instead, I begin with this story because it illustrates so well the paradox that shapes and inspires my work on Torres and other early Latinas/os.

On the one hand, Torres is mythologized with a plaque that hon-ors his participation in St. Mary's and more broadly in Philadelphia: It marks his contributions to early Latin American diplomacy, the broader hemispheric friendship across the Americas that such community and diplomacy fostered, and the continued significance of this friendship into the twentieth century (the plaque's date coincides with the so-called Banana Wars period of U.S. intervention in Latin America and precedes by a few years the institution of the so-called Good Neighbor Policy). On the other hand, despite this pronouncement on the church façade, Torres's grave, his buried body, and the activities in which he participated to develop these diplomatic relations remain unknown, even to historians of the church.

I suggest that this contradiction is not singular to Torres but illustrates how the presence of Latinos and their influence on the United States have been received by broader U.S. culture from Torres's time to our own. Although Torres's categorization as Latino is complicated and risky, the contradiction of mythology combined with relatively little substantial engagement with our history of Torres is one of the clearest indications that we might consider him Latino. Torres also shares with borderlands subjects this contradiction vis-à-vis U.S. history and culture: Integral to national history and to the national imaginary yet constantly either projected as fantasies (of romance, of threat to national unity, for example) or rendered invisible, borderlands subjects and Latinos inhabit a paradoxical position in the larger U.S. national imaginary. We might begin to reframe and revise this understanding of Latinos by examining early figures like Torres. In this chapter, I examine the Philadelphia community in which Torres developed this cultural diplomacy and then engage in a more sustained consideration of Torres and his work.

Manuel de Trujillo y Torres emigrated to Philadelphia in exile from New Granada in 1796, when he was fleeing the Spanish colonial government, which was looking to arrest or kill him for his part in a failed revolutionary plot. He was part of an early but influential wave of Spanish Americans who came to the United States as exiles or visitors and who used their position in the United States to support the fight for Spanish American independence. Torres worked as publicist, purchasing agent, economist, diplomat, and as one of the nation's first Spanish-language translators and teachers. He advocated for Spanish American independence through his writing and through connections he forged with U.S. and Latin American thinkers of various political persuasions, in addition to his contributions to the congregation of St. Mary's. His publications included *An Exposition of the Commerce of Spanish America* (1816).[1] The United States recognized him as official representative of Gran Colombia in 1822, the year of his death.[2] The Jeffersonian-Democrat writer and editor William Duane called Torres the "Franklin of the southern world" in an obituary published in *Niles' Register* and other U.S. periodicals; the appellation positions him within a broader, hemispheric discourse of republicanism and pragmatism that could be readily symbolized by Franklin, 1776, and Philadelphia.[3]

Like many of the other figures working in Philadelphia, Torres is at once significant and difficult to place. An examination of Torres contributes to work such as that of the Recovering the U.S. Hispanic Literary Heritage Project, supported by Arte Público Press, which locates early historical moments of U.S. Latina/o identity. Given the incidence of anti-Latina/o policy and rhetoric in the contemporary United States, such a history is necessary. At the same time, the sense of history Torres's life and work allow is far from simple, and its complexity marks the many and various identities and political positions indicated with the single term *U.S. Latino*, which is far from monolithic. The power relations between Latinos and other U.S. Americans—and between U.S. Americans and Latin Americans—are also far from homogeneous. Torres at once elucidates and complicates our understanding of what might be called a Latino nineteenth century.

Revolucionaros al borde de la independencia: Filadelphia as Borderland

Torres's work and U.S. Americans' perceptions of him deepen our understanding of nineteenth-century Latino, Latin American, and U.S. identities. Positioned alongside the specter of Franklin and of 1776 more broadly, the independent Latin American republics for which Torres was working might seem mere continuations of U.S. independence. At the same time, U.S. investment in Spanish American independence invites us to question this notion of lineage and to consider looking at American independence from a broader hemispheric viewpoint that spans the eighteenth and nineteenth centuries. Torres's conceptualization of Spanish America in his *Exposition* and other works seems to compromise anticolonial resistance to outside forces for hemispheric friendship, a compromise several scholars have read as influential to the Monroe Doctrine.[4] His life and work reflect a duality of thought, language, and culture that informed national foundation and independence.

Hence, Torres's life and work remind us that Latino and U.S. identities were mutually informed decades before 1898 or even 1848 and that their mutual imbrication was at the heart of national independence in the South as well as in the North. Torres's *Exposition* appeared just a year after Madison secured ratification of the Treaty of Ghent to end the War of 1812. Published during the Era of Good Feelings and the development of the Monroe Doctrine, Torres's *Exposition* illustrates national as well as hemispheric imaginaries, reminding us that Latina/o and U.S. identities were interdependent even at the time of early nationalism.

Scholars and activists alike have long noted the ways in which the rhetoric of American independence informed subsequent revolutionary politics, from the decades following the War of Independence to our own time. Here, I examine how the liberatory and reactionary gestures of this rhetoric are not mutually exclusive and argue that the mutual imbrication of Latino and U.S. revolutionary rhetoric urges us to map the transnational influence in independence movements as neither linear nor unidirectional. That is, reading Torres alongside borderlands theory corrects a significant and longstanding misperception: Rather than regard U.S. revolutionary rhetoric as originary and all that follows as secondary, rather than consider influence as always moving southward, my reading of Torres highlights how revolutionary rhetoric and its cultural influence crisscross South and North, Latino and Anglo cultures.[5]

We typically think of U.S. independence as beginning circa 1776 and ending with the founding of the nation. However, a hemispheric examination of independence literatures across the Americas reveals how the work of U.S. independence extends into the nineteenth century, as the United States paradoxically seeks to strengthen its economic and political self-determination through relations with emergent independent Spanish American republics. This became particularly crucial after the War of 1812. What I call "the long era of American independence" extends our chronology of independence, but it also expands it geographically to consider independence from a hemispheric perspective, spanning Philadelphia to Spanish America's Filadelfia.

Here, I use the term *Filadelphia* to refer to the intersection of the physical city and the cultural imaginary of the city in Spanish American circles; the term highlights the interplay between Philadelphia and *Filadelfia*. Filadelphia is the site where two concurrent cultural movements occurred: what Nancy Vogeley in *The Bookrunner* refers to as a "Hispanic vogue" for Spanish-language and Spanish American novels, grammars, and political and philosophical treatises, and what Rodrigo Lazo, following the Cuban exile José María Heredia, calls *la famosa Filadelfia*, which refers not only to the city itself but also to its "symbolic power" as a site of resistance and Enlightenment.[6] This *Filadelfia* also refers to the city's "multilingual history of hemispheric relations" that "disrupt[s] the city by shifting it away from its nationalist associations."[7] Though it is far from geographic borderlands, Filadelphia operates as a kind of borderland where U.S. interest and fascination with Latin America mixes with Latin American fascination with and interest in the United States, particularly around the idea of hemispheric independence. Moreover, the Spanish Inquisition's restrictions on the publication and circulation of texts considered anti-government and heretical encouraged Spanish American authors to look elsewhere for the publication of these materials. With the relative decline of Philadelphia's prominence in the United States, including the move of the capital to Washington and the increasing significance of other cities such as New York and Baltimore, Philadelphia's printers and journalists had excess resources with which to support Spanish-language publications and literature related to Spanish American independence. As a result, Philadelphia (and Filadelphia) became an offshore capital of sorts for the Spanish American independence movement, predicated not only on Spanish Americans' need for access to publication and circulation but also, and of more interest to us here, on U.S. Americans' need to continue to have cultural and revolutionary relevance.

Filadelphia as borderland challenges national divisions of space and time; it reveals a multidirectional temporality of independence across the Americas rather than focus on discrete nation-states. In Filadelphia, the independence movement indexed by 1776 has yet to be completed; it is carried on by printers, writers, and politicians who have transferred their ideals for U.S. independence in the eighteenth century to Spanish America in the nineteenth. The critical concept of the borderlands also questions the relationship between center and periphery that informs colonial and early national histories. Though we typically consider nineteenth-century Philadelphia a center and not a periphery, reading Filadelphia as one of several sites of Latin American independence highlights how, in relation to the United States, its centrality shifts in two significant ways at the same time: The city is losing its relative centrality in U.S. politics, culture, and printing, giving way to other central cities such as Washington, Boston, and New York; Filadelphia serves as a "peripheral center" for the newly emergent and as yet to emerge Latin American republics Colombia, Mexico, and Cuba, among others.

I read Filadelphia as "on the border of independence" in order to recognize the mutual dependencies and the unraveling histories that inform the national foundations across the Americas in the nineteenth century. I want to hold in place the Spanish "al borde de la independencia" to describe this tension. In Spanish, the sense of "on the border" merges with being "on the verge." In a colloquial use, most famously Pedro Almódovar's *Mujeres al borde de un ataque de nervios* (*Women on the Verge of a Nervous Breakdown*), "*al borde*" in Spanish signifies being on the verge of something undesirable. The sense of anxiety that "*al borde*" signifies, along with its conflation of border and verge, is useful here: the anxiety about Latin America being "*al borde de la independencia*," of whether Spanish Americans were capable of self-government, was a strong motivator for action, for both those in favor of and those against independence. Places like Philadelphia allowed for the examination, articulation, and mitigation of those fears, as did the work of transcultural interlocutors such as Torres. Moreover, the conflation of space and time that the phrase "*al borde*" offers is particularly apposite for our reading of Torres and of Filadelphia: Filadelphia serves as a spatial and cultural "borderland" for Latin and U.S. American republicans; it also serves as a temporal borderland between trans-American coloniality and monarchy and between republicanism and postcoloniality (in addition to U.S. imperialism). Filadelphia is also on the border of independence because it points to the limits of independence, to the spaces where American national identities are developed through cross-cultural networks, translation, and exchange.

Translating Independence: The Language and Grammar of Hemispheric Republicanism

Torres's arrival in Philadelphia in the 1790s coincided with an increase in inter-American trade between the United States and the Spanish colonies. Merchants like the Stoughton brothers of New York and Boston, who were also Spanish consuls, coordinated U.S. commerce with Havana, Buenos Aires, Cartagena, and other Spanish American ports. Even then, U.S. commercial interests acknowledged the usefulness of inter-American trade. For example, Spain's diminishing ability to provide supplies for her colonies encouraged the United States to export goods to Spanish colonies. At the same time, loopholes in anti-slavery trade laws, combined with a blatant disregard for them, furthered the import of Africans to the United States on Spanish American ships. This last example, of course, should warn us against viewing inter-American trade as simply a manifestation of revolutionary ideals.

In his life and work, Torres served as an interlocutor between the United States and the Spanish colonies working to gain independence. He forged relationships with prominent and influential U.S. Americans to increase their support for Spanish American independence. These included statesmen such as Henry Clay, John Quincy Adams, and James Monroe and merchants such as Jacob Idler and Stephen Girard of Philadelphia.[8] Torres was also acquainted with journalists such as the influential Democratic-Republicans William Duane, Baptis Irvine, and Hezekiah Niles, all of whom encouraged the publication of his columns in *Aurora* and other newspapers. He was an early but influential Latin American member of the Freemasons.[9] In addition to such formal relationships, Torres hosted gatherings at his home, where U.S. and Latin American writers, investors, and political activists met for strategy sessions and discussions of political and intellectual matters.[10]

These ties allowed Torres to better understand U.S. perspectives and to give U.S. Americans at least initial access to Spanish American ideas and culture. While developing these ties, Torres also continued to nurture his relationships with other Spanish Americans both in the United States and elsewhere. Historians have recently discovered evidence that Torres met Francisco de Miranda during his famous 1805 visit and that he helped Miranda organize the 1806 expedition to South America. We also know that he was acquainted with Simón Bolívar and organized a junta to overthrow Royalists in New Spain with Mariano Montilla and Pedro José Gaul in 1816.[11] Torres was also acquainted with the influential Dominican friar José Servando Teresa de Mier Noriega y Guerra, who stayed with Torres during his extended visit to Philadelphia. Torres assisted Mier in publishing pamphlets and introduced him to Henry Marie Brackenridge, then *alcalde* of Pensacola.[12] Torres served as a bridge between the United States and Latin America, influencing Latin Americans like Mier away from monarchism and toward republicanism and urging U.S. Americans like Madison and Monroe to consider Latin America as nascent republics with which the United States should form partnerships.[13] In an instance both symbolic and material, Torres assisted the trade of Venezuelan tobacco for U.S. gunpowder.[14] Torres's exile in Philadelphia, rather than position him outside the site of Spanish American revolution, presented an alternate, complementary locus to the fight for independence. Evidence of this exists in the fact that, in 1814 (eighteen years after Torres had been living in exile in Philadelphia), Spanish authorities made an unsuccessful assassination attempt against his life.[15]

Torres's connections and his publications indicate that his work was relatively successful and that there was U.S. support for Spanish American independence before official recognition. Torres was instrumental in bringing about this formal recognition in 1822, once Florida became an official territory of the United States. Interest and support for the independent Latin American republics was also predicated by U.S. interest in commercial and political negotiations with other nations, particularly in this case with Britain and Spain. The United States supported revolutionaries who displayed allegiance to the United States and to its plans for hemispheric negotiations, and Torres's argument in favor of commerce with Spanish America (and its argument for Spanish American independence) echoes these interests, presaging U.S. interest in Latin America in centuries to come.

In addition to working as one of the first Spanish-language teachers in the United States, Torres published English- and Spanish-language articles and essays on independence and international relations in the United States, translated and published monographs in both languages, and co-edited one of the earliest Spanish grammars published in the

United States: *Dufief's Nature Displayed in Her Mode of Teaching Language to Man* . . . (1811).[16] The grammar is a Spanish-language adaptation of a French-language grammar by the same title that was popular at the time. Torres's work in publishing, writing, and language instruction illustrate his work as one of cultural translation, which shapes his understanding of Spanish American independence and informs his contributions to that project. That the first Latin American diplomat was also one of the earliest Spanish-language teachers in the United States is more than mere coincidence: It reflects a longstanding interest in and need for what we now call "cultural literacy," a need that can be traced at least as far back as Thomas Jefferson's 1779 arguments for the teaching of Spanish and for establishing the nation's first modern languages program at the College of William and Mary.[17] These translations and bilingual negotiations were not (of course) purely cultural: They also speak to the economic and political forces that informed calls for learning Spanish and developing relations with Spanish America.

The pedagogy behind *Dufief's Nature Displayed* is of particular interest here: Not only does the grammar seek to be an early introduction to the Spanish language for U.S. Americans; it also claims to be "so very economical, that a liberal education can be afforded even to the poorest of mankind; by which it is obtained the great desideratum of enabled nations to arrive at the highest degree of mental perfection."[18] The claim's assertions of economy, common sense, and universality, influenced by Enlightenment political and economic philosophy, also align with Torres's own emphases in developing hemispheric relations through writing and publishing. The grammar's examples, like those of the *Exposition*, are practical and seem to offer an objective and utilitarian argument for broadening U.S. understanding of the Spanish language and of Latin America. This utilitarianism reflects the transnational Enlightenment ideals of the time, again associated often with Benjamin Franklin. They also indicate how cross-cultural learning and exchange were not ends in themselves: They were necessary for national growth.

Torres's cross-cultural negotiations highlight how Latin American interests were dependent on the United States and the ways in which the U.S. national imaginary was dependent on Latin American independence for its own development in the early nineteenth century. This second point is of greater interest here, because it reverses the relation-

ship of dependency as typically regarded in the hemisphere: Mutual imbrication challenges the idea that Latin American states simply modeled
themselves on the United States. As I note below regarding the appellation of Torres as the "Franklin of the southern world," this comparison,
when read closely and critically, tells us more about U.S. reliance on
Latin America than the opposite.

The bicultural relations that developed in Filadelphia also challenge the presumed progression from the age of Enlightenment to the
age of expansion as traditional Anglo historiography tells it, as one of
originating in the thirteen colonies (but especially Massachusetts and
Pennsylvania) and extending southward and westward to the rest of the
hemisphere. As I discuss below, Torres's *Exposition* positions Spanish
America as unique in the world, arguing that in it one can find all of
the best that the rest of the world can offer. It also promotes Spanish-
American exports to the United States as a means of independence. The
contradictions inherent in both of these tenets of Torres's argument offer
an early version of the contradictions and effacements that continue to
inform Latin American–U.S. relations to this day, including NAFTA and
post-NAFTA economics, im/migration and labor issues, and anti-Latino
mythologies about the monocultural origins of the United States.

Mapping Interdependence in Torres's *Exposition*

Torres's *An Exposition of the Commerce of Spanish America; with Some
Observations Upon Its Importance to the United States* (1816) was published by George Palmer, an active Philadelphia printer who published
works on politics and history. Torres's *Exposition* presumes to give its
readers an overview of trade relations; 84 of its 119 pages list tables detailing various exchanges of currency and goods for Spain, France, and the
United States. These are introduced with an essay advocating U.S. trade
with Spanish America and, implicitly, Spanish American independence
from Spain. Though Torres's *Exposition* announces itself as an economic
and commercial work, the first sentence emphasizes its broader applicability: "The different matters of this work, destined to guide merchants
in their commercial operations, will also be very useful to any one who
buys, sells, or exchanges in any way: to the farmer and to the insurer, to
the banker and to the statesman."[19] The universal applicability as stated

in Torres's Introduction calls to mind the vision of Torres as "the friend of all America, of humanity, and virtue," William Duane expresses in a letter dated July 15, 1822, to James Monroe upon announcement of Torres's death.[20] Consistently throughout the *Exposition*, Torres highlights how his economic information will benefit more than just merchants, that the manual has broader implications for independence.

The manual includes a number of "operations," or examples of trade transactions, which offer not only mathematical equations but also written commentary to illustrate the potential outcome of exchange. The operations develop an overall theme of resulting gains in the United States, as seen in the operation detailing the trade of 1,000 Spanish ounces of silver for a gain of $8.47. These operations offer readers a sense of the possibilities of trade relations with Spanish America; they allow readers to imagine commercial exchanges and their outcomes before materially engaging in or even pursuing them. The idea of trading with Spanish America mitigates the anxieties that merchants (and farmers, statesmen, and others) might feel about opening new trade relations. That these operations are so numerous and diverse illustrates how Torres is attempting to walk readers through the many possibilities of trade with Spanish America and its presumed concomitant risk.

The mitigation of anxiety is introduced more explicitly in the preceding essay, where Torres associates the same kind of rhetorical assurance by noting the consistent value of Spanish American minerals. According to Torres, precious metals are "not only the representatives, but the regulators and the equivalents of every other thing; a quality very contrary to the nature of paper money, whose value is always regulated by the degree of confidence the public place in it." He also reminds readers that precious metals "increase . . . the real capital of a nation, and in the same proportion its power." In this claim, Torres invites and encourages other nations—particularly the United States—to acquire Spanish American specie for their own profits: It is the regulator of all other trade. Because he makes this claim in order to argue that the United States *acquire* Spanish American specie, Spanish American independence as Torres describes it here will result in foreign (U.S.) rather than domestic profit. According to Torres, precious metals serve a crucial purpose in global trade relations.

In highlighting that trade with Spanish America would benefit the United States, and in predicating Spanish American independence on that trade and on that benefit to the United States, Torres's argument foreshadows the places where liberal (or neoliberal) and dependency economics might overlap, despite their presumed distinction. Spanish America will gain materially through export, and thus it will achieve economic independence from Spain, but according to Torres, Spanish America will do so by giving away to other nations (particularly the United States) *precisely* what is most valuable in a global market. Torres's transnational view of independence and of interest, though, explicitly obscures this issue, focusing as it does on the significance of independence to other nations.

Torres's tables represent exchange, which makes an explicit point that Spanish American goods are admissible into the market with U.S. dollars and goods. They illustrate the broader welcome into republicanism and global trade that Torres's essay makes more explicit, countering assumptions that Spanish America is stuck in the past. At the same time, the exchange of goods in the tables, more often than not, results in a profit for the United States. Torres's commercial interests primarily express themselves in the copious attention and elaborate detail given to monetary values, measurements, and weights. More than providing a handbook for commerce, the sense of assurance implied in Torres's exposition—the presumption is that examples are provided for the most common operations one might encounter—attempts to inspire confidence in such transactions, particularly in regards to benefits to the United States.

In addition to arguing that Spanish America might offer material gains to other countries, Torres bases the significance of emerging Spanish American independence on universal values. Here, Torres conceptualizes Spanish America as a repository of the best that the rest of the world has to offer and as completely unique in that regard. The paradox of universalism and exceptionalism is not new in Torres; it informs the concept of America from the seventeenth century onward.[21] In his introduction to Spanish America's "Situation, Government, Soil, Climate, Productions, etc.," Torres claims that Spanish America "affords all the different productions of other continents, including those of Asia . . . and yields, in the vegetable and mineral kingdoms, many productions which are peculiar to this continent."[22] According to Torres, Spanish America can claim these natural resources as well as a "diversity of climates . . . from the most intense heat to ice."[23] Appealing to U.S. statesmen and merchants, he posits Spanish America as a microcosm, one in which "all nations . . . partake directly of the rich commerce."[24] Torres' rhetorical goals shape the idea of Spanish America his *Exposition* presumes to introduce. He then expands this universal appeal in a discussion of Spanish American geography and in particular of the Spanish Main.

In what might be called the apex of his introductory essay, Torres defines Spanish America as "the centre between Asia, Europe, and the United States, through which Asia is nearer to Europe and the United States several thousands of miles by the communication between the two great oceans."[25] Though the statement might be considered accurate as it refers to the Isthmus of Panama, Torres's location of this as *central* is noteworthy: It presumes to bring Latin America out of the margins of the global marketplace and position it as its core, raising its global significance. However, as with the argument about the significance of Spanish American minerals, the statement is predicated on a contradiction: The centrality of the Spanish Main and by extension (according to Torres) of Spanish America is defined by its ability to connect other centers of economic and political wealth to each other.

Like Torres's position as interlocutor in Filadelphia, this conflation of core and periphery in Torres's mapping of Spanish America complicates the distinction between Anglo and Latin Americas, predicating Spanish American independence on U.S. investment while yoking U.S. strength to Spanish American independence and development, ultimately resulting in interdependence. It is this blurring and crisscrossing of national and cultural identities and power relations that invite a reading of Torres through the critical concept of the border, that space which disrupts binaries, including those of core and periphery. One of Torres's main arguments for U.S. and other global investment in Spanish America is its central position, but this central position as Torres articulates it is primarily as a conduit that serves other nations. In Torres's view, Spanish America is both center and margin at once. That this view is articulated in Filadelphia, through Filadelphia publishers and because of Filadelphia transnational networks, means that this centrality/peripherality of Spanish America is coterminous with that of the Pennsylvania city.

The "Franklin of the Southern World" and the "Open Wound" of American Independence

Torres's synchrony with U.S. identity seems to have been championed by those whose own relationship to the United States was complicated, who had a singular investment in Spanish American independence as one that would continue their own perceived thwarted republicanism. William Duane, a staunch Jeffersonian Democrat of Irish birth who had been tried under both the Alien Act and the Act of Sedition, noted in a letter dated October 25, 1814, recommending Torres as a cultural liaison to Secretary of State James Monroe, that Torres's "practical experience" and "principles and views" are "perfectly in the Spirit of our Government."[26] At the time of his death, obituaries in dozens of U.S. newspapers praised his life's work as instrumental to the burgeoning friendship between the Americas North and South, or as William Duane described Torres in his obituary, the "Franklin of the southern world."

The comparison to Franklin is something that might have occurred to Torres himself. His *Exposition of the Commerce of Spanish America* delivers the majority of its argument through numerical data: More than 80 of the publication's 110 pages are filled with charts and transactions. This calls to mind Franklin, who in works such as *Poor Richard's Almanack* displays what Paul Pasles in his mathematical biography calls Franklin's "quantitative reasoning."[27] The tables in Torres's *Exposition* show quantitative and not merely philosophical reasons for U.S. support of Spanish American independence, and it is this form of reasoning that most objectively aligns his insights with U.S. interests.

It is no minor point that Duane notes Torres's importance by raising the specter of U.S. revolution.[28] Duane knew firsthand how the era of Federalist national constitution fostered the curtailment of revolutionary impulses, and his interest in Spanish American independence continued his earlier revolutionary ideals. Duane's view locates Torres within a trans-American republic of letters, one in which Spanish-speaking and English-speaking Americans participated through various literary, political, and cultural networks.[29] This republicanism is evident in other of Torres's publications, such as the 1812 *Manual de un Republicano para el uso de un Pueblo libre*, which supported U.S. political practices and purported to translate Rousseauean views of government for the burgeoning republics of the South. Torres's transnational republicanism is also evident in his work for U.S. newspapers, in particular the Philadelphia *Aurora*, which he possibly edited. The *Aurora*, which Duane edited first with Benjamin Bache and then alone (if not with Torres) after Bache's death, continued to publicize Anti-Federalist and Jeffersonian appeals against strong centralized governments through the Federalist period and onward.[30] A sense of Torres's legacy for Duane is apparent in the newspaper itself. For a "rabble rouser" like Duane, the freedom of the revolution had been contained to a certain extent with the ratification of the Constitution. Hence, the aspirations for and possibility of American revolution were transported or transposed southward onto Spanish America. The figure of Spanish America and its accompanying emblems such as Torres served as repositories for the revolutionary ideals of North American radicals such as Duane. This is part of a larger phenomenon, in which U.S. Americans depend on Latin American independence movements in part in order to address their own sense of unfinished revolution.[31] The sense of unfinished revolution was not the only reason for U.S. investment in Latin American independence, and it was not true for all U.S. Americans. But it does inform much of the work and spirit of men like Duane, who were disillusioned with the political climate of the late eighteenth and early nineteenth centuries. This is significant for writers and thinkers in Philadelphia, the center of republican thought that had come to be supplanted by Federalism and by other centers such as Washington, D.C.

At the same time, the negotiation between difference and sameness is necessary for the economic relationships that Latin Americans and U.S. Americans are developing at the time. The "modern world-system" that continues to develop during and informs the long age of American independence, Immanuel Wallerstein reminds us, puts nations in the position of needing to trade with other nations for their own national growth and stability.[32] Because of this, nations also cannot become too proximate: Cultural ideals of U.S. exceptionalism and prominence belie the interdependence on which U.S. expansion depends. Torres's *Exposition* reflects and articulates these contradictions in very interesting ways. Torres postulates the significance of Spanish America as important to U.S. wealth, a framework that suggests Spanish America might ultimately and paradoxically give away what gives it value, while the value is predicated on the basis of potential exchange. At the same time, the indeterminacy exhibited through Torres and respondents to him such as Duane caution us to read this as an early version of what comes to be known as the Monroe Doctrine, as some scholars have suggested.[33]

Torres's descriptions of Spanish America in *An Exposition* and his self-positioning in Filadelphia contributed to assumptions that Spanish American nations in their independence would and should reflect the ideals of other nations, particularly the United States. As such, Torres's work seems to invite a "control through sameness" that the historian Eldon Kenworthy later calls the "America/Américas" myth, which is "a versatile strategy of control that emphasizes identity."[34] However, Torres's expression of this cannot simply be named an instance of U.S. "control"; this reading is complicated first by the fact that this particular articulation of identity stems from a Latin American argument in favor of independence and second by the milieu in which Torres works and the U.S.–Latin American interdependency that informs it. Such interdependency troubles the distinction between same and different, between Spanish America and the United States. As I have argued above, the political and cultural diplomacy that emerges in Filadelphia through figures like Torres illustrates U.S. reliance on Latin America, reversing our understanding of hemispheric influence and allowing us to correct present misapprehensions as we return toward a Latino nineteenth century.

NOTES

1 Manuel Torres, *An Exposition of the Commerce of Spanish America, With Some Observations Upon Its Importance to the United States* (Philadelphia: G. Palmer, 1816).

2 See Charles H. Bowman Jr., "The Activities of Manuel Torres as Purchasing Agent, 1820–1821." *The Hispanic American Historical Review* 48:2 (May 1968) 234–46 and "Manuel Torres, A Spanish American Patriot in Philadelphia, 1796–1822." *The Pennsylvania Magazine of History and Biography* 94 (1970) 26–53.

3 William Duane, "Death of Mr. Torres." *Philadelphia Aurora*, reprinted in *Niles' Weekly Register* July 16, 1822.

4 See Anna Brickhouse, *Transamerican Literary Relations and the Nineteenth-Century Public Sphere* (Cambridge: Cambridge University Press, 2004), 4. Brickhouse cites Nicolás García Samudio, *La Independencia de Hispanoamérica* (Mexico City: Fondo de Cultura Económica, 1945), 171–78.

5 John Carlos Rowe, among others, has recalled the ways in which the rhetoric of the American revolution argues that "the United States in the nineteenth century

employed the rhetoric of 'emancipation' derived from the American Revolution to promise, often falsely, various subaltern groups—African Americans, Native Americans, Chinese Americans, Latin Americans, European Americans, and women—the hope of eventual social justice tied inextricably to national progress and American individualism." See Rowe, *Literary Culture and U.S. Imperialism* (Oxford: Oxford University Press, 2000), 5.

6 Nancy Vogeley, *The Bookrunner: A History of Inter-American Relations—Print, Politics, and Commerce in the United States and Mexico, 1800–1830* (Philadelphia: American Philosophical Society, 2011), 42; and Rodrigo Lazo, "La Famosa Filadelfia: The Hemispheric American City and Constitutional Debates." *Hemispheric American Studies*, ed. Caroline Levander and Robert S. Levine. (New Brunswick, N.J.: Rutgers University Press, 2007), 57.

7 Lazo 69 and 70.

8 Bowman 234 and 237.

9 Vogeley 84.

10 Bowman, "A Spanish American Patriot," 34.

11 Ibid., 31 and 45.

12 Bowman, "Purchasing Agent," 18–22. According to Vogeley, Torres's influence on Mier was extensive and even unintentional, as some of the books that most influenced Mier's later work were stolen from Torres's library. Vogeley 84.

13 Vogeley 86n229.

14 Vogeley n229, referencing Bowman.

15 Bowman, "A Spanish American Patriot," 39.

16 Manuel Torres and L. Hargous, *Dufief's Nature Displayed in Her Mode of Teaching Language to Man* (Philadelphia: T. & G. Palmer, 1811).

17 R. Merritt Cox, "Spain and the Founding Fathers." *The Modern Language Journal.* 60:3 (March 1976) 101–9.

18 Torres and Hargous, *Dufief*, title page.

19 Torres, *Exposition*, 1.

20 Qtd. in Bowman, "Purchasing Agent," 246.

21 See Emily García, "'The cause of America is in great measure the cause of all mankind': American Universalism and Exceptionalism in the Early Nation," *American Exceptionalisms*, ed. Sylvia Söderlind and James Taylor Carson (Albany: SUNY Press, 2011), 51–70.

22 Torres, *Exposition*, 7.

23 Ibid.

24 Ibid., 5.

25 Ibid., 17.

26 Qtd. in Bowman, "Spanish American Patriot," 40.

27 Paul C. Pasles, *Benjamin Franklin's Numbers: An Unsung Mathematical Odyssey.* (Princeton, N.J.: Princeton University Press, 2007), 1–19.

28 The comparison recalls Jesse Alemán's discussion of the uncanny as it figures in the "shared revolutionary histories" between Mexico and the United States, as it

"collapses the otherwise clear distinctions between native and foreigner, domestic and international, America and América, making Mexico in particular a strangely familiar place that troubles the trans-American imaginary of the United States." The Torres/Franklin comparison raises the spectre of revolution in similar ways that mark Spanish America as "strangely familiar." Jesse Alemán, "The Other Country: Mexico, the United States, and the Gothic History of Conquest." *American Literary History* 18:3 (Fall 2006), 406–26, 77.

29 For a broader history of these trans-American literary networks, see Brickhouse and Kirsten Silva Gruesz's *Ambassadors of Culture: The Transamerican Origins of Latino Writing* (Princeton, N.J.: Princeton University Press, 2001), esp. pp. 7–19.

30 Coronado, following Bowman and García Samudio, mentions the possibility that Duane had helped "reorganize" the *Aurora*, 478n3.

31 Emily García, "Novel Diplomacies: Henry Marie Brackenridge's *Voyage to South America* (1819) and Inter-American Revolutionary Literature." *Literature in the Early American Republic* 3 (April 2011): 145–71.

32 Immananuel Wallerstein, *The Modern World-System III: The Second Era of Great Expansion of the Capitalist World-Economy, 1730s–1840s* (Burlington, Mass.: Academic Press, 1989). For Wallerstein's treatment of the modern world-system in connection with the period examined here, see Volume III of Wallerstein's work.

33 For example, Anna Brickhouse, following the popular historian and chancellor at the Colombian Consulate General Nicolás García Samudio, has suggested that Torres may have been a significant influence on James Monroe and John Quincy Adams in drafting the economic and ideological policy. See Brickhouse, 3.

34 Eldon Kenworthy, *America/Américas: Myth in the Making of U.S. Policy toward Latin America* (University Park: Pennsylvania State University Press, 1995), 37.

4

From Union Officers to Cuban Rebels

The Story of the Brothers Cavada and Their American Civil Wars

JESSE ALEMÁN

On July 8, 1864, Washington, D.C.'s *Daily National Intelligencer* ran a short ad announcing books received for sale. Included in William Ballantyne's new stock were *The Life of Lieutenant General U.S. Grant* by Major Penniman for $1.25; *The Maine Woods* by H. D. Thoreau, also for five bits; *Haunted Hearts* by the author of *The Lamplighter*, Maria S. Cummins, and *The Poor White, or the Rebel Conscript* by Emily Clemens Pearson, which topped the list at $2.00 each; and for a buck-fifty, *Libby Life* by Lt. Col. F. F. Cavada.[1] At first glance, the list seems indicative of the era's literary history—a celebratory biography of a rising Civil War star; a meditative travel narrative by a declining transcendentalist; and two narratives by women which prove that even the Civil War couldn't snuff out readers willing to shell out a full day's pay for most skilled laborers for gothic romance and Union propaganda. And then somewhere in between history, transcendentalism, and popular, professional women writers there's *Libby Life*, a prisoner-of-war memoir about Richmond, Virginia's Libby Prison penned by a relatively unknown lieutenant colonel named Frederic Fernandez Cavada, a Cuban-born U.S. citizen whose record of service in the U.S. Civil War pales in comparison to the heroism he and his brother Adolfo garnered in Cuba's Ten Years War against Spanish rule of the island.

Spanning 1868 to 1878, the Ten Years War, or *La Guerra Grande*, as Cubans call it, was a rupture of anti-imperialist movements bubbling on the island since at least the 1830s. Often linked to anti-slavery interests, sometimes fueled by arguments for annexation to the United States, and nearly always fostered by *criollo* desire for economic independence from Spain, Cuba's anti-imperialism took many forms throughout the nineteenth century, culminating with its final bid for independence in 1895—the war José Martí made famous. But Cuba's Ten Years War is an especially interesting event because the island's historic problems over race, slavery, independence, and self-governance took on a different tone in the aftermath of the Confederacy's secession and the subsequent civil war. As Ada Ferrer explains, Cuba's *Guerra Grande* began when Carlos Manuel de Céspedes, a sugar planter, lawyer, and poet, freed his slaves and then "invited them to help 'conquer liberty and independence' for Cuba."[2] They did, along with thousands of others, and thus waged an anticolonial insurgency and independence movement three years after the end of the U.S. Civil War that constituted rebellion against Spain and its ruling *peninsular* class on the island.

The "ever-faithful isle" earned its sobriquet by staving off slave re-bellions, revolutionary movements, and the gravitational pull of the United States, though the two engaged in lucrative trade and commerce throughout the nineteenth century. Cuba had long been the object of northern and southern annexationist designs in the United States, mainly because of the island's sugar and coffee industries backed by plantation slave labor but also because of its strategic maritime location. Presidents James K. Polk and Franklin Pierce both offered to purchase the island from Spain for $100 million and $130 million, respectively, while the 1850s filibustering expeditions led by Narciso López and Mis-sissippi Governor John Quitman were very much part of the clandestine movements to free Cuba for U.S. annexation. The politics of Cuban in-dependence throughout the nineteenth century, though, were not al-ways clear. "The Cuban filibustero," Rodrigo Lazo tells us, "embodied the contradiction of protonationalist (Cuban) discourse and U.S. expan-sionism. . . . The antimonarchical position of exiles was intertwined with the position of U.S. expansionists who relished the thought of roping Cuba in[to] the Union."[3] This is what the Cuban historian Louis Pérez Jr. means when he describes nineteenth-century Cuba as "between em-pires," as the tiny island had to navigate its desire to break from Spain with the internal push and external pull to become part of the United States.[4] Complete independence was one option, as separatists often emphasized, but many *criollos* saw annexation as a strong political and economic lever that would wedge Spain off the island without upsetting the balance of Cuba's slave economy and related racial system of citizenship. At the same time, Cuba was not entirely committed to breaking from Spain, as a sector of slaveholding Cubans, fearing the specter of a race war on the one hand and the loss of Cuban identity on the other, advocated for Spanish reform rather than U.S. annexation.[5]

Either way, Cuba and its accompanying slave system played such a prominent role for the Confederacy that it was included in the Union blockade of New Orleans. Many Cubans saw a common cause in the Confederacy—namely, they "believed in limited government, the right of self-determination, and in defending a staunch Constitutionalist peoples against invasion by a powerful majority," according to Darrel Brock.[6] The Cuban-born and Harvard-educated poet, lawyer, and newspaperman Jose Agustín Quintero was the Confederacy's most important, influential, and successful diplomat to Mexico, brokering deals with the governor of Nuevo Leon and Coahuila for munitions, contraband supplies, and the possibility for the Mexican border state's annexation to the Confederacy, while Ambrosio José Gonzales, who introduced Quintero to the influential Club de La Habana, volunteered his services to the Confederates and ended up as a colonel and chief of artillery under his old friend and schoolmate General P.G.T Beauregaurd (himself a Spanish-French creole). Finally, Loreta Janeta Velazquez's cross-dressing as Lt. Harry T. Buford sartorially links Cuba and the Confederacy as two regions involved in related anticolonial conflicts. At the height of the Civil War, Velazquez even vows to fight for Cuban independence in the same way her Cuban nationalism led her to fight for the South: "I begrudged that this fair island should be the dependency of a foreign power; for I was, despite my Spanish ancestry, an American, heart and soul, and if there was anything that could have induced me to abandon the cause of the Southern Confederacy, it would have been an attempt on the part of the Cubans to liberate themselves from the Spanish yoke."[7]

Cuba's relation to the United States and the Confederacy during the war years is thus not anomalous but analogous insofar as the reverberations of the U.S. Civil War rippled across the Gulf of Mexico to shape the contours and the conflicts of Cuba's Ten Years War. Velazquez's comment also shores up the confusing national politics of the time. Her use of *American* either makes Cuban independence a national cause of the United States or it indicates Velazquez's trans-American identity, suggesting that she understands Cuba's independence as part of a greater

"American" movement, a point further emphasized by her juxtaposition of her "Spanish ancestry" with her American "heart and soul." This
Cuban Cartesian split, so to speak, is what distinguishes her—and her
fellow U.S. Hispanic writers—from Cuban and Mexican nationals residing in the United States during the war years. They are not quite natives,
immigrants, or exiles, to recall Nicolás Kanellos' taxonomy of early U.S.
Hispanics, but transnational subjects born out of the rifts of internecine
conflict.[8] Nowhere is this trans-American experience better seen than in
the lives and writings of Frederic and Adolfo Cavada, two Cuban-born
brothers and Union officers who became Cuban rebels during the Ten
Years War.

The brothers Cavada—there were three of them, actually—were
born in Cienfuegos, Las Villas Province, Cuba, to Isidoro Fernandez
Cavada y Diaz de la Campa of Santander, Spain, and Philadelphia-born
Emily Howard Gatier. "Ironically," Michael Dreese explains, "the three
sons of Isidoro and Emily Cavada would be key figures in the independence movement that sought to overthrow the yoke of colonial power
under which both branches of the family had prospered."[9] Fernandez
Cavada, a loyal *peninsular*, served as the Spanish crown's tax collector
in Cienfuegos, where he met and married Emily Howard, the youngest
daughter of a French émigré, Louis Howard, a landowner who fled the
Saint-Domingue revolt and settled in Cienfuegos, where he traded in
sugar and cattle. After Fernandez Cavada's 1838 death (he was thirty-six
at the time), Emily Howard taught school briefly before she returned
with her sons to Philadelphia in 1841 and married Samuel Dutton, a
banker and ship chandler who became stepfather to Emilio, Frederic,
and Adolfo Cavada. Not much is known about their early years. The
eldest, Emilio, became a New York and Philadelphia sugar merchant
and served as a medic during Cuba's 1895 war for independence, while
Frederic started his U.S. education in a boarding school in Wilmington,
Delaware, and finished it with graduation from Philadelphia's Central
High School in 1846. Afterward, he served as an engineer for the transcontinental railroad along the Isthmus of Panama, where he contracted
malaria and returned to the City of Brotherly Love a little worse for
wear. In July 1861, he and his younger brother Adolfo joined Company C of the Twenty-third Regiment of Volunteers of Pennsylvania,
recruited in Philadelphia, and later they enlisted with the Zouves Com-

pany under Captain Collis in the 114th Pennsylvania Regiment.[10] As Frederic's recruiting officer, O. W. Davis, later recalled, "On the twentieth day of July, 1861, a delicate looking young man entered the business office . . . and asked for a position in the Twenty-third Pennsylvania Volunteers."[11] He proclaimed that he had no knowledge of "military matters": "None whatever" but was willing to pay for the cost of raising his own company; he also affirmed that he did not have a job; was out of work because of his health; and when asked if he "could endure the exposure of a soldier's life," he responded, "I do not know, but have made up my mind to try it."[12]

The brothers Cavada constitute a class a little different from that of the émigrés in New York, New Orleans, Key West, and Philadelphia who agitated for Cuba during the 1850s and 1860s. This émigré class, as Gerald Poyo has shown, was largely responsible for fostering a sense of Cuban nationalism that encompassed the United States and the island through print culture, political pressure, and labor politics. Separatists, annexationists, cultural and political nationalists, abolitionists, and radical anarchists all converged in the United States during the island's heady mid–nineteenth century. Through various newspapers and influential political clubs, they seem to have applied as much pressure on U.S. politics and culture as they did on Cuban military and political change on the island.[13] They were Cubans in the United States politicking for the future of their homeland.

But the Cavada brothers were different on this score. First, they were not émigrés in the sense that there is no indication their mother moved them from the island to Philadelphia out of separatist politics. Quite literally, her domestic arrangement changed, and because Frederic and Adolfo were relatively young, they followed their mother; eldest brother Emilio followed too, as his stepfather trained him in the business world. Second, Frederic and Adolfo grew up in the United States. They attended school in Delaware and Philadelphia, mastered English (Frederic often went by Federico, Frederick, or Fred), secured U.S. citizenship, and saw the U.S. military as a venue for upward social mobility. Third, they came to their revolutionary politics when they returned to Cuba as official U.S. consuls. Much of their writing in the United States makes nary a mention of Cuban independence, but just as reformist leaders were leaving Cuba for the United States en masse in January 1869, the brothers Cavada were resigning their official posts to throw in with the rebels in Trinidad and Cienfuegos.

It is tempting to see them as Americanized Cubans or, in contemporary terms, as Cuban Americans, who lack the sense of entitlement fueling the Cuban nationalism of their contemporaneous émigrés but also find their experience in the United States, especially as part of the U.S. military, wanting. But instead, the brothers Cavada should be seen more as trans-American subjects—hemispheric citizens whose sense of belonging traversed the Americas rather than being bound by its national borders. In this sense, the brothers Cavada provide a more viable paradigm for understanding nineteenth-century U.S. Latino/a identities because they offer a more vexed understanding of "Our America." On the one hand, they were complicit with U.S. power at home, especially as it quelled the Confederacy's rebellion, but on the other hand, they were radical agents of insurgency on their native island. Theirs was an identity forged out of two Americas, but unlike José Martí, who claimed only one America as his, the brothers Cavada imagined themselves within and across two, making their transformation from Union officers to Cuban insurgents all the more significant in the context of the island's war of rebellion.

In themselves, the brothers are a study in contrast. While older brother Frederic suffered an embattled Union career, took ill often, and injured easily, younger brother Adolfo was almost an army overachiever whose field diary charts his penchant for military details and his rapid rise in rank. Penned in English, Adolfo's journal is significant as a document attesting to a U.S. Hispanic participant in the earliest battles of the U.S. Civil War: It spans more than two years, from August 1861, when he enlisted as a Philadelphia volunteer, to New Year's Eve, December 31, 1863, when he closes his diary "ready to begin another year" and wondering what 1864 will bring.[14] In between, the entries chart his transformation from a greenhorn to an experienced battle veteran as he weathers skirmishes and pickets at Warwick River and the subsequent battles of Fredericksburg, Chancellorsville, and Gettysburg, the last of which he figures as the culmination of his military experiences and personal development.

At Yorktown, Adolfo sits on picket along the banks of the Warwick and alternates between fear, adventure, awe, and humor during the month-long campaign. April 8, 1862—"Brisk musketry firing ahead—Began to feel a little green—The skirmishing very lively," but only four days later, the green captain gets daring: "On picket still at Warwick River: Occasionally I go in search of adventure—crawling on hands and knees opposite to the rebel batteries; by Captain Hilderbrand, Fred, and myself was considered fine fun."[15] That same evening, shells, musket fire, and a thunderstorm all rouse Adolfo from sleep as "rapid volleys were fired—artillery began to push further, shells whizzed and burst—the lightening [sic] flashed, the thunder crashed, and the rain plashed.—Altogether about the grandest piece of music in nature's repertoire."[16] The light action he sees is enough to inspire some literary pretention in his journal too. In the previous entry, for instance, "lightening [sic] flashed, the thunder crashed, and the rain *plashed*" in the heat of the skirmish—not *splashed* in the diary but *plashed*, a rhymed onomatopoeia that captures the sound and action of water as it puddles around him amidst rebel fire and a fierce thunderstorm. Finally, come May, Adolfo gives a more lighthearted entry, one that points to either the folly of warfare or its absurdity: "May 1862—"Bang! Whiz, whiz! Look out for your heads! Men rushing ahead eager for the fray; men rushing back eager to get out of it."[17]

By June 2, 1862, Adolfo has grown accustomed to picket duty—"Getting shelled every day but don't mind that now," he says, but six months later at the first Battle of Fredericksburg, he encounters real action on the front, and his journal entry betrays his excitement, trepidation, and his relief for surviving one of the most lopsided Confederate victories of the war: "Fix bayonets—Charge! . . . Hurrah! The Rebel artillery and musketry all concentrated on us. Terrible fire—our men fall by hundreds . . . The air is full of flying bullets . . . men falling in groups. List of wounded: Lt. Humpherys—slightly wounded; Genl Humpherys—two horses killed. Capt. Cavada—allright."[18] His May 7, 1863, entry, one day after Union forces suffer more heavy loses at the Battle of Chancellorville, is more grim: "In camp—Reflections—Another ground movement, another terrible, bloody battle fought by the Army of the Potomac resulting in *so* many killed, *so* many wounded, *so* many prisoners."[19]

It is significant for U.S. Hispanic history that Aldofo Cavada, a Cuban-born U.S. citizen, was a participant in the Civil War's early battles and kept a diary about it to boot, putting to rest both the popular misconception that the war was an Anglo American conflict as well as Walt Whitman's idea that it would remain unwritten: "Such was the War. It was not a quadrille in a ball-room. Its interior history will not only never be written, its practicality, minutia of deeds and passions, will never be even suggested. The actual Soldier of 1862-'65, North and South, with all his ways, his incredible dauntlessness, habits, practices, tastes, language, his appetite rankness, his superb strength and animality, lawless gait, and a hundred unnamed lights and shades of camp—I say, will never be written—perhaps must not and should not be."[20]

With Cavada's diary we have both the written war and the interiority of an "actual" soldier, and here is where the journal takes significance for understanding Cavada's trans-American identity, for his interiority—his excitement, anxiety, fear, and joy—corresponds with the Union cause at the start of the war. It is not coincidental that the diary opens with Cavada at Yorktown, which is more memorable as the last battle of the American Revolution rather than one of the first Civil War skirmishes. Meanwhile, the excitement and gloom he feels at Fredericksburg and Chancellorsville, respectively, mirror the ebb and flow of the Federal army's momentum, as it weathered Confederate General Robert E. Lee's lopsided victory at Fredericksburg only to face a worse fate at Chancellorsville. In short, Cavada figures himself in his military diary as a synecdoche for the Union at the start of the war, but he also fashions himself as a quintessential U.S. citizen who begins as a greenhorn picket at the site of the American Revolution's siege of Yorktown and comes of age at the Civil War's most significant battle.

Just as the Union victory at the Battle of Gettysburg marked a turning point in the war, it also signals a change in Cavada's diary. His July 2, 1863, entry seems self-consciously aware of the impending battle's importance, and, as if to respond in kind, he takes more care to narrate it poetically: "~~The rain fell~~. No sound broke the stillness of the air except the pattering rain drops in the grass. . . . It was a grand sight—one to make one['s] blood warm and tingle through its channels—all sense of danger—the past abolished in that great present—that surrounds us." It is at Gettysburg that Adolfo comes of age as a Union officer. He proclaims a day after the battle: "July 4, 1863—The Fourth of July! A day made doubly dear by the victory of liberty over slavery on the fields of Gettysburg. . . . A short distance from here I could see the hill where I encamped with the 23rd Regiment during the 1st and 2nd of November 1862. Things have changed in my favor since then."[21] That Gettysburg takes place around the Fourth of July is perhaps a historical irony but symbolic nonetheless as Adolfo narrates his transformation through a national imaginary that begins with the American Revolution and culminates with U.S. independence. It is also the first and only time that Adolfo mentions slavery as a *casus belli*, as if his trans-American transformation as a U.S. Cuban citizen corresponds to his awareness about slavery and independence, a point that will return with a difference after the Civil War.

If Gettysburg is the culmination of Adolfo's Union career, however, it marks his big brother's misfortune on the field. July 3, 1863: "No positive information had been received of Fred's fate.—Some thought he had escaped, others had seen him wounded and [taken] prisoner, others still had seen him struck down by a cannon ball—amid so many contradictory statements I still hoped for the best."[22] Aldofo's concern is not new. Throughout his diary, he is called to attend to Frederic, who is often ill, absent, or broke. Adolfo recounts taking leave to go retrieve his AWOL big brother; other times he mentions letters received from his mother, reminding him to watch after Fred; and always, when they share the same field, his diary entries express concern for his brother. Throughout most of time Adolfo is coming of military age, Fred's health wanes. On December 16, 1862, Adolfo hears that his brother has been wounded and goes to visit him at camp; a month later, Frederic comes to stay with Adolfo at camp, and he's "very sick"; a day later, Adolfo secures leave papers for his brother and sends him home to recuperate, under the escort of Lt. Col. O.H.P. Carey of the 77th Pennsylvania Infantry. Four months later, on April 4, 1863, Adolfo must go find Fred and bring him back to camp.

Frederic at first proved to be a precious war participant. In May 1863, he was found guilty of and cashiered for three related charges of "behav[ing] himself in a cowardly manner in the presence of the enemy" at the Battle of Fredericksburg by absenting himself from the battlefield, taking shelter at the rear of the battlefield, and deserting his men under fire for shelter in the rear.[23] By official accounts, he did not comport himself much better at Gettysburg. He was in the melee long enough to get captured, and once again, charges of cowardice were leveled against him. In his July 12, 1863, report, Captain Edward R. Bowen of the 114th Pennsylvania Infantry notes that he "saw Lieutenant-Colonel Cavada, who was then commanding the regiment, stopping by a log house in an orchard on our right. I inquired if he was wounded; he replied that he was not, but utterly exhausted. I begged him to make an effort to come on, as the enemy was only a few yards from him and advancing rapidly. He replied that he could not, and I left him there, and not having heard from him since, I have no doubt he was taken prisoner there."[24] He was, and his commanding officer, Colonel Collis, who himself was accused of cowardice a few months later, filed formal charges against Cavada and waged a nasty letter-writing campaign to the president of the United States, accusing Cavada of cowardice at the battles of Chancellorville and Gettysburg. As Collis explained in a letter to Assistant Secretary of State Seward: "At Chancellorville, on the 3d May, 1863, when the first shot was fired at my regiment, Colonel Cavada disappeared, and when, after two hours' incessant fighting, with but ninety men and four officers left, . . . we marched to the rear, [and] we found Colonel Cavada sitting in the woods more than two miles distant from the line of battle"; he claimed he was "suddenly attacked with a very severe headache."[25] Cavada's capture at Gettysburg, Collis argued, was indicative of the cowardice he displayed at Fredericksburg and Chancellorville, but the fact that the lieutenant colonel was captured alongside General C. K. Graham was probably the only reason Collis's and Bowen's reports fell on deaf ears.

Meanwhile, to pass his time as a prisoner of war, Cavada penned sketches, anecdotes, and stories about prison life on contraband scratches of paper, and a few months after his 1864 release, King and Baird, the same company that printed Collis's incendiary pamphlet against Cavada, published *Libby Life: Experiences of a Prisoner of War*, which Philadelphia's J. B. Lippincott re-published in 1865. As the *Daily National Intelligencer* announced on June 18, 1864, "The narrative abounds with scenes and incidents, the correctness of which is vouched for by his fellow prisoners, and will interest every reader."[26] Dedicated to the Union League of Philadelphia, a prominent organization of uppercrust, Republican Party businessmen who supported Lincoln's war effort to which the brothers Cavada and their stepfather, Mr. Dutton, belonged, *Libby Life* recounts daily life as a prisoner—the boredom, hunger, and small celebrations the Union captives enjoy—with "freedom" as an underlying theme. "My chief aim in these humble pages," Frederic explains, "has been to perpetuate for my companions in captivity, a compliance with their request, a truthful record of our prison experiences,—a record which, while it cannot fail to bring back upon our hearts some of the gloomy shadows which once darkened them in the prison-house, may also renew upon our lips the irrepressible smiles which were wont to wreathe them at times, in spite of hunger, suffering and despair."[27] Cavada's sentiment gives truth to the power of language, especially during wartime, to be subversive and transformative. "In prison camps and torture blocks," James Dawes postulates, "the achievement of communication and recognition through an undetected note or an answered whisper is the first step in rebuilding the world."[28]

All Civil War prison camps were notorious, and Libby Prison was no exception. Part of Richmond, Virginia's prison complex, which included Castle Thunder and the nearby Belle Isle Prison, Libby was a warehouse-turned-jail for Union officers between 1861 and 1864, when it was then used for Confederate military criminals. By all accounts, sanitary conditions due to overcrowding were deadly, so much so that in February 1864, Libby Prison was the site of a sensational and subsequently sensationalized escape attempt by way of a fifty-seven-foot tunnel. "By February 9, 1864," William Hesseltine explains, "the tunnel was opened and a hundred and nine prisoners made their escape during the night. Forty-eight of the hundred and nine officers . . . were captured before they reached the Union lines." Of the ones who did make it, Hesseltine continues, several offered exaggerated official reports, newspaper accounts, and personal narratives about their escape.[29] Cavada was not one of the escapees, but he recounts the escape in his narrative immediately after it occurred, and in his preface he situates his book *contra* the exaggerated accounts. He states that his "sketches . . . were drawn, not with the object of presenting a sensational picture of the military prisons of the Confederacy, but simply to while away the idle hours of a tedious and protracted captivity."[30]

But when we recall that Libby Prison is in the heart of the Confederacy, then Cavada's longing for freedom in the face of captivity must be read against the presence of black slavery (despite Lincoln's Emancipation Proclamation) and, as the aforementioned book *The Poor White* reminds us, within the North's sensationalized accounts of white slavery. Unlike Adolfo, who finds the triumph of "liberty over slavery" on the Gettysburg battlefield, Frederic discovers the opposite as he becomes a Confederate captive and describes his conditions as akin to those associated with the tortures of slavery. He recounts laundry day, for instance, or "whitewashing" day, as he calls it, as a "torture and terror" "invented by the fiendish ingenuity of some monster in human shape" as the prisoners are hosed down from above by the prison guards, while "a dozen negroes from below" scrub out the prison quarters with filthy water.[31] It is a brief but telling scene as Cavada and his Union compatriots literally and symbolically find themselves stuck between black slavery below, white overseers above, and no escape from either. Cavada draws a similar, if not more bizarre, sketch during the 1864 New Year's Day "Grand Ball" in the prison's kitchen. With a small band, accompanied by a man "well blacked up" as a "negro woman" and another dressed as "a comical representation of [her] colored beau," the prisoners engage in a "heathenish" dance that leaves the "Sioux and Camanches [sic] . . . utterly outdone."[32] On a lower floor, two men engage in a chess game that rivals Thoreau's symbolic "ant war" in *Walden*:

> On the floor below, two sane men are near the termination of a highly interesting game of chess; . . . Black's hand is outstretched, tremulous with ill-controlled excitement: White turns pale, for those nervous outstretched fingers clutch a portentous black rook, and in another instant the white king will be mated. . . . When lo! From the ceiling overhead, where it was hung, down comes a huge ham, and drops like a bomb-shell into the very midst of the contending hosts! The pieces are scattered right and left; the board, and the rickety table on which it stood, are overset; and the black and the white general both spring to their feet with a cry of horror. . . . The *war-dance* was still going on overhead, and a gigantic Indian warrior having leaped into the air, and come down directly above the suspended ham, had jarred it from the nail on which it hung, and had thus ruined the most brilliant game of chess ever played in the prison.[33]

The New Year's celebration gives way to a carnival scene of racial disruption and destruction, with the U.S. Civil War figured as a chess game, not between northern and southern whites but between blacks and whites in a metaphysical struggle for dominance over a binary racial system troubled by the presence of Native America. Cavada's seemingly simple sketches, then, represent in miniature allegories of race war that situate his imprisonment as enslavement to the United States' prevailing racial order, making his final acquisition of freedom even more ironic because he is "bought out" during a prisoner exchange in 1864 and becomes "once more substantially and positively—FREE!"[34]

Immediately after his return to Philadelphia, Frederic challenged Colonel Collis to a duel for officially and publicly accusing Cavada of cowardice. The duel never occurred, and Cavada briefly re-enlisted in the Union Army under his friend General David Birney, but near the war's end, Secretary of State Seward named Frederic U.S. consul to Trinidad de Cuba, and he promptly tendered his resignation from the Union Army to take up his new post and return to his native island in 1866. It was a homecoming for him and also an awakening as his dispatches to the U.S. State Department urge the State officials to aid Cuba's independence movement.[35] The freshly appointed consul and former Union officer was becoming rebellious, and after the outbreak of Cuba's Ten Years War on October 10, 1868, Frederic resigned his post and joined Cuba's insurgency, alongside Adolfo, who also returned to the island after the Civil War as the American vice consul in Cienfuegos. As the *New York Herald* reported on February 12, 1869, "It is reported that the leaders of the [Cuban] revolution in the sugar districts of Cienfuegos, Villa Clara and Trinidad are Adolfo Cavada and his brother, Frederick [*sic*] Cavada. The former was recently American Vice Consul at Cienfuegos. He was a Colonel of a Philadelphia regiment of zouaves during the civil war in America. The latter was until last week the American consul at Trinidad de Cuba, and has just resigned."[36] Big brother Emilio joined the cause by using his New York and Philadelphia sugar businesses to supply funds, munitions, and other contraband to his brothers, while Adolfo commanded a small force of rebels in the province of Las Villas. However, it was middle brother Frederic—the poet, POW, and would-be "coward"—who emerged as the commander-in-chief of Cuba's rebel army; he became known as "General Candela," or the "Fire King," for the scorched-earth, guerrilla tactics he practiced against the island's economic staple, the sugar cane fields. The *Cincinnati Daily Enquirer* reported in a piece titled "War to the Knife and the Knife to the Hilt":

"The insurgent General Cavada has issued the following order to the forces under his command: 'It is probable that the owners of plantations will begin to grind sugar cane at an early date and the General expects his subordinates to burn the cane fields as soon as the cane is dry.'"[37]

A burn policy and other forms of property destruction were neither politic nor popular during the Ten Years War. Rebel President Carlos Manuel de Céspedes worked to muster support from fellow landowners and slave owners by assuring them that the rebellion would respect property, including food, farms, land, and, of course, people. The insurgent leadership was forced to balance two different impulses of their rebellion—namely, to protect the interests of the landed *criollo* class and keep at bay the idea that the rebellion opened the opportunity for immediate emancipation of black slaves.[38] This was especially true of mid-island locales such as Cienfuegos and Trinidad, which were in between eastern Cuba, the hotbed of the insurrection, and the more prosperous western Cuba, which became the Spanish stronghold. "Insurgent leaders were hopeful of obtaining material and financial support from their wealthy counterparts, and hence were reluctant to enact measures capable of antagonizing sugar planters in the west. Any prospect of obtaining the support of western planters required respect for their estates and their slaves. In 1869," Pérez concludes, "Carlos Manuel de Céspedes proclaimed the death penalty for any attack against sugar estates and slave property."[39]

Threats to people and property were not only bad politics in Cuba, but they also made the Cuban rebellion unpopular in the United States at a time when rebel leaders were soliciting U.S. recognition of belligerency and intervention on behalf of the insurgency. An October 29, 1869, *New York Tribune* article, for instance, reports that

> We have singular news from Cuba that the negroes near Cienfuegos have driven off a body of insurgents, which, we imagine, answers in some way to the general order of the patriot Cavada for burning the cane-crop. These things, however, are not the worst of our friends of Spanish descent as seen through the transparent ingenuity of those from whose stock and kind they are supposed to have descended. . . . The Cubans may make them worse still if they quarrel overmuch among themselves; and if there

is any danger of this for want of a strong executive arm in the Junta, by all means, let the arm be found and put in its right place.[40]

Bad politics and worse press do no good for mustering support of the rebellion on the island or in the United States, yet Frederic manages to practice both as General Candela, as if the rebellion he wages is against the United States and Cuba's elite criollo class.

The Fire King did not exactly put down the pen for the knife, as the aforementioned *Cincinnati Daily Enquirer* headlined. Instead, in 1870, somewhere between organizing a rebel army and leading it, Frederic found the time to write a travel narrative for *Harper's New Monthly Magazine* praising the national wonders of Cuba's Bellamar Caves and inviting U.S. visitors to see the cave for themselves. "Easy of access from Havana by railway," Cavada explains, "and commodiously and safely prepared for the reception of visitors, [the Bellamar cave] fully repays one from a day's absence from the busy scenes of the capital."[41] The article makes no mention that Cuba is embroiled in civil war, led in part by Cavada himself, and for this reason it might be better understood less as a travel puff piece and more as a complex autobiographical allegory of hemispheric history and trans-American rebellion. As the article continues, it recounts Cavada's descent into the cave. At first, Cavada frames the tourist's gaze, noting the cave's natural wonders, its passageways, columns, and the unique formations of its stalactites and stalagmites, but the farther Cavada descends, the more gothic the experience becomes, most notably when he crosses a formation known as the "Gothic Temple." Soon, formations begin to take shape, and he encounters the "'Mantle of Columbus,'" a solid formation that has crystallized into a mass "as white as snow."[42] Beyond it is the "Devil's Gorge," a symbolic point of no return as he descends farther to discover at his journey's end the "Avenue of Hatuey," a passageway that leads him to "a tall, keen stalagmite called the 'Lance of Hatuey.'"[43] In the deepest part of Cuba's Cave of Bellamar, Frederic finds the most celebrated figure of indigenous rebellion in Cuba.

A Taíno chief from Hispaniola, Hatuey became Cuba's national hero for raising a guerrilla war of rebellion against the Spanish in 1511, until his capture and execution on February 2, 1512. He emerged as a protean symbol of Cuban nationalism throughout the nineteenth century as a way of recalling the horrors of the Spanish black legend; re-imagining Cuban *criollos* as indigenous insurgents; and spinning a romantic, heroic history to the island's legacy of insurgency. Pedro Santacilia's 1859 *Lecciones orales sobre la historia de Cuba*, which was published in New Orleans, emphasizes Hatuey's rejection of Catholic conversion, and Juan Cristóbal Nápoles Fajardo's poem "Hatuey and Guarina," also published around 1856, imagines Hatuey's putting his love of patriotism before his love for Guarina.[44] Francisco Sellén, a revolutionary Cuban poet exiled to the United States in 1868, penned and published in New York *Hatuey*, a drama in verse that represents the indigenous insurgent as a martyr for independence, patriotism, and the treachery of betrayal within his rebellion.[45] Cavada's *Harper's* article might be seen in the same vein but with a difference in the sense that it narrates Cavada's coming to revolutionary consciousness. His is a symbolic journey beneath Cuba and, by extension, within his own interiority as he takes the path for U.S. visitors to the cave, schluffs off Columbus's mantle, and in the end finds Hatuey's lance for warfare. In much the same way that Adolfo's diary charts his coming of age as a Union officer, "The Cave of Bellamar" narrates Frederic's transformation from U.S. citizen to Cuban rebel ready to take up Hatuey's war of guerrilla tactics.

Thus, at the same time as the *Harper's* article, General Candela also penned and published in Spanish an insurgent manual to guerrilla warfare and a field guide for officers.[46] The pamphlet gives military definitions of terms such as *hilera* and *fila*, line and ranks; *frente* and *flanco*, front and flank; and *vanguardia* and *retaguardia*, vanguard and rear guard—the usual military terms, with the glaring omission of *retreat* and *surrender*, that indicate Cavada was attempting to introduce military protocol to his insurgent troops. His field guide for officers emphasizes this point, as he recommends that officers follow a clear chain of command, establish military tribunals, and, probably the most telling of his experiences in the Union Army, that officers keep written copies of their orders to collect as a record of their rebellion—all of this while advocating the use of guerrilla warfare whenever possible.

It is not difficult to comprehend how both pieces can come from the same pen at the same time if we understand Cavada's life and imagination within the context of a trans-American formation. He is not torn between "Nuestra America and the America that is not ours," as Martí would later put it. Rather, both Americas are his in ways that produce two different bodies of writing: one in English, published in one of the leading upper-middle-class magazines of the time in the United States; the other in Spanish, written to make Cuba's insurgent war against Spain more efficient in terms of military policy and guerrilla tactics. One announces allegorically his coming to revolutionary consciousness on the island; the other employs strategies he learned in the Union to wage rebellion. His is a trans-American identity with a voice in both worlds (U.S. and Latino), as Cavada is not so much torn by his double-ness as he is formed by it in the same way that the outbreak and outcome of the U.S. Civil War inflected the issues of race, anti-imperialism, slavery, and self-governance fueling Cuba's own war of rebellion.

In this regard, Frederic underscores a profound understanding of the relation between the U.S. Civil War and Cuba's Ten Years War—both are American civil wars that share a genealogy much as the Cavada brothers themselves do, for if the U.S. Civil War is the arena for Adolfo's coming of age, it is the Cuban war that turns Frederic into a general and later commander-in-chief whose scorched-earth practices rivaled Sherman's march to Savannah. It also made him a trans-American hero, claimed by Cuban nationals as a prodigal son; by Philadelphians as a freedom-fighting brother; and by Unionists as a comrade in arms. It is thus not surprising that his capture by Spanish forces in late June 1871 garnered national headlines across the United States and a petition for his release became a *cause célèbre* for high-ranking Union brass, including Generals Graham (his former Libby Prison compatriot), Sheridan, and Sherman, all of whom petitioned President Ulysses S. Grant to seek Cavada's release. But to no avail. A week before his fortieth birthday, Frederic was executed without trial on July 1, 1871 (almost eight years to the day he was captured at Gettysburg). In his last letter to his wife, dated June 30, he writes, "I am here as a prisoner of war due to circumstances that without a doubt are familiar to you."[47] They are no doubt uncanny to him too, a sickly, inexperienced lieutenant colonel of the Philadelphia Volunteers who passed his time in a rebel prison writing anecdotes finds himself a prisoner of war again—this time as a rebel commander-in-chief who never quite realized the irony of quelling one rebellion in the States but leading another on the island. His last words were reportedly,

"Adios mi Cuba, hasta siempre."[48] One story even says he tossed his cigar and hat into the air before the bullets flew. His obituary ran in the *New York Herald*, the *Cincinnati Daily Gazette*, the *Leavenworth Times*, the *Boston Daily Journal*, Philadelphia's *Public Ledger*, and the *Philadelphia Inquirer*, which closed its paean to him with the following: "He lived and wrought and died for the cause of Cuban independence. He was a brave soldier, a true patriot, and an estimable gentleman."[49]

Ten months later, the New Orleans *Picayune* made brief mention that Adolfo Cavada was also killed in action,[50] and even though the Ten Years War ended in 1878 without securing Cuban independence or the immediate abolition of slavery, the revolutionary spirit of the brothers Cavada in action and in writing laid the foundation for the anti-imperial movement of Martí's generation. But at the risk of making too much of Frederic's transformation, from would-be coward to the fire-king, it is worth noting that his return to Cuba and subsequent insurgent leadership fulfilled a nostalgic fate he expressed in his first published poem, "The Cuban's Adieu to His Native Land," which appeared in the Philadelphia *Evening Bulletin* in 1847:[51]

> Adieu to thee! Queen of the sea,
> Adieu to the thoughts of the past,
> Though for e'er thy remembrance shall last,
> Whenever on earth I may be.
> Adieu to thee! Isle I hold dear,
> 'Till thy people at Liberty's call,
> By causing Iberia to fall
> 'Neath the flag of the free shall appear.
> And now thou'rt gone, perhaps for ever,
> But await with a patient heart,
> Till Columbia by valour and heart
> The chains of the tyrant shall sever!

At first glance, the poem reads like the scores of other Cuban exile poems published in Spanish-language organs throughout urban centers like New York and New Orleans. It imagines Cuba's someday gaining its independence from Spain, perhaps with the United States' assistance, and combines the political rhetoric of revolution with the romantic, if not overly sentimental, view of the island. But there are two differences here. The first is that it is penned by a fifteen-year-old boy rather than an adult poet, lawyer, property owner, politician, or military man, as the majority of Cuban exile writers were in the 1840s and 1850s. The second is that it is penned and published in English. In other words, Cavada's poem, like the brothers Cavada, marks a transitional generation of U.S. Cubans in the nineteenth century—not quite at home but not quite in exile either. They are "deterritorialized," as Lazo puts it, meaning that the Cavada brothers and their writing move "in and out of one nation and then another."[52] But such motion is not seamless, for to traverse one nation to another means to betray them both, to rebel against their borders in the name of a larger, hemispheric sense of citizenship. We see such a movement in Cavada's poem, for in it is a glimpse at how the fire of rebellion fueled the poet to travel from Cuba, to Philadelphia, and back to the island again, with independence in mind the entire time.

NOTES

1 *Daily National Intelligencer*, July 8, 1864.

2 Ada Ferrer, *Insurgent Cuba: Race, Nation, and Revolution, 1868–1898* (Chapel Hill: University of North Carolina Press, 1999), 15.

3 Rodrigo Lazo, *Writing to Cuba: Filibustering and Cuban Exiles in the United States* (Chapel Hill: University of North Carolina Press, 2005), 7.

4 Louis A. Pérez Jr., *Cuba between Empires, 1878–1902* (Pittsburgh: University of Pittsburgh Press, 1983), 29–31. See also Pérez Jr., *Cuba: Between Reform and Revolution*, Third edition (New York: Oxford University Press, 2006), 83, and Christopher Schmidt-Nowara, *Empire and Antislavery: Spain, Cuba, and Puerto Rico, 1833–1874* (Pittsburgh: University of Pittsburgh Press, 1999), 27–32.

5 Schmidt-Nowara, *Empire and Antislavery*, 31.

6 Darryl E. Brock, "José Agustín Quintero: Cuban Patriot in Confederate Diplomatic Service," in *Cubans in the Confederacy*, ed. Phillip Thomas Tucker (Jefferson, N.C.: McFarland and Company, 2002), 44.

7 Loreta Janeta Velazquez, *The Woman in Battle: The Civil War Narrative of Loreta Janeta Velazquez, Cuban Woman and Confederate Soldier* (Madison: University of Wisconsin Press, 2003), 248.

8 Nicolás Kanellos, "An Overview of Hispanic Literature of the United States," in *Herencia: The Anthology of Hispanic Literature of the United States*, ed. Nicolás Kanellos (New York: Oxford University Press, 2002), 16.

9 Michael A. Dreese, *Torn Families: Death and Kinship at the Battle of Gettysburg* (Jefferson, N.C.: McFarland and Company, 2007), 137.

10 See Joseph John Jova, "Foreword," *Libby Life*, by F. F. Cavada, (Lanham, Md.: University Press of America, 1985); Louis Alfredo Martinez, "Federico Fernández Cavada: Loyal to Two Flags," in *Hispanic Presence in the United States*, ed. Frank de Varona (Miami: Mnemosyne Publishing Company, 1993); O. W. Davis, *Sketch of Frederic Fernandez Cavada, A Native of Cuba* (Philadelphia: James B. Chandler, 1871). The Historical Society of Pennsylvania holds a small collection of Cavada-related material, and the University of Miami houses the Fernando Fernández-Cavada collection.

11 Davis, *Sketch of Frederic Fernandez Cavada*, 10.

12 Ibid., 11.

13 Gerald E. Poyo, *"With All, and for the Good of All"*: *The Emergence of Popular Nationalism in the Cuban Communities of the United States, 1848–1898* (Durham, N.C.: Duke University Press, 1989), 4.

14 Adolfo F. Cavada, Diary, unpublished, Fernando Fernández-Cavada Collection, Cuban Heritage Collection, University of Miami Libraries, Coral Gables, Florida.

15 Ibid.

16 Ibid.

17 Ibid.

18 Ibid.

19 Ibid.

20 Walt Whitman, *Memoranda During the Civil War*, ed. Peter Coviello (New York: Oxford University Press, 2004), 7.

21 Adolfo Cavada, diary, unpublished.

22 Ibid.

23 Thos. M. O'Brien and Oliver Diefendorf, *General Orders of the War Department*, Volume 2 (New York: Derby and Miller, 1864), 160.

24 *The War of Rebellion: A Compilation of the Official Records of the Union and Confederate Armies* (Washington, 1889), Series I, Vol. XXVII, Ch. XXXIX, 503.

25 Charles Henry Collis, *The Case of F. F. Cavada* (Philadelphia: King and Baird, 1865), 12.

26 *Daily National Intelligencer*, June 18, 1864.

27 Cavada, *Libby Life*, 10.

28 James Dawes, *The Language of War: Literature and Culture in the U.S. from the Civil War Through World War II* (Cambridge, Mass.: Harvard University Press, 2002), 2.

29 William Best Hesseltine, *Civil War Prisons: A Study in War Psychology* (New York: Frederick Ungar Publishing, 1964), 131. The escape was fictionalized in Peter Burchard's juvenile novel *Rat Hell* (New York: Putnam, 1971), with Cavada perhaps making an appearance as the character Sears, an artist. See Burchard 36.

30 Cavada, *Libby Life*, 9.

31 Ibid., 33.

32 Ibid., 126–27.

33 Ibid., 127–28. Italics in original.

34 Ibid., 200.
35 Joseph John Jova, "Foreword," *Libby Life*, n.p.
36 *New York Herald*, February 2, 1869.
37 *Cincinnati Daily Enquirer*, October 29, 1869.
38 See Ferrer, *Insurgent Cuba*, 24.
39 Pérez, *Cuba between Reform and Revolution*, 90.
40 *New York Herald Tribune*, October 29, 1869.
41 General Fredrico F. Cavada, "The Cave of Bellamar," *Harper's New Monthly Magazine* (November 1870), 826.
42 Ibid., 828.
43 Ibid., 833.
44 Rebecca Earle, *The Return of the Native: Indians and Myth-Making in Spanish America, 1810–1930* (Durham, N.C.: Duke University Press, 2007), 76.
45 Francisco Sellén, *Hatuey, poema dramatíco* (New York: A da Costa Gómez, 1891).
46 F. F. Cavada, *Ejercito Libertador de Cuba: Breve instruccion de guerrilla y guia de los jefes y oficiales de campaña* (Guaimaro, Cuba: Imprenta del Cubano Libre, 1870).
47 Frederic Cavada Letter to Wife, June 30, 1871. Fernando Fernández-Cavada Collection, Cuban Heritage Collection, University of Miami Libraries, Coral Gables, Florida. Translation provided by the Cuban Heritage Collection.
48 *Times Picayune*, July 26, 1871.
49 *Philadelphia Inquirer*, July 12, 1871.
50 *The Daily Picayune*, April 4, 1874.
51 Joseph John Jova, "Foreword," *Libby Life*, n.p.
52 Rodrigo Lazo, *Writing to Cuba*, 55.

5

Almost-Latino Literature

Approaching Truncated Latinidades

ROBERT MCKEE IRWIN

How to talk about "Latino" literature in a period that predates the general usage of the term as a category of cultural production or identity? If there is likely to be a general consensus on whether a given literary text might be categorized as Latino in the early twenty-first century, applying this category to another historical context is in itself an exercise that calls for definition. For example, one might argue that José Martí, who lived fourteen years in New York City and wrote many of his most acclaimed works from the United States, was a proto-Latino and that his *Versos sencillos* and various essays (e.g., "Nuestra América") and *crónicas* (e.g., "Coney Island") can therefore be categorized as Latino writing,[1] or that John Rollin Ridge's *The Life and Adventures of Joaquin Murieta* was a Latino novel because its protagonist, who was born in Mexico but lived out the last and most historically significant years of his life in the United States, was a proto-Latino. But either case might produce detractors, as Martí is best known as a Cuban writer and is indeed a symbol of Cuban nationalism, and Ridge, who was part Cherokee, is most often seen as a foundational figure of Native American literature as his Murieta novel was the first novel published in English by a Native American author.

Another case of interest might be that of what might be deemed the first Mexican novel set in the borderlands, *La campana de la misión*, first drafted by José María Esteva in 1858 and published in his native Xalapa, Veracruz, in 1894. It recounts the shipwreck of Mexican travelers on their way to San Francisco, leaving a young couple stranded in the desert terrain of the Baja California peninsula. They frantically ring the bell of the abandoned San Borja Mission in vain, and after they lose hope for rescue, the romantic hero, Eduardo, sets off alone in search of help. He perishes in a storm, and his fiancée, Laura, left alone in the abandoned mission, is never heard from again. The plot is not one of migration, but the story of Mexican travelers enduring perilous conditions and eventually dying while trying to get to California might be thought of as anticipating the life stories of the many undocumented migrants who in recent decades have died trying to reach the United States. The novel's protagonists are neither impoverished nor uneducated, but rather of Mexico's elite; Laura and Eduardo, a poet, hoped to reach San Francisco, where Laura's father had launched a business. Yet they are almost Latinos: Had *La campana*'s author been a Californio, or had its plot led its romantic protagonists to settle in San Francisco, a case might be made for classifying this as an early Latino novel. *La campana* has never been categorized in this way, nor has anyone ever identified it as a precursor to the genre as neither its author nor its protagonists ever lived in the United States. Indeed, Esteva, who was from Veracruz, when exiled from Mexico for having collaborated with the government of Emperor Maximilian during the French Intervention, fled to Cuba and not the United States, as so many Latin American expatriates did in the nineteenth century.

The case of Chilean Vicente Pérez Rosales, whose Gold Rush memoir is treated by Juan Poblete elsewhere in this volume, likewise fails to fit neatly into the category of Latino author. Even if some of his writings are occasionally anthologized in Latino literature collections (for example, in *Under the Fifth Sun: Latino Literature from California*, edited by Rick Heide), he remains known to his readers, including those reading him in such anthologies, as a "Chilean" and not a "Latino" author. If studies on contemporary Latino cultural production take as a starting point the self-evident nature of the appropriateness (i.e., the Latinidad) of their objects of study, studies focused on the nineteenth century, which can consider Latino subjects only through anachronisms and extrapolations, are forced to think carefully about the notions on which such terms (*Latino subject, Latinidad, Latino literature*) are based. Whether or not Vicente Pérez Rosales ought to be thought of as a Latino is not really of great importance, however. Instead, what this volume seeks is to think beyond rigid categories in order to better understand the history of race and racialization, migration and citizenship, and national and transnational identity in the United States.

I will therefore take a moment to try and define what seems to be self-evident: how the notion of Latino might be distinguished from a separate category of Latin American. The notion of Latin American is reasonably clear for a discussion in a context of migration, especially when posited in opposition to U.S. American. There is an Anglophone America that is defined in contrast with what José Martí called "Nuestra América." The opposition, of course, breaks down in the context of the notion of Latino America, which describes identities and cultural contexts that cross territorial divides. If the border between Mexico and the United States separates U.S. America from Latin America, the physical and cultural presence of Latin Americans in the United States establishes a separate category of identity and culture that operates both within and in opposition to each of the other two: the Latino.

The distinction between *Latino* and *Latin American* has to do with territoriality but also with subjectivity.[2] A Latin American who visits the United States does not become a Latino by her mere fleeting presence in U.S. territory, whereas an individual who was born in Latin America but comes to the United States as an infant and lives the rest of his life in the United States may not identify as Latin American at all, but only as Latino. While some Latinos living in the United States may simultaneously retain their Latino American identity to some degree, for those born in Latin America who later relocate to the United States, there must be some dividing line to determine when a Latin American may become a Latino. Does it happen after a period of time? Does it have more to do with acts of assimilation, or with a desire to break to some degree with one's Latin American roots and establish oneself in the United States? Is it a class-based identification open to only certain immigrants? Why is it that Mexican immigrant Alurista is so profoundly Latino, while Isabel Allende, who has lived in the United States for more than twenty years, still identifies as Chilean, despite having lived fewer years of her life in Chile? Paul Allatson's *Key Terms in Latino/a Cultural and Literary Studies* defines a Latino/a as "the broad panethnic identity that includes [. . .] any citizen or resident [of the United States] with Latin American heritage."[3] Thus it would seem that identity is key: Once a Latin American–born immigrant to the United States is ready to assume a U.S.-based identity, letting go (of course not completely) of a feeling of belonging to a birth country enough to set down roots as a racialized minority in the

United States, she then becomes Latino. But for the immigrant, does this conversion happen at a particular moment, or is it better understood as a process? To help think about this last question, we'll begin with another one: What happens to a Latin American who desires to immigrate to, and establish himself as a resident in, the United States and begins to do so but ultimately cannot? Is this category of person, one whose process of becoming Latino is thwarted, of interest to Latino studies? It would seem that these truncated, disrupted, obstructed Latinidades call attention to the precariousness of the category for many, and the deeply embedded bigotry that continues to marginalize Latinos in the United States, even today as they enter ever more prominently and in greater numbers into the mainstream of national culture.

Continuities: Liminality and Violence

I turn to the liminal category of "almost immigrant" or failed immigrant in order to point to the stories of migration we do not know so well—and the gap here lies not only in Latino studies, but in American and Latin American studies as well—stories of disrupted immigration, stories that have become increasingly relevant in our current moment of xenophobia and border violence. I am thinking, for example, of the stories we will never hear told of the seventy-two "illegal immigrants" (as they were identified by Mexican authorities), fifty-eight men and fourteen women from El Salvador, Honduras, Guatemala, Brazil, and Ecuador, who were massacred, apparently by the Zetas drug cartel, in Tamaulipas in August 2010. This story made international headlines, although it had not been the first such mass killing of migrants in Mexico: previous, less-publicized cases include those of the discovery of fifty-five bodies in an abandoned mine in Taxco, and of fifty-one bodies recovered from near a trash dump in the outskirts of Monterrey.[4] Theirs are lost stories of those who perhaps dreamed of becoming Latinos but never had the chance to claim this identity.

Meanwhile, the U.S. Immigration and Customs Enforcement agency (ICE) has been deporting immigrants in record numbers. The annual number of deportations has been rising steadily over the past thirty years, from only about 18,000 in 1980, to about 30,000 in 1990, to more than 188,000 in 2000, to 387,242 in 2010.[5] The year 2011 saw a record number of 396,906 deportations, a figure that rose to 409,849 in 2012, as the Obama administration continues to strive to meet a quota of 400,000 deportations per year.[6] Meanwhile, hundreds of thousands of immigrants—476,000 in 2010—left the United States "voluntarily"—that is, at the request of the Department of Homeland Security, but without an official removal order. ICE Director John Morton brags in a report that in 2010, ICE arrested a record number of employers for hiring undocumented immigrants, and that workplace inspections (more commonly known as "raids") were running at record levels in 2011, part of his "record-breaking immigration enforcement strategies" designed to "help strengthen and secure our homeland."[7] Meanwhile, in 2012, an election year in which campaign rhetoric included a proposal to construct an electrified fence along the border in order to execute instantly anyone trying to sneak across, deaths among undocumented immigrants attempting to cross the border (usually due to hypothermia, but also attributed to snake bites, heart attacks, traffic accidents, or violent crime) continue to be a major problem. Reports based on data from 2010 note that "although the number of people attempting to cross the United States–Mexico border illegally has declined in recent years, the number of unauthorized migrants found dead continues to increase" as immigrants avoid better-known (and -patrolled) crossing points, instead following more remote and dangerous routes through the desert.[8]

These migrants' struggles of, to use ICE terminology, "removal" (formal deportation) or "return" (voluntary departure)—or Mitt Romney's 2012 presidential campaign buzzword *self-deportation*—or even death are stories about which we hear little. We know that hundreds of thousands of immigrants, most of them Mexican (73 percent of removals and 75 percent of returns in 2010), are being hunted down, incarcerated in ICE's outsourced and mostly for-profit private prisons, and tossed back across the border, but we learn little about their stories through Latino (or American or Latin American) literature. These temporary migrants, these almost-Latinos, are liminal figures who exist only in the interstices of the cultural categories that structure academic knowledge. Migrants such as those captured by ICE do get across the border, as Pérez Rosales did, but get spit back where they came from. In Mexico, for example, such returnees may be branded back in Mexico as *pochos*, losing as it were some essential piece of their Mexican identity, but they are almost never made part of a Latinidad that grants them a prominent place in Latino literature.

While the California Gold Rush was a unique historical circumstance, in a way it set the tone for later waves of migrations. The feelings of hope, trepidation, and excitement expressed by Pérez Rosales upon arriving in San Francisco in February 1849 are commonplace in Latino literature that recounts experiences of immigration to the United States. Similarly, the various tribulations experienced by Pérez Rosales, such as the sacking of Little Chile by Yankee marauders, might offer some parallelisms to those lived by contemporary Latin American immigrants to the United States, as esthetically reconstructed through Latino narrative. However, Pérez Rosales's violent displacement from California after less than a year, and his subsequent reinsertion into Chilean society a few months later, is ultimately what defines his story as one of travel and not of migration.

He writes of his re-accommodation back in Chile: "On my downward path I had reached the lowest rungs on the fragile ladder of fortune; in California I had reached what seemed to me the lowest rung of all, that of personal service as a waiter, and it never occurred to me that an even lower one remained for me to tread, that of a minor civil servant!"[9] While his tone is ironic, there is a story of involuntary displacement that he mostly elides. His tragic and somewhat shameful return trip to Chile is told in fewer than two pages—in deep contrast with his upbeat recounting of his voluntary voyage to and arrival in San Francisco, material enough for two entire chapters, or 28 pages. And this latter tale of removal is not a common trope of Latino literature, the details of which remain mostly outside of the way we think of the experience of migration in the Americas. We know, for example, that 72 migrants were executed in Tamaulipas and that 400,000 immigrants were deported each year from 2012 to 2014, but we don't know their stories.

Vicente Pérez Rosales

Vicente Pérez Rosales's memoirs provide an early portrait of what California represented to those arriving in the United States from Latin America. The setting, of course, is the Gold Rush, the first moment of the history of California as a U.S. territory, a history propelled by massive immigration, from the Anglophone east, the Asian Pacific west, and, especially, the Spanish-speaking South. Pérez Rosales's memoirs, parts of which were written as early as 1849, were published for the first time as a part of *Recuerdos del pasado* in Chile in 1882 and later in an unabridged form as *Diario de un viaje a California 1848–1849* in a limited edition (one hundred copies) in Chile in 1949 and in more widely available edition only in 2007. The former text was translated into English as *Times Gone By* in 2003.

Let me begin with a passage from *Times Gone By* that expresses the hopes and fears of those coming to Gold Rush–era California:

> California was an unknown country, almost a desert, full of dangers, and prey to epidemic diseases . . . personal security could be found only in the barrel of a gun or at the point of a knife, yet robbery, violence, sickness, death itself were secondary considerations when compared to the seductive gleam. . . . At the moment of departure no one gave a thought to the dangers and travails awaiting us. Unanimously we cheered the fresh breeze that was moving us along, and we lost sight of our native land without revealing with a sigh or tinge of remorse that we understood the magnitude of our collective rashness. (217–18)

The Chileans, who were among the first to set out for California when rumors of the discovery of gold began to circulate in late 1848, had little idea what California would be like, as the former isolated and sparsely populated Mexican territory had only just started to become a destination for travelers of any kind. However, the promise of riches was irresistible for many Chileans, who began reading in local newspaper headlines such as that of a front-page editorial printed in *El Comercio* of Valparaíso on November 16, "Emigración a California," that drew attention to the opportunities for enrichment in California and signaled the threat of an impending mass exodus of Chilean adventurers.[10]

Regardless of the intentions of individual Chilean "argonauts," those who remained did not assume that Chile might become wealthy when their prodigal sons returned with pockets full of gold but instead worried that their soon-to-be-prosperous compatriots would never return. Even as an anti-emigration drama was staged in Valparaíso titled "*Yo no voy a California*" (I am not going to California) in late December 1848, newspapers continued to deplore the wave of emigration and the resultant loss of population (estimated already at 2,000), cash (emigrants had left with more than a million pesos), and potential income (estimated at more than $6 million).[11] The very same day as the publication of an editorial in *El Mercurio* announcing the statistics cited above and the premier of the play, December 28, 1848, Vicente Pérez Rosales embarked for California, arriving in San Francisco on February 18 of the following year as one of the first "49ers." Pérez Rosales writes: "Once we had passed through the thick low lying fog that like a curtain almost always hangs over that place, . . . our eyes fell on the most beautiful view that could be offered them at so difficult a moment . . . the straits of the Golden Gate, which, glorious and imposing, seemed to be opening wide to receive us. We had reached California!" (222–23). His optimism was shared by his fellow-travelers: "For me good fortune has always been a delusion, but this did not keep me from sharing in the general happiness as I stood contentedly contemplating the scene. If an impartial spectator . . . had dropped at that moment from the moon, he could easily have read . . . in each of those agitated hearts: 'My dream's come true!'" (226). This enthusiasm, expressed thusly, was an early incarnation of what would later come to be known to so many Latin American emigrants as "the American dream."

The context appears quite clear. Chileans were not going to California to exploit the land and return home; with a somewhat fantastic aspiration for self-enrichment, they were emigrating. While Pérez Rosales upon embarking on his adventure never makes clear whether he intends to return to Chile (and there is no telling whether or how he edited his diaries upon returning to Chile, where they were later published), these entries express a possibility, a dream, that he would make himself a fortune and a new marvelous life in California.

However, his dreams were not to come true. He soon comes to realize that gold is not readily available for everyone who shows up, and that Chileans, despite their experience and skill as miners, have no advantage whatsoever. As foreigners they find themselves at a distinct disadvantage in a territory newly occupied by a nation that has only just come into its possession and is determined to assert its authority and ownership. Nativism, according to the California historian Leonard Pitt, was "born in the months of 1849 and early 1850 when mining was most individualistic, government most ineffectual, and immigration most rapid."[12] And the immigration of Spanish-speakers (and later Asians) provoked great feelings of xenophobia among Anglo Americans, who marked them as more significantly foreign than, say, European or Australian immigrants. By April 1849, a group of Yankees carried out a local purge "of all Chileans, Mexicans, and Peruvians" on the grounds that they were "trespassers" in the mines.[13]

While U.S. Americans, fresh from war with Mexico, felt a special need to establish that Mexicans, to whom California had belonged until only a few months earlier, were no longer in charge, and many still saw them as adversaries, the extension of this animosity toward Chileans and other Spanish-speakers seemed to be justified by a cultural similarity: It was too difficult for Anglo Americans to try to differentiate among different groups of Spanish-speakers, who, it was thought, were culturally united through not only language but also religious excess (Catholicism) and a common heritage of Spanish-style colonialism. Not only had the Spaniards notoriously mixed with the indigenous peoples they had conquered, but their homeland had its own history of Moorish invasion that inculcated Arab and African elements into the ethnic bloodline. Writes Pérez Rosales: "The hostility of the common run of Yankees toward the sons of other nations, and most especially toward Chileans, had intensified. Their argument was simple and conclusive: the Chilean descended from the Spaniard, the Spaniard had Moorish blood, therefore the Chilean had to be at the least a Hottentot or at best something very much like the timid and abased Californio" (272).

Eventually driven from the mines by nativist thugs, the Chileans, who had formed their own makeshift settlement in San Francisco known as Chilecito (Little Chile), continued to be harassed and threatened wherever they went. After an unprovoked and violent attack on Little Chile that resulted in bloodshed on both sides, the local English-language newspaper produced headlines proclaiming: "American blood shed by vile Chileans . . . Citizens beware!" (273). Threatened, pursued, assaulted, the Chileans and their desire to make it in the "Golden State" persevered; in Pérez Rosales's words: "to be sure, they were robbed of all they possessed; but in California that was a matter of no consequence . . . [And] no one favored returning to Chile; instead we unanimously resolved to struggle anew" (273).

Unfortunately, the dream of Vicente Pérez Rosales and other Chileans could ultimately not be sustained. After less than a year in California, Pérez Rosales is finally forced to return when his Little Chile is assaulted by arsonists: "The fire spread in all directions with the same sickening speed with which we sometimes see it spread in Chile in some of our wheat fields at harvest time. In the midst of that immense roaring bonfire, stoked by the explosion of barrels of gunpowder that filled the air with sparks and flaming timbers, everything was soon invaded by burning boards carried by the wind. The fire surrounded us on all sides, and like everyone else we saved ourselves only by the speed of our flight" (294).

Almost Latino

Pérez Rosales's was in the end a travel diary, not a tale of immigration, although it might have been the latter had his luck here been different. Had Pérez Rosales stayed and lived out the rest of his years in the United States, or at least lasted more than a year in California, this text might be read by literary historians as an early precursor of Latino literature. In fact, Marissa López has identified Pérez Rosales precisely in those terms; she does so not by locating him within an imagined community of Spanish-speakers and their progeny who live in the United States with a clearly established minority status but as a part of a "transnational *latinidad*" that challenges such nationally construed configurations.[14] However, in more conventional terms, this text is no more Latino than Humboldt's travel narratives are Latin American. Instead, Pérez Rosales and many other Chileans of Gold Rush–era California did not "emigrate" as the Chilean press had feared but only visited California. They therefore remained Chilean without ever becoming Chilean American—that is, they are not proto-Latinos, but only almost-Latinos. And as such, their experience models that of many others who have set out for California with optimistic dreams that are shattered as they end up deported, driven back home, or killed. Pérez Rosales was an almost-Latino; indeed, he is a foundational figure of almost-Latino literature.

Latino is an imaginary category that may be understood as a political identity, a market segment, a distinct culture, an ethnicity, or a demographic grouping, but it does not apply to tourists or other short-term visitors to the United States. Objectively, those who manage to stay and find some stability in a new life may be categorized or may identify as Latinos; those who don't have no choice but to remain Latin Americans. Those who live in the interstices of these two categories without ever managing to fully cross over from the latter into the former represent often painful stories of migration that are rarely considered yet are an important aspect of everyday life in the Americas. Migrants such as the many who get caught by U.S. Immigration and Customs Enforcement agents and are deported, or those who make it to "El Norte" only to find it a hostile environment in which they choose not to stay, or those who die in transit, whether because of harsh conditions of crossing the desert or because of the risks they face in dealing with those on whom they must depend for help along the way are all current-day examples of this pattern.

Pérez Rosales's "travel diary," a first-person account about the Chilean minority living in the California Territory in 1849, is normally read both in Chile and in the United States through the category assigned to it by its publishers. For example, the 2007 Chilean edition of *Diario de un viaje a California* argues that we must "incorporarlo al canon nacional [chileno], lugar que le corresponde" (incorporate it in the Chilean national literary canon, where it belongs),[15] while the 2003 English translation of Pérez Rosales's memoirs is published in Oxford University Press's "Latin American Library" series, along with works by major figures of Latin American history and literature such as Simón Bolívar, Andrés Bello, Fray Servando Teresa de Mier, Domingo Faustino Sarmiento, Joaquim Maria Machado de Assis, Clorinda Matto de Turner, Cirilo Villaverde, Jose de Alencar, and Ricardo Palma. An earlier 1976 text, *We Were 49ers! Chilean Accounts of the California Gold Rush*, which includes an English-language translation of an excerpt of *Diario de un viaje a California*, refers to Pérez Rosales and the other Chileans whose accounts of Gold Rush experiences it features as "some of the most famous names in Chilean literature."[16] Pérez Rosales is presented uniformly not as an immigrant but as a Chilean visitor to California. Whether or not this was how Pérez Rosales thought of himself in early 1849, it was clearly what Anglo American xenophobes intended for him.

In the end, it makes little difference what we call Pérez Rosales or others like him. What is important is that we take into account these stories of truncated or impeded processes of Latinidad. Kirsten Silva Gruesz, in setting out to explore how to define Latino literary history, critiques the commonly employed categories of "immigrant" and "exile" for their lack of precision in historicizing the texts that end up anthologized under one rubric or the other; as she puts it: "An exile may well imagine the future differently from a voluntary immigrant—but how many writers have access to knowledge of their place in this taxonomy at the time they are writing?"[17] While some seasonal workers may think of themselves as living in exile, they may later end up deciding to stay, with or without documents to legitimize their presence, in the United States. Meanwhile, others may come to the United States with every intention—or at least hope—of staying but may not find a way to do so. There is no way to know whether Pérez Rosales's diary was written in hopes of earning its author a place in the Chilean or Latin American literary canon, of documenting a story of exile and repatriation, or of narrating an immigrant's "American dream" come true.

Thinking Transnationally

My point here is that categorizations based on identity categories that we all know are fluid, or geographical sites in an era of multidirectional flows, do not help us to understand some of what might be considered the greatest human rights abuses occurring today in our hemisphere. What I am proposing through my rescue of Pérez Rosales's writings, which I teach not in a class on Latino literature or Latin American literature but in one titled "California and Latin America" whose context allows students to explore relationships of ethnic otherness, migrations and transculturations, cultural and military imperialism, and so on, is an engagement with interstitial spaces such as those implied in stories of Latin American migrants who do not quite become—or only barely become—Latinos in order to better understand some of the more disturbing social problems of times that see Jan Brewer, who championed and signed Arizona's brutal anti-immigration law, elected by a comfortable margin, and presidential candidate Mitt Romney's reviving the Ku Klux Klan's slogan "Keep America American" as part of his anti-immigration rhetoric.

Juan Poblete has proposed the "concept of a globalized Latino/a America," a transnational approach to Latino studies that, as Frances

Aparicio argues, recognizes the importance of locating Latino studies in relation to the traditions of both American studies and Latin American studies.[18] Poblete has in his previous work argued that "the US and Latin America are intertwined in inextricable ways by the new flows of people, capital, goods and communications" and that "the new global condition of Latinos" calls for new epistemologies and critical approaches, not unlike those suggested here.[19] As the question of contemporary dynamics of cross-border movement, voluntary and involuntary, as discussed above in the context of both the nineteenth century and the present makes clear, Latinidad is perhaps most productively addressed not only as a fixed ethnic identity but also as an unstable, sometimes volatile, and often incomplete transnational process.

NOTES

1 See Laura Lomas, *Translating Empire: José Martí, Migrant Latino Subjects, and American Modernities* (Durham, N.C.: Duke University Press, 2009).

2 On the complexities of meaning evoked by the terms *Latin American* and *Latino*, see, for example, Walter Mignolo, *The Idea of Latin America* (Malden, Mass.: Blackwell, 2005); Claudia Milian, *Latining America: Black-Brown Passages and the Coloring of Latino/a Studies* (Athens: University of Georgia Press, 2013); Juan Poblete, "Latin/o Americanism/o" in *Dictionary of Latin American Cultural Studies* (Gainesville: University Press of Florida, 2012), 197–204; as well as the essays collected in Juan Poblete, ed., *Critical Latin American and Latino Studies* (Minneapolis: University of Minnesota Press, 2003).

3 Paul Allatson, *Key Terms in Latino/a Cultural and Literary Studies* (Malden, Mass.: Blackwell, 2007), 140.

4 "Zetas Massacre 72 Illegal Immigrants in San Fernando, Tamaulipas," *Borderland Beat*, August 26, 2010. http://www.borderlandbeat.com/2010/08/zetas-massacre-72-illegal-immigrants-in.html.

5 Bryan Caplan, "Deportation Statistics." *Library of Economics and Liberty*, August 21, 2011. http://econlog.econlib.org/archives/2011/08/deportations_st.html.

6 Dan Moffett, "Deportation of Illegal Immigrants Breaks Another Record in 2012," *About.com*, December 24, 2012. http://immigration.about.com/b/2012/12/24/deportations-of-illegal-immigrants-break-another-record-in-2012.htm.

7 John Morton, "Statement of John Morton, Director, US Immigration and Customs Enforcement, Before the House Committee on the Judiciary, Subcommittee on Immigration Policy and Enforcement: 'Oversight Hearing on US Immigration and Customs Enforcement: Priorities and the Rule of Law.'" *Homeland Security*, October 12, 2011. http://www.dhs.gov/ynews/testimony/20111012-morton-ice-oversight.shtm.

8 Genevieve Quinn, "Broken Borders, Broken Laws: Aligning Crime and Punishment Under Section 2L1.1(b)(7) of the US Sentencing Guidelines." *Fordham Law Review* 80.2 (2011), 925.

9 Vicente Pérez Rosales, *Times Gone By: Memoirs of a Man of Action*. Trans. John H. R. Polt (Oxford: Oxford University Press, 2003), 296; hereafter cited parenthetically.

10 Jay Monaghan, *Chile, Peru, and the California Gold Rush of 1849* (Berkeley: University of California Press, 1973), 44.

11 Ibid., 174–75.

12 Leonard Pitt, "The Beginnings of Nativism in California." *Pacific Historical Review* 30.1 (1961), 23.

13 Ibid., 25.

14 Marissa López, *Chicano Nations: The Hemispheric Origins of Mexican American Literature* (New York: New York University Press, 2011), 49–59.

15 Vicente Pérez Rosales, *Diario de un viaje a California 1848–1849* (Santiago, Chile: Tajamar Editores, 2007), 10.

16 Edwin A. Beilharz and Carlos U. López, eds. *We Were 49ers! Chilean Accounts of the California Gold Rush* (Pasadena, Calif.: Ward Ritchie Press, 1976), front cover.

17 Kirsten Silva Gruesz, "The Once and Future Latino: Notes Toward a Literary History *Todavía Para Llegar*" in Lyn Di Iorio Sandín and Richard Pérez, eds., *Contemporary US Latino/a Literary Criticism* (New York: Palgrave Macmillan, 2007), 129.

18 Juan Poblete, Introduction to *Critical Latin American and Latino Studies*, xxiii; Frances Aparicio, "Latino Cultural Studies" in Poblete, ed. *Critical Latin American and Latino Studies*, 19.

19 Juan Poblete, "US Latino Studies in a Global Context: Social Imagination and the Production of In/Visibility." *Work and Days* 24.1–2 (2006), 243.

6

Toward a Reading of Nineteenth-Century Latino/a Short Fiction

JOHN ALBA CUTLER

Already the title of this chapter names a fugitive archive. As just one example, consider the weekly Spanish-language newspaper *El Hispano-Americano*, which was founded by Victor Ochoa in 1891 in Santa Fe, New Mexico, and, according to available bibliographic information, stayed in print for almost thirty years, ceasing publication in 1920. Of this thirty-year run, only a handful of issues from 1891 and 1892 have been preserved, available on microfilm at just nine universities in the country and in digital format to university libraries subscribing to Readex's Hispanic American Newspapers archive. *El Hispano-Americano* published original and reprinted short fiction in each of its issues, usually dedicating the third of its four broadsheet pages to the genre. It is impossible to tell if this practice continued for the newspaper's entire print run, but even if it happened for only the first two years, that would mean the newspaper published more than one hundred short stories, many of them by local writers. And *El Hispano-Americano* is only one of numerous Spanish-language periodicals that printed short fiction in the nineteenth century.

To refer to this fragmentary archive as short fiction might even be *mis*naming it. Nineteenth-century Spanish-language newspapers published a variety of short narrative forms—including *costumbrista* sketches and *crónicas*—for which "short fiction" is an insufficient gloss. This formal diversity suggests the importance of generic analysis. Fredric Jameson describes genres as "literary *institutions*, or social contracts between a writer and a specific public, whose function is to specify the proper use of a particular cultural artifact."[1] The short prose narratives that proliferated in nineteenth-century Spanish-language print culture illuminate how Latino/a reading publics were constituted at the crossroads of U.S. and hemispheric American literary history. To explore this idea, I provide analyses of two texts emerging from distinct regional print cultures. The first is a series of sketches by Carlos F. Galán called "Recuerdos de California" (Memories of California), printed in *La Voz del Nuevo Mundo* in San Francisco in 1881; it presents a startling portrait of a language-based, politically resistant Latino/a community in California in the wake of the U.S.–Mexico War. The second is a short story by Venezuelan expatriate Nicanor Bolet Peraza titled "Historia de un guante" (The Tale of a Glove), which appeared in Bolet Peraza's literary magazine *Las Tres Américas* in New York in 1895 and which advances a stunning critique of industrial modernity.[2]

To the extent they represent broader trends in nineteenth-century Latino/a short fiction, these texts are significant for both their social content and their literary form. "Recuerdos de California" and "Historia de un guante" wrestle with the question of what it means to be modern, particularly under conditions of discrimination, marginalization, and dislocation. Significantly, both texts configure their sense of modernity in relation not only to the local conditions of U.S. Latino/a communities but also to print cultures plugged in to hemispheric and even world literary currents. Galán's and Bolet Peraza's works attempt to show that Latinos are not belated newcomers to modernity but rather full participants in what Pascale Casanova describes as unified literary time, "a common measure of absolute time that supersedes other temporalities, whether of nations, families, or personal experience."[3] The stories' publication dates bracket the dawn of *modernismo*, the Latin American literary movement predicated on aesthetic innovation and a critique of U.S. imperialism and materialism.[4] But the principal genres of *modernismo* were poetry and *crónicas*, not short fiction. Galán's and Bolet Peraza's texts illustrate how short fiction served as a crucial "'small' place of experimentation" for U.S. Latino/a writers during this period.[5] In both cases, the literariness of the texts is paramount, because it is the *modernista* literary aesthetic that reveals the stories' "*deseo del mundo*," to use Mariano Siskind's term, their desire to approach a horizon of world literature that might overshadow their marginal, parochial origins.[6] At stake in nineteenth-century Latino/a short fiction is thus a form of social power routed through the symbolic capital of literature.

Costumbrista Sketches and the Coloniality of Power

Accounts of the short story in U.S. literary history tend to follow a straightforward, linear evolutionary model: romantic (Irving) to gothic (Poe, Hawthorne, Melville) to regionalist (Twain, Jewett) to realist (James, Chopin) to naturalist (Dreiser, Crane) to the modern, literary short story (Fitzgerald, Hemingway). The very definition of the short story emerges from this generic history, in Edgar Allan Poe's description of a unified, autonomous narrative that might be read in one sitting.[7] It would be a mistake for two reasons to attempt to shoehorn the narrative forms of Spanish-language print culture into this generic account—first, because those forms were heterogeneous and evolved along different tracks in different locations; and second, because this kind of generic history presumes a teleology with the "literary" short story as its end point, but short prose forms in Latin American and U.S. Latino/a literature continue to be experimental and diverse throughout the twentieth century. A reading of nineteenth-century Latino/a short fiction must grapple with this heterogeneity as its central fact.

Carlos F. Galán's narrative sketches "Recuerdos de California" are a case in point. Galán (1831–?) was born in Spain and moved to Mexico in 1845 to attend the military academy at Chapultepec in Mexico City, going on to fight with the Mexican Army during the U.S.–Mexico War (1846–48).[8] He spent time working in the gold fields of California during the early 1850s but found working and living conditions for Mexicans shocking and unbearable. Well educated, Galán edited several newspapers in the Mexican states of Baja California and Sinaloa before serving briefly as interim governor of Baja California directly after the restoration of the Republic in 1867. He moved back to California in the 1870s and in 1881 became editor of *La Voz del Nuevo Mundo*, one of the most influential and longest-running Spanish-language newspapers in the region.[9] Galán transformed the newspaper during his short tenure as editor from a four-page broadsheet to an eight-page magazine format with larger fonts and fewer advertisements. The paper continued to report on news from throughout the hemisphere, but under Galán it focused increasingly on events in Mexico and the embattled position of the Mexican community in the United States. As with many Spanish-language periodicals in the nineteenth century, *La Voz del Nuevo Mundo* complicates Nicolás Kanellos's distinctions among the immigrant, exile, and native presses, largely because its readership comprised elements of each of these communities.[10] In editorials, for example, Galán often addressed immigrant miners from Chile and Mexico, uniting their concerns over discrimination with a consciousness of the continued dispossession of the native *californio* population.

Under Galán's editorship, *La Voz del Nuevo Mundo* emphasized Latino/a modernity and cosmopolitanism. The paper supported free trade and the protection of workers' rights, particularly those of immigrant laborers in California; and in editorials, Galán characterized these ideas as constituting the very essence of modernity. In his editorial of August 13, 1881, for example, Galán criticized nativist currents in the United States calling for an end to naturalization for various undesirable nationalities, but he did so in terms that emphasized how immigration was inextricable from the most ambitious projects of transnational modernization, stating,

Las vias férreas en Méjico y Guatemala y la apertura de canales en Nicaragua y Panamá—todos debidos á capitales estrangeros—van necesariamente á atraer á esos países grande inmigracion, de la misma clase que los Estados Unidos ya repugnan. Si esta gran nacion, grande en todo—en terrenos, en vias de comunicacion y en toda clase de productos naturales, industriales y civiles, y en poblacion—teme y quiere abolir la constante inmigracion que ha contribuido á hacerla lo que és, ¿se hallan las pequeñas repúblicas de América en mejores condiciones para resistirla?[11]

The railroads in Mexico and Guatemala, and the opening of canals in Nicaragua and Panama—all indebted to foreign capital—will necessarily attract a great deal of immigration to those countries of the same type that the United States is now rejecting. If this great nation, great in everything—in land, in communication technologies, and in all kinds of natural, industrial, and civic resources—fears and desires to abolish the constant immigration that has helped make it what it is, will the small republics of America be found in better conditions to resist it?

In retrospect, Galán's optimism about the potential for immigration to Latin American republics to upset the balance of power in the Americas appears to naïvely underestimate U.S. willingness to exert economic and military power abroad, as in the building of the Panama Canal. Yet Galán cannily ties technological modernity—the railroad, the canal, communications technology—to the complex routes of capital and labor throughout the hemisphere. Modernity does not flow from the metropolitan center of the United States southward but rather emerges transnationally, if unevenly, in multiple sites and through multiple modalities.

La Voz del Nuevo Mundo's hemispheric ethos anticipates the Latin Americanism of José Martí, José Enrique Rodó, and other *modernistas* and is apparent in the paper's reprinting of Latin American news obtained through exchanges with newspapers all along the Pacific coast. Each issue of the paper devoted three full pages of text to updates from individual nations. This hemispheric consciousness finds a literary manifestation in the newspaper's dedication to the *costumbrista* sketch, which, as Enrique Pupo-Walker notes, was "the most appealing of all short narrative forms" for nineteenth-century Latin American readers.[12] The *cuadro de costumbres* is a difficult genre to define, a mishmash of ethnographic description, reportage, and first-person narrative. Spanish scholar Evaristo Correa Calderón's classic definition describes the *costumbrista* sketch as "literatura de breve extensión, que prescinde del desarrollo de la acción, o ésta es muy rudimentaria, limitándose a pintar un pequeño cuadro colorista, en que refleja con donaire y soltura el modo de vida de una época, una costumbre popular o un tipo genérico representativo" (literature of brief length, which dispenses with plot development, or in which the plot is rudimentary, dedicating itself to painting a small, colorful sketch, reflecting with wit and ease the way of life of an epoch, a popular custom, or a representative generic type).[13] The *costumbrista* sketch's historical consciousness is crucial to this definition. Salvador Bueno argues that "[t]odos los intentos destinados a definir la literatura de costumbres están abocados al fracaso si no tienen en cuenta como observara Menéndez y Pelayo, su *modernidad*" (all attempts to define *costumbrista* literature are destined to fail if they do not take into account, as Menéndez and Pelayo might observe, its *modernity*).[14] That modernity often stems from the temporal distance between the narrative voice of the *costumbrista* sketch and the epoch or customs it describes, which allows readers to identify with the narrator's contemporaneity.

Galán showed a predilection for *costumbrismo* as both an editor and a writer. He regularly reprinted *costumbrista* sketches, including works by Ramón Mesonero Romanos and Ricardo Palma, perhaps the premier Spanish and Latin American *costumbrista* writers, respectively. Galán experimented with this *costumbrista* historical consciousness himself in "Recuerdos de California," three sketches which together represent some of the most explicitly political imaginative literature of the Latino/a nineteenth century. The sketches appeared in *La Voz del Nuevo Mundo* on May 21, May 28, and June 11, 1881, and all are narrated from the perspective of a former resident of the Sonora mining camp, presumably Galán. In the May 21 Recuerdos, the narrator recalls nostalgically, "El invierno de 1849 a dejado hondos recuerdos en los que lo pasaron al pié de las heladas montañas de la Sierra Nevada" (The winter of 1849 to 1850 has left a deep impression on those that passed it at the feet of the snowy mountains of the Sierra Nevada).[15] In the May 28 Recuerdos, the narrator characterizes himself as "uno de tantos gambucinos en busca de la volátil diosa Fortuna" (one of so many miners in search of that fickle goddess, Fortune).[16] These details situate Galán in a specific community and historical moment; this is not the privileged world of the *californios* by now well known from the works of Mariano Vallejo and Maria Amparo Ruiz de Burton but rather a multinational working class community that feels the sting of U.S. dominance differently from the loss of land and status.

The communities Galán describes in his sketches anticipate modern Latino/a communities, unrestricted by particular nationalities. "El campo de Sonora," the narrator notes in the opening paragraph of the May 21 Recuerdos, "era uno de los más concurridos por los mejicanos, especialmente y como su nombre lo indica por los Sonorenses" (The Sonora camp was one of the camps most crowded with Mexicans, especially, as its name suggests, by Sonorans).[17] Martínez, the hapless protagonist of the story, is one of these. Martínez falls in love with the daughter of a Chilean miner who disapproves of their relationship. They elope, and when she becomes pregnant, Martínez returns to attempt a reconciliation with her father. When the Chilean sees Martínez ride into town, however, he goes into a frenzy, shouting that Martínez is a thief. A crowd gathers and mistakes the Chilean's meaning, thinking Martínez has stolen the horse on which he rode in. In a shocking conclusion to what has been a mostly comic story, Martínez is summarily lynched, and his wife has a nervous breakdown and dies in an insane asylum, while the Chilean is never heard from again. Bracketing the violence for a moment, it is significant that the Sonorans and Chileans move within the same social world in the story, alongside Spanish-speakers of other nationalities. Language is a powerful unifying factor for this community, so much so that its boundaries are broader even than what would usually count as Latino/a today: "Las introducciones no eran de estilo entonces y bastaba hablar español para llamar a cualquiera paisano, viniese de Magallanes ó de Filipinas, y entablar conversación con él" (Formal introductions were not the style of the day, and it was enough to speak Spanish to hail whatever compatriot, whether he be from Magallenes or the Philippines, and strike up a conversation with him).[18] This sense of a linguistic community powerful enough to bind together individuals from countries thousands of miles apart anticipates the Latin Americanism of *modernismo*, though here it is configured within a specifically Pacific paradigm.

This sense of community animates the narrator's reflections on "*la ley de Lynch*," or lynch law. In the middle of the story, the narrator pauses to observe, "En aquellos meses, los robos de caballos eran muy comunes; los americanos, a veces con razón y a menudo sin ella, culpaban de ellos á los de la raza española" (In those months, horse thefts were very common; the Americans, sometimes with reason but often without it, blamed the thefts on those of the Spanish race).[19] The resonance of "*la raza española*" is particularized by the story's sense of linguistic community. "*La raza española*," in other words, is not those of Spanish racial descent but rather those bound together by the Spanish language.[20] This reading is bolstered by a similar commentary in the June 11 Recuerdos, when the narrator claims that "el oro de California, que los mejicanos encontraban con la mayor facilidad, les suscitaba envidia y mala voluntad de los menos afortunados, que eran especialmente los irlandeses, y el término de *greaser*, aplicado indistintamente a todos los de raza española, era para estos un sangriento insulto" (The gold of California, which the Mexicans were most adept at finding, provoked envy and bad will against them from the less fortunate, especially the Irish, and the term *greaser*, used indiscriminately against all those of the Spanish race, became for them a cruel insult).[21]

The third Recuerdos narrative is particularly interesting as a fiction-alization of the infamous lynching of Josefa Segovia in Downieville, California, in July 1851. In the story, Segovia becomes Josefa Juvera, an immigrant from Atotonilco el Alto in Jalisco, Mexico. She is described as a young woman known for her "hermosura, patriotismo, y finos mo-dales" (beauty, patriotism, and fine manners), in contrast with histori-cal accounts characterizing Segovia as a lower-class prostitute.[22] In the narrative, Josefa marries a young man from Sinaloa, and the two make a home together. A year later, pregnant and happy, Josefa falls prey to a mob of drunk, raging Irishmen who resent the Mexicans for their good fortune in mining. The night of the Fourth of July, the mob breaks down Josefa's door, and while some of the men hold her husband fast, one of them attempts to rape Josefa in her bed. Her husband pleads with her to defend herself, which she does by plunging a knife into the throat of her assailant. Enraged by the violent act, the mob convenes a kangaroo court, which quickly convicts Josefa of murder, and despite the protesta-tions of several prominent men called to the scene, she—like Martínez in the former story—is quickly hanged.

Part of the story of modernity that Galán's narratives implicitly tell centers on the transnational movement of people and capital. In the June 11 Recuerdos, that movement involves European alongside Latin Ameri-can immigrant labor, as Irish immigrants are the narrative's primary an-tagonists. The narrator states that the Irish in California "comprendían muy poco las obligaciones y deberes que su nueva condición [de ciu-dadanía] les imponía. Más papistas que el Papa, tomaban del americano todos sus ódios, muchas de sus preocupaciones y muy pocas de sus vir-tudes" (little comprehended the obligations and duties imposed upon them by their new status [as citizens]. More Catholic than the Pope, they took from the American all of his prejudices, many of his worries, and very few of his virtues).[23] Galán's sensitivity to the tenuous whiteness of the Irish here is as impressive as his nuanced portrait of the diver-sity of the Latino/a community in the other narratives. They allow the narrative to displace anxieties about assimilation onto another group, which becomes the tool of Anglo American bigotry. Note too that for the Irish, citizenship is a "new condition," a description that character-izes their savagery in the story as barely repressed primitivism. The nar-rative thus establishes Latino/a modernity not only through its historical consciousness but also by implicitly comparing Latinos to a group that has not yet become fully modern.

The story dramatizes the visceral horror of the lynching, emphasizing the violence of the "coloniality of power," to use Aníbal Quijano's term, that predominated in 1850s California.[24] Galán's narrative makes some significant changes from the historical documentation of the Josefa Segovia case, most of which comes from an account given by J. J. McClosky, a Downieville resident.[25] In Galán's sketch Josefa's "victim," a man described as "un *galgo* más audaz o más ébrio que los demás" (one *greyhound* or dog, more bold or drunk than the others) attempts to sexually assault her, while historical records indicate that during an argument, Segovia challenged Fred Cannon to come into her house, where she stabbed him.[26] In Galán's sketch, as in McClosky's account, a doctor attempts to save Josefa's life by pointing out that she is pregnant and that hanging her would therefore mean killing the innocent child, but Galán's story concludes with further detail: "Pero aún no estaba saciada la sed insana de los bárbaros. Notó uno de ellos, que el feto se movía en las entrañas de la madre sacrificada, y a patadas le quitaron la vida, que sin ellas hubiera perdido muy pronto" (But even then the bloodlust of the barbarians was not satiated. One of them noted that the fetus still moved within the dead mother's womb, and they kicked it until it was dead, which would have happened soon anyway).[27] The murder of the fetus not only compounds the viciousness of the crime, but the irony built into the final sentence suggests the crime's senselessness within a regime of obvious racial oppression.

The most pointed change in Galán's sketch from the historical accounts of the Segovia lynching is the location of the hanging itself. Historians describe the hanging as happening from a bridge, with men lining the river on both sides to watch. But in Galán's sketch both the kangaroo court and the lynching take place on a special platform set up for the Independence Day celebrations:

> La plataforma en que horas antés se habían proclamado los sacros e inalienables derechos del hombre, el juicio por jurados, dos instancias para los juicios criminales, etc. etc., fue el lugar escogido para patíbulo. Allí en un momento, colgaron una cuerda de la rama de un árbol y se arreglaron

de modo, que sujeto el dogal al cuello de la víctima empujasen a ésta de la plataforma y la caída bastara a desnucarla.[28]

The platform from which hours earlier the sacred and inalienable rights of man had been proclaimed—trial by jury, two appeals for criminal judgments, etc. etc.—was the place chosen for the gallows. There, after a moment, a rope hung from a tree limb, arranged in such a way that when the victim's neck was put in the noose and her body pushed from the platform, the fall would suffice to snap her neck.

Josefa's death dramatically symbolizes the failure of the promises of equal protection and inalienable rights. This is evident not only in the location of the death but also in its process. The fall from the seat of justice is meant to break her physically and to remind Latino/a readers of *La Voz del Nuevo Mundo* of their own repeated falls from American grace. The June 11 Recuerdos exhibits the generic syncretism that characterizes the *costumbrista* sketch, but it also shows an evolution from Galán's earlier sketches. The sketch combines reportage and fiction, but where the first two installments in the series have the loose narrative structure typical of many *costumbrista* sketches, the June 11 Recuerdos is a more unified narrative, driving forward from Josefa's initial engagement to her untimely death. The narrator is also a much more muted presence in the final sketch. Although he breaks forth in an impassioned critique of lynching in the story's final sentence—"Tal es la justicia de los hombres!" (Such is the justice of men!)—he does not figure as a character in the action of the story as he does in the first two sketches.

This generic experimentation emerges as a response to the local conditions of the California Latino/a community. Bueno argues persuasively that in the Spanish colonial context of Cuba, "En la imposibilidad de enfrentar directamente el gobierno colonialista, ya que la censura imponía férrea mordaza imposible de quebrantar, los costumbristas encontraban en su práctica literaria un vehículo adecuado para la diatriba, la denuncia solapada" (In the impossibility of confronting the colonial government directly, since the censure imposed an unbreakable iron grip, the *costumbristas* found in their literary practice an adequate vehicle for diatribe, for disguised critique).[29] Writing in Spanish in the United States,

Galán would not have had the same fear of censorship, partly because of a stronger tradition of freedom of the press but, more important, because he could assume that his audience would be restricted to sympathetic Spanish-speakers. The *costumbrista* sketch is useful for Galán not because it is a mode of discreet political critique but because it is a mode of historical representation that reaffirms the modernity of narrator and readers alike. The sketches resonate powerfully into the present through their portrait of Latino/a modernity as forged in the crucible of U.S. expansion and the violent exclusion of Latinos from the U.S. body politic.

Modernismo and Latino/a *Deseo del mundo*

The 1880s saw a boom in U.S. Spanish-language periodicals. Beyond California, regional Spanish-language print cultures thrived in New Mexico and New York. In the latter, expatriate Latin American writers found a ready community of fellow-travelers and a publishing infrastructure stretching back to the 1830s. As the increase in short fiction publications coincided with the increasing dynamism of hemispheric print culture, one way of reading the turn toward short fiction is that it marks a new relationship between Latino/a writers in the United States and the technologies and textures of modernity and *modernismo*. As the nineteenth century drew to a close, the pace of modernity seemed to accelerate, marked by massive changes in infrastructure in the West and Southwest (the railroad, wage-labor, new printing technologies) and by new literary forms, such as the Symbolist-inflected poetry of Rubén Darío that burst onto the scene in 1888 with the publication of *Azul*. The majority of the short fiction sponsored by U.S. Spanish-language periodicals comprised either translations of works by European writers or reprints of works by established Spanish and Latin American writers. A catalogue of these writers would be extensive, ranging from European (especially French) writers such as Victor Hugo, Anatole France, Émile Zola, and Carmen Sylva (Regina Elisabet of Romania) to Latin American writers like Manuel Gutiérrez Nájera and Roberto Payró. The Spanish-language press in the United States participated vigorously in what Meredith McGill has described as the "culture of reprinting" in the nineteenth-century United States.

McGill regards the culture of reprinting as a kind of *laissez-faire* arrangement that worked to the benefit of savvy writers. For example, writing against the grain of conventional scholarship, she asserts that Poe "is both subject to and seeks to benefit from the peculiar structure of this market."[30] Siskind provides another way to think about the culture of reprinting within *modernismo*, however, arguing that it represents an important facet of Latin American cosmopolitanism, an "attempt to undo the antagonistic structures of a world literary field organized around the notions of cultural difference that Latin American cosmopolitan writers perceive to be the source of their marginality, in order to stake a claim on Literature with a capital L."[31] For Siskind, *modernismo* is characterized by two contradictory impulses: the desire to assert a unified Latin Americanism and the desire to achieve the kind of literary autonomy and universality that Casanova identifies as the currency of world literature. Spanish-language periodicals demonstrate both of these tendencies, but with the added complication that U.S. Latino/a writers operated not only in the context of the dialectical relationship between Latin America and the world literary powers of Europe but also with the increasing technological, cultural, and military domination of the United States.

The Venezuelan expatriate writer Nicanor Bolet Peraza provides a good example of what Siskind describes as Latin American *deseo del mundo*, or "desire for the world," where the "world" is both "a signifier of abstract universality [and] a concrete and finite set of global trajectories traveled by writers and books."[32] Bolet Peraza is best known for his work as editor and publisher of two important Spanish-language periodicals in New York during the 1890s—*La Revista Ilustrada* and *Las Tres Américas*—that participated in the culture of reprinting. Through these periodicals, Bolet Peraza proved instrumental in supporting the burgeoning hemispheric literary culture of *modernismo*, publishing works by such luminaries as José Martí and Juan Antonio Pérez Bonalde. He also made a name for himself as a writer, and scholars have generally characterized his work as bridging the gaps between realism, *costumbrismo*, and *modernismo*. Domingo Miliani credits Bolet Peraza for helping the Latin American short story assume its modern form, noting, "En Bolet Peraza el cuento se presenta con precisa independencia de otras modalidades narrativas en prosa. Condensación de las acciones, efectividad del conflicto, poder de síntesis en las secuencias, ésos son los rasgos significativos resaltantes" (In Bolet Peraza the short story is manifest clearly independent of other prose narrative modes. Condensation of action, unity of conflict, synthetic power in sequence: these are the significant features foregrounded).[33] Carlos Sandoval traces Bolet Peraza's evolution from *costumbrista* to short story writer specifically to his New York years and the stories he published himself in *Las Tres Américas*, including "*Las tres vidas de Antón*," "*El monte azul*," "*El espejo encantado*," and "*Historia de un guante*."[34] These critical appraisals are helpful for understanding a neglected writer, but they both work by reaffirming the familiar teleological narrative about the modern short story's evolution.

"*Historia de un guante*" exemplifies not so much the purity of the modern, literary short story as it does the two senses of *deseo del mundo* that animated *modernismo*. First, *deseo del mundo* manifests in the story's self-conscious literariness. The plot is simple. The narrator recalls attending a dance as a young man and picking up a glove dropped by a beautiful young woman. The glove has a sweet, overpowering redolence, and the young man falls instantly in love with the woman after pressing it to his nose. At this point, the glove takes on a life of its own and begins a dialogue with the narrator, recounting its life history since being violently cut away from its mother, a goat, until the dance, where the glove could sense by the heat of its mistress's palm that she had fallen in love with one of her dance partners. The glove actually taunts the narrator for mistaking the smell of its mistress's lover for the smell of the mistress herself, and for thinking that he might have a chance to woo her. The story concludes by returning to the retrospective frame; the narrator observes that he since that day long ago uses the glove only to polish his eyeglasses, a punishment for the glove's cruelty.

The story's *modernista* sensibility manifests in highly stylized descriptions and ambivalence about female sexuality. This is clear from the first paragraph of the story, which thrusts readers *en medias res* into a description of the dance:

Habia llegado ya la hora del cansancio, del fastidio y del sueño. Las bujías habian sido cambiadas tres veces, el *buffet* estaba agotado; los músicos exhaustos, los trajes femeninos en desorden, los peinados desmayados, los lindos rizos que la bandolina sostuvo hasta donde fue químicamente posible, caían sobre los ojos medio dormidos haciendo en ellos el estorboso efecto de las moscas; la concurrencia comenzaba a desfilar por delante de los dueños de la casa, ensayando cada cual una sonrisa de despedida, una mueca de trasnochado.[35]

The hour of fatigue, ennui, and sleepiness had already arrived. The candles had been changed three times, the "buffet" was empty, the musicians exhausted, the women's dresses in disorder, their coiffures failed. The delicate curls that the bandolín had sustained as long as chemically possible fell over half-closed eyes, making them as annoying as flies. The crowd began to shuffle out before their hosts, everyone making a half-hearted smile of farewell, a sign of their exhaustion.

The opening description establishes a sense of exhaustion in the narrator, who looks back on his youth from old age with nostalgia but also embarrassment. That exhaustion pivots on the spent female bodies, the disordered dresses, and limp hairstyles as signs of a revelry both energetic and strangely passionless. The women's *"lindos rizos,"* or beautiful curls, are sustained by the bandolín *"hasta donde fue químicamente possible,"* emphasizing the decaying artifice of their appearance, which demands chemical intervention.

When the narrator learns that the glove can talk, he demands that it recount its history, which it does in the following terms: "Un curtidor, después de mil atomías me zabulló en tanino, una cosa muy amarga; me dió a comer alumbre, una cosa que frunce y da carraspera; me ahogó en tinta gris perla, me prensó y aplanchó, y me entregó a un cortador que me despedazó, y de allí me tomó una costurera que me acribilló a puntadas" (A tanner, after a thousand indecencies, washed me clean. He gave me alum to eat, which made me retch and grow hoarse. He drowned me in pearl gray dye and ironed me, and then delivered me to a leatherworker who cut me in pieces, and from there took me to a seamstress who pierced me everywhere with stitches).[36] As if the glove's voice were not enough personification, this description characterizes its creation as a violent, bodily process. It is drowned, dismembered, poisoned, and perforated as if caught up in some perverse *auto-da-fé*. As Sandoval points out, the glove's tortuous creation is also a damning critique of the inhuman working conditions of industrial capital, because not only is she subjected to the various poisons and dangers of the manufacturing process, but so are the *curtidor*, the *cortador*, and the *costurera*.[37] The beauty of the resulting glove resembles nothing so much as the chemically altered curls of the dancers at the beginning of the story, another body standing in for the dehumanizing artifices of modernity.

A comment the narrator makes to the glove stakes this critique of modernity to theories of democratic citizenship. At first the glove demurs when the narrator asks it to recount its history, saying, "Mi madre fue una cabrita infeliz," to which the narrator responds, "No te aflijas por lo humilde de la cuna. Vivimos en épocas democráticas en que el mérito es quien da la estirpe" (My mother was an unfortunate goat. . . . Do not be distressed by your humble origins. We live in democratic times in which merit determines the stock).[38] The narrator's comment plays on the absurdity of the talking glove. What possible virtues could the glove hope to demonstrate to overcome the fact of its origins, its nonagency? And at this point, the story's difference from other *modernista* texts is crucial, for as Rachel Price persuasively argues, "[M]odernismo was object-oriented typically in its interest in precious luxury items or through its attempt to approximate advertising's *strategies*, while disavowing everyday material culture through flights to a world of princesses and swans."[39] Running counter to this disavowal, "*Historia de un guante*" degrades a luxury item by revealing its emergence from the industrial processes of material culture. The narrator's flippant aphorism depends on the glove's status *as object*, catalyzing the narrator's disillusionment. Not only do the glove's bodily sacrifices count for nothing in the end, but after learning that his object of desire loves someone else, the narrator does not even attempt to pursue her. No matter his origins or his merits, his chances at fulfillment are foreclosed before he even makes an attempt to win her. The narrator's comment calls attention to the spirit of the age as he emphasizes the "*épocas* democráticas" in which they live, times implicitly contrasted to bygone, nondemocratic epochs. The story doubles up and ironizes this temporal distancing in its subtitle, "Recuerdos de Mocedad," which suggests that the narrator has arrived at a more mature, fuller modernity than even what he remembers from his youth or adolescence.

As significant as the story's relation to *modernista* aesthetics is its surprising publication trajectory. Sandoval credits *Las Tres Américas* with the first publication of the story, followed closely by its appearance in the Venezuelan literary magazine *El Cojo Ilustrado* in July 1895.[40] This account puts the story squarely within circuits of Latin American literary circulation. Yet *"Historia de un guante"* was published at least twice in the United States before it appeared in *Las Tres Américas*: once in *El Hispano-Americano* in Las Vegas, New Mexico (April 21, 1892), and once in *Las Dos Repúblicas* in Los Angeles, California (serialized on November 19 and 22, 1892). Given the dates of publication, it is probable that Antonio Flores, the editor of *Las Dos Repúblicas*, acquired the story from *El Hispano-Americano*, though no attribution is given to the other paper. It is also unlikely that Victor Ochoa, the editor of *El Hispano-Americano*, was the first to publish the story. Like other *Nuevomexicano* newspapermen, Ochoa reprinted news and literature from regional and Mexican periodicals. Ochoa likely reprinted *"Historia de un guante"* from a Mexican periodical, though up to this point I have not been able to find the source.

The occluded history of *"Historia de un guante"*—a minor story not usually even collected in anthologies of Bolet Peraza's work—and its routing through Mexico and the Southwest and reappearance in New York suggest that the itineraries of *modernista* literary exchange were not always predictable. In relation to Latino/a literary history, *fin-de-siglo* New York is something of an overdetermined space, a site of cultural and political ferment felt the hemisphere over. By contrast, although much work has been done on the dynamism of New Mexican print culture in the same time period, that work tends to emphasize the localism of *Nuevomexicano* writers and editors and their strong regional identity.[41] Neither of these narratives is wrong, but the migrations of *"Historia de un guante"* imply that they are incomplete—that New Mexico energetically tapped into hemispheric literary culture via Mexico City, another important hub for the triangulation of U.S., Caribbean, and Latin American cultural production. McGill's characterization of the culture of reprinting as "a distinctive literary culture that cannot adequately be perceived through the optics of national literary study" applies as well to nineteenth-century U.S. Latino/a literature as to U.S. literature more broadly.[42]

Given Bolet Peraza's participation in the New York Latino/a community, it is tempting to see *"Historia de un guante"* as exhibiting *modernismo*'s impulse to, as Gruesz puts it, "[define] Latin Americanness through its spiritual opposition to the economically dictated values of the United States."[43] By this reading, the story's harsh representation of industrialism and its satire of the idea of meritocracy could be seen as directed against U.S. materialism and inequality. Such a reading would certainly have resonated with readers of Victor Ochoa's newspaper *El Hispano-Americano*, which was openly critical of both the continued federal disenfranchisement of *Nuevomexicanos* and the modernization projects of the Porfirio Díaz regime in Mexico. Like many *Nuevomexicano* journalists, Ochoa was a Mexican exile and supported the Catarino Garza borderlands revolt in the 1890s, activism that led to Ochoa's imprisonment for violating U.S. neutrality laws.[44] Yet any significance we might read into Ochoa's reprinting of *"Historia de un guante"* runs into problems when balanced against its subsequent reprinting in *Las Dos Repúblicas*. Founded in March 1892 by Antonio Cuya and Antonio J. Flores, the Los Angeles paper was avowedly pro-capitalist and pro-Díaz, often criticizing other newspapers, such as Los Angeles's *El Monitor*, for opposing Díaz's free trade, modernizing agenda. Where *El Hispano-Americano* is text-heavy with news, editorials, stories, and poetry, *Las Dos Repúblicas* is almost entirely dominated by advertising, including prominent advertisements for Spanish lessons for interested businessmen. The paper printed a fair amount of literature, serializing novels and printing short stories and poetry, but the pittance of news and commentary that the paper offered, along with the preponderance of advertising, lends the literature an air of mere entertainment, as opposed to the belletristic mission of Bolet Peraza's *Las Tres Américas* or the politicized context of *El Hispano-Americano*. Literature is a disposable object in *Las Dos Repúblicas*, as evidenced by the poor editing job done on the two installments of *"Historia de un guante,"* which appear in the paper rife with spelling and orthographical mistakes, even misspelling Bolet Peraza's name as "N. Boute Peraza."[45]

Nevertheless, it is significant that *all* of these newspapers found space for *"Historia de un guante"* in their pages. What unites them is the conviction that short fiction such as Bolet Peraza's has tapped into the realm of universal literariness, the true sign of Latin America's emergence into modernity. "*Historia de un guante*" especially would play into this desire for literary cultural capital through its obvious Symbolist influences. For example, the narrator's mania at the end of the story, when he announces that he still keeps the glove "para el prosaico oficio de limpiar mis gafas de cincuenton," strongly echoes Poe's many manic narrators.[46] This is not to say that the story's political critique is unimportant but rather that the cultural work it, and many other short stories, does within Latino/a print culture extends beyond its content to its formal and literary historical innovations and influences.

Just as Galán's recourse to *costumbrismo* presents a challenge for literary histories centered on a conventional narrative of regional realism, so do Bolet Peraza's *modernista* fictions challenge traditional literary histories positing the development of "American" short fiction from realism to naturalism to modernism. Spanish-language newspapers circulated *modernista* writing beginning in the 1890s, and writers such as Bolet Peraza experimented with *modernista* ideas and forms. To acknowledge this fact is to insist that Latino/a modernity is not a belated, reactionary development but part and parcel of a world system of modernity in which center and margin have always been inextricably linked. In other words, a complete history of the *American* short story needs to account not only for the evolution of the short story in English but also its coexistence with a variety of other short narrative forms, including in Spanish the *costumbrista* sketch and the *modernista* short story. This more comprehensive history would need to acknowledge that in the United States *modernismo* precedes modernism, and that Latino/a writers were interested in many of the same thematic and formal innovations that now-canonical U.S. writers would take up a generation later.

Attending to nineteenth-century Latino/a short fiction is also important inasmuch as literary scholarship has been disproportionately devoted to the major genres of the novel and the lyric poem. This is not to say that the novel and lyric poem are not important but rather to reiterate that as a fugitive archive, short fiction has the potential to enrich and broaden our understanding of the Latino/a nineteenth century. At the same time, scholarship on *modernismo* has tended to focus on the genres of poetry and the *crónica*, with short fiction relegated to a minor role within that movement. But there is good reason, particularly within the U.S. context, to renew our focus on short fiction. In her examination of the "asymmetrical" relationship between the short story and the novel, Mary Louise Pratt observes that one reason the short story has historically been regarded as a minor genre is "the very concrete fact that a novel constitutes a complete book (or books), while a short story never does. A short story is always printed as part of a larger whole, either a collection of short stories or a magazine, which is a collection of various kinds of texts."[47] Andrew Levy makes a similar point when he argues that Poe's creation of both the modern literary magazine and modern short story shows that the two are "symbiotic projects," because the blossoming of industrial capitalism in the nineteenth century made for an economic system perfectly tailored to the "disposable artifact" of the short story.[48] Studying nineteenth-century Latino/a short fiction thus entails studying U.S. Spanish-language print culture and helpfully reminds us that *modernismo* unfolded through hemispheric print culture as much as through the publication of independent volumes.

Most important, Galán's and Bolet Peraza's stories illuminate a central tension in the unfolding of Latino/a modernity. While such writers as Galán trenchantly depicted the oppression of Latinos in the United States, those stories always participated in a larger literary culture of reprinting in which the vast majority of stories, including those of Bolet Peraza, were not centered on the oppositional relationship between Latinos and the dominant culture, or between Latin America and the United States. The world literary horizons of Latino/a short fiction are a good reminder that even while *modernista* writers first anticipated and then critiqued U.S. imperialism, the United States during this era remained a relatively marginal literary force. Dominant accounts of *modernismo* assert that, in Julio Ramos's words, during this era literature "[became] the fundamental vehicle for an anti-imperialist ideology, defining the Latin American 'being/identity' through its opposition to the modernity of 'them': the United States or England."[49] In recent years, however, Siskind and other scholars have argued that *modernismo* extends beyond this dialectic, aspiring to belong to "a world posited in the vague language of a desire to transcend the limitations not only of the local but also of the neocolonial relations, whether with Spain or new powers like France or Britain."[50] Reading Galán and Bolet Peraza side by side, we see how nineteenth-century Latino/a writers grappled with modernity emerging at precisely this juncture of the particular and the universal—the local conditions of Latino/a dispossession in the United States facing off with the global aspirations of their narratives.

NOTES

1 Fredric Jameson, *The Political Unconscious: Narrative as Socially Symbolic Act* (Ithaca, N.Y.: Cornell University Press), 106.

2 For reprints and translations of these narratives, see John Alba Cutler, "Confronting Frontier and Industrial Violence: Latino Narratives" in *The Heath Anthology of American Literature, Seventh Ed., Volume C, Late Nineteenth Century: 1865–1910* (Boston: Wadsworth, 2014): 999–1014.

3 Pascale Casanova, *The World Republic of Letters* (Cambridge, Mass.: Harvard University Press, 2002), 93.

4 Literary historians generally cite the publication of Rubén Darío's *Azul* in 1888 as the beginning of *modernismo*.

5 Mary Louise Pratt, "The Short Story: The Long and the Short of it," *Poetics* 10 (1981): 190.

6 Mariano Siskind, *Cosmopolitan Desires: Global Modernity and World Literature in Latin America* (Evanston, Ill.: Northwestern University Press, 2014), 3.

7 E. A. Poe, "Twice-Told Tales: A Review," in *Edgar Allan Poe: Essays and Reviews* (New York: Library of America, 1984), 569–77.

8 The most useful source for biographical information about Galán is a deposition he gave in a legal case in San Francisco in 1874, found in *Compilation of Reports of Committee on Foreign Relations, United States Senate, 1789–1901*, Vol. II (Washington: Government Printing Office, 1901): 493–99. Some information can also be found in Leonidas Hamilton, *Border States of Mexico: Sonora, Sinaloa, Chihuahua, and Durango* (San Francisco: Bacon & Co., 1881).

9 The paper began, as Kirsten Silva Gruesz notes, as *El Nuevo Mundo*, a biweekly paper founded by Mexican poet José María Vigil in 1864 (Gruesz, *Ambassadors of Culture: The Transamerican Origins of Latino Writing* [Princeton, N.J.: Princeton University Press, 2002], 177). Sometime soon afterward, however, editorship was taken over by Francisco P. Ramírez, the political radical who edited the influential paper *El Clamor Público* in Los Angeles during the 1850s. *El Nuevo Mundo* merged late in the 1860s with another San Francisco paper called *La Voz de Chile y de las Repúblicas Americanas*, edited by a Chilean immigrant named Felipe Fierro, and briefly went by the name *La Voz de Chile y del Nuevo Mundo* until settling on the name *La Voz del Nuevo Mundo*. Galán became the editor of *La Voz del Nuevo Mundo* early in 1881, after Fierro found himself in debt and poor health. Fierro died in San Francisco soon thereafter. After editing the paper for a year, Galán left California and apparently returned to Mexico.

10 See Nicolás Kanellos, "A Brief History of Hispanic Periodicals in the United States," in Kanellos and Helvetia Martell, *Hispanic Periodicals in the United States,*

Origins to 1960: A Brief History and Comprehensive Bibliography (Houston: Arte Público, 1993), 6.

11 Galán, untitled editorial, *La Voz del Nuevo Mundo*, August 13, 1881: 4. I have retained the original spelling and orthography for all of the nineteenth-century texts quoted in this chapter. Unless otherwise noted, all translations are mine.

12 Enrique Pupo-Walker, "The Brief Narrative in Spanish America: 1835–1915," in *The Cambridge History of Latin American Literature*, ed. Roberto González Echevarría and Pupo-Walker (New York: Cambridge University Press, 1996), 504.

13 Evaristo Correa Calderón, *Costumbristas españoles: Estudio preliminar y selección de textos* (Madrid: Aguilar, 1950), xi.

14 Salvador Bueno, *Literatura Costumbrista Cubana* (Morelia: Ediciones Casa San Nicolás, 2000), 10. Italics added.

15 Galán, "Recuerdos de California," *La Voz del Nuevo Mundo*, May 21, 1881: 7.

16 Ibid.

17 Ibid.

18 Ibid.

19 Ibid.

20 This is similar to what Gruesz describes in relation to the New Orleans newspaper *La Patria*: "When the paper was retooled . . . in January 1846, it had a new subtitle: *Organo de la población española de los Estados Unidos*, and a more solemn editorial voice. This would seem to suggest that the paper was directed at Spaniards, yet a self-advertisement reprinted in every issue that spring implies that the adjective describes language, not nationality. The editors repeatedly stressed that "La población española de Nueva Orleans es indudablemente la más variada de cuántas existen no sólo en esta ciudad sino en toda la Unión" (the Spanish population of New Orleans is undoubtedly one of the most diverse not only in this city but in the whole of the Union) (*Ambassadors of Culture*, 113–14).

21 Galán, "Recuerdos de California," *La Voz del Nuevo Mundo*, June 11, 1881: 7.

22 Ibid.

23 Galán, "Recuerdos," June 11, 1881: 7. "Más papistas que el Papa": literally, "more popish than the Pope," but intending to convey that a person is overly zealous in his or her regard for a custom or law, or in this case, that the Irish have become more zealously American than natural-born citizens.

24 Aníbal Quijano, "Coloniality of Power: Eurocentrism and Latin America," trans. Michael Ennis, *Nepantla: Views from the South* 1.3 (2000): 533. Quijano uses the term to refer to the persistence of modes of racial and economic domination formulated in colonial contexts.

25 For histories that depend on McClosky's account, see William B. Secrest, *Juanita* (Fresno, Calif.: Sage-West, 1967), 25; and Rudolfo Acuña, *Occupied America: A History of Chicanos*, Fifth edition (New York: Pearson Longman, 2004), 137.

26 Galán, "Recuerdos," June 11, 1881: 7.

27 Ibid.

28 Ibid.

29 Bueno, *Literatura Costumbrista Cubana*, 17.

30 Meredith McGill, *American Literature and the Culture of Reprinting* (Philadelphia: University of Pennsylvania Press, 2007), 150.

31 Siskind, *Cosmopolitan Desires*, 6.

32 Ibid., 3.

33 Domingo Miliani, *Tríptico venezolano* (Caracas: Fundación de Promoción Cultural de Venezuela, 1985), 51.

34 Carlos Sandoval, "Ingenios, entes, y negocios," *Revista de Literatura Hispanoamericana* 3 (1998): 66.

35 N. Bolet Peraza, "Historia de un guante," *Las Tres Américas* 30 (1895): 780.

36 Ibid.

37 Sandoval, "Ingenios," 66.

38 Bolet Peraza, "Historia de un guante," 780.

39 Price, *The Object of the Atlantic: Concrete Aesthetics in Cuba, Brazil, and Spain, 1868–1968* (Evanston, Ill.: Northwestern University Press, 2014), 13.

40 See Bolet Peraza, "Historia de un guante," *El Cojo Ilustrado* 85 (1895): 400–1. Many thanks to my colleague Nathalie Bouzaglo for pointing me to this source. In her book *Ficción adulterada: Pasiones ilícitas del entresiglo venezolano* (forthcoming, Beatriz Viterbo), Bouzaglo reads "*Historia de un guante*" brilliantly in relation to *El Cojo Ilustrado*'s tendency toward commodity fetishism.

41 See, for example, Doris Meyer, *Speaking for Themselves: Neomexicano Cultural Identity and the Spanish-Language Press, 1880–1920* (Albuquerque: University of New Mexico Press, 1996) and A. Gabriel Meléndez, *Spanish-Language Newspapers in New Mexico, 1834–1958* (Tucson: University of Arizona Press, 2005).

42 McGill, *Culture of Reprinting*, 1.

43 Gruesz, *Ambassadors*, 192.

44 On the complications of Ochoa's biography, see Meléndez, *Spanish-Language Newspapers*, 87–88.

45 N. Boute Peraza [*sic*], "Historia de un guante," *Las Dos Repúblicas*, November 22, 1892.

46 Bolet Peraza, "Historia de un guante," 780 (". . . for the prosaic office of cleaning my old-man spectacles . . .").

47 Pratt, "Short Story," 186.

48 Levy, *The Culture and Commerce of the American Short Story* (New York: Cambridge University Press, 1993), 21–22.

49 Ramos, *Divergent Modernities: Culture and Politics in Nineteenth-Century Latin America* (Durham, N.C.: Duke University Press, 2001), 46.

50 Siskind, *Cosmopolitan Desires*, 138.

7

When Archives Collide

Recovering Modernity in Early Mexican American Literature

JOSÉ ARANDA

Although an archive is an expression of an idea in its most sophisticated material mode, the experience of an archive is wholly a different matter. Ironically it is the experience of archived material, and not its content per se, that I would argue underwrites the institutional logic for having archives in the first place. Beyond the quantitative and qualitative possibilities of any knowledge set lies the web of human relationships such a knowledge set engenders. This distinction was in dramatic display for me one summer many years ago in the stacks of the Rice University Fondren Library. I was following up on a footnote by the recoverers of the nineteenth-century writer María Amparo Ruiz de Burton, author of *Who Would Have Thought It?* (1872) and *The Squatter and the Don* (1885). Rosaura Sánchez and Beatrice Pita cited Ruiz de Burton's attendance at Abraham Lincoln's presidential inaugural ball and her familiarity with leading politicians of the time as evidence of her political wherewithal.[1] Intrigued by such a claim, I wondered if there was any mention of her in the letters, journals, and diaries of such well-known figures. Beyond the recovery of her two novels and Ruiz de Burton's own claims, was there a way to verify these relationships? So I embarked on what I thought was a wild goose chase. Surely Ruiz de Burton's connections were due to her husband's position as an Anglo American and West Point officer. There was no way that she herself enabled these relationships. After all, it was amazing enough that she, a woman born in Loreto, Baja California, who immigrated to Alta California after the U.S.–Mexico War to marry this New Englander from Vermont, had over time written two novels in English. All the same, I looked. And I looked in the manner that I was trained to look, beginning with the index. Imagine my surprise when I saw Burton, Mrs. Henry Stanton. The index was to Roy P. Basler's *The Collected Works of Abraham Lincoln* (1953), and this is what I found:

To Simon Cameron
Hon. Sec. of War.   Executive Mansion

My dear Sir: June 1, 1861
Mrs. Captain Burton is very desirous that her husband may be made
a Colonel. I do not know him personally; but if it can be done without
injustice to other officers of the Regular Army, I would like for her to be
obliged.

Yours truly
A. Lincoln.

In less than the minute it took for me to read this memorandum from Lincoln, I understood myself within the textual and cultural power of the archive. Again, it was not just the content of the memorandum, which was important, but the glimpse into a web of human connections made by this one author of Mexican descent. I also knew, because I had read all the scholarship at the time, that I was the first to verify Ruiz de Burton's connection to Lincoln. That was a thrill that echoed with the thrill of the content of the memorandum itself. She had gone to Lincoln to make a request on behalf of her husband. On the basis of her request, she, not Henry Stanton Burton, was obliged. In that moment, I knew that this historical figure was unlike anyone the Chicano/a movement or Chicano/a studies had prepared me to understand. Finally, I also knew that Sánchez and Pita had "read" incorrectly her and the archive they had assembled. As I would go on to argue, María Amparo Ruiz de Burton was no "sub-altern." She wrote and negotiated her world with a defined and sophisticated alternative history, but she was clearly a daughter of the Enlightenment and a colonialist. She was not a Chicana.[2] In my mind, the emergent archive of nineteenth-century Mexican America had collided with the counternationalist, Marxist-leaning, activist archive of the Chicana/o movement. It was then that I understood that I and other recoverers were embarking on a long-term revision of Mexican American literary history.

The Recovery Project and its archive has made its way into the broader study of American literature, and nowhere has its impact been more noticeable than in studies of the U.S. nineteenth century. A substantial number of Recovery scholars contributed to Caroline Levander and Robert Levine's 2007 collection, *Hemispheric American Studies*.[3] Since then the complexities over language, citizenship, race, gender, class, and national belonging by this Recovery archive continue to pose major challenges to how to restructure the meaning of nineteenth-century American literature. In this regard, the Recovery Project should be viewed as an extraordinary example, if not the most important, of what Ralph Bauer calls "'inter-American literary studies'—the comparative investigation of 'literatures and cultures of this hemisphere' as one unit of study" that responded to Gustavo Pérez's question, "Do the Americas have a common literature?"[4] Given the institutional and linguistic origins of the Recovery Project, its academic mission and scholarly scope floats between and around the perimeters of American literary studies on the one hand, and Latin American studies on the other, thus borrowing and informing theoretic and methodological practices on all sides, as well as making available authors and primary texts heretofore locked away in archives, or forgotten, or ignored because of hispanophobia.

With this rich dynamic in mind, I make the case for how to problematize and unpack what the Recovery Project has meant for the field of Chicana/o literary studies in particular, and Latina/o studies in general. Of key interest here is the transformation of a Mexican American archive that no longer solely revolves around a Chicana/o movement politic or set of poetics to organize the critical identities or keywords of the field.[5] Understanding this transformation of the archive is also critically important at this historical juncture given how the terms *Latina*, *Latino*, and *Hispanic* are currently in use to identify the most dramatic demographic change in U.S. society since the early twentieth century. Since the conclusion of the 2012 presidential election, the renewed frequency and deployment of these terms to identify a large ethnic voting bloc for regional and national elections has reinvented perennial favorite questions to ask: Who are Latinas/os? Where do they live? Where do they come from? What do they want? How do we understand them as "American"? What is their history? Use of such of terms as markers for identities represents a political desire for coherence of a multitude of data points that can be categorized and managed toward political ends and are hence vulnerable to conservative forces and values that seek to homogenize all Latina/o communities under one rubric, thereby sacrificing difference in favor of political gains.[6]

In academia, there is a similar tendency to discipline emergent archival materials into already accepted and familiar tropes, patterns, identities, and historical outcomes. There is of course a politic to all archives, whether in its creation, or its maintenance, or its deconstruction. Over the past twenty years, the work of Recovering the U.S. Hispanic Literary Heritage has presented one challenge after another to the archives of the Chicana/o movement that were absorbed and institutionalized by a variety of academic disciplines. To be sure, the Recovery Project has had a similar effect in Puerto Rican studies, Cuban American studies, and Dominican studies.[7] Although the Recovery Project grew out of the efforts of activists and scholars involved in the broader civil rights movement, the contents of this emergent archive belong to other times and other politics. As a result, while much of this archive is familiar, much of it is equally unfamiliar. In order to grapple with this divergence between an institutional drive for coherence versus the diversity of difference found in the archive, I argue for the need to embrace the anarchy in the archive as an opportunity, and not something to malign or steer clear of. Despite inevitable anachronisms, these same current terms—*Latina, Latino*, and *Hispanic*—can be viewed as a point of departure for historicizing differences among and between communities of Spanish-speaking origin that were absorbed territorially through conquest by the United States or absorbed through successive waves of immigration.

Now as the Recovery Project enters its third decade, the archive of Hispanic America deepens, yes, but it also resists singular coherence. What survives in the record is as diverse as the individuals and individual circumstances that have produced that record. In the case of Mexican America, part of the anarchy of the nineteenth-century archive lies in that it intersects with the emergent national narratives of both Mexico and the United States, but these intersections are rarely acknowledged in their own times and never claimed by either the national or regional imaginaries of each country. The biography of Juan Nepomuceno Seguín of Texas, nineteenth-century landowner, soldier, and politician, reflects a contorted set of identities: Is Seguín to be remembered as one of the surviving heroic defenders of the Alamo? Or is he better remembered as the mayor of San Antonio, falsely accused of aiding and abetting Santa Anna's failed 1842 attempt to retake Texas? Or should Seguín be lauded for his eventual political maturity when he fights on the Mexican side of the U.S.–Mexico War of 1846? Further, can an individual of Mexican descent be both hero and sellout to three countries—Mexico, the Republic of Texas, and the United States—and still be hailed by a Chicana/o movement–inspired historiography? For those wishing to work on Seguín's memoirs as a historical and literary text, all these identities come into play, especially if one engages the national and regional imaginaries that constitute the foundations of his writings.[8]

This chapter attempts to understand such contorted identities by understanding the meaning and effect of modernity in early Mexican American literature. My aim is to go beyond understanding modernity for Mexican Americans solely in terms of the invasion of proto-industrialized capital to regions like the Southwest or West or the border with Mexico, and to look beyond modernity's usual negative alteration of local economies, politics, cultures, and language without denying this fact or minimizing its consequences. When contemplating the range of identities available to people of Mexican descent in the post-1848 era of the United States, one needs to account not only for the influence of the evolving border between the United States and Mexico, and not only for the broad influence of native peoples in the Southwest and West, but also for the regional differences that become visible from Texas to California over the latter half of the nineteenth century, especially as settler identities take root because of westward expansion. By the end of the nineteenth century, one can find in print culture alone all of the following possible identities: Mexican, Mexican expatriate, Mexican rebel, Mexican exile, Mexican American, Californio, Tejano, Spanish American, Latin American, Chicano/a, Pachuco/a, Cholo/a, and Pocho/a, to name a few. To navigate the differences each term entails is in the end a useful way to recover the histories of ethnic formation otherwise marginalized or, worse, forgotten, but each term in itself also has the capacity to give way to a deeper anarchy that all archives are beholden to for their meaning over time.

Such a multiplicity of identities after 1848 is, I would argue, a symptom of the broader effects of modernity on the conquered territories. To make sense of the evidence of modernity in texts made available by Recovering the U.S. Hispanic Literary Heritage since 1991, I am beholden to the work by Latin Americanists, like Enrique Dussel, Aníbal Quijano, and Walter Mignolo, who have unpacked the relationship of modernity to colonialism in the Américas and who have developed terms such as *coloniality* and *coloniality of power* to better understand how the Enlightenment and liberal concepts such as the rights of man and social-change mechanisms like revolutions were compromised by their roots in territorial conquest and the rise of capitalism. Mapping the effects of this modernity on Mexican America is also key to understanding why the Recovery Project has transformed the archive, and further how this evolution is poised to trigger a transformation of U.S. nineteenth-century studies in years to come.

Mexican American Modernity

Among the many twists and turns in any discussion of modernity and Mexican American communities post-1848 but pre–Chicano movement lies the difficulty of understanding the role of literature for a people caught so precariously betwixt and between the nation-state. In most literary studies today, it is taken for granted in the West and its former colonies that literature was a primary mechanism and means for establishing the foundational narratives of the nation-state. By contrast and for decades after the U.S.–Mexico War, Mexican American communities existed outside the state-sanctioned narratives of nation-building. "Mexican" by language, culture, and religious habits, these people had nevertheless no binding influence on the republic of the Estados Unidos Mexicanos. Their status as "American," as procured by the 1848 Treaty of Guadalupe Hidalgo, only occasionally, and very infrequently at that, secured the rights and privileges of U.S. citizenship. Despite what would seem completely debilitating circumstances, to produce outside the realm of the nation-state or to produce in a literary landscape without clear foremothers or forefathers, people wrote in most of the popular genres of the time, including the press.

Recorded in these literary and print productions, I argue, are the pressures and reactions to living under the peculiar weight of a modernity that is itself lodged between the United States and Mexico. Early Mexican American literature thus provides a series of historical and cultural frames from which to evaluate the ongoing consequences of a modernity defined and fueled by a "coloniality of power" that serviced the imaginaries of a globalized Europe. These cultural productions also evidence a variety of regional rationales for their own existence as separate from but not ignorant of the nation states of the United States and Mexico. The "coloniality of power" that resides in these texts is often double-edged, fighting off an Anglo American colonial presence, only to hide, make natural, or complicate older Spanish–Mexican colonial narratives.

My goal here is simple. I mean to apply the logic of Walter Mignolo's method for rendering visible what Eurocentric modernity would otherwise keep invisible. I mean to offer a thick description of a "territory" that underwent a profound reconstitution, in order to then land on another Mignolo term, *colonial difference*, and argue for a way to name the kind of modernity that was visited on a "territory" conquered by war and words in the mid–nineteenth century of North America. Speaking on the relationship between modernity and the emergence of the nation-state in Latin America, for instance, Rob Marsh writes: "In the national narratives of Latin American nations it has been extremely important to emphasize the modernity of the nation, to catalogue and emphasize the specificities and the qualities of its civilization and to narrate the defeat of barbarism. . . . To govern is to subject the supposedly barbarous elements of America to the rule of a civilization defined solely on European terms."[9] For Quijano, the above process of subjugating the barbaric other is always part and parcel of the growth and consolidation of labor under capitalism. All the same, modernity's continual identification with the "something new and different" and its proliferation of "changes in the material dimensions of social life" required constant guarding and redirection by elites of those same others it sought to control and profit from.[10] Quijano writes: "For those exploited by capital, and in general those dominated by the model of power, modernity generates a horizon of liberation for people of every relation, structure, or institution linked to domination and exploitation, but also the social conditions in order to advance toward the direction of that horizon. Modernity is, then also a question of conflicting social interests. One of the interests is the continued democratization of social existence. In this sense, every concept of modernity is necessarily ambiguous and contradictory."[11] Mignolo's work on modernity and coloniality mirrors both Marsh's and Quijano's assessments of modernity and its construction of the "social," but with an emphasis on the processes of exchange, transaction, accommodation, and refutation in order to dramatize the presence of colonialism as always a dynamic, multivalent, multi-situated, as well as invoking and engaging a disparate range of actors. He writes:

> The history of the Americas and the Caribbean from 1492 on is not only the history of Western European linguistic, economic, and religious expansion, but also the history of the ways of life adopted by those who were there before the expansion occurred. . . . And it is finally the history of those "in-between": the natives or immigrants who had to deal with colonial situations and the postcolonial intellectuals who had to negotiate a cognitive space between the fragments of the European legacy and the forces of Amerindian ruins.[12]

Altogether this body of Latin American theory agrees on the range and extent of forces brought to bear to convert, correct, and manage a "new world" in the image and aggrandizement of Europe. In this context, what we often accept as the "transnational" character of Mexican American literature has to do with processes like transition, transitoriness, and transparency imposed by coloniality. More specifically, the "trans" has to do with the transitions that occurred when one colonial matrix gave way to yet a more powerful one in 1848; it has to do with the transitory promises of a modernity that accompanied the Anglo American colonial matrix but also the sense of betrayal and confusion that the prior Spanish–Mexican order, also a product of modernity, was so vulnerable and could be defeated; and finally, it has to do more with the transparency of the raw naked power of the nation-state when you are the subject of its colonialism as its perpetual "other." The structure of the modernity I will be describing here echoes what Dussel calls "transmodernity," where "trans" refers to those things/processes/inventions that are related to but external, hence considered extraneous and unimportant, to the maintenance of a Eurocentric modernity.[13] In what follows, modernity is linked to an analysis that posits its rise not just with capitalism and racism, but as an invention that arose from Europe's colonization of the Américas.

Although Marsh, Quijano, Mignolo, and Dussel are speaking of modernity in relation to Latin America, I deploy them here in order to consider the status of modernity in those territories lost by Mexico and gained by the United States in 1848, and to take up more concretely Mignolo's sense of those caught "in-between." Up to that moment in history in 1848, one can and should claim that Mexico was on the road to its own definition of modernity and nationalism from the moment Padre Miguel Hidalgo launched a war of independence in 1810. Mexico secured independence from Spain in 1821, but it was not until 1824 that the Mexican political process codified its first constitution as a republic. It was the Constitution of 1824 and its liberal policies that drew American and European settlers to Mexico's northern territories like Texas. It was in this relatively secure period that Mexico began to develop and deepen the instruments of its national identity. For example, Raymond Craib writes: "Mexico's first geographic society—Instituto Nacional de Geografía Estadística (later to become Sociedad Mexicana de Geografía y Estadística)—had been created in 1833 by Valentín Gómez Farías, a president who believed that the accumulation of a production of geographic and statistical knowledge of the nation's territory was critical for national development."[14] In the context of the perceived "horizon of liberation" such documents offered and imagined, it is no wonder that the repeal of the 1824 Constitution by President Antonio Lopez de Santa Anna later in 1833 ushered in a series of secessionist movements in Mexico, including the successful Texas War of Independence in 1836. Ten years later the various regional nationalist agendas that were set in motion in 1776 and 1810, respectively, came to a head during the U.S.–Mexico War. Using Texas as fulcrum, the United States was able to consolidate and expand its territorial claims on the continent, thereby superimposing its own narratives of nation-building (Manifest Destiny) over lands and peoples that up to that point in time had also proceeded under the sign of modernity, but a modernity that was only weakly supported by a nationalist superstructure called Mexico. Nevertheless, the signs and artifacts of the previous Spanish–Mexican colonialisms and modernities were many and deep, from language to religion, from land use practices to land grant documents, from racial practices according to a "castas system" to architecture, the arts, and print culture, the residual presence of things Spanish, Mexican, Mestizo, and Indio, could not be Americanized overnight.

Yet, and despite the dizzying multitude of examples of this residual past from Texas to California, February 2, 1848, marks the official narrative of separation from the nation and modernity that continues under the sign of Mexico. For those people, communities, and cultures that remained and survived in the years after 1848, another colonialism and a different iteration of modernity becomes their burden to negotiate, just as it becomes a burden, an experience to witness the slow erosion, the fading of their residual shared cultural past. And perhaps these twin burdens could have been acceptable under the logic of democracy and citizenship, but the "horizon of liberation" that Quijano speaks about as constitutive of modernity was actively opposed and obstructed by Anglo American ideologies of racial superiority and by the industrial and agricultural economies of the United States and their desires for cheap and ever-available labor. As they were for other ethnic and immigrant groups, institutions were set up to require former Mexican nationals to assimilate into a nationalist set of American identities but also to discipline, punish, and alienate those deemed beyond the reach of civic incorporation. This alienation from the modernity of America was never completely totalizing but almost so. During moments of crisis, like war, people of Mexican descent have always been deemed appropriate for the military. This has been true since the Civil War and repeated ever since. Conversely, during other moments of crisis, like the Great Depression of the 1930s, Mexicans and Mexican Americans have been rounded up like criminals and without due process deported to Mexico. Other institutions, like the courts, the schools, banking, and voting, were notoriously steeped in the racism of their day.[15] Were conditions like these the only thing to deal with under the regimes of Anglo American modernity, the Mexican American community would have been one thing, but the economic and political instability of the waning years of Porfirio Diaz's dictatorship in early 1900s, followed by the Mexican Revolution, introduced successive waves of Mexican refugees that had the effect of destabilizing local strategies to Americanize the population of Mexican descent in the United States, as well as ironically re-Mexicanizing large areas of the Southwest and West by people in exodus. What is important to notice about this Mexican immigration is that it imported the competing modernities of Mexico itself, and over time the sustained movement of people, goods, technologies, and ideas created an uneven but palpable circuit between the conditions of modernity affecting Mexican Americans and those affecting Mexican nationals.

Without a doubt, this competing and conflicted circuit is a regional expression of the "alternative modernities" first explored by Dilip Parameshwar Gaonker in the late 1990s, but with one sharp difference: The status of the "nation-state" does not cohere in any normal sustained manner.[16] To be more precise, whereas "state" functions and institutions, like laws, courts, and taxes, abound whether north of the border, or even south of the border during a civil war, the concept of the nation, *la nación*, existed as a practical imaginary for most, something to move toward, and for some as a memory of a dream never quite realized. By comparison to Anglo Americans or Mexicanos who inherit the Mexican Revolution, national belonging is continually questioned and questionable on either side of the border. As a result, regional identities become all the more important to communities of Mexican descent and all the more diverse given the 2,000-plus-mile border shared with Mexico. Over time in Texas, Mexican American life becomes symbolically and politically organized around the Texas Revolution (1836), and "remembering" the Alamo colors everything about being Mexican in the state; in New Mexico, centuries of an aristocratic landed gentry survive the Anglo American invasion by transforming themselves into Spanish Americans; in California, extreme demographic shifts, first introduced by the Gold Rush in 1849, succeed in "minoritizing" the once-combined majority of Californios and Native Americans to such a degree that by the early twentieth century Spanish California with its deteriorating missions and fake folklore like Helen Hunt Jackson's *Ramona* (1884) becomes a commodity for tourists, land speculators, and easterners looking for a new life; in this environment, one could only be "Mexican," a pejorative.

By historicizing and mapping the whole of the territory, not just focusing on the border, or borderlines, or borderlands ceded to the United States by the U.S.–Mexico War, but nonetheless open to and engaging in dialogue with the evolving nation-states of both Mexico and United States, one can understand what Mignolo means by "colonial difference," and why cultural production within this identified space carries so much import. He writes:

> The colonial difference is the space where the coloniality of power is enacted. It is also the space where the restitution of subaltern knowledge is taking place and where border thinking is emerging. The colonial difference is the space where local histories inventing and implementing global designs meet local histories, the space in which global designs have to be adapted, adopted, rejected, integrated, or ignored. The colonial difference is, finally, the physical as well as imaginary location where the coloniality of power is at work in the confrontation of two kinds of local histories displayed in different spaces and times across the planet.[17]

In essence, all cultural production within this space appears embedded with its own relationship to modernity and coloniality of power. In the case of cultural production by people of Mexican descent, and because it comes from a dominated context and precisely exterior to any nation-building outcome, it is a production in search of naming its own historical conditions, but because of the heterogeneity of its communities and the political and economic contingencies these communities had to deal with, it is one that never came to fruition.

All the same, and in retrospect, and because of the accumulated attempts to recover a history of Mexican Americans, it is now possible to name this modernity and thereby complete the analysis that is made possible by understanding the relationship of modernity and coloniality to each other. Quijano writes: "And since 'modernity' is about processes that were initiated with the emergence of America, of a new model of global power (the first world system), and of the integration of all the peoples of the globe in that process, it is also essential to admit that is about an entire historical period. In other words, starting with America, a new space/time was constituted materially and subjectively: this is what the concept of modernity names."[18] Thus, I take up Quijano's definition of modernity as an imperative to describe the "new space/time [that] was constituted materially and subjectively" on the territories the United States won by war, but equally important I take up Quijano's optimism that these more shadowy, darker, and troublesome modernities of the periphery can be named, and that the naming itself is essential to any critique. It is within the contact zone of evolving and competing modernities associated with those lands re-territorized by the United States that I like to name its experience and negotiation by people of Mexican descent in the United States as a modernity of subtraction, a subtraction whose point of origin and evolution is the territorial designs of coloniality beginning in 1492, but whose consequences take on an additional traumatic turn in 1848.

Reading Geographically, Naming Modernity

I would argue that Mignolo's colonial difference underwrites how we might apply a geographic vision to analyzing histories and interpreting texts that are themselves imbued by their communities and their writers with a differential awareness of recolonized terrains. It is within this differential awareness that a modernity of subtraction for Mexican Americans becomes visible. With such a method, we can notice in the available primary and secondary sources about and by Mexicans and Mexican Americans several broad trends of historical and cultural value in this early period. Foremost among these is that despite the hegemonic pull to see all historical matters as a confirmation and validation of the United States, North America was the site of not one or two but multiple European-inspired colonial enterprises, from roughly 1492 to 1898. And further, these colonial enterprises often conspired against one another for New World domination. This observation should guide our thinking when considering how we might identify the archives deemed central to Mexican Americans. Specifically, it is important to understand that the United States and Mexico became part of a prolonged colonizing contest over territories, now regarded as the Southwest and West, roughly beginning in 1821 and culminating in 1848. Despite our nationalist conditioning since 1848, these disputed territories were not "*tierras incognitas.*" On the contrary, these territories had been under colonial scrutiny and pressure ever since the Ponce de Leon and Coronado expeditions and subsequently colonized and "civilized" to various degrees up to the start of the U.S.–Mexico War in 1846.[19]

In the context of archives that have competed and continue to compete with ethnic minority versions of U.S. history, it is critical to keep center stage that the U.S.–MexicoWar was not over empty, unpopulated spaces, or under-utilized land. The war was about peopled lands, deep harbors with towns long used to exporting and importing to a global market whether on the Gulf of Mexico or the Pacific from San Diego to San Francisco. It was over natural and mineral resources. And it was most certainly about markets and the expansion of markets—as I have learned so well from Stephanie Le Manager.[20] This is a long way of saying that the war was predicated on the fact of what already existed in the coveted territories west and south of the Mississippi River. The Anglo American territorial impulse was in part, I argue, a political unconscious that coveted what Spanish and Mexican colonialisms had been able to construct over three centuries of effort. What the United States gained came at the expense of what Mexican America came to lose, but also lose substractively over time by existing at the periphery of the nation-states of Mexico and United States.

Nonetheless, the remnants of these prior colonial domains often enter our critical discussions, whether in Chicana/o studies or postnational studies, by way of language centered on such terms as *oppositionality*, or *alterity*, or *resistance*, and yet almost never through historical narrative or historical treatments of archives. Rarely are the analyses attuned to the particularities of a prior historical moment—with all the structures of feelings and materiality one assumes with any historical moment of any particular people in any one particular place and time. In the absence of a thoroughly shaped knowledge project of Mexican Americans, postmodern, poststructuralist, and postcolonial theories have been very useful, giving us means to comprehend the social and political conditions of a minority community in era of late capitalism. But the very contemporary origin of these theories has given us only a provisional comprehension of the order of things.

Like Raymond Williams's use of the term *residual*, early Mexican American literature is full of deep remnants—prior moments of another world that was already full, fully present in its own cultural and political underpinnings—and, equally important, also always, already evolving into future states of an evolving colonial ideology that was Mexico's political discourse in 1846.[21] What we find in early Mexican American literature, then, are these rare glimpses into a state of collective being that was "anterior," "antes," before the reality that began in 1848 with the signing of the peace treaty. Because of the war, though, this anterior state becomes fragmented, demoted in social value, and displaced to the peripheral of the newly arrived official history of the United States. For the newly constructed class of U.S. citizens of Mexican descent, "*el tiempo anterior*," the time before, which had been everything, suddenly becomes an irretrievable past, and not just the basis for nostalgia of a golden age, but a past whose recalling cannot help but create a bifurcated sense of well-being, and at the center of that split is the issue of lost lands and, more significantly, an erosion of a sense of place—a sense of place that was timeless, if far from perfect, under a Spanish–Mexican cosmology. Thus loss, erosion, and dislocation anchor the significance of a modernity of subtraction for Mexican Americans. Within this particular rendering of colonial difference, the anteriors we find in early Mexican American literature cannot help but do war against an Anglo-Puritan world order. The anterior of early Mexican American literature here opposes, yes; resists, yes; and even proposes itself as an alternative to many a drifting son or daughter of latter-day Congregationalists, but never do these "anteriors" achieve a confidence in themselves, because the future for Mexican Americans, despite the U.S. Constitution and the Treaty of Guadalupe Hidalgo, is not about belonging to the conquering nation. Instead, for well over one hundred years, the conquering nation treats its citizens of Mexican descent as barely tolerated foreigners. Because this modernity of subtraction is so tied to territorial loss, one can imagine the cultural work at play whenever these anterior states are represented or articulated, especially in the case of geography.

All the same, to claim territorial loss as the epicenter of a modernity of subtraction for post-1848 communities of Mexican descent, including those communities that form as a result of successive waves of Mexican immigration into the United States, is to decry the injustice of that loss but also to claim the lighter side of the coloniality of power that would justify one colonial enterprise over another. Because the matrix of modernity/coloniality, especially its darker elements, always seeks to make itself invisible to notice, hence impervious to critique and intervention, how does the burden of modernity ever get expressed and exposed by these same communities? This question returns us to the archive where the flows, and in particular the excesses, of modernity/coloniality are recorded and preserved but also very often in contest and conflict with its own formation. Like water poured into a cup, one can perceive the work of modernity/coloniality when it flows and fills a space previously empty of its influence, but because this flow is never content, very often this space is filled to excess, and this excess then flows layers upon layers of modernity/colonialty over the same space of colonial difference. Because these overflows happen in specific spaces at specifics times, the matrix of modernity/coloniality is always most visible at the point of excess, especially when the point of excess is the space of overlapping and competing colonialisms.

It is here at a point of excess—in a space that was already territorialized, cultured, racialized, and gendered once by Spain and then again by an independent Mexico—that the post-1848 writer of Mexican descent in the United States, for instance, appears as both colonizer and colonized, as beneficiary and victim of settler colonialism, as white and nonwhite, and as gendered, and therefore disciplined, in accordance with a European patriarchal system. Excess, I would argue, is what symbolically, figuratively, and rhetorically characterizes the writings of such individuals, and to some extent the individuals themselves. From María Amparo Ruiz de Burton to Sandra Cisneros, one finds in Mexican American literature a surplus of representations of excess, be it of violence, or poverty, or sadness, or irrationality, or silence, or death. Thus, the excess of one time/space continuum will very often reveal a history of excesses. In this sense, to remember the Alamo vis-à-vis Juan Seguín, who wrote unsuccessfully to set the official record straight, can never just be about Anglo Texans in 1836, but also about the mission system that constructed it in the first place, and the native peoples the Catholic Church subjugated and converted. Perhaps not surprising in this context, an anarchy of the archive is frequently at play when contemplating the collisions between excesses that occurred in the transformation of a Spanish–Mexican colonial space into the Manifest Destiny of Anglo America.

As with the example of the Alamo, nowhere are the intersections of geography, modernity of subtraction, and excess more provocative than in colonial place names. Although to glimpse a modernity of subtraction at work one could start reading geographically anterior moments anywhere in the Mexican American archive, Spanish place names have become over time active archival sites in themselves and illustrative of what is at stake when studying modernity/coloniality post-1848. Why, for example, is San Francisco called San Francisco? For that matter, why is California California? To put it more broadly, why didn't the state constitutional convention of 1849 rename everything in California with place names more in keeping with an Anglo-Saxon Protestant colonial imaginary? To the victors go the spoils, right? What happened to the European zeal of renaming conquered lands? Everything began seemingly so briskly with New Spain, New England, and New France. Did nineteenth-century colonialism just wear itself out? Should we charge the "Forty-Niners" with laziness, or were they just too focused on the gold to be bothered with a few Spanish place names? Here a lack of obvious excess turns out to be an excess of a different order. To go down the path of answering the foregoing questions, one will invariably need to think postnational, transnational, and postcolonial. Further, one will have to think about the implicit and explicit instrumentality of language that institutionalizes social relations around any given geographic location with but the drop of a name. Then coupled with cartography, one will have to imagine how language transfers, supports, and maintains the cultural and political imaginaries that are imparted to any named place but especially colonized and recolonized locales. Here, the naming of place symbolizes the power of the colonizer, the power to set in motion a set of usable histories and fictions for an evolving colonialist community. For such a community, the naming of place feeds the desire for a shared symbolic narrative of purpose, and with this purpose in place, geography then becomes a virtual springboard toward the future.

San Francisco is as good an example as any. To ask about its origins is to remember its full name: La Misión de San Francisco de Asis (Mission Dolores). To know this origin is to acknowledge the Franciscan mission system that colonized and pacified the native populations of California, who were converted to Catholicism and forced to perform feudal labor for the mission lands.[22] To place San Francisco on the map of "El Camino Real" is to link it to all the other surviving Spanish place names from here to San Diego. And eventually, one might be motivated by sociology or economics to wonder how these missions sustained themselves, and why the nearby harbors became even more attractive in the latter days of the Spanish viceroy in Mexico City. To ask and know these facts is to awaken to the lucrative trade that sprung up in the early 1800s between Yankee ship captains, early Californio colonists who commandeered mission lands from the Franciscan order beginning in the 1790s, and Cantonese merchants who traded spice for cattle hides, tallow, and foodstuffs from the Yankee captains who themselves had traded with or bought from the ranching "dons" of California. In short, San Francisco is San Francisco because during the nineteenth century's own era of globalization, this city became a port of entry and egress for the world. The Gold Rush in 1849 only magnified what was already a reality: San Francisco was a global city, and little has changed that status. Today, to stroll its streets is to walk into its past, confirm it, and propel its reality into the future. For example, have you ever wondered why Gene Roddenberry, creator of the television series *Star Trek*, located the fictional headquarters of Starfleet in San Francisco? It's not a coincidence. It's because of geography, real and imagined, and the role that cultural geographies of the nation-state play in conjecturing the future.

The survival of Spanish place names after 1848 must be evidence, however subtly, of the imaginative power of the former colonialisms that dominated the Southwest and West, an excess that prevailed. Yet, it also behooves us to entertain the possibility that their survival was part of a coloniality of power that ushered in a new phase of colonialism in the Americas. In other words, 1848 Anglo American colonialism could not at some global level risk invalidating the logic of a former European colonialism that held sway in one manifestation or another for almost 400 years. It might be easier to see now that 1848 necessarily required some acknowledgement of the global colonialism that was already in place—a globalism that in actuality had fed and propelled the variant known as the United States of America. Here, San Francisco survives once as a place name because of its role in the "futuring" of a superior colonialism, and then again through a highly selective and nuanced cultural-political process that insists on some vestiges of prior colonialisms worthy of institutional memory. Over time, tourist sites that feature "old California" become appealing because their static presence confirms rather than deconstructs the inevitability of an Anglo California. Even historical curiosity is dulled by a nostalgia that is ironically in the service of the future not the past. This selective process of remembering prior colonial histories and/or non-European indigenous histories in the case of Native America might be a distinctive feature of settler countries like the United States. If so, the unevenness that appears through any casual geographic reading of place names should be understood, I argue, as continuous with the logic of 1848, and not some aberration due to local demographics or weakness in the power of colonialism itself. Instead, the unevenness that appears graphically on maps of North America since 1848 is part and parcel of a global colonialism that conditioned, shaped, and to some real degree disciplined the evolution of Manifest Destiny of the United States, at least until 1898—that other historic moment when the premiere colonialism of North America was undisputedly confirmed as south of Canada but north of Mexico. Nonetheless, people of Mexican descent residing in the United States were disenfranchised by one nation and abandoned by the other legally, culturally, and linguistically from participating as elites in the global colonialism that consolidated in the nineteenth century. Theirs was (has been) a subtractive experience of post-1848 modernity/coloniality. Hence, their relationship to surviving place names like San Francisco, or Los Angeles, or Albuquerque, or El Paso, or San Antonio is like the darker effects of modernity/coloniality in all of the Américas, an evolving legacy, rooted in the past to be sure, but also equally moving toward a future of uneven consequences, uneven fates.[23]

Because of the past twenty years of the Recovery Project, one vital reason for pursuing a study of modernity in early Mexican American literature lies in the various strategies and philosophies developed in the long period after the U.S.–Mexico War. There is in this archive a solace and inspiration one can derive from how and why people of Mexican descent chose to experience the aftermath of war by staying north of the border. These people chose not to emigrate south according to the terms of the Treaty of Guadalupe Hidalgo. Later the archive is filled by the experience of others who fled the devastations of another war by making el Mexico de afuera, despite all its complications, their new home. From 1848 on, one is able to note in folklore, letters, print culture, and literary production an apprehension not just of the political realm but of the new Anglo American political imaginary that is revising and realigning centuries old discourses on race, gender, class, religion, citizenship, power, sovereignty, and more. For Mexican Americans, modernity is less about any particular angst over imperial designs or dread about cultures of capitalism, as it might be for Anglo Americans and more about the anxiety and frustration of becoming/being the unrecognized underclass other for two nation-building projects: the United States as it emerges as an imperial world power, and Mexico as it stages a hemispheric socialist response to the imperial impulses of the West.

Understood in this broad context, the archive of the pre-movement era might collide with that of the Chicano movement because of the differences I have highlighted, but these collisions are momentary, and demonstrative of an archive still very much under construction. Like my archive moment with María Amparo Ruiz de Burton and Abraham Lincoln, which was momentarily disorienting but nonetheless thrilling, these archival collisions should be seen as vehicles by which both the familiar and the unfamiliar are rendered strange and new, and thus available for new interpretations, new methodologies, all linked by the conditioning forces of coloniality and modernity in the Américas.

Thus, the Recovery Project provides opportunity after opportunity to recover the effects of modernity in early Mexican American literature. Precisely because this period of texts and contexts is self-consciously rendered/situated in place and region, we ourselves are situated to understand modernity for early Mexican American literature as an alternative political unconscious that is trying to narrate the uneven erosions and fusions of two historically competing colonialisms. It is a narrative nonetheless advancing the politics and poetics of an "in-between" community, a community between Mexico and the United States that also struggles to deal with its orphan status, unclaimed by either nation-state. It is from this "in-between" continuum of location/dislocation that we can access the modernities captured by the cultural production in early Mexican American literature. It is from a modernity of subtraction that we can appreciate those aspects of the archive that seem by comparison, to either modernist figures in the United States or Mexico, out of place, forever anomalies. Instead of reading negatively the disconnection or isolation of Mexican American writers from María Amparo Ruiz de Burton to María Cristina Mena to Daniel Venegas, and of course, to Jovita González and Américo Paredes, their lack of connection is a symptom of their modernity rather than a comment on their fitness to chronicle the world they lived. A modernity of subtraction encourages us to resist hegemonic normalizing tendencies to pacify and discipline the archive to a narrow set of identities and to embrace instead the messy, contradictory, volatile character of the Mexican American archive.

NOTES

A special thanks to Rodrigo Lazo and Jesse Alemán for their wisdom, skill, and patience in shepherding this chapter to fruition. And to all my C19 *colegas* for your support and comments *mil gracias*.

1 Rosaura Sánchez and Beatrice Pita, introduction, The *Squatter and The Don* (Houston: Arte Público Press, 1992 [1885], 5–51.

2 See José F. Aranda Jr., "Contradictory Impulses: María Amparo Ruiz de Burton, Resistance Theory, and the Politics of Chicano/a Studies," *American Literature* 70.3 (1998): 551–79.

3 Caroline F. Levander and Robert S. Levine, eds., *Hemispheric American Studies* (New Brunswick, N.J.: Rutgers University Press, 2007).

4 See Ralph Bauer, "Hemispheric Studies," *PMLA* 124.1 (2009): 234–50.

5 José F. Aranda Jr., "Grappling with the Archive of Mexican America," in Special Issue, *The Specter of the Archive*, ed. John-Michael Rivera, *English Language Notes* 45.1 (Spring/Summer 2009): 67–78.

6 See Sophia J. Wallace, "It's Complicated: Latinos, President Obama, and the 2012 Election," in *Social Science Quarterly* 93.5 (December 2012): 1360–83.

7 See José F. Aranda Jr., "Recovering the U.S. Hispanic Literary Heritage," in *The Routledge Companion to Latino/a Literature*, ed. Suzanne Bost and Frances R. Aparicio (New York: Routledge, 2013), 476–84.

8 For more on Seguín and similar figures of Mexican descent, see B. V. Olguín, "Sangre Mexicana/Corazón Americano: Identity, Ambiguity, and Critique in Mexican-American War Narratives," *American Literary History* 14.1 (Spring 2002): 83–114.

9 See Rob Marsh, "Lecture on *Ariel* (1900) and *Calibán* (1971)," http://www.mml.cam.ac.uk/spanish/SPS/nation/Ariel-Caliban.html (9/29/09): 1.3.

10 See Aníbal Quijano, "Coloniality of Power, Eurocentrism, and Latin America," *Nepantla: Views from South* 1.3 (2000): 546, 547.

11 Ibid., 548.

12 See Walter Mignolo, "Afterword: Human Understanding and (Latin) American Interests—The Politics and Sensibilities of Geocultural Location," *Poetics Today* 16:1 (Spring 1995): 180.

13 See Enrique Dussel, "World-System and 'Trans'-Modernity," *Nepantla: Views from South* 3.2 (2002): 221–44.

14 See Raymond B. Craib, "A Nationalist Metaphysics: State Fixations, National Maps, and the Geo-Historical Imagination in Nineteenth-Century Mexico," *Hispanic American Historical Review* 82:1 (2002): 35–36.

15 For a classic rendering of such historic moments, see Rodolfo F. Acuña, *Occupied America: A History of Chicanos*, Seventh edition (Upper Saddle River, N.J.: Pearson, 2010).

16 See Dilip Parameshwar Gaonker, "On Alternative Modernities," *Public Culture*, 11.1 (1999): 1–18.

17 See Walter Mignolo, "Preface," *Local Histories/Global Design* (Princeton, N.J.: Princeton University Press 2000), ix.

18 See Aníbal Quijano, "Coloniality of Power, Eurocentrism, and Latin America," *Nepantla: Views from South* 1.3 (2000): 547.

19 David J. Weber, *The Spanish Frontier in North America* (New Haven, Conn.: Yale University Press, 1992).

20 Stephanie LeMenager, *Manifest and Other Destinies: Territorial Fictions of the Nineteenth-Century United States* (Lincoln: University of Nebraska Press, 2004)

21 See Raymond Williams, *Marxism and Literature* (London: Oxford University Press, 1978).

22 See Edna Kimbro, Julia G. Costello, and Tevvy Ball, *The California Missions: History, Art, and Preservation* (Los Angeles: Getty Conservation Institute, 2009).

23 For a thorough treatment of a similar phenomenon but on a much broader scale, see Andrew Sluyter, "Colonialism and Landscape in the Americas: Material/Conceptual Transformations and Continuing Consequences," *Annals of the Association of American Geographers* 91.2 (2001): 410–28.

8

Feeling Mexican

Ruiz de Burton's Sentimental Railroad Fiction

MARISSA K. LÓPEZ

No es la raza Mexicana diferente de la Americana para que se crea que solo en nuestro cuerpo se reconcentran las enfermedades.

(The Mexican race is not different from the American race and one should not think that disease takes hold in only our bodies.)
—Mexican Laborers' Petition to the Mexican Consul in the United States[1]

A quarter of the way into María Amparo Ruiz de Burton's novel *The Squatter and the Don* (1885), the titular Don, Mariano Alamar, makes a business proposal to a gathering of squatters who have settled on his land. When he is met with resistance and scorn, "Don Mariano reddened with a thrill of annoyance."[2] A few pages later, his youngest daughter, Mercedes, meets the son of one of these squatters, Clarence Darrell, whom she will later marry. Clarence and Mercedes feel a strong mutual attraction, and Mercedes' "face was suffused with burning blushes" (93). Clarence saves his blushes for Mercedes' father. He "blushed with pleasure and bowed" when Don Mariano compliments his combination of fine feeling and business sense (98). Clarence can, however, muster romantic changes of complexion. Faced with a competitor for Mercedes' affection—a Mr. Selden, who blushes in response to Mercedes' blushes in a San Francisco theater—"Clarence's face also flushed, and then turned pale" (145). Clarence's passion comes in part from his father, William, who "felt the hot blush come to his face" when he defends Don Mariano toward the end of the novel (271). The protagonists in *The Squatter and the Don*, as evidenced by these examples, do a significant amount of blushing.

The novel understands this blushing as an index of refined sentiment, a symbol of that which sets *Squatter's* protagonists apart from the railroad monopolies wreaking havoc on the social and geographic terrain of late-nineteenth-century California, companies like the Central Pacific, which one character describes as having "no soul to feel responsibility, no heart for human pity, no face for manly blush" (*Squatter* 296). Blushing also, as John González notes, is a way for the novel to assert the whiteness of its protagonists.[3] A brown face does not register a blush quite as spectacularly as a white face. Decades after *The Squatter and the Don* was first published, however, brown faces became just as much casualties of the "soulless, heartless, shameless monster" that was the Central Pacific as the blushing faces of the Alamares and their allies (*Squatter* 296).

In June 1916, for example, a Mexican laborer living in a camp for railroad workers in Palmdale, California, came down with a case of typhus. This caused no small amount of anxiety in the city, spurring a rash of hygiene education programs aimed at the laborers and providing ammunition to those arguing for tighter controls on Mexican immigration.[4] As several of the laborers noted, however, in a petition to the Mexican consul from which I take my epigraph, disease is not a feature endemic to Mexican bodies at the exclusion of Anglo Americans. Poor sanitation and squalid living conditions, rather than a genetic tendency toward slovenliness, rendered the Mexicans in Palmdale more vulnerable to typhus, the laborers argued. These petitioners were seeking help ameliorating the situation in the camp, while also objecting to the ways in which public health programs had taken control of the sociopolitical meaning of *mexicanidad*. To be Mexican, at this moment in Palmdale, was to be diseased.

Both these laborers and the genteel Mexicans in *Squatter* leverage their corporeality. While the rail workers assert their material bodies as evidence of their humanity, *Squatter's* investment in the body relies on the immaterial, on the Mexican body's access to the abstractions of whiteness, its ability to register emotion rather than manifest physical feeling. These two Mexican communities are separated by time and class, but taken together they evoke the story of what the railroad's arrival means for Mexicans in California over the course of a generation spanning the turn of the last century: First, the railroad divests the landed Mexican gentry of Alta California of their material wealth, then it creates a public image of Mexicans as diseased, dirty, and displaced. That divestment and public transformation is part of the tale *Squatter* is telling. The novel understands itself, as did its contemporary reviewers, as an anti-rail diatribe and a defense of Mexican whiteness. Even as it asserts the whiteness of its central characters, however, *Squatter* is conscious on some level of their impending racialization. Those instances where racial distinctions become fuzzy make visible the ebb and flow of a range of artificial categories seen as grounded in the seemingly incontrovertible truths of the human body; the differences between emotion and physical feeling, for instance, or technology and the human begin to seem tenuous as well over the course of the novel.

These binaries begin to unravel in a series of overlapping domains: The novel is consciously interested in rail as a social institution, but its discussion of actual trains is much more evocative; Ruiz de Burton wants her readers to take emotion seriously as political argument, and yet her treatment of illness and physical deformity is much more striking; and finally, the novel is heavily invested in presenting the Alamares as white but instead documents the evolution of something we might call Mexican feeling. Trains, feelings, and bodies intersect in San Diego, where much of *Squatter's* action is set, and which comes to serve in the novel as a kind of affective field that has a profound influence on these three domains. San Diego's putative healing qualities function as an ironic backdrop to the disintegration and reformation of the binaries the novel is so invested in maintaining.

The Squatter and the Don thus relies on a set of seeming contradictions that hinge on a paradox of the human body: It appears self-contained but actually exists symbiotically with its natural and mechanical environment. In this interconnection, about which *Squatter* seems not explicitly aware, we might see the novel as aesthetically *dismodern* rather than sentimental, realist, or even modern, as scholars have read it. By *dismodern* I mean to invoke Lennard Davis's articulation of the term as a critique of postmodernity. The postmodern subject, Davis argues, is a "ruse to disguise the hegemony of normalcy."[5] That is, according to Davis, postmodern subjectivity assumes the equality of various subjectivities as deviations from a universal norm; the fundamental political problem, Davis argues, is not one of inequality, but the assumption of a norm from which there is a standard deviation. Dismodernism asserts "that difference is what all of us have in common." Rather than postmodernism's focus on cultural difference, Davis argues for fundamental physical difference and "dysfunction," and for "dependence, not individual independence" as an ethical foundation.[6]

The stakes of this argument for Davis lie in the replacement of a Foucauldian binary of docility and power with one of "impairment and normalcy." Davis is deeply engaged with postmodernism's impact on our social, political, and physical futures; but dismodernity offers a way of looking backward as well as forward. In reading the physical body as the site where the political and the aesthetic converge, Davis is motivated by an understanding of the modern and the postmodern as retreats from the political. Ramón Saldívar positions himself against such readings of the modern in *The Borderlands of Culture*, his intellectual biography of Américo Paredes. Saldívar frames the U.S.–Mexico borderlands as a site where European and Pan-American ideas of modernity come together, producing an "alternative version of modernity, which [Saldívar] describe[s] as a 'subaltern modernity'" that gives the lie to critiques of modernism as apolitical and ahistorical.[7]

Both Davis and Saldívar deploy the body—disabled and racialized, respectively—as critical interventions into dialogues about aesthetics and identity. Both understand the ways in which modernity relies on an idea of a subaltern subject incompletely recuperated by the postmodern. Saldívar locates this phenomenon solidly in the Americas, in the border region between the United States and Mexico, specifically. Davis's dismodernity provides an additional way to articulate those ideas and to bring racial and ethnic alterity into dialogue with other modes of physical difference, a dialogue that productively frames *The Squatter and the Don*, which comes at the cusp of the modern age. There Ruiz de Burton grapples with capitalism's transformation of the human and its reworking of physical space. Race and ethnicity factor deeply and constitutively into *Squatter*'s analyses, though the novel is read mainly as an avoidance of race or a celebration of whiteness. For scholars of nineteenth-century Latina/o literature, then, dismodernity and the Latina/o modern make possible a reading of *The Squatter and the Don* in which the vagaries of the human body are understood as national allegory that transcends Ruiz de Burton's limited intentions.

Trains

Ruiz de Burton intended, as her subtitle makes clear, for *Squatter* to be "A Novel Descriptive of Contemporary Occurrences in California," a novel, in other words, about the railroad and the aftermath of the U.S.-Mexico War. Scholars have tended to focus on the latter at the expense of the former. Such treatments usually center on the United States' failure to live up to the terms of the Treaty of Guadalupe Hidalgo, which ended the U.S.-Mexico War of 1846–48 and guaranteed the property rights of Mexican landowners who chose to remain in the newly ceded territory. The creation of the Land Commission in 1851 to adjudicate disputed grants and the subsequent divestment of *rancheros* like Ruiz de Burton and the characters she portrays in her novel are where *chicanidad* is often thought to begin. For *Squatter*'s narrator, however, that divestment is inextricable from the railroad's arrival in California. Not long after taking land from the "Spanish people," observes the narrator, on the grounds that so much should not belong to so few, "this same congress mind you, goes to work and gives to railroad companies millions upon millions of acres of land" (163). Though the narrator's umbrage is rooted in the perceived wrong done to Mexican Americans, the complaint participates in the broader anti-rail feeling that swept late-nineteenth-century California.

Rail, then, is a cornerstone of *Squatter*'s Mexican American concerns, but it is also how the narrator inserts those concerns into a national conversation, and many people were talking about trains when Ruiz de Burton was writing. The railroad, one of the most significant technological innovations of the nineteenth century, was a prominent feature of the era's cultural production. Trains, observes Amy Richter, are everywhere in nineteenth-century U.S. fiction, serving as shorthand for technical and corporate innovation, social diversity, and national integration, especially after the Civil War.[8] In "To a Locomotive in Winter" (1892), for example, Walt Whitman praised a train's "black cylindric body" and "long, pale, floating vapor-pennants, tinged with delicate purple" as the "type of the modern—emblem of motion and power—pulse of the continent."[9] For Whitman a train was a "fierce-throated beauty," but writing earlier in the century, Nathaniel Hawthorne approached Clifford and Hepzibah's train ride in *The House of the Seven Gables* (1851) more abstractly, as Clifford opines that the train can "spiritualize travel" (227). Feeling themselves "drawn into the great current of life itself" (223), the siblings observe what the narrator refers to as "the usual interior life of the railroad" (224), which strikes them as "life itself" (225).[10]

Whitman and Hawthorne, as were many authors, are taken with the technical wonder of the train and the social diversity it invites as travelers mingle in the cars and are ferried from one place to another. Rail narratives were not always so sanguine, however. Richter notes that although trains had the much-promoted potential to erase social and sectional divisions, their ability to collapse the distance between places and people often highlighted dissent and social anxieties of the period (15). Frank Norris's *The Octopus* (1901) is an obvious example. In *The Gilded Age* (1873), as well, Mark Twain and Charles Warner take aim at rail-inspired land speculation and fraud as well as the unchecked power of rail corporations, themes also at the heart of William Dean Howells's *The Rise of Silas Lapham* (1885).[11] The social anxieties expressed in railroad narratives centered on racial issues, however, just as often as they did on corporate greed.

While trains were indeed a means of integrating the nation—think of the trains that bring Caroline Meeber into Chicago and New York in Theodore Dreiser's *Sister Carrie* (1900), or even the trains that bring Mercedes Alamar, in *Squatter*, to the East Coast vacation homes of her sister's in-laws—they were also often a site of segregation. Harriet Jacobs's experience purchasing tickets from Philadelphia to New York in *Incidents in the Life of a Slave Girl* (1861) illustrates this neatly when she discovers that first-class train tickets "could not be had for any money" because "colored people" are barred from first class. "This was the first chill to my enthusiasm about the free states," she writes.[12] Thirty years later, in *A Voice from the South* (1892), Anna Julia Cooper recounts similar exclusions.[13]

Segregation, corporate angst, and technological wonder characterize the bulk of nineteenth-century railroad fiction. This diverse array of texts can also be broadly described as concerned, like *Squatter*, with the changing nature of life in the United States in the wake of new relationships between corporations and citizens. *Squatter's* narrator is as outraged as those of *The Octopus* and *The Gilded Age* over the railroad monopolies' rapacious greed, yet the narrator remains aloof from the class and race concerns of writers like Jacobs and Cooper. Moreover, *Squatter's* narrator is not at all seduced by the "rumble and the tumult" of the open cars in which Clifford and Hepzibah ride (Hawthorne 225). When the characters in *Squatter* board trains, they enter private cars that mirror the comforts of home and keep them paradoxically separate from the rest of the train-riding public into which they wish to assimilate.

Squatter's interest in rail lies less with individual characters' interactions with trains and more with the railroad corporation as a social institution whose relationship with California, as William Deverell recounts, was rather contentious. Opposition to the railroad was a defining feature of California politics, particularly in the 1870s, when *Squatter* is set, and when tensions reach such a pitch as to force a constitutional convention in the state in the hopes of reigning in rail's extensive influence. The state initially welcomed the railroad with little opposition as a modernizing force for good, but it turned out to be a difficult force to reckon with. Apart from the railroad's noise, speed, and occasional dangers, California residents soon began to realize the cost of harboring such a huge corporate giant as the Central Pacific. The recognition was slow, however, because the Central Pacific Railroad was really the first thing like itself in the United States: a massive, all-encompassing, hugely influential entity. The Central Pacific railroad fundamentally and irrevocably altered California's political landscape just as surely as the train forever changed time, space, and subjectivity.

Though early opposition to the railroad was voiced by competing transportation interests—such as steamship and other freight and cargo lines like Wells Fargo—when the railroad failed to deliver on its utopian promises to the people of California, public opinion began to turn. Railroad opponents, however, constituted a multifaceted majority that was often at odds with itself. "Individuals might agree that there was a railroad problem," writes Deverell, "but disagreed on just exactly what this supposedly singular problem looked like."[14] The "problem" had much to do with the fact that by the late 1870s the Central Pacific was California's largest landowner, employer, and company. When the constitutional convention failed to regulate rail adequately, the economic downturn of the "terrible seventies" created a traumatized class of working poor who gravitated toward the xenophobic populism of Dennis Kearney and the Workingmen's Party.[15]

Though *Squatter*'s genteel characters and narrator are economic victims just as much as Kearney's followers, neither the party nor Kearney appears in the novel. *Squatter* does, however, express anger over the very same events that rallied Kearney's followers, such as the massacre at Mussel Slough and the revelation of the Colton letters.[16] Adding insult to injury, the Central Pacific, in the words of *Squatter*'s narrator, "refuse[d] to pay taxes on their gigantic property" (337), a reference to their claim that taxes imposed upon them by the new constitution were illegal.[17]

Squatter, as contemporary reviewers received it, thus actively participates in the statewide anti-rail dialog, despite refusing a connection to the working classes of California. *The San Francisco Chronicle* referred to it as an "anti-monopoly novel," and *The Daily Examiner* noted that in addition to its being about the violations of the Treaty of Guadalupe Hidalgo, *Squatter* treated "the injury which San Diego and the lower coast counties suffered by the absorption of the Texas Pacific into the Southern Pacific, and the general demoralization . . . caused by the introduction of the railroad monopoly as a factor in the political affairs of this State and Coast."[18] *The Daily Alta*'s reviewer was less sympathetic, complaining that "the fervid eloquence of the author is reserved to depict the baleful effect which the non-construction of the Texas Pacific Railroad has had upon Southern California" and suggesting that "expound[ing] some pet views regarding what ought to be the morality of business" is the novel's main objective.[19]

True, the narrator does not withhold opinions about business. After all, in the end San Diego and its inhabitants are brought to ruin by the railroad, the inhuman business at *Squatter*'s heart. Why, however, does the narrator harbor such hatred for the railroad, and does this hatred serve as nothing more in the novel than a vehicle by which the narrator can express "pet views" about capitalism's purported amorality? Gentlemanly Clarence, who mixes business, pleasure, and personal relationships, is presented in contradistinction to the impersonal, unfeeling

Central Pacific, which the narrator blames for San Diego's financial ruin, but such blame seems unfounded. "In our opinion," writes *The Daily Alta*, "this [holding the railroad responsible for San Diego's collapse] is hardly a fair deduction, however much distress might have befallen upon the victims of reckless speculation."[20] *The Daily Alta* does have a point; by 1885 the Atchison and Topeka railway had arrived in southern California and the population in Los Angeles was steadily growing as rail networks increased throughout the decade.[21] There was enough rail activity in and around San Diego by the late 1880s to make the narrator's vehemence, and James Mechlin's eventual suicide, seem excessive.

The motivating energy behind the novel's disquisitions on rail's excesses comes not from the business of rail but from the physical experience of riding trains, the emotional and social dislocations of which *Squatter*'s narrator glosses over. As Wolfgang Schivelbusch and many others have observed, trains make possible wholly novel conceptions of the self as an object incorporated into a larger system of motion, of space as a thing easily traversed and overcome, and of landscape as simultaneously static and moving.[22] In the late nineteenth century, trains were the consummate symbol of a modernity that was fast eroding the individual's significance. As Mark Seltzer notes, rail travel produces an uncertain, anxious agency in that while one experiences motion on the train, it is motion caused by an external force. The individual is not responsible for his or her own movement, and it is a movement unlike any other: One can see that one is moving, but one does not feel it.[23] Apprehending what Seltzer calls "panoramas in perspective" produces at once a sense of spatial mastery and subordination to motion.

Hawthorne, to illustrate, describes Clifford and Hepzibah's simultaneous excitement and disorientation as they see "the world racing past them" on the train. A village vanishes "as if swallowed by an earthquake"; buildings are "set adrift" and the natural landscape is "unfixed from its agelong rest and moving at whirlwind speed" (224). The two travelers take this all in with a mixture of wonder, excitement, and fear. Mercedes Alamar, on the other hand, remains unfazed as she witnesses a similar display on her train ride from San Francisco to New York, a trip her mother has arranged in order to disrupt the budding romance between Mercedes and Clarence Darrell. After they part, on a train, Mercedes retires alone to her compartment, so overcome by grief that she does not notice what the narrator describes as a "flying wall of verdure," trees engaging in "grotesque antics" for her entertainment, transforming "that portion of the Pacific slope into a flying gymnasium" (155). Clifford and Hepzibah marvel at the drifting landscape, but Mercedes does not even see the topsy-turvy foliage that does much more than simply float past. Writing about views from a moving train, Michel de Certeau describes the kind of immobile landscape appreciated by Clifford and Hepzibah. Trees and such "do not move. They have only the movement that is brought about from moment to moment by changes in perspective."[24] Like Seltzer, de Certeau emphasizes the estrangement from one's own body provoked by the uncertainty about where movement is located, yet Mercedes resists that estrangement. She sees nothing, serene in her immobility while things move around her.

Resist is perhaps too grandiose a word for what can arguably also be read as Mercedes' melodramatic teen angst. Yet her behavior in this scene is striking if we grant, as Mark Seltzer argues, that turn-of-the-century American culture is characterized by an acute awareness and anxiety over "the 'discovery' that bodies and persons are things that can be made" (3)—that is, of the mechanization of the body, the subordination of nature to industry. The railroad rendered human bodies as cogs in a machine, and I began this chapter by exemplifying how railroads were able to control the meaning and significance of Mexican bodies in particular. *Squatter* consciously works against rail's growing influence with character monologues and narratorial asides denouncing the Central Pacific. This pushback, however, remains largely directed at the railroad as a social institution; trains as mechanical objects complicate things significantly. We can read Mercedes' sensory apathy on the train as a way for the novel to resist the railroad—as a way, in other words, to posit human against machine. In other moments, however, human and machine come together quite productively in *Squatter*.

Mercedes might resist the train's disorienting power, but in several instances the narrator uses machines to explain human emotion. In a fit of anger, for example, Clarence's father, William, is described as "an overturned locomotive which had run off its track, and become hopelessly ditched" (216). The train that carries Clarence away from Mercedes is deployed similarly as emotional icon when the narrator calls it a "magician" that not only understands the lovers' pain upon separation but also gives it voice with its whistle. Mercedes' "heart gave accelerated throbs when she heard those shrieks . . . it seemed to her as if expressive of [Clarence's] pain at being torn from her . . . the locomotive understood it all and shrieked to say he did so, because he knew that she too wished to shriek like that" (154). In these instances characters who take issue with the railroad are nevertheless intimately, and sentimentally, connected to trains.

The narrator sees those trains, as does Hawthorne, as almost spiritual. Overwhelmed by the changes heralded by trains' speed and power, Clifford, in *The House of the Seven Gables*, thinks, "the world is growing too ethereal and spiritual to bear these enormities a great while longer." In his mind, trains, like mesmerism, embody electric energy: "the demon, the angel, the mighty physical power, the all-pervading intelligence." All three—trains, electricity, mesmerism—have rendered, in his opinion, "the world of matter a great nerve, vibrating thousands of miles in a breathless point of time" (230). This nerve, according to Clifford, is the telegraph, which takes thoughts from people's heads, like mesmerism, and transports them across space and time, collapsing distance and materializing the abstract, like the train. *Squatter's* narrator makes a similar connection in a description of Mercedes' heart "beat[ing] with telegraphic velocity" (262) when she is separated from Clarence again later in the novel. Mercedes might be numb to the train's power, but she embodies a sister technology that, in Hawthorne's rendering at least, expresses the train's mystical reach.

Calling Mercedes' heart "telegraphic" performs the anxieties and preoccupations Seltzer describes and reveals an even deeper conflict about whether a clear distinction between bodies and machines can be made. *Squatter* asserts that emotion makes the difference between human and machine, and it understands emotion as distinct from the kinds of physical feelings the Palmdale laborers experienced during their bouts with typhus. The physical body, in other words, plays a second, racialized fiddle to the primacy of emotion, understood in the novel as the purview of whiteness. This distinction the novel makes is a false one, however. Physical and emotional feelings are as inextricable as human and machine, and the boundaries between them all are as porous as those between Native, Anglo, and Mexican. Emotions, moreover, much as the novel understands them as separate from physical feeling, can be read as traces of the political work performed by the sick and disabled body in *Squatter*.

Feelings

The body in *Squatter*, as a repository of human feeling, is a hedge against a modernity characterized by an unfeeling rationalism that pervades economic and racial thought. The novel cannot maintain that distinction between human and machine, however, which is also theoretically suspect. Sentimentality is not the opposite of the modern, and human emotion might well be the product of the very capitalism with which *Squatter*'s narrator takes issue. The notion of a purely rational modernity has been challenged by theorists such as Eva Illouz, for example, who argues for the existence of an "emotional capitalism" as the process by which economic and emotional relationships define and shape each other. Excavating modernism's "emotionality" changes "standard analyses of what constitutes modern selfhood and identity," Illouz argues.[25] In *Squatter*, excavating the imagery of trains helps articulate the importance of the body, and subsequently of race, in the novel. At *Squatter*'s core are questions not just about the railroad's impact on California politics and culture but also about the relationship between trains and people. Every appearance of trains in the novel is an occasion to wonder how the train redefines the human, and what difference *mexicanidad* makes. How, in other words, is the Mexican body articulated in the exchanges between people, trains, and railroads in *The Squatter and the Don*?

Critical discussions of the body in *Squatter* have been held largely in sentimental terms. They have, moreover, used the linkages between whiteness and feeling, forged by such canonical sentimental authors as Helen Hunt Jackson and Harriet Beecher Stowe, to argue against a reading of *Squatter* as a resistant text, a turn that David Luis-Brown complicates in *Waves of Decolonization*. Sentimentalism, as Luis-Brown succinctly defines it, "comprises a cluster of tactics by which writers effect reform by representing the public sphere in terms of domestic tropes—emotions, love, and family—and thereby claim moral authority through representations of areas of life that were commonly construed as irrelevant to politic[s]."[26] Critics have linked the emergence of sentimental fiction with the consolidation of English and North American middle classes, and since the 1990s scholars have been concerned to show the imperial implications of these domestic concerns.

Long dominated by the debate, epitomized in the work of Ann Douglas and Jane Tompkins, concerning whether sentimentality degraded a strong, idealistic American culture, or encouraged deeper social engagement, later work on sentimentalism sought to push the boundaries of the field beyond the private home and printed text.[27] In *States of Sympathy* (1997), for example, Elizabeth Barnes reads the affect of eighteenth-century fiction as foundational to American political philosophy. Similarly, Laura Wexler's *Tender Violence* (2000) argued that women's photography at the turn of the last century articulated a domestic vision imbricated in the period's imperial racism. Luis-Brown's work keeps pace with this critical turn toward linking affect with imperialism, but he notes that while sentimentalism was "ideally suited to representations of populations victimized by empire" (36), the form could also be turned against imperial ends by writers of color who sought to instantiate a non-Anglo, feeling subjectivity.

Though Luis-Brown calls sentimentalism a "highly protean form" (47) whose politics shift with the social location of its author, a key assumption with which he must contend, and which *Squatter* blithely reinforces, is that the capacity to feel is congruent only with whiteness. Thus, sympathetic as he is to Ruiz de Burton's project, Luis-Brown, along with others who have written about it, reads *Squatter* as complicit with, rather than resistant to, Anglo American imperial racism. The arguments of David Luis-Brown, John González, Jesse Alemán, and others that *Squatter*'s sentimental turn is meant to align the Alamar family with Anglo gentility—to reify, rather than unsettle, whiteness—are not untrue, but these arguments are made wholly within the confines of the sentimental, and a playful, tongue-in-cheek tone lurks beneath the surface of the novel's dalliance with it as well as with the tidy resolutions of the historical romance, its sister form. "Really, I think our romance is spoiled," jokes Mercedes' brother-in-law George after Clarence and Mercedes have overcome Doña Josefa's objection to their relationship. "It would have been so fine—like a dime novel—to have carried you off bodily," George quips, playfully diffusing the melodramatic potential of the scene (132).

The Squatter and the Don thus keeps the sentimental at arms length, simultaneously seeking access to its white privilege while conceiving itself as generically distinct in key ways. The reader is meant to take *Squatter* seriously. George's comments make that plain, as does Mercedes' reading material. When Mercedes, flustered by her feelings for Clarence, hides behind her book, her sister Carlota says that her "novel must be very interesting." Madame Halier, Mercedes' tutor, retorts, "It is not a novel—it is French history" (113). *Squatter*, in its very subtitle, self-consciously treads the line between literature and history. And feelings, it further asserts, are not to be trifled with; they are the stuff of high-minded texts.

All of which begs the question: What work is the body doing in *Squatter* if we are to consider it beyond the confines of the sentimental? As both John González and Jesse Alemán have noted, the novel deploys the body—specifically, as González argues, the body's ability to blush—in order to assert the Alamares' whiteness, but the novel's assertions are fraught and not entirely successful. Just as the binary of human and machine is a false one, so too is the division between the races porous in *Squatter*. For example, Alamar patriarch Don Mariano's reference to "we, the *natives* of California, the Spano-Americans" is meant to erase the actual native presence in California, not to identify the Alamares as Native American. In the same conversation, however, he ventriloquizes popular beliefs about the Mexican ranchers as "lazy, thriftless, ignorant natives" who own too much land (162). Don Mariano's speech is a moment where the narrative almost becomes conscious of Mexican American racialization: His self-conception of "native" is giving way to Anglo readings of Mexican Americans, which are just as derogatory and problematic as the novel's views of Native Americans. In a similar moment of dawning consciousness, Victoriano, Mariano's son, notices that the family cows look "just like ourselves, the poor natives" as they are being led to slaughter (208).

In these moments *Squatter* works against itself as the characters articulate the novel's awareness of emerging racial hierarchies even as the narrator struggles to assert their whiteness. Don Mariano and his son have emotions about the political realities that disempower them, emotions meant to set them apart from the racialized, laboring classes. If, however, as Melanie Dawson argues in her reading of *Squatter* as a realist novel, "sympathy can be a modern condition . . . that [confronts] the cultural inequities that the novel addresses," then emotions can, as Eva Illouz asserts, be a function of capital in the same way that race is.[28]

Granting that emoting bodies are constructed by capital just as much as laboring bodies troubles *Squatter's* desire to use the sentimental body as a defense against an encroaching modernity represented by the railroad. There is, however, a kind of knowledge articulated in the body that the corporation (despite the obvious corporeal pun) cannot access. *Squatter's* protagonists may experience emotions that correspond to the novel's conscious political arguments, but the bodies in this novel feel things that the novel cannot fully articulate. In the cataloging of the physical feelings and conditions of *Squatter's* characters, their bodies emerge as affective registers of the changing political climate of late-nineteenth-century California.

Bodies

Squatter's use of physical health as a political metaphor is, of course, a sentimental convention. When, for example, Mercedes tells George and Clarence, "I dislike wines" (133), she speaks the language of temperance activists that pervades late-nineteenth-century U.S. fiction, as does Elvira, who asserts that when "we women have suffrage . . . we will make things uncomfortable for inebriates and tobacco smokers" (141). "Life," Clarence's father observes, moreover, "is not worth living without health" (71). As Jennifer Tuttle notes, the arc of *Squatter's* plot can be understood as beginning in an idyll of good health, then descending into despair and illness caused in no small part by the arrival of Anglo settlers (71).[29] The Alamar and Mechlin families are particularly afflicted by the political headaches the squatters introduce. James Mechlin's "very fine nervous organization ill-fitted him for the rough contact" of settlers (78), and, the narrator explains, "it was a noted fact, well recognized by the two families, that misfortunes made them all more or less physically ill" (315). Beneath these conventional surface concerns, however, considerations of race, nation, and physical health come together in a complex network on display in Clarence's bout with typhus, which he contracts in Yuma, Arizona, after his forced separation from Mercedes (264). His illness symbolizes his forlorn, lovesick state, but it also construes him as a Mexican ally.

As illustrated by the Palmdale laborers, in the early twentieth century typhus was seen as a Mexican disease in the southwestern United States. As Alexandra Stern has documented, however, as early as the 1890s Mexico had instituted typhus quarantine and fumigation sites along its border with the United States, twenty years before the United States began taking such measures.[30] Mexico, in other words, saw typhus as a threat from the north, a belief expressed in Clarence's contracting the disease in Arizona. Typhus helps depict Clarence as a romantic hero, but it also unearths a host of thorny political questions linked to disease, nation, and the racialized body. Clarence's illness, like his later travels through the "majestic ruins" of Mexico (284), allows him to cross physical and metaphysical borders of illness, fear, debilitation, and eventual union with Mercedes; it is the eye of the storm separating order from chaos in the novel, sickness from health, Mexican from Anglo. In contrast to this abstract, turbulent zone of transformative disease, Ruiz de Burton posits the very concrete space of San Diego as a healthy, regulating environment framing the novel's concerns about health, racial integration, and the relationship between human and machine.

San Diego's "salubrious air" (67) and "genial climate" (68) promote healthy living, as do its trees, which are "the healthiest in the world." The land is naturally well drained—"You never hear of any malarial fevers in San Diego"—and will be even more so, residents hope, when money earned from the railroad will finance sewers (70). San Diego is the kind of place, contends *Squatter*'s narrator, where a man like James Mechlin, who "had lost his health" (67), can recover it. San Diego is also the kind of place that can redeem a squatter like Clarence's father, William. Though he comes to settle on the Alamar *rancho* along with Gasbang and Matthews, his former employees, William "felt no sympathy, no liking for any of those men" (69). The narrator distinguishes him early on by identifying him with the refined Mechlins and Alamares as one who experiences sympathy. Further, just as James Mechlin's illness is caused by delicate nerves, William is similarly sensitive. Startled by a rifle shot soon after arriving in San Diego, he says, lightheartedly, "I didn't know I had nerves. I believe that is what women call it" (71). William even blushes "the blush of remorseful shame" (271) later in the novel when he realizes his misconduct.

San Diego's "salubrious air" has the power to restore James Mechlin's physical health and to inspire William to embody the force of his fine feelings when, for example, he feels "a pang shoot through his heart" watching George play with his (George's) infant son (270). William also recognizes his own frailty and dependency when Gabriel binds him in his *lazo* during an argument. The full-body bruise William suffers is nothing compared with the emotional pain he suffers from the rift the argument causes between him and his family. William's recognizing the errors of his squatting ways and the equality of Mexican and Anglo Americans is predicated on his own physical and emotional healing. Both James Mechlin and Wiliam Darrell are thwarted along this San Diego road to bodily and mental health, however, by the disease of Anglo settlement.

It is not, however, entirely fair to blame "Anglo" settlement for the deterioration of health in *Squatter*. The Mechlins and the Darrells are Anglo American, after all. The end of the U.S.–Mexico War does open the gate to Anglo immigrants to California, but the distinction made in *Squatter* is more one of class than race. The novel works, in fact, to unite squatters and Mexican Californians against a common enemy that renders them, according to Don Mariano, "all sufferers, victims of a defective legislation and subverted moral principles" (74). This toxic, political amorality is represented in the novel by the Anglo settlers who, paradoxically, have the most to say about health.

When William first arrives in San Diego, he is greeted by Gasbang and Matthews, his former employees, who have invited him to settle with them on the Alamar *rancho*. Gasbang's "broad, vulgar face . . . compressed, thin, bloodless lips, his small, pale, restless eyes and flat nose" suggest the low nature revealed as the plot unfolds. "Matthews' visage was equally noticeable for its ugliness," opines the narrator (69), and at the end of the novel he has gone "back to his old love of whisky . . . burning poison circulated in his veins," and his sister has him committed to an insane asylum (269). Yet it is through the decidedly unhealthy Gasbang and Matthews that the reader learns about most of San Diego's naturally sanitary drainage and healthful climate.

Such unreliable promoters as Gasbang and Matthews cast doubt on San Diego's long-term health. While James Mechlin recovered his nerves, and William Darrell had an emotional epiphany there, it seems as soon as San Diego's health becomes an object for reflection, or commodification, it evaporates. As *Squatter's* plot unfolds, each character's health begins to deteriorate and health becomes an illusion, an ideal toward which the characters strive. James Mechlin, for example, falls ill before the start of the novel, and the reader first encounters him on an upswing. "[Y]ou were sick but now you are well. Don't be lazy," his wife chides in his first scene (66). Disappointment after disappointment drives him to suicide at novel's end, however (305). Likewise, the "cold in his lungs" (280) that Don Mariano catches on a cattle drive evolves into a "congestive chill" (300) that eventually kills him (304).

More significant than the characters who die are those who recover, albeit unsteadily. Mercedes, for example, suffers through two nervous fevers before marrying Clarence. Clarence, meanwhile, feels "sick in mind and body . . . thoroughly heartsick" (260) at having to leave Mercedes and is struck with a case of typhoid fever so serious that "he lay on a sick bed, delirious with a raging fever that seemed to be drying the very fountain of his young life" (267). That Clarence and Mercedes emerge from illness while James and Don Mariano die suggests an analogy between the economic transformation of California and a devastating sickness, a glass through which the nation must pass darkly in order to be reconceived, or made anew.

Reading Clarence's and Mercedes' recoveries and their eventual marriage as the happy culmination of illness and California's transition to U.S. rule is overly optimistic, however. Don Mariano's son Gabriel's fall offers the narrator a chance to make that perfectly clear. Forced to work as a manual laborer, Gabriel tumbles off a ladder while carrying bricks, a fall in which "the entire history of the native Californians of Spanish descent was epitomized" (325). Gabriel, near death, physically and spiritually broken, embodies the history of Mexican California. While California's transformation offers Clarence and Mercedes a nominally happy ending, the novel, through bodily descriptions of other characters, paints the advent of the United States as a disabling tragedy, not unlike the trials of Little Eva in Stowe's *Uncle Tom's Cabin*.[31]

Even though Clarence and Mercedes are reunited at novel's end, and the Alamar family is saved from financial ruin by Clarence's wealth, a note of sadness pervades the conclusion. The characters must still grapple with the deaths of Don Mariano and James Mechlin, and Doña Josefa, Mercedes' mother, reflects, from a position of relative comfort, on what the railroad has wrought. "Her husband would have been alive, and Mr. Mechlin, also, and her sons would not have been driven to poverty and distress, and perhaps lost their health forever" if the railroad "had not blighted San Diego's prosperity" (335). The railroad indirectly creates an absence, through the death and disablement of key characters, that underpins the new reality the characters must forge for themselves as they move into the twentieth century.

Squatter renders the absence, or loss, caused by the railroad in starkly physical terms. The nervous condition afflicting James Mechlin at the beginning of the novel seems almost quaint when compared with the self-inflicted rifle wound that ends his life, as if the physical ailments of the past are somehow not adequate to capture the enormity of devastation in postwar, post-rail California. James's son, George, also takes a bullet, and though his wound is not fatal, it results in a lifelong limp, a danger "to him far more terrible than death" (274). George's wound, unlike his father's, is not self-inflicted. Shot by Matthews, the alcoholic squatter committed to an insane asylum by his sister, George, like Victoriano, will forever bear the physical scars of California's transformed landscape. Tano's legs go mysteriously numb on the same cattle drive that corrupted his father's health. The condition, which brings occasional "attacks more or less serious of the same lameness which deprived him of the use of his limbs," is chronic and incurable (285).

George and Tano, the afflicted sons of the dead patriarchs James and Don Mariano, represent a new, physically compromised generation: the future of California. Despite the twinge of physical nostalgia here, and the suggestion that a previously intact body now lies defeated on the train tracks, death and dismemberment seem woven into the historical fabric of the United States when Mercedes, Elvira, and their East Coast traveling party encounter a group of veterans as they tour the nation's capital. The "five or six old men with very white beards" walked toward the group "as if weakened by sickness; one walked on crutches and one had lost an arm" (196). The party learns that the men are veterans of the

U.S.–Mexico and U.S. Civil wars; they are at the Capitol petitioning for a pension that Congress is working hard to deny, despite knowing "how valuable were the services of those who went to Mexico to conquer a vast domain" (197). The very act of nation-making, these bodies suggests, involves physical destruction. Though the characters in *Squatter* experience emotions of despair over Mexico's physical compromising to the United States, their physical trajectories undercut this, indicating that the nation is an always already imperfect body, predicated on frailty, built by maimed veterans, and moving forward through its wounded citizens.

Latina/o Modernities

The sick, broken, and dead bodies in *The Squatter and the Don* are meant to symbolize, without a doubt, the ways in which the railroad, monopoly capitalism, and Anglo racism eviscerated the Mexican Californian culture that had taken root through the first half of the nineteenth century. This formulation, however, rests on the assumption of an ideal, perfect body symbolizing national unity and political peace. Such a body does not exist in *Squatter*, even though the novel's bodily logic seems to demand it. Furthermore, the veterans at the Capitol suggest the impossibility of such national bodies.

From the physical impairments in *Squatter* the reader deduces that nations comprise a series of faulty bodies, whose imperfections reference an intact wholeness, an impossible physical perfection, an ideal absence at the heart of the nation. Such perfection is the dream of a modernity represented in *Squatter* by the railroad and its regulation of space, time, distance, and bodies. In its corporate form, the railroad, according to James Mechlin, has "no heart for human pity" (296) and yet, in its corporeal form, the actual trains are all too human, as when they shriek in consort with Mercedes' pain (154).

Squatter thus demands the possibility of physical perfection and mechanistic apathy—an intact Mexican California destroyed by the "heartless" railroad—while simultaneously proving both illusory. A dismodern aesthetic illuminates the ways in which Mexican and Anglo bodies are constituted in and through the trains cutting across the physical and abstract spaces in *Squatter*—San Diego and the corporate spaces of rail. Trains, feelings, and bodies are interdependent in the novel, not opposed to one another. In concert with ideas of a Latina/o, or subaltern, modernity, as articulated by Ramón Saldívar, dismodernity makes possible a metahistorical reading of the physical travails of *Squatter's* characters. That is, rather than reading Mariano's death or Tano's crippling as Mexican American political grievance of limited scope and impact, we can read *Squatter's* broken bodies and sympathetic machines as arguments about the frailty of nations. In the Latino nineteenth century, ·then, through this reading of Ruiz de Burton, we begin to see other stories, other frameworks emerging alongside the stories of racial oppression and opposition we've come to anticipate. We see the human body, the material world, capital, the natural world, and social institutions like companies and nations all taking shape and expanding simultaneously. They appear as concentric circles, or expanding networks wherein the body, as *Squatter* argues, is always already imperfect, and the nations that contain them are always already composite, multiform, and interdependent.

NOTES

1 Quoted in Natalia Molina, *Fit to Be Citizens? Public Health and Race in Los Angeles, 1879–1939* (Berkeley: University of California Press, 2006), 67.

2 María Amparo Ruiz de Burton, *The Squatter and the Don*, Second edition (Houston: Arte Público Press, 1997), 87. Hereafter cited parenthetically.

3 John M. González, "The Whiteness of the Blush: The Cultural Politics of Racial Formation in *The Squatter and the Don*" in *María Amparo Ruiz de Burton: Critical and Pedagogical Perspectives*, ed. Amelia Maria de la Luz Montes and Anne Elizabeth Goldman (Lincoln: University of Nebraska Press, 2004), 153–68.

4 Molina, *Fit to Be Citizens?*, 61.

5 Lennard J. Davis, "The End of Identity Politics and the Beginning of Dismodernism: On Disability as an Unstable Category," in *The Disability Studies Reader*, Second edition, ed. Lennard J. Davis (New York and London: Routledge, 2006), 241.

6 Ibid., 239.

7 Ramón Saldívar, *The Borderlands of Culture: Américo Paredes and the Transnational Imaginary* (Durham, N.C.: Duke University Press, 2006), 17.

8 Amy G. Richter, *Home on the Rails: Women, the Railroad, and the Rise of Public Domesticity* (Chapel Hill: University of North Carolina Press, 2005), 4.

9 Walt Whitman, *Leaves of Grass* (New York: Library of America, 1992), 583.

10 Clifford and Hepzibah have fled after Judge Pyncheon, their wealthy cousin, dies mysteriously in their house. The novel centers on this house, haunted by history

and restless ancestors. Hawthorne balances the lugubrious weight of the past in the novel with dazzling new technologies like photography and trains. Nathaniel Hawthorne, *The House of the Seven Gables*, 1851 (New York: Signet Classics, 1961). Hereafter cited parenthetically.

11 Inspired by the events at Mussel Slough, *The Octopus* concerns the land struggles between wheat farmers in the San Joaquin Valley and the fictional Pacific and Southwestern railroad. In *The Gilded Age*, Twain and Warner describe a small Missouri town's desperate attempts to boost property values by attracting a railroad, while conversely, Howells shows how railroads use their monopoly power to drive down property values in *The Rise of Silas Lapham* when the titular Lapham's financial problems are deepened by a railroad's plans to build near his property.

12 Harriet A. Jacobs, *Incidents in the Life of a Slave Girl: Written by Herself*, 1861 (Cambridge, Mass.: Harvard University Press, 1987), 162.

13 Cooper's collection of essays focuses on the education and empowerment of African American women as the key to racial uplift.

14 William Francis Deverell, *Railroad Crossing: Californians and the Railroad, 1850–1910* (Berkeley: University of California Press, 1994), 16, 41.

15 Ibid., 42. Kearney, an Irish immigrant living in San Francisco, led a third-party worker's movement in the late 1870s, the Workingmen's Party of California, which "attacked the Chinese, vilified capitalists, and blasted alleged political corruption" (Deverell 43).

16 In May 1880, in a culmination of tensions that had been building for years, six people were killed when U.S. marshals came to evacuate settlers off land that belonged to the Southern Pacific (Deverell 57). The Colton letters, between David Colton, and Collis Huntington, made public by Colton's widow, detailed lobbying and other efforts on the part of the Central Pacific throughout the 1870s, including questionable financial dealings and strong suggestions of bribery (Deverell 61).

17 The California Supreme Court eventually upheld the Central Pacific's position, to the astonishment and anger of the state's people (Deverell 62).

18 Quoted in *Conflicts of Interest: The Letters of María Amparo Ruiz de Burton*, ed. Rosaura Sánchez and Beatrice Pita (Houston: Arte Público Press, 2001), 568, 565.

19 Quoted in Ibid., 567.

20 *Conflicts*, 567.

21 Deverell, 62.

22 A German cultural historian and sociologist, Schivelbusch detailed in *The Railway Journey* (1977) the emergence of an industrialized consciousness that takes shape around train travel and the regulation of space and time instigated by the railroad.

23 Mark Seltzer, *Bodies and Machines* (New York: Routledge, 1992), 17. Hereafter cited parenthetically.

24 Michel de Certeau, *The Practice of Everyday Life* (Berkeley: University of California Press, 1984), 112.

25 Eva Illouz, *Cold Intimacies: The Making of Modern Capitalism* (Cambridge, UK: Malden, 2007), 2.

26 David Luis-Brown, *Waves of Decolonization: Discourses of Race and Hemispheric Citizenship in Cuba, Mexico, and the United States* (Durham, N.C.: Duke University Press, 2008), 37. Hereafter cited parenthetically.

27 In *The Feminization of American Culture* (1977), Ann Douglas argues that sentimental fiction written by women undermined the strong, cultural foundation Puritan thinkers had honed; eight years later Jane Tompkins, in *Sensational Designs* (1985), built on Douglas's scholarship but argued that sentimentality fostered, rather than destabilized, an ethics of political responsibility.

28 Melanie V. Dawson, "Ruiz de Burton's Emotional Landscape: Property and Feeling in *The Squatter and the Don*." *Nineteenth-Century Literature* 63.1 (2008), 52.

29 Jennifer S. Tuttle, "The Symptoms of Conquest: Race, Class, and the Nervous Body in *The Squatter and the Don*," in Montes and Goldman, 71.

30 Alexandra Stern, *Eugenic Nation: Faults and Frontiers of Better Breeding in Modern America* (Berkeley: University of California Press, 2005), 59.

31 Eva's near-drowning and eventual untimely death signal the loss of U.S. innocence in the face of the peculiar institution of slavery.

9

Pronouncing Citizenship

Juan Nepomuceno Cortina's War to Be Read

ALBERTO VARON

In the decades after the U.S.–Mexico War, the border between the United States and Mexico was anything but assured. From California to Texas, inhabitants of and immigrants to the newly conquered territories struggled to adapt to the political and social changes affecting the border regions. To varying degrees, social unrest and open conflict between Native, Mexican, and Anglo American inhabitants troubled the new U.S. Southwest. In one effort to settle territorial uncertainty and assert the fixity of the border, the United States completed the Gadsden Purchase in 1854 to acquire territory in present-day New Mexico and Arizona for the completion of the transcontinental railroad, to secure trade routes to California, and to appease Mexican concerns with Indian raids in the area.[1] Yet despite numerous official attempts to affirm the national boundaries, the United States often struggled to incorporate the diverse social and cultural life found within the newly shaped nation. Just five years later, events in south Texas would rekindle the racial tensions that had persisted since the war, resulting in armed conflict and the involvement of the U.S. Army in an affair that drew national attention.

When a disagreement between a Mexican American and an Anglo resident devolved into violence in the fall and early winter of 1859, the escalating racial tensions between Anglo and Mexican Americans living along the border would convert Juan Nepomuceno Cortina—rancher, soldier, occasional cattle-rustler, and longtime resident of the border region—into what U.S. public opinion would label a bandit. In July of that year, Cortina chanced upon Deputy Sheriff Bob Spears beating a former family employee. Cortina intervened and, after Spears supposedly racially insulted Cortina, Cortina shot Spears in the shoulder. Fearing repercussion, Cortina fled to Mexico, whence he planned a daring raid that would shape the region and beyond for decades to come. Several months later, on September 28, Cortina returned to Texas ahead of a group of approximately seventy-five armed men, storming into Brownsville to settle a feud with Adolphus Glaveke, a German immigrant and longtime resident of the area who, in collusion with others, conspired to despoil the Mexican-origin community. Anglo American citizens used the raid to appeal to Washington for heightened security along the border, and, in response, the local police force, the Mexican military in Matamoros, the Texas Rangers, and the U.S. Army under Robert E. Lee were all mobilized to repel Cortina from the area. Consequently, Cortina found himself at the center of a transnational public dispute about the border and the place of Mexican Americans in the United States.

To make sense of the ensuing conflict, all parties quickly began a print campaign to advocate for their respective positions. Many in the English-language press sought to demonize Cortina and bring national attention to the status of Anglo settlers in the region, and the Spanish-language press similarly sought to advocate for the rights of Mexicans and Tejanos whom Cortina represented. In order to combat the pejorative characterization that circulated among the press, on November 23, 1859, Cortina issued a written proclamation in which he offered a scathing portrayal of south Texas. In the proclamation, one of several he would issue throughout his career, Cortina declares that the state was overrun by "flocks of vampires, in the guise of men."[2] These vampires "scattered themselves in the settlements" across the state, "without any capital except the corrupt heart and the most perverse intentions." When Cortina chastises the relatively recent Anglo settlers who flocked to the frontier as corrupt "vampires," he indicts them as a parody of manhood—a failure of these "vampires in the guise of men" to live up to dominative notions of male public identity.

In his proclamations, Cortina does more than invoke cultural understandings of manhood; he transforms the meaning of banditry even as he relies on its cultural significance. Cortina presents himself as a figure of transnational, democratic manhood by situating his actions within a U.S. revolutionary narrative that imagines the U.S. national project as but one of ongoing, hemispheric, republican, revolutionary projects. Here I identify the ways in which Latinos in the nineteenth century sought to imagine themselves as citizens of a U.S. nation, though often by extending the cultural imaginary across the border. Within a transnational or hemispheric frame, Cortina's actions and words take on a different light beyond the limitations of outlaw and bandit.

The place of Cortina's documents as literary performances, and the ramifications of understanding them within broader Latino print culture, has been historically neglected. Until very recently, historical memory has typically understood Cortina through the biased and often racist descriptions of official government documents. Cortina's dubious biography, similarly informed by these accounts, leaves him an ambiguous figure of republican idealism, yet the accusations of impropriety, illegality, or even treason must be remembered as a product of the racist political and social environment in which he lived. Nonetheless, Cortina (and the conflict he initiated) has subsequently been fixed in dominant U.S. history as an outlaw or bandit whose efforts demonstrated the inassimilability of the newly formed Mexican Americans. Conversely, Mexican American cultural tradition regards him as a rebel or social bandit who opposed the nation-state and its discriminatory policies. I suggest Cortina be understood in the tradition of U.S. anti-racist figures, like John Brown of Harpers Ferry, to which I return below; this is made apparent when his actions and the print legacy it inspired are examined. Cortina attempted to make himself and his fellow Mexican Americans legible on the national stage by pronouncing a kind of being, by inserting himself into familiar national manhood and expanding its categories of recognition. Rather than see Cortina as outside the U.S. nation-state, I suggest that through his proclamations he sought to interpellate Mexican Americans as national subjects.

Though the proclamations were in direct response to the events of 1859, they were informed by Cortina's lifelong experience living in an area far removed from a national center and of grappling with the lingering after-effects of tremendous national change. Born on May 16, 1824, in the state of Tamaulipas, Mexico, Juan Nepomuceno Cortina moved to the area around what is now Brownsville, Texas, at a very young age, spending much of his adolescence between there and the city of Matamoros in what was then Mexico. Cortina witnessed the arrival of Anglo settlers, many by invitation of the Mexican government, and the subsequent shifts in political allegiance and social landscape. During the

U.S.–Mexico War, Cortina fought for the Mexican Army under General Mariano Arista in the battles of Resaca de la Palma and Palo Alto, afterward returning to Brownsville as a rancher and occasional cattle rustler on both sides of the border. The experience of fighting on the losing side of this conflict left Cortina in a peculiar position, now formally a citizen of a new country and asked to choose between prior national loyalty and his connection to home and community.

Jerry Thompson's work provides the most current and complete account of Cortina's life and examines his life in relation to myriad changes affecting southern Texas in the mid–nineteenth century. Thompson points out the "immense nuances, contradictions, paradoxical views, and incredible survival instincts" that characterized Cortina but ultimately concludes that unlike many of the Mexican American civil rights leaders who would champion the Mexican American cause in the late twentieth century and who "tried to engender change by working within the existing social and political system, Cortina resorted to armed defense and rebellion at the end of a pistol," rendering him a "social bandit."[3] Thompson's biography is expertly researched, but absent from his study is an analysis of Cortina's position within hemispheric Latino print culture and as an early actor in American literary history. Within the Mexican national tradition, and more locally the Tejano, social banditry had a long-established cultural and political tradition and functioned as a mode of political will. As a military leader, Cortina was one of the first Mexican Americans to enter the U.S. national imaginary and offers a different history of Latinos in the United States. Moreover, in his literary performance, Cortina was actively drawing on and participating in a longstanding literary expressive tradition, one more easily recognizable to his Mexican contemporaries than to his American audience.

The Cortina Wars, as this episode is usually referred to, is more productively understood as Cortina's war to be read. Stories about Mexico, Mexicans, and the newly created Mexican Americans proliferated in both popular fiction and nonfiction in the decades following the U.S.–Mexico War, and Cortina became somewhat of a regional hero, making an appearance in several popular fictions that inscribe him as either outlaw or hero of resistance. Cortina was the central character in John Emerald's *Cortina, the Scourge of the Rio Grande* (1872), and he has cameos in both Jovita González and Margaret Eimer's *Caballero* (ca.

1936) and Américo Paredes's *George Washington Gómez* (ca. 1939), the last two being key texts of the early-twentieth-century Mexican American modernist movement. Yet in his own textual explanation of events, Cortina attempts to inscribe his actions within recognizable frameworks of national manhood. According to Dana Nelson, early U.S. national manhood became understood as a fraternal association of white men and intimately connected to civic duty, and "after the passage of the Constitution, the nation began forming and reforming institutional devices for policing men who failed in their national self-discipline. Such individuals were exteriorized from the civic body as alien—figured in terms of effeminacy, sedition, insanity, and criminality."[4] By focusing on the national center, her analysis provides a foundational account of how the nation imagined its citizenry as male public beings. But on the geographical margins of the United States, on the borderlands where national authority was less fixed and competing national interests reigned, such national manhood was less secure. How then were Mexican Americans to be viewed and included in the national whole? I identify the ways in which Latinos in the nineteenth century sought to imagine themselves as citizens of a U.S. nation, though often do so by extending the national cultural imaginary across the border. It is here that Cortina becomes so instructive.

Cortina's first proclamation was published on September 30, 1859, and a second proclamation followed shortly thereafter on November 23. In issuing these, Cortina called upon the Mexican *pronunciamiento* (proclamation) tradition to make himself and his actions legible in both English and Spanish to both U.S. and Mexican audiences. The documents were originally published as broadsides but immediately were printed and distributed in English- and Spanish-language newspapers. The proclamations were first published in the Matamoros newspaper *El Jaque* but thereafter reprinted in translation and with a rebuttal by the editor in Brownsville's *American Flag*.[5] A flurry of newspapers and official government correspondence began reporting on the events. Shortly thereafter, a copy of the proclamations and some of the key responses were included in the official U.S. *Congressional Record*, elevating the regional conflict to national significance.[6]

Cortina's actions were transmitted across the nation, in newspapers in Texas, New Orleans, Baltimore, New Mexico, South Carolina, and New

York, among others. On October 16, 1859, the New Orleans *Daily Pica-yune* published an editorial about Cortina's actions that framed the conflict as one of border control and enforcement, notably what the author, "a gentleman, long resident in Western Texas, and long acquainted with subject on which he writes," considered the "lamentable and humiliating" fact of the nation's failure to protect its southern border. In an effort to drum up sympathy for the Anglo position in the conflict, the author laments how those who "were induced to settle [there] under the protection of the stars and stripes, . . . now appeal in vain for some powerful arm to stay the law defiant and life destroying hand."[7] Calling for U.S. Army resettlement of the border posts, and in response to the departure of the Matamoros Army, one resident of Brownsville writes to "let the great guns again watch over our dear sister Matamoros, and the soldiers of Uncle Samuel keep marauders here in check, or practically the line of boundary between the United States and Mexico must be moved back to the nueces [*sic*]," recalling the much-contested strip of land between the Nueces and Rio Grande that contributed to the outset of hostilities a decade earlier.[8] The New Orleans *Daily True Delta* reported that "our whole Mexican border to the distance of about 1500 miles, is completely shorn of the least protection, let the emergency be what it may, and it may well be remarked that a parallel case is nowhere to be found in the civilized world."[9]

Those living nearer to the centers of the U.S. nation would have been perplexed by the events occurring at the nation's edges. The Arkansas *State Gazette* published an interview with Mr. Kinney, editor of the *Brownsville Flag*, the newspaper that originally reported the Cortina conflict.[10] New Yorkers were perhaps troubled to learn that "to the loyalty and just conduct of the neighboring military and civil authorities of Mexico we are greatly indebted for our present security"[11] while Columbus, Georgia's *Daily Inquirer* reported the events, explaining the item to its readers as "highly important intelligence" and adding that "meetings were held daily in Brownsville and contributions were taken up for the support of the Mexican troops."[12] The *Philadelphia Inquirer* somewhat sarcastically states that "orderly citizens had nothing to fear, his object being to chastise his enemies—the Sheriff and the Lawyers," absolving Cortina's vindictiveness but undermining the impulse for justice and order that Cortina sought to explain.[13]

Though by most accounts Cortina was thought to be illiterate, he nonetheless is credited with the content of these proclamations, if not their scribing. Authorship is attributed either to a Mexican journalist and revolutionary, Miguel Peña; one of the well-educated Cortinistas such as Jesús Ballí; or Cortina's brother José María, though most scholars and Cortina contemporaries consider Peña the most likely source.[14] Regardless, there is little doubt that the ideas contained within the proclamations were Cortina's own. The content of the proclamations, in part and sometimes in whole, was repeatedly transcribed and repeated in a variety of official and personal correspondence. The general public was uncertain of what to make of the documents, and the opposing parties struggled to explain the documents for their respective audiences.

For Cortina, it was the press that carried his message to the region and the nation, the press that both vilified him and sought to defend him. His proclamations were part of the larger circulation of newspaper stories, government correspondence, and popular fiction that covered and responded to the events in south Texas. The vibrant print culture that included newspapers "were community leadership institutions [and] assumed an importance parallel to that of the church and the mutualist society in providing leadership, solidifying the community, protecting it and furthering its cultural survival."[15] Cortina periodically disrupted and controlled the mail service, intercepting the mail carriers all along the Rio Grande, from the Gulf of Mexico at least as far upward as Rio Grande City.[16] As in all wars, knowledge and information is vital to victory, but in a time when letters were the primary means of communication, the dissemination of texts was doubly integral to controlling the course of events.

One method of distributing information was by public proclamation. Proclamations were a fairly common genre, especially in Mexico but elsewhere as well. The large sheets were designed to be displayed in prominent public spaces where they could be read aloud to the illiterate sectors of the population. As a statement of official policy and public concern, proclamations were used to communicate government actions with the population. Most famously in the United States is the decree that ended slavery, the Emancipation Proclamation, yet in Mexico the proclamation also had a public life. The Mexican nation-state itself was founded by a proclamation, now known as Miguel Hidalgo's "*Grito de*

Dolores," that was published and read aloud in 1810. In 1846, at the outset of the U.S.–Mexico War, Francisco Mejia, commander of Matamoros and at one time of the Mexican Army of the north, offered a scathing indictment of U.S. colonial aggression and its impact of international sovereignty through a proclamation that was intended to be distributed throughout the army and civilian populations, an act with which Cortina was likely familiar.[17]

Cortina's proclamations fit into the description of Latino print culture adeptly and meticulously described by Raúl Coronado. Building upon what Coronado has called a "history of textuality," not just a history of high fiction but of the networks of distribution and consumption across a wide array of genre and form and the "surrounding ideas that inform" writing, Cortina's proclamations can be understood as part of a broader print world that extends from Mexico City to Washington and beyond.[18] Underscoring the importance of writing in the development of a Latino modernity, Coronado has shown how Latinos in Texas and "the rest of the Southwest, too, began to seek out printing presses. . . . as a means to imagine a world where political authority rested in the inhabitants of the new nation-state."[19] Cortina provides a "language that would allow these individuals to practice new personhoods, to enact new ways of imagining community" that draw upon a cultural, political, and literary tradition that exists within and between nations, however fraught, incomplete, unsatisfactory, and ultimately unsuccessful such calls might have been. What people read varied widely, and non-narrative literary forms, including the (bilingual) press, were key vehicles for the dissemination of ideas in the region. If the printing press was used as a way of articulating and asserting competing visions of sovereignty, Cortina's proclamations suggest a notion of national belonging fully within the U.S. nation-state yet informed by his experience as a Mexican citizen. Understanding the transnational print culture of Cortina's proclamations helps elucidate the double logic that motivates its content—asserting U.S. citizenship while claiming his Mexican-ness.

Yet, the double logic of a transnational cultural orientation was lost on many of Cortina's contemporaries. For many readers concerned with an impending race war (Cortina's raid happened within weeks of John Brown's attack at Harpers Ferry), it was easier to understand the racial tensions of the region as an unfortunate escalation of a duel, a common literary and cultural trope for southern manhood. Some tried to dismiss his actions as nothing more than a personal feud gone awry. *The Southern Intelligencer* described the raids as "private revenge," a letter from the self-organized "committee of safety" to President James Buchanan states it as an attempt to remedy a "private grudge,"[20] and the *New Orleans Picayune* contends the "quarrel is wholly a family one."[21] But undermining the press's characterization of Cortina as outlaw or personal vendetta is a tension about his manhood. The Anglo press acknowledged that Cortina was "lionized by principal citizens there, we are told, as a hero."[22] Cortina's behavior is "formidable and dangerous" and he possessed "extraordinary influence."[23] The *Southern Intelligencer* states that "the man shows great skill as well as courage" nervously noting that "he seems to wait his time and opportunity, and this with a self-reliance and firmness of purpose which may well give a pause," puzzling over the "enigma" of how he maintains his force.[24] The author endows Cortina with many of the masculine ideals prevalent in the national imaginary at that time—he possesses "skill," "courage," and entrepreneurial acumen to maintain a large military force without the support of the state, but at all times his abilities are kept in check by his self-control and commitment to his goals. The author's warning to "give a pause," then, asks what it means when a racialized body possesses the very characteristics used to assert heteronormative privilege.

Cortina's forces, whose numbers were estimated at anywhere from 100 to 1,500 men, not only posed a military threat but also served as an example of his masculine performance, merging what Amy Greenberg has seen as often-competing ideas: "restrained" and "martial manhood."[25] This appropriation of competing manhoods troubled many Anglos. In a letter to Texas Ranger John "Rip" Ford seeking military aid, Mr. Hale complained about the "insecurity of life and property, the stagnation of trade," and, most tellingly, the "*disastrous effect upon our national character abroad*, which this state of affairs has produced."[26] Mr. Hale appeals to his reader's sense of "national character," the perception of integrity, pride, and manhood which Cortina's raids "exposed at every moment [and] in which their lives, fortunes, and honor are to be risked."

In defining the Mexican American "race," Cortina uses the vocabulary of manhood that would have been immediately recognizable to his southern and northern contemporaries as manly.[27] Explaining Texas

Mexicans to his readers, Cortina describes them as possessing "genial affability," "humility, simplicity, and docility, directed with dignity," an "irresistible inclination towards ideas of equality," and "adorned with the most lovely disposition towards all that is good and useful in the line of progress," qualities that would ring as manly virtues. At the same time, he demands justice for those who wronged him or "leave them to become subject to the consequences of our immutable resolve"—in short, challenging them to a duel.[28]

Cortina's proclamations draw on dominant U.S. notions of manhood in the justification of his actions. As he writes, Cortina industriously dedicates himself to "constant labor" and paints himself as hardworking, unwavering, and invested above all in the prosperity of his fellow man who are also "honorably and exclusively dedicated to the exercise of industry." His bandit manhood is then confident and courageous, not the rigid machismo often associated with banditry, but rather in deliberate concert with a feminized sense of mutual freedom, what he called "sisterhood of liberty." Cortina readily accepts the label of bandit, stating "If, my dear compatriots, I am honored with the name, I am ready for the combat," but he added that only if offered with an explanation of its qualities."[29]

Both Cortina and the nation tried to understand his exploits in terms of national manhood, but antebellum notions of manhood were intimately connected to national citizenship, which in its strict association to a single nation-state limited the degree to which Cortina was read. However, Cortina's sense of national belonging transgressed national boundaries, thereby challenging his readers' notions of both manhood and citizenship. In his first proclamation, Cortina claims he aims only "to chastise the villainy of our enemies" who "form, so to speak, a perfidious inquisitorial lodge to persecute and rob us, without any cause, and for no other crime on our part than that of being of Mexican origin."[30] Cortina makes abundantly clear the racial prejudice that dominates the Texas social structure but excuses his use of violence as the state's inability to meet its obligations to its own citizens, stating bluntly, "inasmuch as justice, being administered by their own hands, the supremacy of the law has failed to accomplish its object." He elevates democratic values above national affiliation in efforts to justify his actions and make them legible across national borders.

The failure of the nation-state animates his position as a U.S. citizen, and Cortina's proclamation is as much a declaration of U.S. citizenship as it is a declamation of racial injustice. Cortina imagines himself within the ideals of emancipatory citizenship, as "a part of the confederacy" that champions the rights of its citizens, calling on the government "for the sake of its own dignity, and in obsequiousness to justice," to come to the aid of Texas Mexicans. His statements bear quoting at length as it sets the terms for a vexed nationalism:

> And how can it be otherwise, when the ills that weigh upon the un-fortunate republic of Mexico have obliged us for many heart-touching causes to abandon it and our possessions in it, or else become the vic-tims of our principles or of the indigence to which its intestine distur-bances had reduced us since the treaty [*sic*] of Guadalupe? when, ever diligent and industrious, and desirous of enjoying the longed-for boon of liberty within the classic country of its origin, we were induced to naturalize ourselves in it and form a part of the confederacy, flattered by the bright and peaceful prospect of living therein and inculcating in the bosoms of our children a feeling of gratitude towards a country beneath whose aegis we would have wrought their felicity and contributed with our conduct to give evidence to the whole world that all the aspirations of the Mexicans are confined to one only, that of being freemen; and that having secured this ourselves, those of the old country, notwithstanding their misfortunes, might have nothing to regret save the loss of a section of territory, but with the sweet satisfaction that their old fellow citizens lived therein, enjoying tranquility, as if Providence had so ordained to set them an example of the advantages to be derived from public peace and quietude.[31]

For "diligent and industrious" Cortina, it is the failure of the Mexican nation-state that has led Texas Mexicans, perhaps with regret, to "aban-don" Mexico and become U.S. citizens. The shift in national affiliation was not taken lightly, but a calculated risk lest Texas Mexicans "become the victims of our principals," the victims of national loyalty over self-preservation. In Cortina's words, Texas Mexicans worked diligently to prosper and uphold order, but when circumstances of fate required them to switch national allegiance, they did so willingly. Cortina's sense of citizenship moves fluidly between nations, perhaps a consequence of the war or an early articulation of cultural nationalism, but Cortina publicly states his willingness to leave behind ties to Mexico (the "old country") and to "their old fellow citizens" in exchange for the "advantages derived from public peace," "liberty," and being "freemen." "Desirous of enjoying the longed-for boon of liberty within the classic country of its origin," Texas Mexicans value democratic ideals over the authority of any single nation-state, crediting the United States with the creation of republican ideals and thereby explaining their desire to become American. His commitment to the U.S. nation-state would have been complete had Texas Mexicans not been "defrauded in the most cruel manner" and left with no option other than to retaliate and "destroy the obstacles to our prosperity."[32]

Casting himself as a champion of justice, Cortina seeks to rewrite the Mexican American male as a defender of the rights putatively guaranteed by the state. Through literary figuration and performance, Cortina charges banditry with both moral and revolutionary purpose and transforms his actions into patriotic protest by revealing a language of rebellion familiar to U.S. audiences. Cortina self-consciously sought to envelop his raids within a rhetoric of revolutionary right that framed his activities within nationalist movements, both U.S. and Mexican. Cortina's proclamations fit squarely within various regional, nationalist movements of the mid–nineteenth century, including Texas's own independence movement and those of 1850s Mexico, especially the Plan de Ayutla (1854) that called for the overthrow of Santa Anna and that sets the stage for Benito Juárez's liberal government and Constitution of 1857. The Plan de Ayutla sought to establish a democratic republic "sin otra restricción que la de respetar inviolablemente las garantías individuales" (without other restriction except the inviolable respect for individual rights) but uses masculinist tropes in defining national belonging, grounding its claims by "usando de los mismos derechos de que usaron nuestros padres en 1821" (using the same rights that our forefathers used in 1821), the year the Spanish recognized Mexican independence.[33] Where Cortina staunchly defends the "sacred right of self-preservation," he uses the word *inviolable* three times in just these two proclamations: discussing the "inviolable laws"; how "Hospitality and other noble sentiments. . . . are inviolable to us"; and "orderly people and honest citizens are inviolable to us in their persons and interests," foregrounding ideological commitment over personal retribution.[34]

At the same time, Cortina's banditry attempts to locate Mexican American manhood within a tradition of patriotic resistance and national defense resounding of the founding fathers and the United States' national origin story. Cortina's proclamation recalls Thomas Paine, who in *Thoughts on Defensive War* praises "a point to view this matter in of superior consequence to the defence of property; and that point is *Liberty* in all its meanings."[35] Historians have shown that for Paine, "creating a viable national identity for Americans other than through their customary association with Britain [a competing national presence] was a crucial part of the revolutionary process," yet here the revolutionary process itself becomes a crucial part of the creation of a viable national identity.[36] Eric Foner states that among Paine's contributions to revolutionary America, "the politicization of the mass of Philadelphians— from the master craftsmen to a significant segment of the laborers and poor—was the most important development in Philadelphia's political life in the decade before independence."[37] Foner holds that this politicization helped mobilize a nascent nation otherwise culturally indistinct from England; that process was made possible through literature and through the inception of an imagined reading public. Cortina's proclamation makes an analogous statement that attempts to mobilize the local populace, composed mostly of Texas Mexicans with a minority Anglo U.S. population, in support of his ideals and in opposition to an absent national government unable to provide for the defense of its borders. In Cortina's narratives, the revolutionary process itself becomes a crucial part of the creation of a viable Mexican American identity, one that elevates democratic ideals above national boundaries.[38]

The proclamation makes clear that Texas Mexicans are separated by "accident alone, from the other citizens of the city," and that they act explicitly "*not* having renounced our rights as North American citizens." Cortina and his followers "disapprove, and energetically protest, against the act of having caused a force of the National Guards from Mexico to cross unto this side to ingraft themselves in questions so foreign to their country that there is no excusing such weakness on the part of those who implored their aid."[39] Cortina's U.S. citizenship is juxtaposed with that of Anglo Texans who looked to Mexican enforcement, whose proximity provided a more rapid response to the area disagreements. As Cortina would tell it, his choice for self-defense is a more American action than that of those who sought the aid of a foreign government, and he reframes the threat to U.S. sovereignty not in his assault on Brownsville but on the Anglo Texans' call to the Mexican National Guard, inviting a foreign army into the country. While in some aspects Cortina's literary banditry functions within transnational revolutionary movements, his literary performance of that rebellion reinforces U.S. authority in the region. By reigniting revolutionary discourses, Cortina suggests a U.S. national project still in the making and locates the United States within ongoing hemispheric revolutions.

Though Cortina may not have explicitly modeled his proclamations on the founding documents of the United States, the proclamations resound with the rhetoric of republican revolution that situates Mexican American armed protest not apart from but within democratic national projects. Cortina was heavily invested in hemispheric revolutionary movements and was committed to the liberal reforms. Throughout the 1860s, he fought alongside Juárez and against the French intervention, until Porfirio Díaz imprisoned him in 1876. His proclamations need to be understood within transnational movements for democracy, one pursued both in the United States and in Mexico, both against the nation-state but also in cooperation with it. Transforming revolutionary manhood into an act citizenship, Cortina was able to textualize his actions to resonate with public understandings of national obligation, manhood, and the duties of citizenship. As the Brownsville Committee of Safety put it, many could now "believe him to be the man he represents himself in his proclamations."[40] Yet despite Cortina's efforts to make his actions recognizable if not sympathetic to a U.S. audience, he is primarily regarded in the popular imaginary as an outlaw, a temporary aberration to the otherwise inevitable affirmation of southern Texas as a U.S. national space, a struggle over interpretation that has persisted for more than a century and a half. The Cortina Wars, however, would herald the racial and economic tensions that just a few years later would lead to civil war; in this light, Cortina must be reimagined as part of a broader struggle against racial inequality. During the occupation of Brownsville, the *New York Times* stated, "public attention is at this moment diverted from the outbreak at Harpers Ferry to one of another sort."[41] Unlike Harpers Ferry, which Cortina's actions anticipated by about three weeks and which remains in historical memory as a justified yet doomed revolt conducted in the name of freedom and justice, Cortina's actions are labeled seditionist and secessionist.[42]

When John Brown began organizing his rebellion against slavery, he composed a document intended to give direction and explanation for his actions. Brown's "Provisional Constitution and Ordinance for the People of the United States" is a lengthy treatise that reaffirmed the principles of the United States' own constitution. Brown hoped the document would "provide an administrative and moral framework for the egalitarian, interracial provisional state that Brown planned to establish. . . . and would serve as a model charter for the free and reunited nation as a whole."[43] An active abolitionist, Brown aspired to end slavery, to extend the principles of freedom and equality to the universality stated in the founding documents, and to serve as both a practical and representative model for how such changes could be enacted. Toward the end of his "Provisional Constitution," Brown states "the foregoing articles shall not be construed so as in any way to encourage the overthrow of any State government, or of the General Government of the United States, and look to no dissolution of the Union, but simply to Amendment and Repeal. And our Flag shall be the same that our Fathers fought under in the Revolution."[44] Brown makes explicit his commitment to the country, his position as a concerned citizen of the United States, and his intention to preserve the union with an expanded and renewed sense of justice and equality. Brown's raid on the arsenal ultimately failed; he was quickly surrounded and captured (by Robert E. Lee no less, who would go almost directly from West Virginia to southern Texas), tried (despite his protestations, his attorney submitted a plea of insanity), and shortly thereafter hanged for treason. The immediate national response to Brown's raid was mixed if not polarized, some decrying the insanity and immorality of the plot while others lauded his abolitionist aspirations, and by most accounts hastening the national rift that led to civil war. Though immediately following the events at Harpers Ferry many stood aghast at the audacity and violence of Brown's actions, subsequent historical memory has vindicated his actions as a pivotal step toward emancipation.[45]

Perhaps the differences in historical memory can be explained by the ambiguous legal and racial status of Latinos, or perhaps it is the affiliation with a rival nation and the way such sentiments shift racial characteristics to national ones that deny Cortina a place within U.S. history. However, as literary performances, Cortina's proclamations need to be reconsidered for the way they expand and revise claims for U.S. manhood and citizenship. Cortina textualized his actions to make them familiar, to resonate with public understandings of national obligation and with the duties of citizenship. Cortina bases his claims to citizenship on "the sacred right of self-preservation," the natural rights that both precede and derive from national law. Cortina goes to great lengths to downplay the violence in his actions. He is "horrified at the thought of having to shed innocent blood" and reports to be "loth [sic] to attack," odd words for a career soldier.[46] He laments the way the events were portrayed, stating "it behooves us to maintain that it was unjust to give the affair such a terrible aspect, and to represent it as of a character foreboding evil."[47] Rather than think of the bandit as a figure who operates outside of accepted social order, as an entity who uses violence out of a disregard for society and its institutions, Cortina emphasizes shared democratic ideals that cross race and nation. As banditry moves from armed resistance to literary representation, it presents the possibility for Mexican American manhood to move from regional conflict to national manhood by imagining Mexican Americans within the American body politic. In his writings, Cortina is made the champion of American democracy and republican virtue rather than a figure of resistance to the nation-state, a distinction that enables a revised conception of the role of Latinos in U.S. cultural history.

NOTES

1   See Richard Griswold del Castillo, *The Treaty of Guadalupe Hidalgo: A Legacy of Conflict* (Norman: University of Oklahoma Press, 1990) and David Potter, *The Impending Crisis* (New York: HarperCollins, 1976).

2   U.S. Congress, House, *Difficulties on the Southwestern Frontier*, 36th Congress; 1st Session, 1860, H. Exec. Doc. 52, 70–82; hereafter cited as *DSF*. All citations are from the English version of Cortina's Proclamation reproduced in *DSF*. Cortina issued two proclamations in late 1859, one dated September 30 and the other quoted above, and would continue to issue proclamations periodically during his active military and political career over the subsequent three decades. An original copy of the 1859 proclamations can be found in the National Archives. The proclamations are also reproduced in Jerry D. Thompson, *Juan Cortina and the Texas-Mexico Frontier, 1859–1877* (El Paso: Texas Western Press, 1994).

3 Jerry Thompson, *Cortina: Defending the Mexican Name in Texas* (College Station: Texas A&M University Press, 2007), 251–52.

4 Dana D. Nelson, *National Manhood: Capitalist Citizenship and the Imagined Fraternity of White Men* (Durham, N.C.: Duke University Press, 1998), 13.

5 Brownsville, *American Flag Extra*, October 1, 1859.

6 *Difficulties in the Southwestern Frontier* is part of the official records of the first session of the House of Representatives, 36th Congress, executive document #52.

7 Western Texan [pseud.], "The Defences of Western Texas," *New Orleans Daily Picayune*, October 16, 1859, 3.

8 "The Late Attack on Brownsville: Cortina, the Leader, and His Character," *New Orleans Daily Picayune*, October 19, 1859, 1.

9 "Texas Items," *New Orleans Daily True Delta*, 14 October 1859, 5.

10 "Affairs on the Rio Grande," *Arkansas State Gazette Democrat*, October 22, 1859.

11 "Retirement of the Mexican Guerillas," *New York Tribune*, October 19, 1859, 6.

12 "Attack Upon Brownsville by Guerrillas: Five Men Murdered," *Columbus Daily Enquirer*, October 15, 1859, 2.

13 "From Northern Mexico, and Brownsville, Texas," *Philadelphia Inquirer*, October 20, 1859, 1.

14 Thompson, 46–47.

15 Nicolás Kanellos with Helvetia Martell, *Hispanic Periodicals in the United States* (Houston: Arte Público Press, 2000), 7.

16 U.S. Congress, House, *Troubles on the Texas Frontier*, 36th Congress; 1st Session, 1860, H. Exec. Doc. 81, 7–10.

17 Messages of the President of the United States, *Mexican War Correspondence*, Exec. Doc. 60, 127.

18 Raúl Coronado, *A World Not to Come: A History of Latino Writing and Print Culture* (Cambridge, Mass.: Harvard University Press, 2013), 20.

19 Ibid., 26.

20 *DSF*, 21.

21 Ibid., 40.

22 Ibid., 39.

23 Ibid., 21.

24 "Later from Brownsville. Another Fight—Cortina Victorious!! Full Particulars," Austin *Southern Intelligencer*, November 9, 1859, 2.

25 Amy S. Greenberg, *Manifest Manhood and the Antebellum American Empire* (Cambridge: Cambridge University Press, 2005), 11.

26 *DSF*, 42, emphasis added.

27 For a discussion of southern manhood, see Craig Thompson Friend and Lorri Glover, eds. *Southern Manhood* (Athens: University of Georgia Press, 2004); Craig Thompson Friend, ed., *Southern Masculinity* (Athens: University of Georgia Press, 2009), and Nina Silber, *The Romance of Reunion* (Chapel Hill: University of North Carolina Press, 1993).

28 *DSF*, 72.

29 *DSF*, 80.
30 Elsewhere he talks of "secret conclaves" and "shadowy councils," both of which would resonate with male homosocial secret societies then prevalent. See Mark Carnes, *Secret Ritual and Manhood in Victorian America* (New Haven, Conn.: Yale University Press, 1989).
31 Cortina, "Proclamation," *DSF*, September 30, 1859, 71–72.
32 This excerpt, like much of the Pronunciamientos, is written in long, sprawling sentences, with numerous appositional phrases interrupting the flow of his assertions. The appositions provide useful description and needed contextualization of the events Cortina narrates, but the syntactic breakup of the narrative imparts a sense of dislocation that formally reflects Cortina's own condition of provisional control. At once conversational, distancing, and disruptive, the text undermines the authority of the written document even as it utilizes it to assert its command of the events. Through repeated intervention in the structure of his own narrative, Cortina reminds the reader of the failures of the nation-state and interjects on behalf of the Texas Mexican community, calling for new interpretations and new voices.
33 Unless otherwise noted, all translations from the Spanish are my own.
34 While he espoused the republican values of Benito Juárez's presidency and the Constitution of 1857, in 1876–77 Cortina sided with soon-to-be dictator Porfirio Díaz, believing Díaz to be the best hope for a liberal, democratic government in Mexico. In a proclamation, Cortina "invite[s], in the name of the public liberties, all Mexican[s] who love their institutions, and who in other times fought with me in defense of liberty, to rally around the flag which is unfurled by the well-merited General Porfirio Díaz, because it is the symbol of the constitution of '57, under whose shad alone can be given to the people of Mexico a truly republican government." The "Proclamation, Azcapotzalco, 18 May 1876," is quoted in Thompson, *Juan Cortina*, 88.
35 Thomas Paine, *The Writings of Thomas Paine, 4 Volumes*, ed. Moncure Daniel Conway (New York: G. P. Putnam's Sons, 1894), 56.
36 Edward Larkin, "Inventing an American Public: Thomas Paine, the Pennsylvania Magazine, and American Revolutionary Political Discourse," *Early America Literature* 33.3 (1998): 270.
37 Eric Foner, *Tom Paine and Revolutionary America* (New York: Oxford University Press, 2005 [1976]), 56.
38 While I argue that Cortina wrote in a revolutionary literary tradition, he was not alone. Cuban filibusters such as Miguel T. Tolón explicitly drew on or translated Paine's work. For a discussion of Paine's influence on Cuban revolutionaries, see Rodrigo Lazo, *Writing to Cuba: Filibustering and Cuban Exiles in the United States* (Chapel Hill: University of North Carolina Press, 2005).
39 Cortina, "Pronunciamiento," September 30, 1859.
40 *DSF*, 75.

41 "The Texas Border Outbreak," *New York Times*, November 9, 1859, 4. The news was also reprinted as "The Brownsville Affair—the Leader," *Chicago Tribune*, November 12, 1859, 2.

42 Numerous claims were made that northern Mexico was a refuge for runaway slaves. To illustrate one way in which Mexico was portrayed as a haven for lawlessness and racial ambiguity, the New Orleans *Daily Picayune*, February 14, 1859, recounts a racist anecdote of a runaway slave, Big Jim, who became an officer in the Mexican Army. When the United States invaded Monterrey during the U.S.–Mexico War, the newspaper mockingly stated, "no doubt Big Jim is now a general. In Texas, he was known far and wide as an appropriator of other people's chickens."

43 Evan Carter, *Patriotic Treason: John Brown and the Soul of America* (New York: Free Press, 2006), 242.

44 John Brown, "Provisional Constitution," Article XLVI.

45 For a collection of concurrent accounts and Brown's influence on his contemporaries, see John Stauffer and Zoe Trodd, eds., *The Tribunal: Responses to John Brown and the Harpers Ferry Raid* (Cambridge, Mass.: Belknap Press of Harvard University Press, 2012); for Brown as a pioneer of civil rights, see David Reynolds, *John Brown, Abolitionist* (New York: Vintage, 2006).

46 *DSF*, 70.

47 Ibid.

10

Raimundo Cabrera, the Latin American Archive, and the Latina/o Continuum

CARMEN E. LAMAS

In this chapter I argue for the importance of the Latin American archive for Latina/o studies.[1] I do so for two reasons. First, a concerted entry into this archive furnishes new information concerning the Latina/o experience. This is so because many Latina/os, particularly but not exclusively in the nineteenth century, lived their lives across national boundaries, not infrequently traveling from their home countries to the United States and back again. Because they often wrote in Spanish (as opposed to English), their works are published primarily, though not exclusively, in their home countries or in countries where the Spanish language is the primary linguistic medium. As such their lives, both written and lived, are to be recovered from the Latin American archive and would otherwise be unknown in the absence of this resource. Second, the types of materials we find in the nineteenth-century Latin American archive demand that we ask new questions of the Latina/o experience, and they command new answers to such questions. Specifically, to study the Latin American archive in the course of recovering Latina/o voices and lives of the nineteenth century calls one to question the very nature of Latina/o identity and what this implies, in turn, for not only Latina/o studies but American and Latin American studies as well.

This dual phenomenon—the capacity for the Latin American archive to lead to the recovery of new Latina/o voices and lives *and* to illustrate new dimensions of, indeed a new mode of understanding, Latina/o identity—is well illustrated in four works by the Cuban intellectual Raimundo Cabrera (1852–1923). Cabrera was prolific: He was a novelist, poet, and autobiographer; he composed *zarzuelas*; and he was an accomplished journalist. The works here selected, while not representative of his entire oeuvre, nevertheless serve to encapsulate his own complex relationship to the United States. I demonstrate how the Philadelphia publication and later English translation of Cabrera's well-known work *Cuba y sus jueces: rectificaciones oportunas* (1887) (trans. *Cuba and the Cubans*, 1896) opens the historical record to two long-time U.S. residents, the brothers Pedro José and Eusebio Guiteras, whose work has to date been studied only from a Latin American perspective.[2] Analyzing this text further allows for the recovery of the translator of the work, Laura Guiteras, who was previously unknown in the study of Latina/o literature and history.

Second, I examine Cabrera's serialized fictive war memoir *Episodios de la guerra. Mi vida en la manigua* (1897–98), arguing that with it Cabrera, who lived less than two years in the United States, inserted himself into the longstanding Latina/o communities in New York and Florida of the late 1890s.[3] In effect, Cabrera transformed himself, a short-term Cuban exile, into a prominent member of Latina/o political and cultural circles through the war memoir genre. Third and finally, I study Cabrera's Spanish translation of Andrew Carnegie's very popular *Triumphant Democracy or Fifty Years' March of the Republic* (1886), which appeared under the title *Los Estados Unidos. Reducción de la obra "Triumphant Democracy" de Mr. Andrew Carnegie; con notas, aplicaciones y comentarios* in 1889, arguing that Cabrera's rendering interpolates not only Cabrera into Carnegie's text but also the United States into Cuba and, more important, Cuba into the United States.[4]

These three studies together illustrate the complex manner in which Latina/o identity was formed in the nineteenth century. Indeed, the lives of the persons examined in this chapter, most particularly Cabrera himself but also his translator, Laura Guiteras, and her two uncles, illustrate what I refer to as the Latina/o continuum. Frederick Aldama speaks of a "continuum of literary production" when he refers to how such writers as Gary Soto, Rolando Hinojosa-Smith, and Jimmy Santiago Baca, among others, began writing in the 1960s and 1970s and continue to publish to the present day. He believes that in this extended literary production, these authors are "transgressing period[s] bound by historical dates and offering instead a continuum of Latino literary production."[5]

I propose a different deployment of the term in that I speak of a Latina/o continuum that is constituted and comes about simultaneously in and beyond space and time, suggesting that figures like Cabrera represent a sort of identity that is not entirely Latin American (in this case Cuban) and not entirely U.S. American. Nor is it merely transnational, which is ultimately still tied to the geographic/spatial; rather, it is a sort of identity that simultaneously occupies multiple spatialities while inhabiting and crossing diverse temporal moments. It had, to be sure, a significant hand in shaping Latinidad in the nineteenth century and down to the present day.

The Philadelphia Editions of *Cuba y sus jueces*

When Raimundo Cabrera stepped on U.S. soil in 1896 his arrival was preceded by the publication in the United States of an extended Spanish-language edition (1891) and an English translation (1896) of his best-known book, *Cuba y sus jueces*. Both works were published in Philadelphia by the Levytype Company, a company referred to in the November 1898 issue of *The Printer and Bookmaker* as "the official organ, in Spanish, of the Cuban Junta in New York."[6] The work in question offered a historical overview and sociological analysis of Cuba and its people, customs, and history. A response to the pro-Spanish pamphlet published in Madrid, *Cuba y su gente (Apuntes para la historia)* (1887), by the Spaniard Francisco Moreno, Cabrera wrote the work in order to counter negative depictions of Cubans as lazy, lacking culture, and having a proclivity toward criminality.[7] *Cuba y sus jueces* had been published first in Havana in 1887, and in that year alone appeared in four editions, along with four additional print-runs in the next decade. In what follows I will examine the two U.S. editions, illustrating the ways in which they each were modified for their U.S. audiences and how these modifications—and the identity of the translator—serve to make evident a Latina/o community in late-nineteenth-century Philadelphia (and beyond) about which virtually nothing was known before engagement with these sources.[8]

By inquiring as to the identity of the work's translator, Laura Guiteras, we can begin to trace the intellectual exchanges occurring between Latina/os in the United States in the mid- to late nineteenth century. While the voices and lives of individuals like Laura Guiteras have been largely lost to history, works by such individuals as Cabrera, who also published two diaries of his U.S. travels, help us to reconstruct their lives and those of their communities.

Cabrera had met the Guiteras family on his 1891 visit to Philadelphia, a meeting he documents in his published compilation of letters, which detail his travel experiences from Key West to New York and is titled *Cartas a Govín. Impresiones de viaje. Primera serie* (1892).[9] Cabrera also published a second series of letters titled *Cartas a Govín. Sobre la exposición de Chicago. Impresiones de viaje. Segunda serie* (1893) detailing not only his experiences at the 1892 Chicago Exposition but also his travels through the Midwest and then in upstate New York.[10] These works, a must-read for scholars of nineteenth-century Latina/o literature and history, are filled with rich geographic and cultural details, including short observations about race relations in the United States. Moreover, they allow us to reconstruct the presence of longstanding Latina/o communities he encounters not only in Philadelphia but also in Thomasville, Georgia, where he comes across 300 Cuban cigar workers.

Laura Guiteras was the daughter of Antonio Guiteras; she was born in Matanzas, Cuba, in 1856. Her family, pro-independence advocates, fled to the United States with the outbreak of the Ten Years War. She first resided in New York City and later married William K. Martin of Philadelphia. She dedicates her translation of Cabrera's book to her uncle Eusebio Guiteras, and, as it turns out, Laura Guiteras was herself a member of a well-known family in Cuban literary and cultural circles, for she had *two* intellectually prominent uncles on her father's side: the aforementioned Eusebio and his brother, Pedro José Guiteras. While these two Cuban intellectuals have been claimed by Cuban studies, their U.S. experiences have gone largely undocumented by Cuban studies scholars, and they have not been recovered for Latina/o studies.[11]

Eusebio Guiteras was an educator and the author of the very popular multi-volume Spanish-language readers *Libros de lectura* (1856, 1857, 1858, and 1868). Published in the United States and Cuba, they were used in schools throughout Latin America in the nineteenth century. According to Luisa Campuzano, the first volume had thirteen editions by 1898.[12] These books were used not only to teach children who knew Spanish how to read but also to teach Spanish to English speakers in the United States. Eusebio first traveled to the United States in 1848, returning to Matanzas in 1853. He lived in Cuba in the 1860s but permanently returned to the United States in 1869 and lived there until his death in 1893.

Also well known to scholars of Cuba but almost entirely unknown in Latina/o and American studies was her second uncle, Pedro José Guiteras, who lived in the United States from 1853 to 1890. While residing in Rhode Island, he wrote *Historia de la conquista de la Havana (1762)*, published in 1856, as well as the two-volume *Historia de la isla de Cuba* (1865–66). He revised his two-volume *Historia* from 1882 to 1883 while residing in Baltimore, and the second editions were finally published in Cuba in 1927 and 1928 by the anthropologist Fernando Ortiz.[13] Pedro José Guiteras died in Charleston, South Carolina, in 1890.

Pedro José's recovered residence in the United States will lead scholars to ponder a fundamental question, one that will open a new area of scholarship: How does an author's residence in the United States (in this instance for almost forty years) affect his or her work (in this case the writing of Cuban history in and from Rhode Island)? Pedro José lived, wrote, and published books on Cuban history from the U.S. antebellum period to the height of the Civil War and through Reconstruction while Cuba was in the midst of its own struggle for independence from Spain, a struggle that included long debates about Afro-Cuban participation in the movement. During most of his lifetime, universal freedom was not granted for Cuban slaves, but instead the *Ley Moret* of 1870 established a process of gradual abolition through the *patronato* system.[14] One can only imagine the theoretical and disciplinary implications of the answer to such a question, especially in relation to Pedro José's own experience with race and race relations in the United States. Recognizing from *where* texts are written, as Rodrigo Lazo has so elegantly analyzed in his work on Cirilo Villaverde, leads one to question *how* location and residence affect the work at hand—in this case, not the writing of fiction but that of history itself.[15]

Laura Guiteras's 1896 translation of Cabrera's book is not the first of his works to have been published in the United States. In 1891 a Spanish-language edition of *Cuba y sus jueces* was published in Philadelphia by the Levytype Company—the publisher that subsequently printed the English translation under the title *Cuba and the Cubans*. And this 1891 Spanish-language edition was edited by none other than Laura's uncle Eusebio Guiteras.[16] Differing from the multiple previous editions that were published in Havana, this edition (the seventh) contained 107 engravings (including photographs) interspersed throughout the text. It further added an appendix that recorded sometimes extensive information for each engraving. While both Pedro José and Eusebio Guiteras are briefly mentioned in earlier editions of *Cuba y sus jueces*, in the Philadelphia edition their photographs appear prominently, in the body of the work, and brief biographical entries appear in the appendix: Cabrera refers to Eusebio on page 88 of the Philadelphia edition, this in a list of "retóricos, profesores y gramáticos," and he includes his picture on page 86 of the same edition, marked as illustration No. 37, noting the following in the appendix:

> No. 37.—Eusebio Guiteras.—Born in Matanzas on March 5, 1823: he was educated at the school *Carraguao*. He collaborated until 1865 in the most notable publications of his epoch. He published a leveled Spanish grammar text whose success is demonstrated by the multiple editions published in Latin America. His travel account about his trip through Europe, Asia and Africa is interesting, as well as his book *A Winter in New York*. Author of texts on religion and other well-received books. He currently resides in Philadelphia.[17]

In this brief entry Eusebio is presented as a cosmopolitan author whose travel and texts span the globe. Meanwhile, the 1896 English translation features the intervention of Cabrera's Latina translator, Laura Guiteras, for it is her historical interpolation that contextualizes Eusebio Guiteras's life and works in a U.S. Latina/o context.

First, in the opening pages of *Cuba and the Cubans* we find the following dedication: "To / the memory of her beloved uncle / Eusebio Guiteras / this translation is dedicated / by his niece / Laura Guiteras."[18] By choosing to dedicate the translation to her uncle and by identifying herself as his niece, Laura Guiteras not only converts Eusebio into a historical marker in Cuban culture, this due to his prominence as the individual to whom the work is dedicated, but she does so for herself as well, by placing her name next to his; significantly, she does so in English.

Second, instead of offering merely the six sentences cited from the 1891 Philadelphia edition, and in place of the brief asides in that entry that refer to New York and Philadelphia, Laura includes in her 1896 translation a full biographical sketch of her beloved uncle of six-and-a-half pages in length, which appears as the description of engraving No.

37. As above, this sketch includes references to Eusebio's travels through-out France, Italy, Spain, Greece, Turkey, Egypt, Syria, and Jerusalem, as well as his life and literary and educational activities in Cuba; but it additionally includes a significant historical intervention for American studies because she highlights Eusebio's intellectual exchanges with Henry Wadsworth Longfellow, emphasizing that Eusebio was instrumental in the publication of William H. Hurlbert's now much-cited article on Latin American poetry, "The Poetry of Spanish America," which appeared in 1849 in the *North American Review*, edited by Longfellow.[19]

While Hulbert's article was an important intervention for Latin American studies, because it presented Latin American authors to a U.S. readership, revisiting Eusebio's friendship with Longfellow and deciphering his influence on the publication of the piece through a detailed reading of their correspondence would help us to better understand such an important figure for American studies as Longfellow from the context of his intellectual exchanges with such individuals as Eusebio Guiteras. This time, however, through a Latina/o studies perspective.[20] Also of interest to American studies, and in the same vein, is the reference to Eusebio's correspondence with William Cullen Bryant, Washington Irving, George Ticknor, Hubert H. Bancroft, and John Greenleaf Whittier (333).

Laura then comments on Eusebio's popular Spanish readers, citing the financial success of the books and noting that "many editions have been issued by Appleton & Co. of New York; the largest in 1886, counting upwards of 18,000 volumes. This is an unprecedented success in the Island of Cuba" (335). She then catalogs his published and unpublished works that were written in the United States, including his novels, a re-translation of a Spanish rendering of the Bible, and a reader for the study of the English language (336–37). She closes the biographical sketch by highlighting the fact that Eusebio Guiteras was a member of the Historical Society of Pennsylvania and of the American Catholic Historical Society (337).

The recovery of Eusebio Guiteras for Latina/o and American studies is particularly significant not only because it is facilitated by the textual intervention of a Latina but also because it directs the historian to archival resources that have not been accessed by Latina/o studies scholars to date; after she places Eusebio and his works and life squarely in the

United States, in English, we find that No. 37 contains a footnote which states that the biographical sketch was originally published in *The Records of the American Catholic Society of Philadelphia* in 1894 (330 n1). Here, then, we discover not only that Laura Guiteras was not merely a translator of Cabrera who married a Philadelphian and lived in that city but also that she was a member of a larger Latina/o *community* that existed in her day in Philadelphia, evidence of which may be found in church archives. Indeed, Laura was active in the Catholic Church in the 1870s to 1890s, and a thorough review of this archive would allow scholars to reconstruct the lives of the Latina/o communities of which Laura and her family were a part.

It is only by way of accessing the Latin American archive, where Cabrera's *Cuba y sus jueces* is first published (in Spanish), and by following the literary thread to the English translation of the work, that we gain new insight into another aspect of the Latina/o experience of the nineteenth century. For, while Latin American scholars have ignored the U.S. dimensions of these figures—indeed, they have shown no interest in the English translation of *Cuba y sus jueces*—and while Latina/o studies scholars have not taken an interest in these individuals, who wrote in Spanish, a study of their lives at the intersection of Cuba and the United States opens new avenues of research into nineteenth-century Latinidad.

Cabrera's New York Rendition of the Cuban War Memoir

Shortly after arriving in New York, Cabrera started and edited the newspaper *Cuba y América*, which he launched on April 1, 1897, and which ran in the United States until September 1898, when Cabrera returned to Cuba and continued production from there. *Cuba y América* contained the serialized war memoir *Episodios de la guerra. Mi vida en la manigua*, which was subsequently published in book form in Philadelphia and in Mexico, both in 1898.[21] Written by Cabrera but published under the pseudonym Ricardo Buenamar (which was an anagram of Cabrera's first and last names), this memoir has drawn only brief commentary from contemporary scholars, who note that it must be counted among that author's collected works.[22] However, the memoir is significant. Though it has collected dust in the Latin American archive for close to 120 years, its insertion into Latina/o and American studies brings to the fore, first, the Latina/o readers he reached in that the newspaper in which it appeared documents the goings-on of the Latina/o community of his day. Second, Cabrera deploys the war memoir to inscribe himself and his work into contemporaneous Latina/o cultural productions and political debates. This last dimension of the text is particularly salient for Latina/o studies.

Episodios de la guerra. Mi vida en la manigua details the experiences of one Ricardo Buenamar, the supposed author and protagonist of the serialized war memoir who is said to be a young man recently arrived in New York after fighting in the still raging War of 1895. We are told he was born to a Spanish father and a Cuban mother, and the memoir speaks against the abuses inflicted on Cubans and Spaniards alike as they fight one another, many dying from starvation and illness.

Because Cabrera never experienced an extended war campaign and because he was a longtime Autonomist,[23] he needed to legitimize his participation and role in the Cuban émigré community in which armed struggle served as a legitimizing marker; a fictive war memoir was therefore a truly strategic and effective means of influencing the formation of the Cuban republic from afar and without ever having to fight in the war itself.[24] Moreover, after renouncing Autonomism, Cabrera faced a serious challenge. Because it was obvious in 1897 that Autonomism was no longer a viable option for the island, Cabrera had to reposition himself politically if he wished to occupy any significant role in the future Cuban republic.[25]

Viewed in this light, the publishing of *Cuba y América* and the war memoir in particular must be seen as something more than the production of another publicity piece that pushed for Cuban independence, especially when one takes into account the first installment of the memoir.[26] While both the Philadelphia and Mexico City book versions begin the war memoir with the April 15, 1897, installment, *Cuba y América* has an April 1, 1897, entry, excluded from the published versions and forgotten by history, in which Ricardo Buenamar is said actually to be a longtime Cuban resident of New York who returns to the island, not a Cuban *criollo* fighting for independence on the battlefield.

In this "erased" version, Buenamar visits Cuba with a Mr. Parker, a tobacco magnate from Georgia, a visit that in turn leads them to meet Máximo Gómez, the general of the Cuban Army. Buenamar never reveals his ethnicity or nationality, so Gómez refers to the two visitors as "the two yankees" (13); and Cabrera establishes the existence of a wide distance between Cubans who have resided for a long time in the United States, on the one hand, and Cubans from the island, on the other, by having Gómez address his Cuban American counterpart and his companion as foreign guests: "North Americans are in all places our best friends, and Cubans long for the occasion to honor them" (12). Buenamar responds by toasting Cuban independence in his *"español difícil"*—a Spanish whose difficulty the reader would nevertheless question because it does not deter Buenamar from writing his memoir in Spanish. Then, Gómez gives them a writ of passage, noting that help should be offered to the two American citizens, Mr. Parker and Mr. R. Buenamar, so they can return to pending business concerns in the United States.[27] Cabrera ends the episode in New York, from where Buenamar recalls that every time he thinks about meeting Gómez, his heart palpitates for the general and for the Cuban Army (14).

This lost/excluded episode is ripe with the theoretical possibilities at once present in Cabrera's life and the life of his works and their readers, because Raimundo Cabrera/Ricardo Buenamar suddenly embodies multiple subject positions and places at different times and at once. These positions range from North American, Cuban, Americanized-Cuban, long-term exile, short-term exile, pro-independence advocate, and repented ex-Autonomist, to newly arrived immigrant.[28] The list proliferates as Cabrera negotiates, through this pseudonym and this genre, the multiple linguistic, social, racial, cultural, and political spaces of the diverse Latina/o communities in the United States.

All three versions, the serialized one in *Cuba y América* and the books published in Philadelphia and Mexico, include another episode that speaks to such multiple juxtapositions of identity. The entry titled *"El inglesito"* (The little Englishman) (June 15, 1897) in diminutive form, refers to an individual who supposedly fought in both the Ten Years War and the War of 1895. During the Ten Years War he was known as Henry Reeve, born and educated in Brooklyn. A bookkeeper by trade, he is said to have joined the expedition of General Jordan, where he was given the nickname "El inglesito," because though he spoke Spanish, he never lost his American accent. According to Cabrera/Buenamar, at one point, he is captured and pretends he is mute, because he knows his

Spanish captors will kill him if they hear his accent. He later escapes and commits suicide in order to avoid imprisonment. Yet immediately after this description and in the same installment, Cabrera/Buenamar mentions that he knows an alternative version of Henry Reeve's war experiences. In this one he is killed in battle and left for dead, but, being only injured, he escapes into the woods, survives, and continues fighting for the Cuban cause.

Then, in the same installment, a second "*inglesito*," is mentioned, and he is referred to as the "*segundo tomo*" of Henry Reeve. This "second volume" is said to have gone by the name Julio Dodle. He is "*tenido por norteamericano*" (taken for a North American) (72), but Cabrera/Buenamar clarifies that Dodle was actually born in Matanzas, Cuba, of foreign parents and schooled "*afuera*" or outside the island. He was working in Cuba as a mechanic in a sugar refinery when the War of 1895 began. "*Su acento estranjero*" (foreign accent) (72) once again signals his foreignness. In this version, Henry Reeve/Julio Dodle travels back to New York in order to gather armaments for the insurrection, only then to return to Cuba to continue fighting (77). Cabrera/Buenamar concludes that he most likely remains fighting in Cuba even up to the time of his recording the latest installment of the memoir. Because that installment explains that the leaders of the revolution thought he was the same person, Henry Reeve/Julio Dodle (13), this character, embedded in the real-life events of the War of 1895 that the fictive war memoir "documents," is meant to bridge the political, social, racial, and cultural spaces between the United States and Cuba, just as Cabrera/Buenamar is supposed to do the same.

Henry Reeve was a historical person. He was born in Brooklyn in 1850; he did go to Cuba with General Jordan in 1869; he was injured but escaped. He died on the Cuban battlefield in 1876. His life and legend continue to this day because Fidel Castro created the Henry Reeve Brigades in 2005 as a response to the Hurricane Katrina disaster: These Cuban doctors continue their service in Haiti and Pakistan. In addition, Enrique Clio wrote a 2009 novel about Reeve's exploits on the Cuban battlefield titled *The Faraway War*. In this juxtaposition between history/fiction, time/space, author/pseudonym, we find best exemplified a Latina/o continuum, the different spaces, both temporal and physical, inhabited by Latina/os at the same time through travel, memory, and the literary circulation of their works that predate and postdate their time in the United States. For with the *inglesito*, Cabrera/Buenamar subverts fixed notions of time and space folding the past into the present and vice-versa, as well as inhabiting both Cuba and New York at the same time, and at different historical moments, all of them existing simultaneously—but to be found in the Latin American archive.

Cabrera as Translator

In 1889 Cabrera published a translation of Carnegie's well-known and fantastically popular 500-plus-page book *Triumphant Democracy or Fifty Years' March of the Republic*. His translation, however, was not straightforward. Instead, he rendered into Spanish only the particular selections of the work that he deemed to be important for Cuba's economic, political, and social future. In the end, he appropriates Carnegie's book altogether, radically transforming it into a book about Cuba. This appropriation speaks to Cabrera's Latina/o intervention in a very specific manner, an intervention made possible only when we enter the Latin American archive.

A glimmer of Cabrera's purpose in rewriting Carnegie's book may be found in the preface to his translation, in which he reflects on his own interventions in Carnegie's text.[29] Omitting Carnegie's own preface and replacing it with his own, he clarifies that the translation is a "reduction" of Carnegie's book (xviii), emphasizing that because of the bitterness he experienced when thinking of Cuba as he read Carnegie's text, he separated himself in great part from the author's plan and purpose. Instead, he decides to choose from the original the most important facts and narratives, in order to compare the progress of the American people with the disgrace experienced by the society in which, Cabrera says, "he nacido, en la que vivo y para la cual escribo" (he was born, lives in and for whom he writes) (xix). He states that his purposeful rewriting of Carnegie's book serves as work directed not at the Cuban middle or intellectual class but at the Cuban masses that do not have access to relevant texts or information (xix). He then admits to including additions to and commentaries on Carnegie's text in order to emphasize the need for Cuban self-government via Autonomist rule (xix–xx). The manner in which Cabrera accomplishes his mission affects our reading of his work as a Latina/o text, because in the end, as in the English translation of *Cuba y sus jueces* and the publication of his fictive war memoir, Cabrera's translation of Carnegie brings the United States into Cuba and Cuba into the United States.

Cabrera accomplishes this translation/transposition in a systematic and strategic fashion. First, he keeps most of Carnegie's chapter headings, yet he ignores and does not include any of Carnegie's closely chosen epigraphs. From Milton to Spenser to Stuart Mill to Shakespeare, entries meant to set the tone for the content of the chapters, Cabrera simply erases them for his readers. Second, while he is relatively true to the original in the first chapter of the translation, Cabrera's intervention slowly picks up speed, until the Carnegie text eventually is rendered unrecognizable. Starting in the second chapter, Cabrera alters Carnegie's language. For example, after quoting one of Herbert Spencer's many Eurocentric assertions about the importance of biology for economic success, Carnegie begins "The American People" with the following two sentences: "Fortunately for the American people they are essentially British. I trust they are evermore to remain truly grateful for this crowning mercy" (23). Cabrera translates, "El pueblo de la Unión americana es esencialmente inglés" (The American Union is essentially British) (19).[30]

He then commences with his extensive practice of reducing paragraphs and complete pages of Carnegie's book into one- or two-sentence summaries. In these types of erasures, Cabrera manipulates Carnegie's message in order to create a certain vision of the United States that he wishes his Cuban readers to accept. Knowing that Carnegie's racial and national elitism is unpalatable to the audience he is trying to reach, Cabrera's translation of Carnegie is both ideological and political. As he notes in his preface, he wishes to use Carnegie's message of economic and social success to educate the average Cuban reader as to the greatness of the Republican project currently taking place in the United States (xix). To do so, he has to edit accordingly.

While the first type of intervention is one of erasure—the exclusion of the epigraphs as well as the reduction of entire paragraphs and pages into mere sentences—a second type of intervention involves the addition of new passages, cut from the whole cloth, to the text. These additions are first found in the form of added footnotes that are inserted in key places, moments in which Cabrera replaces Carnegie's comparisons between England and the United States with ones between the United States and Cuba. Cabrera's interventions finally move from erasure and added footnotes to direct additions to the actual body of the work: He begins to speak about Cuba's situation without signaling when he is translating Carnegie or when he, the translator, is adding text.

By Chapter 3, *"Ciudades y aldeas"* ("Cities and Small Towns"), it is not clear whether Carnegie is writing about *Cuba's* population, history, and present state, or if it is Cabrera who does so. For example, Carnegie speaks to the magnificent increase in urban populations in metropolises such as Philadelphia, Chicago, Milwaukee, Jersey City, and New York, but Cabrera summarizes these fifty pages in a few paragraphs and then abruptly interjects, "Estas cifras casi fabulosas nos llevan á pensar en la triste suerte de nuestro país" (43) (These almost fantastic numbers make us think of the sad fortune of our country). The reader first thinks it is Scotland and England to which Carnegie is referring, but Cabrera forecloses on such a logical interpretation when he subsequently notes, "[S]iete ciudades fundó en la Isla de Cuba el renombrado conquistador Diego Velazquez . . ." (43) (Seven cities were established in the island of Cuba by the renown[ed] conquistador Diego Velázquez . . .). With this sentence the reader is left to understand that it cannot possibly have been Carnegie who wrote the words in question; and yet the transition of authorial voice is seamless. The translator transforms himself into the author of the work and brings the reader with him, because the data that follow are not footnoted and the *"nos"* and *"nuestro"* (both meaning our) bring the Cuban reader and Cabrera together in the intervention. For in the use of *our* instead of *my/mine* the reader is invited to become a translator himself, to accept Cabrera's interventions as true, and thereby partake of his rewriting of the text, a willful and complicit act between reader and translator.

As the conflation between translator, text, and reader continues, through the use of *nos* and *nuestro*, among other narrative strategies, Cabrera graciously invites Carnegie into *his*, meaning Cabrera's, book by referring to him in the third person in his narrative. For example, when speaking about the production of tobacco in the United States, Carnegie says derisively, "Chewing is already a thing of the past, and the pipe and cigar are doomed. Before many generations the smoker will be considered as disgusting as the chewer is today" (196). Cabrera replaces

Carnegie's negative assessment with the following neutral comment: "el cultivo del tabaco (cuyo uso Mr. Carnegie cree llamado a desaparecer) produjo en la Union en 1880—17.500,000 pesos" (108) (The cultivation of tobacco (whose use Mr. Cargengie believes will disappear) produced in the Unión in 1880—17,500,000 pesos"). More and more Cabrera becomes not simply the selective interpreter but a trusted tour guide who educates his Cuban reader in a manner that attenuates any negative reading of the United States, creating a community of readers that reads Cuba through a U.S. lens and the United States through a Cuban lens, all while marginalizing Carnegie by way of assuming his authorial identity, making him and his book a prop for Cabrera's education of the Cuban masses.

It is his contemporary, friend, and fellow Autonomist Francisco Calcagno who best captures what Cabrera does with Carnegie's work when he admits to the challenges of Cabrera's translation in his introduction to the 1889 second edition of *Los Estados Unidos*, noting, "[V]erdaderamente no es este libro ni una traduccion ni una reduccion de su original; es, pudiera decirse, una vasta leccion de alta política, escrita sobre motivos de Andrew Carnegie: la obra de ese autor le sirve de base ántes que de original" (ix) (Truly this book is neither a translation nor a reduction of the original; it could be said that it is a vast lesson on high politics, written with the same motives as Andrew Carnegie's: The work of this author [Carnegie] serves as a base more than an original). Yet, beyond serving as the foundation or point of departure for Cabrera's own text, I would argue that Calcagno more accurately explains Cabrera's interventions when he writes, "el autor al presentarnos un resúmen de la obra de Carnegie, se ha esforzado en hacerla local, la ha cubanizado" (xv) (when the author presents for us a summary of Carnegie's work, he has made the effort of making it local, he has cubanized it). Then he ends with the following: "al concluir su lectura el corazon se siente satisfecho de la obra, y agradece su esfuerzo al autor y á su intérprete" (xv) (upon finishing the reading of this text, the reader feels satisfied by the work, and appreciates the effort made by the author and his interpreter). As Calcagno's observations and own conflation between author and translator indicate (whether accidental or purposeful), Cabrera's narrative takeover of Carnegie's work exemplifies how a text from the Latin American archive can bring not only the United States into Cuba but Cuba into the United States.

The Spanish publication of Cabrera's *Cuba y sus jueces* coupled with the English translation of that work as *Cuba and the Cubans*, both published in Philadelphia, locates the presence of Latina/os living in the United States who, though forgotten by history, are recovered as readers of his work. Of particular importance is his translator, Laura Guiteras, who published a biographical sketch of her uncle in English in the 1894 edition of *The Records of the American Catholic Society of Philadelphia*, thereby opening a new archive for Latina/o historiography. Laura's dedication of her translation to her uncle Eusebio Guiteras also leads us to the recovery of her two uncles, Eusebio and Pedro José Guiteras, for Latina/o history and literature, for while these individuals hold prominent places in Cuban literary and historical studies, the decades-long presence in the United States of these important figures has neither been recognized nor theorized but must be if their works are to be properly contextualized and understood. To include their U.S. experiences in the study of their works will of necessity add another dimension to the interpretation of Pedro José's histories of Cuba and Eusebio's prolific print career (in the United States).

Cabrera's fictionalized war memoir, in turn, speaks to the deployment of a politically marked genre in order to "rewrite" one's history and inscribe one's self into a Latina/o community. In doing so, he forms—accesses—a Latina/o continuum, in which the association of identity with a single location or a rigid notion of chronological time is challenged by travel, memory, and the literary circulation of his works.[31] Finally, Cabrera's translation of Andrew Carnegie's *Triumphant Democracy* traces Cabrera's interpolation of not simply the United States into Cuban history but Cuba into U.S. history.

As this chapter has suggested, works by individuals like Raimundo Cabrera have been primarily studied through a Latin American lens and housed within that archive, often as part of national historiography. When we take into account the complexity and varied nature of Cabrera's archive, however, we find texts that speak of the multiple locations, both temporal and spatial, that these works inhabit, as well as the U.S. location and temporality of his Latina/o readership. Consequently, the historical and literary archive of such nineteenth-century writers beckons contemporary scholars not simply to recover these texts for Latina/o studies but to challenge the exclusions that continue to occur at the archival level in American and Latin American studies.[32] Conceptualizing the Latin American archive within and on the Latina/o continuum, a space that Cabrera's works so magnificently and fluidly inhabit and reveal, forecloses the effacement of these historically priceless works and invites scholars to compose a new writing of both American and Latin American history, both literary and historical, from the Latina/o continuum, one whose disciplinary and theoretical implications we are just beginning to discover.[33] For, the Latin American archive—written in Spanish, published in Cuba, the United States, and elsewhere—not only furnishes the information but also supplies the perspective that allows one to see precisely the degree to which Cubans in the United States in the nineteenth century lived in and between worlds simultaneously.

NOTES

1 "The Latin American archive" refers to the physical archives held in Latin American countries as well as archives in the United States housing texts that are considered Latin American because of their being in Spanish and/or their authors/publishers being from/in Latin America. It likewise includes the Latin American studies archive, meaning the study of authors and historical events from a mainly nationalist historiography. As such, I am arguing that the task at hand for scholars is to enter these archives, conducting a rereading of texts that is transnational, trans-American, and transatlantic in scope. This type of inquiry invites scholars to ask different questions about and emerging from these archives.

2 Unless otherwise noted, hereafter all translations are mine. Cabrera, *Cuba y sus jueces: rectificaciones oportunas*, First edition (Havana: Imp. "El Retiro," 1887); Cabrera, *Cuba and the Cubans*, trans. Laura Guiteras (Philadelphia: Levytype Company, 1896).

3 While *manigua* in contemporary usage can refer to the countryside, in nineteenth-century Cuba it meant "to take to the hills" or to join the independence movement. An appropriate translation of this title would be *War Episodes: My Life on the Battlefront*. This serialized war memoir appeared in *Cuba y América* (New York, 1897–98), a newspaper started and edited by Cabrera.

4 Carnegie, *Triumphant Democracy or Fifty Years' March of the Republic* (New York: Scribners, 1886); Cabrera, *Los Estados Unidos. Reducción de la obra "Triumphant Democracy" de Mr. Andrew Carnegie; con notas, aplicaciones y comentarios* (Havana: Imp. de Soler Álvarez, 1889).

5 A second reference to a continuum appears in Ramón A. Gutiérrez's "Comment: A Response to 'Gay Latino Cultural Citizenship,'" in *The Gay Latino Studies: A Critical Reader*, ed. Michael Hames-García and Ernesto Javier Martínez (Durham, N.C.: Duke University Press, 2011), 198–203. In his response, Gutiérrez references

the lesbian continuum coined as such by Adrienne Rich and then speaks of placing Latino male sexuality on that continuum.

6 *The Printer and Bookmaker: An Illustrated Magazine Devoted to the Arts Preservative and Kindred Topics* 27: 3 (1898): 136.

7 Moreno, *Cuba y su gente (Apuntes para la historia)* (Madrid: Tip. de Enrique Teodoro, 1887).

8 In 2010 the Latina/o newspaper *Al Día* published *200 Years of Latino History in Philadelphia* (Philadelphia: Temple University Press, 2010). However, it includes only three figures from the late-eighteenth and the nineteenth century: Francisco Miranda (Venezuela), Manuel Torres (Colombia), and Father Félix Varela (Cuba) (12–17).

9 Cabrera, *Cartas a Govín. Impresiones de viaje. Primera serie* (Havana: Tip. "La Moderna," 1892).

10 Cabrera, *Cartas a Govín. Sobre la exposición de Chicago Impresiones de viaje. Segunda serie* (Havana: Tip. de "Los Niños Huérfanos," 1893) (hereafter cited parenthetically).

11 My article "The Guiteras Brothers and Latina/o Historiography" (in progress) more fully explores the lives and significance of the works of these important figures for Latina/o literary studies and historiography.

12 Campuzano lists J. K. and P. J. Collins as the Philadelphia publishers of the first three *Libros de lectura* and Matanzas, Cuba (no publisher), for the *Libro cuarto de lectura*. Luisa Campuzano, "Los Guiteras, Plácido, y Matanzas." Academia Cubana de Lenguas. September 28, 2009. Conference Presentation. Web. October 15, 2014. http://www.acul.ohc.cu/guiteras_y_placido.pdf. Guiteras and Ramón Meza y Suárez Inclán mention that Appleton & Company in New York had also published the four readers. Laura Guiteras, "Brief Sketch of the Life of Eusebio Guiteras," *Records of the American Catholic Historical Society of Philadelphia*, 5, no. 2 (Philadelphia: American Catholic Historical Society of Philadelphia, 1894), 102 (hereafter cited in the text as "Brief Sketch"); Meza y Suárez Inclán, *Eusebio Guiteras. Estudio biográfico* (Havana: Imp. Avisador Comercial, 1908), 23, n.1.

13 Guiteras, *Historia de la conquista de la Habana (1762)* (Philadelphia: Parry and MacMillan, 1856); *Historia de la isla de Cuba con notas e ilustraciones*, 2 vols. (New York: J. R. Lockwood, 1865–66); *Historia de la isla de Cuba*, Second edition, ed. Fernando Ortiz (Havana: Colección de Libros Cubanos, 1927–28).

14 For a detailed study of this time period, see Ada Ferrer's *Insurgent Cuba: Race, Nation and Revolution 1868–1898* (Chapel Hill, N.C.: University of North Carolina Press, 1999) and Rebecca Scott's *Slave Emancipation in Cuba: Transition to Free Labor* (Princeton, N.J.: Princeton University Press, 1985).

15 Lazo, *Writing to Cuba: Filibustering and Cuban Exiles in the United States* (Chapel Hill, N.C.: University of North Carolina Press, 2005), 184–85. Julio Ramos likewise interrogates the issue of location in his article "Migratories" in *Re-Reading José Martí. One Hundred Years Later, 1853–1895*, ed. Julio Rodríguez-Luis (Albany: State University of New York Press, 1999), 53–66.

16 Meza y Suárez Inclán, 27.

17 Cabrera, *Cuba y sus jueces: rectificaciones oportunas*, Seventh edition (Philadelphia: Levytype Company, 1891), 296.
18 Guiteras, "Brief Sketch" (hereafter cited parenthetically).
19 Eusebio was forced to travel to Cambridge because of his wife's (Josefa Gener) poor health in 1848.
20 Iván Jaksić in *The Hispanic World and American Intellectual Life, 1820–1880* (New York: Palgrave Macmillan, 2007) links key Latin American figures to Longfellow and references Eusebio's visit to Longfellow in June 1849 (103). However, he does not expand on the depth or significance of their intellectual exchange apart from noting that he provided Longfellow with copies of Cuban books.
21 *Episodios de la guerra. Mi vida en la manigua. (Relato del coronel Ricardo Buenamar)* (Filadelfía: Compañia Levytype, 1898); *Episodios de la guerra. Mi vida en la manigua* (Mexico: Tip. El Continente Americano, 1898).
22 *Diccionario de la literatura cubana*. Instituto de Literatura y Lingüística de la Academia de Ciencias de Cuba (Havana: Editorial Letras Cubanas, 1980), 259; *Historia de la literatura cubana: Tomo I. Desde los orígines hasta 1898*. Instituto de Literatura y Lingüística (Havana: Editorial Letras Cubanas, 2002), 376.
23 With the signing of the Pacto del Zanjón—the peace treaty that ended the Ten Years War in 1878 (this war was Cuba's first of three insurrections against Spanish colonial rule)—Cabrera, along with influential friends, founded the *Partido Liberal Autonomista*, a party that advocated economic and political autonomy from Spain while simultaneously maintaining Cuba as a Spanish colony. For a detailed study of Autononism in Cuba, see Marta Bizcarrondo and Antonio Elorza, *Cuba/España. El dilema autonomista* (Madrid: Editorial Colibrí, 2001).
24 Agnes Lugo-Ortiz, in her seminal work *Identidades imaginadas. Biografía y nacionalidad en el horizonte de la guerra (Cuba 1860–1898)* (San Juan: Editorial de la Universidad de Puerto Rico, 1999) speaks to the significance of the war in the context of journalistic writing in the United States and Cuba. While she does not include Cabrera's text in her study, she highlights the importance of journalistic pieces that depict the struggle of those fighting on the Cuban war front.
25 Dolores Nieves references this phenomenon but does not elaborate on its political and historical significance when she writes: "La primera [novela] que escribe . . . es *Mi vida en la manigua*. Son las memorias del apócrifo coronel Ricardo Buenamar. Alguien que Raimundo Cabrera hubiera querido ser; pero que no fue" (25) (The first novel he writes . . . is *Mi vida en la manigua*. They are the memoirs of the apocryphal coronel Ricardo Buenamar. Someone that Raimundo Cabrera would have liked to have been; but was not). Nieves, "Prologue," *Sombras que pasan* by Raimundo Cabrera (Havana: Editorial Letras Cubanas, 1984).
26 Stressing the significance of the war memoir genre but not referencing Cabrera's text, Ferrer writes, "Clearly they [insurgents writing war memoirs] saw their writing as more than representation; they saw it also as weapon and war strategy, as a central part of the very process of insurgency they were seeking to describe. More than simply a set of texts, then, this prose of insurgency was itself a kind of

historical event, emerging in a particular context and as part of overlapping and
sometimes competing political projects" (115).

27 The issue of passing is relevant because Cabrera is passing for Ricardo Buenamar,
meaning that he needs to pass as a pro-independence advocate in order to safely
make his way in the Latina/o community he is negotiating in the United States.

28 An explanation of the term Americanized-*criollo* is found in my article
"Americanized-*criollos*: Latina/o Figures in Late-Nineteenth-Century Cuban
Literature," *Revista Hispánica Moderna* 61.1 (2008), 69–87.

29 Cabrera, *Los Estados Unidos. Reducción de la obra "Triumphant Democracy" de
Mr. Andrew Carnegie; con notas, aplicaciones y comentarios* (Havana: Imp. de
Soler Álvarez, 1889) (hereafter cited parenthetically).

30 All translations are mine.

31 I propose one more step for the full theorization of the Latina/o Continuum, one
that moves beyond the archival, though emerging from it, and that is best represented by the term *philosophical horology*. I first coined this term at the International Latina/o Studies Conference in Chicago in 2014. While I am addressing the
full exploration of the term in a separate article, the term serves as a jumping-off
point for the theorization of the manifold ways (beyond the temporal and spatial)
in which the Latina/o experience, as depicted by the intersection of these multiple
archives, challenges and in fact subverts the concept of the Western subject as
constructed to date. Carmen Lamas, "Raimundo Cabrera's New York Rendition
of the Cuban War Memoir," Presentation at the Imagining Latina/o Studies, Past,
Present and Future. Chicago, July 18, 2014.

32 For a longer list of "Latin American" writers who lived and published in the
United States but whose U.S. experience has not been taken into account to date,
see my entry "Nineteenth-Century Latina/o Literature" (*Oxford University Press
Bibliographies*, forthcoming). http://www.oxfordbibliographies.com/obo/page/
latino-studies .

33 In relation to the silencing of history based on the archive, see Michel-Rolph
Truillot, *Silencing the Past: Power and the Production of History* (Boston: Beacon
Press, 1995).

The author gratefully acknowledges the assistance of John Nemec in the
preparation of this chapter.

11

Flirting in Yankeeland

Rethinking American Exceptionalism through Argentine Travel Writing

CARRIE TIRADO BRAMEN

By the latter half of the nineteenth century, "the American flirt" was synonymous with the youthful and unmarried woman, epitomized in Henry James's *Daisy Miller*. This iconic figure had also become emblematic of the United States, as a way to render the notion of the nation-state into a distinct personality type that was playful, pretty, and young. Rudyard Kipling, who was besotted by the American girl's self-possession, independence, and charm, observed in his travel narrative about the United States that "it is perfectly impossible to go to war with these people, whatever they may do. They are much too nice."[1] Not everyone shared Kipling's belief in American niceness. Sigmund Freud for instance in "Thoughts for the Times on War and Death," written during the First World War, invoked the simile "like an American flirt" to describe a shallow and insubstantial life in a culture that denies death and therefore denies mourning. Where Kipling valued the American girl for her flirtatious charm, as a figure antithetical to war and violence, Freud considered "the American flirt" a symptom of war, as the neurotic outcome of a culture's inability to channel grief toward reflection.

The young flirt as representative of the United States illustrates the "uneasy coexistence of nationhood and womanhood," wherein the female body is both a symbol of national unity and a seductive emblem of trouble.[2] This essay explores the female flirt as a contested site of U.S. modernity, which is to say, as a figure of progress, independence, and self-determination on the one hand, and on the other, as a sign of materialistic desire, frivolity, and even neurosis. I want to take this superficial type seriously as a "social hieroglyphic," to use Marx's phrase from

Capital, that needs to be "deciphered."[3] The American flirt became codified in the late nineteenth century as a national type that was largely articulated by travelers to the United States. The flirt is a form of national branding, wherein the nation acquires a commodified form visible in a system of international symbolic exchange. Rendering a nation through an array of personality traits gave the abstract nation-state a characterological form, which is also a form of interpellation that occurs nationally as well as internationally. In the case of the social hieroglyph of the flirt, it was produced from transnational perceptions of U.S. sociality that became encoded as American typologies.

The pervasiveness of the flirt in travel writing about the United States affords the opportunity to ask methodological questions about the rhetoric of national exceptionalism and its related forms—national distinctiveness, uniqueness, and specialness. One might position oneself as anti-exceptionalist or post-exceptionalist, but scholars still need to engage with the rhetoric of national distinctiveness as a relational process that is articulated in terms of other nations.[4] American exceptionalism, as Amy Kaplan has argued, is founded on the paradox of uniqueness and universality; and it has largely been configured in terms of American insularity to underscore how the United States stands apart from the rest of the world through its superiority as a moral beacon of democratic ideals.[5]

One way in which American exceptionalism has been methodologically challenged is through a hemispheric paradigm that highlights interconnection rather than U.S. insularity. Sandhya Shukla and Heidi Tinsman's notion of an "Americas paradigm," for instance, emphasizes the "interconnected nature of North and South power relations."[6] Such a paradigm invites scholars to focus on the impact of U.S. imperialism on the region, but also "to reverse the gaze," to see the multiple ways in which Latin America has affected the United States. Although their approach is largely based on the binary of U.S. exceptionalism versus hemispheric interconnection, I want to expand Shukla and Tinsman's "Americas paradigm" to demystify U.S. exceptionalism by highlighting its relational formation: to show how Latin American gazes have actively articulated and produced forms of U.S. exceptionalism in the process of articulating their own national forms of uniqueness. All exceptionalisms are relational, even those that claim not to be.

My task is not to dismiss exceptionalism but to analyze it, to see how the rhetoric of national uniqueness is produced and reproduced relationally as a form of national branding that reiterates at the level of typology what the commodity does at the level of the object. Travel writing about the United States is an especially useful genre for studying the relationality of exceptionalisms because it reverses the dominant gaze by showing the United States as the cultural "other" that defines through its otherness, in this case, Argentine nationhood. This reversal has the effect of estrangement, of defamiliarizing the United States by raising the question: What does the United States look like as an object of the Argentine imagination, as a point through which Argentine exceptionalism is formulated?

In "The Argentine Writer and Tradition," Jorge Luis Borges understood this relational quality in terms of "Argentine peculiarity," which is "a particular way of relating oneself to what was foreign." Borges's understanding of Argentine uniqueness has itself a history dating back to the mid–nineteenth century, when the Romantic poet Esteban Echeverría celebrated in 1848 this quality of national introspection through international recognition: "We will always have one eye fixed on the progress of nations and the other focused on the heart of our own society."[7] Domingo Faustino Sarmiento, one of the first Argentine chroniclers of the United States, who later became president of Argentina, disparagingly describes this quality as Argentina's "national vanity," epitomized in the self-conscious figure of the "coquette" who contemplates herself in the mirror and embodies the arrogance and self-importance historically associated with Buenos Aries.[8]

The flirt appears repeatedly in late-nineteenth-century Argentine travel writing to the United States, namely in the work of the diplomat and chronicler Vicente Gregorio Quesada (1830–1913) and the novelist and journalist Eduarda Mansilla de García (1838–92). Both were part of the cosmopolitan elite who felt equally at ease in Buenos Aires and Paris. They represent, according to David Viñas, the "*genteel tradition*" of Argentine travel writing during the 1880s and after, when the traditional trip to Europe was replaced with one to North America.[9] I selected these Argentine travel writers in order to expand the discussion of nineteenth-century travel writing from the predominant transatlantic axis to a hemispheric one in order to explore how contested power relations between North America and South America played out in narratives about cultural encounter. How did the issues of national sovereignty, Pan-Americanism, and cultural influence unfold in the trivial details of travel description? Did the apparently innocuous American flirt, which surfaces so saliently in Argentine travel writing, disarm the looming threat of the United States as an emergent global power, or what José Martí calls "the formidable neighbor" and a "monster"? What happens to the "contact zone" when the encounter is not dramatically asymmetrical in terms of Europeans and the indigenous subaltern, but between two settler nations in the Americas?

Beginning with Domingo Faustino Sarmiento's travel narrative written about his first visit to the United States in the 1840s, which serves as an Ur-text of Argentine travel writing to the United States, the American flirt contributes to "the spectacle of liberty in North America." Sarmiento observes that in cities, "women of all conditions go about the streets and roads alone from the age of twelve: they flirt until the age of fifteen, are then married and travel."[10] This sense of women's spatial freedom in the city regardless of class is emblematic of democratic freedom more generally, where perambulatory liberty is a sign of mobility in terms of both geographic expansion and social access. In contrast to the highly prescribed lives of young Argentine women of the elite class who in the French tradition stay within the purview of a *dueña* or guardian, American women are comparatively free of parental restraint. But when we consider the fact that Sarmiento concludes his observation by saying that young American women are "then buried in a new home to raise a family," he clearly feels that such freedom is short-lived, demarcating a sanctioned period of liberty that is then rescinded when the responsibilities of matrimony and motherhood arrive.[11]

Sarmiento's commentary on the young American flirt—a type that is always gendered female—is a point of reference for Quesada and Mansilla. I begin with Quesada's official recollections, a tradition that he inherits from Sarmiento, to establish the dominant template of Argentine travel writing as a genre of ambassadorship and diplomatic propriety. *Recuerdos de mi vida diplomática: Misión en Estados Unidos* (1904) recounts Quesada's years as an ambassador to the United States (1885–92) through his letters to President Julio Roca. Then my chapter moves back eleven years to Quesada's unofficial account of his time in the United

States in *Los Estados Unidos y la América del Sur: Los yankees pintados por sí mismos* (1893). Written under the pseudonym Domingo de Pantoja, a sort of alter ego, Quesada's work shows how travel writing can be employed as a vehicle of anti-diplomacy, as a satirical critique of a nation's policy. This switch from diplomacy to anti-diplomacy radically alters the character of the flirt, who changes from a charming woman to the maligned New Woman refusing to flirt with men. The chapter concludes with Eduarda Mansilla's *Recuerdos de viaje* (1882), which was written nearly twenty years after she left the United States and represents the first published travel narrative by an Argentine woman. For Mansilla, the flirt signifies attraction and repulsion, an ambivalent figure whom she ultimately rejects for an alternative type of North American womanhood, namely post-Confederate womanhood. The defeated southern white woman is tragic for Mansilla, because her aristocratic social grace is now reduced to domestic drudgery in the aftermath of the Civil War. For Quesada and Mansilla, the American flirt becomes the trope through which Argentine anti-Americanism and identification are played out in complicated and inconsistent ways.

Vicente Gregorio Quesada and the Art of Flirtation

An intellectual historian of colonial Argentina prior to becoming a political figure, Vicente Gregorio Quesada began his diplomatic career in 1883 during the first presidency of General Julio Roca. He was first sent to Brazil (1883–85) and then to Washington, D.C. (1885–92), when he became ambassador to the United States during the presidencies of Grover Cleveland and Benjamin Harrison. Published in 1904 when Quesada was seventy-four years old, *Recuerdos de mi vida diplomática: Misión en Estados Unidos, 1885–1892* focuses on the social life of the United States with anecdotes about the personal lives of politicians. Early on, Quesada introduces the flirt as emblematic of American social life, where he characterizes its hospitality and politeness in gendered terms: "Encontré fácil la vida social, hospitalarias las gentes, corteses é instruidas las damas en general: y muy lindas, muy simpáticas, las señoritas para las que el flirt es un entretenimiento" (I have found the social life easy, the people hospitable, the women in general courteous and educated: and very pretty and very kind, the young women for whom el flirt is entertaining).[12]

Interestingly, Quesada never translates *flirt* into the Spanish *coqueta* or even the French *coquette*, suggesting its untranslatability. He does, however, give the English word *flirt* a Spanish inflection by adding the masculine article *el* for *el flirt*, but this is complicated by the term's distinctly feminine cast as inextricably linked to "*las damas*" and "*las señoritas*." Associated with prettiness ("muy lindas, muy simpáticas"), the flirt becomes synymous with an aesthetic language of pleasure, which he describes as entertainment ("*entretenimiento*") in recollecting the American girl's frank manner of speaking and her ability to sustain a lively conversation.

What intrigues Quesada is how this feminine figure can so frankly engage in heterosocial play without fear. Although he acknowledges the flirt's charm, he is ultimately more fascinated by how the men respond to her. North American men demonstrate politeness without aggression ("la galantería no es una agresión"). *El flirt* is shown a great deal of male respect, especially if she is young and pretty: "Jamás conocí país donde se tuviese más general respeto por el bello sexo" (I have never known a country where there was so much general respect for the belle sex). He then returns to this point a few pages later: "La libertad que disfrutan las señoritas en los Estados Unidos está perfectamente garantizada por el respeto de los hombres, impuesto por las leyes, la tradición y las costumbres sociales" (The liberty that the young women enjoy in the U.S. is perfectly guaranteed by the men's respect for them, which is imposed by laws, tradition and social customs) (16). Men, through their respect, grant women their liberty, a sense of "positive responsibility," which is tacitly enforced through the law: If a man isn't careful, he can end up in a duel, or where there isn't a duel, then with a bullet wound. While the flirtatious woman acts without fear, the man, by contrast, behaves because of fear. His gentlemanliness is produced out of the threat of the violence that will come if he fails to regulate his own behavior.

Besides acknowledging that the American flirt's liberty is predicated on males' fear of their own impropriety, Quesada offers his readers an intriguing definition of *flirtation* that further aestheticizes this feminine figure. Attributing the definition to "*una amable señorita*" (a lovely young woman), Quesada describes flirtation as "attention without intention." He repeats this definition, both times in English, which is apt given the untranslatability of the term *flirt*. But how does this definition—attention without intention—result in the flirt's further aes-theticization? During the same period in which Quesada wrote about the American flirt, the German cultural theorist Georg Simmel pub-lished an essay on flirtation wherein he aligns the practice with Kant's definition of art as "purposiveness without purpose." Whether it is flirta-tion or art, there is no particular end in sight but rather the sustaining of possibility, an open-endedness that defers decisions. In a similar vein, the psychoanalyst Adam Phillips has argued that flirtation is "the calcu-lated production of uncertainty, inherently covert and without conclu-sion."[13] Quesada's definition of the flirt as "attention without intention" is a deferral of closure as a game without end, in which flirting is not the means to matrimony but a source of pleasure for its own sake. Within the U.S. context, it represents a way for young women to defer marriage; it buys time for the single woman, a way to delay the drudgery of domes-tic responsibilities, a strategy that Sarmiento observed a generation ear-lier. Quesada comprehends flirtation less in temporal terms and more as an aesthetic practice, where flirtation is a work of art performed through a woman's body, a playful performance wherein women possess charis-matic power over men. This combination of playfulness and power is what intrigues Quesada about the American flirt, but does his interest in the American flirt ultimately go beyond aesthetic appreciation?

Quesada's Alter Ego: Domingo de Pantoja and the Anti-flirt

The flirt is a sign of both pleasure and deep anxiety stemming from women's authority over men. Where the *coqueta* emerges from the highly stratified society of aristocratic Europe, the flirt is a product of a democratic society, or so Quesada suggests, where conventional social hierarchies based on class and gender distinctions diffuse into a disor-derly world of role reversals. As Quesada writes later in *Recuerdos*, "Se dice que la presiding lady of the Executive Mansion is the first lady of the land, porque en esta democracia las señoras tienen el rango del marido, y se llaman la generala, etc." (It is said that the presiding lady of the White House is the first lady of the land, because in this democracy the women have usurped the husband's rank and are called the gen-eral) (123). He adds a footnote attributing this rather controversial claim that American men are hen-pecked, including the president, to another travelogue entitled *Los Estados Unidos y la América del Sur: Los yankees pintados por sí mismos* (1893). Quesada amusingly uses the formalities of academic citation to refer to his own disguised work, which is written under the pseudonym of Domingo de Pantoja.

In contrast to his diplomatically written memoir *Recuerdos*, his pseudonymously written account, *Los Estados Unidos*, is an outspoken critique of U.S. dominance in the hemisphere, published soon after Quesada returned to Buenos Aires after serving six years as ambassador in Washington, D.C. Scholars have dismissed this book for being superficial and inaccurate. North American historians such as David Pletcher have described this "scathing memoir" as evidence of Quesada's anti-Americanism, which Pletcher attributes to "European propaganda."[14] Argentine historian Alicia Vidaurreta discredits the book for its errors and prejudices (although she does not elaborate on the nature of these alleged errors), arguing that it is a far less reliable historical source than Quesada's more authoritative and official account, written in 1904.[15] But the fact that Quesada cites this earlier work in his formal account of his diplomatic years suggests that these texts are not as distinct as Vidaurreta suggests. Pantoja's outrageous and opinionated voice surfaces obliquely in the official account in the form of a footnote, which is to say, that it appears paratextually, as the return of the ambassadorial repressed.

When taken together, Quesada/Pantoja is an intriguing, bifurcated figure. On the one hand, Quesada is an erudite anti-modern in the vein of his contemporary Henry Adams. His *Recuerdos* represents a well-behaved text written by a former ambassador that abides by the conventions of diplomatic propriety. On the other hand, Quesada's alter ego, Domingo de Pantoja, resembles a sarcastic and irreverent Mark Twain who scoffs at the very propriety that Quesada, the ambassador, has mastered. Even his first name, "Domingo," playfully invokes the former president of Argentina who wrote about his travels to the United States in 1847—Domingo Faustino Sarmiento. Where Sarmiento's travel narrative diplomatically praises the United States as a model for Argentine democracy, Pantoja's *Los Estados Unidos* refuses to coat its critique of U.S. power dynamics in tactful diplomatic prose. Instead it offers a travel narrative that is unapologetically opinionated and critical. The fact that Quesada wrote his irreverent account first suggests that the polite official version could be written only once Pantoja had spoken: that Quesada's respectability and self-control are predicated on Pantoja's outrageous impertinence.

Pantoja's narrative provides a fascinating study of how travel writing establishes a discursive space from which to critique U.S. hegemony. *Los Estados Unidos* is a vitriolic condemnation of the romanticized language of Pan-Americanism with its motto, "America for the Americas," which Pantoja translates as "America for the Yankees." Despite the vision of hemispheric unity apparently encoded in Pan-Americanism, Pantoja argues that the Yankees are ignorant of those they want to dominate, perceiving South Americans as *"algo semi-salvaje"* (something semi-wild).[16]

Published in the same year as the Chicago World's Fair, a point that appears in the book's opening advertisement, *Los Estados Unidos* reverses the U.S. gaze that characterizes the 1893 Fair, and that reduces cultural others to curiosities along the Midway. Now, the United States is the object of curiosity. Pantoja's version commences with an Argentinian, Victor Gálvez, a close friend of Pantoja's and himself the author of a travelogue, attesting to the authenticity of the narrative. But this verifying figure happens to be another one of Quesada's fictitious characters. Gálvez, nonetheless, tells the story of Pantoja's life with such detail that it seems entirely plausible. Beginning with Pantoja's migration from Spain to Argentina after the death of his father, Gálvez attests to Pantoja's identification not with Europe but with Argentina, an identification underscored through the source of Pantoja's wealth, which derives organically from Argentine soil, namely through real estate deals. He is, in other words, a "self-made man" (*EU* xv).

Given his wealth, Pantoja had no interest in publishing this narrative but did so at the urging of his friend. According to Gálvez, Pantoja wrote the document solely to "combatir la monomanía yankee, las tendencias yankees y la imitación á lo que es yankee" (combat the Yankee monomania, Yankee tendencies and the imitation of all that is Yankee) (*EU* xiii). Pantoja lays claim to the term *American* by stating in the opening page: "I am as American as they are." Pantoja's consternation at the audacity of the U.S. inhabitants referring to themselves as Americans and thereby excluding the rest of the hemisphere is a recurring tension throughout the narrative. This gesture of naming a nation after a hemisphere is symptomatic of the imperial practices that characterize the

United States, which for Pantoja take on a pathological hue as a sign of monomania linked to power and egotism (*EU* 10). Pantoja's response to this pathology is to claim the term *America* for Argentina and the rest of the Americas.

Despite Pantoja's assertiveness and the sharpness of his critique, his narrative is more diagnostic than curative, with the hope only of containing the United States' psychological pathology within its borders rather than allowing it to spread. The imperial boundlessness of Manifest Destiny, for instance, needs to be countered with the language of limits, which means, at one level, to particularize Americans as Yankees by establishing clearly, to quote Gálvez, "cuál es el límite geográfico del yankee" (that which is the geographic limit of the Yankee) (*EU* xiii). Or to use Gálvez's blunt way of describing Pantoja's objective: "para mostrar los *lunares* y las *verrugas* de Uncle Sam ó de *Jonathan*" (to show the moles and warts of Uncle Sam or Brother Jonathan) (*EU* xiii). Here, political critique takes on an individualized cast, wherein Pantoja converts inter-American issues into interpersonal conflicts, and the language of diplomacy is reduced to a typological discourse of national character.

Where Quesada in *Recuerdos* uses the aesthetic language of flirtation to describe U.S. sociality, he (as Pantoja) invokes the anti-aesthetic in *Los Estados Unidos* to demystify the United States as a hemispheric ideal—as the model of Pan-American mimesis—and to emphasize instead its abject qualities. Pantoja describes his method as "realism," and he takes his reader through a litany of taboo topics, such as the suicides of young people, back-street abortions, and urban prostitution, which he describes by quoting long passages from the sensationalist newspaper the *New York Herald*. But what shocks Pantoja more than these sensational topics is the U.S. style of flirtation, a topic that he addresses at the start of his book. Like Winterbourne in Henry James's *Daisy Miller*, Pantoja wonders whether flirtation is a sign of promiscuity or innocence. "I arrived at the belief," writes Pantoja, "that 'la flirtation' was the most innocent entertainment," the equivalent of German men kissing each other as a sign of friendship (*EU* 29). But this German analogy does not in any way make the custom of flirting more comprehensible: "Me creía, lo confieso, en una tierra extraña" (I confess, I thought I was in a strange land) (*EU* 29). He admits that flirtation, wherein men exercise heroic virtue by restraining their own libidinal desires, must have altered the animal instincts of human beings (*EU* 29). How else can he explain this strange custom? As in *Recuerdos*, Quesada's discussion of flirting focuses on his admiration of male restraint, where playfulness remains playful rather than turning into lustful aggression. Quesada finds this unsettling because it signifies a behavior without an outcome, a playfulness for playfulness' sake, a point that Simmel makes matter-of-factly, where there is no clear trajectory toward marriage.

But as Pantoja's critique of U.S. arrogance and egotism develops and intensifies, his discussion of the flirt changes. Toward the latter third of the book, when he describes the experience of traveling by train and carriage and then staying in hotels, Pantoja observes the absence of flirting. In the highly social spaces of hotel lobbies, for instance, or in crowded cars on the train, young women traveling alone simply read novels or newspapers, an act that he perceives as a form of anti-sociality.

> Se ha juzgado siempre que en sociedad no es permitida la lectura, porque es una demostración de desdén por los que estan presentes; y si ese desdén existe en el hogar y en sociedad—cuál es el resultado? El ensimismamiento que caracteriza al yankee, y en cuanto á la mujer, la ansiedad de la *flirtation* para escaparse del abrumador aislamiento del libro como pretesto, del silencio como resultado y de la frivolidad egoista como *medium*. (199)

> I have always considered that in society, one should not be permitted to read because it demonstrates disdain for the others who are present; and if that disdain exists in the home and in society, then what is the result? The absorption that characterizes the yankee, and as regards the woman, the anxiety of flirtation that leads one to escape from the overwhelming isolation of the book as an excuse, from its resulting silence, and from its shallow egotism that is its *medium*.

Although he admits that in some cases the woman may be genuinely absorbed in her reading, in the majority of instances, however, women use the book or the newspaper as a shield, as a way to isolate themselves from those around them. He finds such a scene unnatural, going against the innate sociability of human beings. Where the flirt in *Recuerdos* exhibits a type of fearlessness, the anti-flirt traveling alone with a book as a companion is a pathological figure, one whose social anxiety forces her to withdraw into her own artificial cocoon. What is lost in this anti-social gesture? For Pantoja, it is "las mil agradables incidencias de la vida social" (the thousand agreeable incidents of social life) (*EU* 198). Sounding like a therapist analyzing a patient, Pantoja outlines the traits of this pathology as a form of self-absorption and egotism, a behavior that rejects those neighboring individuals seated around her wanting to converse by pushing them away with her silence.

This scene, which Pantoja describes as a "ridiculous painting" (198), illustrates a nonrelation or a failed encounter, wherein the book or the newspaper is used as a tactic of isolation rather than as a mode of communication. For Pantoja, the woman reading in public is a metaphor of U.S. foreign policy in the Americas, based on isolationism and taking the form of protectionist policies in curtailing the trading options of "the little republics." The U.S. woman as anti-flirt also signifies for Pantoja the egotism behind such national ideologies as Manifest Destiny, which has its corollary in the nomenclature of the nation.

At one level, the anti-flirt is emblematic of U.S. arrogance and imperial policies, wherein individual anti-social behavior represents national monomania. At another level, however, Pantoja's critique of the American woman who reads rather than talks can be seen as a sign of his own sexism. Pantoja presents sociability as a female mandate, implying that in hotel lobbies or on trains, women have to make themselves socially available to men; their social function is to please and to entertain. Another way to interpret the anti-flirt would be to see the reading woman as a defiant type, one who asserts her own desire for silence over her social role of feminine niceness. Why should she converse with a stranger? Why must she flirt? In this case, one needs to reverse the gaze again and interpret Pantoja symptomatically: The reading woman emasculates the Latin man, creating a non-encounter that is experienced as rejection, which is then projected back onto the anti-flirt as a sign of American egotism and anti-sociality.[17] Women are typically seen in relation to others primarily in terms of familial ties, so the figure of the woman traveling alone threatens Pantoja, because she is at once available and unavailable, a potential relation that turns out to be a nonrelation.

Eduarda Mansilla and "*La rubia coqueta*"

For Eduarda Mansilla, the American flirt is "*la rubia coqueta*" (the blonde flirt) who is young, playful, and excessive, particularly in terms of fashion, whether it is wearing too much makeup or too much jewelry. The blonde flirt represents a national type that is synonymous with "Yankeeland," wherein particular personality traits become emblematic of the nation. In contrast to Quesada, whose narrative emerges from years of diplomatic work, Mansilla, the wife of a diplomat, travels with a large entourage of children, a nanny, maids, and a chaperone, in addition to close friends. One account reports that she even traveled at some points with a cow in case her children wanted fresh milk.[18] Mansilla frames her perspective from the vantage point of a tourist, despite the fact that she lived in the United States for five years. She does not recount, for instance, the daily life of Washington, D.C., but rather focuses on her experiences touring Saratoga Springs, Niagara Falls, and New York City. The phrase "*como touriste*" appears throughout her travel account, which has led Mónica Szurmuk to conclude that Mansilla's *Recuerdos* is the first example of leisure travel writing from Argentina.[19]

In structuring the touristic account of the United States around the figure of the flirt, Mansilla's narrative raises the question of whether tourism is itself a form of flirtation, a playful and pleasurable engagement with a place without a firm commitment to residency. The elusiveness of the flirt translates into the transience of the traveler, and both are opposed to a teleological notion of outcomes, whether it takes the form of permanence or destiny. Furthermore, the flirt and the tourist both operate within a semiotic system of types, wherein they observe and participate in cultural practices as spectacles, as symbolic acts that translate particularities into representative forms. Mansilla, as a tourist who casts the blonde flirt as a national hieroglyphic, is not herself immune from the social gaze. Mansilla is fully aware that while she observes the American girls she herself is the object of their gaze. She is both the surveyor and the surveyed: "Las muchachas inmóviles y parleras, sólo interrumpian su charla para mirarme de arriba abajo y decirme con su mirar frio é inquisitorial: *Baja como puedas*" (The young girls stationary and talking, only interrupt their chit-chat to gaze at me up and down and to say to me with a cold and curious look: *Go down as you can*).[20]

This exchange of gazes represents a site of inter-American encounter, of hemispheric interpellation, where the Argentine traveler in imagining the Yankee as a female type is also constructing a model of Argentine nationhood.

Eduarda Mansilla's *Recuerdos de Viaje* participates in this national discourse of Argentine exceptionalism—a national obsession about its own identity that is deeply influenced by what others think—and projects it onto the American flirt. She sustains the tensions between having and not-having, between accessibility and inaccessibility. On the one hand, the American flirt is a distinctly Yankee phenomenon, yet she is also familiar, embodying the very paradoxes and tensions that characterize late-nineteenth-century Argentina. She is a sign of attraction and repulsion, and in Mansilla's work, the "American flirt" acquires a hemispheric inflection, as an analogical figure of identification. Where Quesada's two travel narratives underscore Argentina's distance from its northern counterpart through the strangeness of American flirtation, Mansilla finds the United States strangely familiar. Similarly, the trains resemble those in Argentina, and both diverge from those seen in Europe. This recognition of New World likeness both represents an important moment of sympathy and identification and reflects the growing similarities between the two countries.[21]

Mansilla introduces the flirt not through a description of the American girl but through the architectural feature of the bow-window, which she associates with Anglo American domesticity. "Flores en vistosos jarrones y lujosas macetas, mesitas con libros y chucherías, adornan aquel misterioso buen retiro de la Americana *flirtation*, tan grata cuanto peligrosa" (17) (Flowers in bright vases and luxurious flower pots, small tables with books and trinkets adorn that mysterious quiet place of American flirtation, as pleasant as it is dangerous). With its large windows that create a niche above the street, the bow-window allows sunlight into the home, while also breaking with the monotony of the rectangular shape of the walls. Veiled with tulle and muslin curtains in the summer, the bow-window represents through the contrived display of various objects a scene of domestic order and beauty. One is invited to peep into the American home and catch a glimpse of this aesthetic display of domestic coziness. American flirtation, epitomized through the bow-window, is both an invitation and a refusal, an inaccessible accessibility, wherein one is invited to glance in the window for a fleeting moment as a passer-by.

As a mother traveling with children, Mansilla, however, enjoyed privileged access into the domestic interiors of American homes. She offered her largely female readers detailed descriptions of American domesticity, while also teasing her readers with only a cryptic portrayal of the bedroom.[22] Although this peek into the home is presented as a privileged position, Eduarda Mansilla's travels were highly circumscribed by what was considered proper for a woman of her class. Though far more financially secure than her British counterpart Fanny Trollope, in many ways Mansilla has more in common with her than with her fellow countryman Vicente Quesada, who writes in the style of Jacob Riis's *How the Other Half Lives*, by venturing into the crowded tenements of Mulberry Street. By contrast, Mansilla was limited to sanctioned tourist sites such as Saratoga Springs and Niagara Falls.

If Mansilla's own ability to travel was limited, so was the act of translation, as Mansilla herself acknowledges. Although she translates the American *flirt* into Spanish as "*la rubia coqueta*," at other points in her narrative she admits to the difficulty of translating the word *flirt* into either French or Spanish. She contemplates translating it into the French *coquette*, but this word "es considerado en Yankeeland como algo de muy duro y severo" (110) (is considered in Yankeeland as something very hard and severe). Implied in this comment is the sense that the American flirt is innocent, playful, and girlish, when compared with the French *coquette* with its connotations of severity, hardness, and experience. She also defines *flirt* to her Latin American readers as both a verb and a noun. She admits that the word is untranslatable: "no me ocurre cómo traducirlo" (110) (it doesn't occur to me how to translate it), and she ultimately follows the model of the French playwright Victorien Sardou, who keeps the word *flirt*. Although Mansilla was known for her translating skills and despite the fact that she wrote one novel in French, she admits to the challenge of translating the flirt accurately into any other language. The problematic nature of national comparison finds its parallel in the dilemma of translation, a dilemma that dramatizes the paradoxical nature of the flirt as both accessible and inaccessible, visible but elusive. Mansilla's own inconsistent use of the "flirt–coqueta" distinction is itself another layer of this paradox.

The difficulty of translating the word *flirt* underscores the distinctiveness of this Yankee type, yet there is something about the act of flirtation that characterizes women across national boundaries. Juana Manso, who is considered to be Argentina's first nineteenth-century radical feminist, commented that flirting is an instinct, inherent to all women to such an extent that "one cannot be a woman without also being a flirt."[23] For a feminist like Manso, the feminine, the feminist, and the flirtatious were inextricably bound together. But the flirt also has a distinctly Yankee cast for Manso, which anticipates Freud's dismissal of this type as shallow and superficial. In her own travel account to the United States in 1845, Manso describes the distinct attributes of the U.S. flirt: "Las mujeres todas son coquetas, remilgadas y sin sentimientos; su amor lo reparten entre el dinero y el tocador" (The women are all flirts, fussy and finicky and without feelings; their love is divided between money and the boudoir).[24] Manso's notion of the U.S. flirt may have served as an antecedent to Mansilla's account. But Mansilla is far less dismissive of the U.S. flirt, because she finds her excess familiar, a characteristic of New World women more generally.

The American flirt, defined as a hemispheric type, takes the styles of Paris and exaggerates them, a tendency that "ocurre siempre en el exterior" (109) (occurs always in the periphery). In using the term *el exterior* (periphery), Mansilla seems to be drawing a comparison here between settler nations such as Argentina and the United States vis-à-vis their relations to Europe. Mansilla is poking fun at the colonial mimicry that takes place among the bourgeoisie of the "exterior" in imitating the high fashion of Paris, because their imitation is so excessive that it acquires a vulgar valence, whether it is in the extreme amount of tulle, a fabric produced in the nineteenth century from Tulle, France, or in the abundant display of jewelry: "las Yankees tienen muchas alhajas" (109) (The Yankee girls have a lot of jewels). This same tendency toward excess is also evident in the U.S. woman's use of cosmetics from perfumes and elixirs to face powders in every shade of white. The supreme symbol of this love of cosmetics is the blonde hair-dye that is used abundantly among "la mujer Yankee," when dark hair mysteriously changes after a few hours into "una trenza en hilos de oro" (77) (a braid made from threads of gold). Artificial blondes constitute a style that "passed from the U.S. to Paris," an example of the "exterior" influencing the metropolitan center, a detail that Mansilla includes to demonstrate the transatlantic dynamics of women's fashion. By drawing these sorts of comparisons within the "exterior"—as the New World periphery to Europe's metropolitan center—Mansilla is using travel writing to draw analogies rather than distinctions. Where Quesada underscores the differences between Argentina and the United States, Mansilla accentuates the points of comparison, most notably in the excessive fashion of the female flirt.

Argentine Exceptionalism and New World Whiteness

Mansilla's emphasis on the artificiality of the American flirt's blonde hair suggests another point of identification between the elite *porteña* and her U.S. counterpart, that of race.[25] The artifice of the U.S. flirt creates a New World space for embracing artifice over authenticity, which for Mansilla takes the form of artificial whiteness. The trope of whiteness in Argentina is itself a sign of unease and anxiety, particularly in the context of turn-of-the-century race science that privileged Anglo-Saxons and Nordics over the "Latin" races. "Argentine governments since the 1850s," according to the historian Julia Rodríguez, "had advocated increased immigration from northern European countries because they believed that such an infusion would bring 'healthy' traits to the population and thereby rid Argentina of its inferior Latin, Indian, and African racial character. The elites convinced themselves that they were a European nation, and hence racially superior to the rest of Latin America."[26] Mansilla shared Sarmiento's ideal of engineering modern Argentina by recruiting northern European immigrants, and thus eradicating the indigenous element and diluting the southern European presence.[27] But 80 percent of the immigrants in the 1880s came from Italy and Spain, thus preventing Argentina from aspiring to a northern European racial ideal. Although derived from the swarthier hues of European whiteness, Argentine exceptionalism historically emerged from this sense of racial superiority over the rest of Latin America. For the philosopher Enrique Dussell, a transplanted Argentine who lives in Mexico, "Argentina pretended to be white, forgetting that the mestizaje there is simply tremendous."[28] According to the cultural theorist Néstor García Canclini, another Argentine intellectual now living in Mexico, Argentine whiteness is simulated whiteness, a fantasy of racial purity.[29] This racial fantasy is largely based on defining Argentine whiteness against what Dussell calls the "indigene" of Latin America. What Mansilla finds in the artificial blondes of North America is this same yearning for a Nordic ideal that has to be manufactured in order to be achieved. The *fin-de-siècle* beauty myth is racially encoded in ways that complement the "race" science of the time. Furthermore, the artificial blondes of North America legitimate Argentina's own aspirations to artificial whiteness. If authenticity is the bastion of Europe, then at least New World nations like the United States and Argentina can positively acknowledge their inauthenticity, in the sense that their postcolonial mimicry is unapologetically excessive. Where the older Juana Manso, who was Sarmiento's contemporary, found the U.S. flirt to be vulgar, Mansilla finds in this vulgarity a certain refreshing defiance of European mores in the very act of imitating them. Where Argentines of her class mimicked the French elite with such exactitude that the French couldn't believe that Mansilla wasn't French, the Yankee form of mimicry does not aim for accuracy. This indicates a certain Anglo American confidence, including the racial confidence of the U.S. elite, in their own whiteness that the Argentines lacked. Argentine mimicry of Parisian manners was compensatory, demonstrating a need for validation that tried to conceal artifice rather than to flaunt it. Despite this difference, Mansilla nevertheless finds in the U.S. flirt a playful form of mimicry that provides a refreshing counter-example to the far more serious and anxiety-ridden modes of Argentine mimicry of European mores.

Just as the flirt playfully encourages uncertainty, so the response to her is equally ambivalent. On the one hand, Mansilla takes pleasure in this figure's ambiguity and unpredictability; but on the other hand, she finds her vulgarity to be deeply unsettling. This is most apparent when Mansilla describes the American flirt's eating habits. Where Pantoja sees the anti-flirt as a metaphor of American anti-sociality, Mansilla interprets the flirt as a model of U.S. sociality, but a form of sociality that can have repulsive aspects. Mansilla satirically captures the scene of a Yankee girl eating voraciously at a hotel:

Las preciosas niñas yankees de delicadísma tez y delgada cintura, se alimentan especialmente de ostras, cangrejos y langostas. Nunca podré olvidar el asombro que me causó en mi primera comida, en el hotel de Nueva York, ver devorar á una elegante muchacha de dieciocho años, la mitad de una langosta, chupando hasta las antenas, con una delicia, que con elocuente expresión se trasparentaba en su bellísimo semblante. (23)

The precious yankee girls of such a delicate complexion and slim waist seem to live on especially oysters, crabs and lobsters. Never will I ever forget my surprise at my first meal at a New York hotel, when I saw an elegant young lady who was eighteen years old devour half a lobster, sucking even the antennas with such pleasure that her beautiful face had such an eloquent expression.

This scene, which Mansilla describes as a spectacle akin to the realism of Zola, combines innocence with carnality, where frilly flirts become not only desiring objects but also devouring subjects taking pleasure in satisfying their voracious appetites. Mansilla betrays her own prudish notions of femininity in her abject description of female appetite. But Mansilla is also fascinated by this vulgar spectacle, wherein a delicate woman ravenously ingests a lobster rather than carefully and self-consciously eating it in small morsels. This uninhibited scene of dining is both sensuous and disgusting, a juxtaposition that highlights the blonde flirt as a dichotomous sign of attraction and repulsion.

The Argentine Ideal: Post-Confederate Womanhood

Although Mansilla devotes most of her travel narrative to the Yankee flirt as a playful type that is both fascinating and repulsive and associated with the northern cities, she ends her travel narrative with an alternative model of Anglo American femininity, namely the white southern woman. Recollecting her time in the United States during the Civil War, Mansilla closes her narrative by declaring, "yo era sudista" (I was a southerner). Despite the region's association with slavery, she writes, the South "monopolized elegance, refinement and culture" (122). Mansilla's playful tone suddenly changes to one of mourning, particularly for the former Confederate aristocrat whose status has dramatically fallen in the aftermath of the Civil War. In the penultimate paragraph of her travel narrative, she writes:

Cayó vencido, aniquilado ese Sud tan simpático á pesar de sus errores; y sus mujeres más hermosas, más educadas, más opulentas, tuvieron que vivir del trabajo de sus manos. Algunas damas de la mejor sociedad, de Nueva Orleans, se vieron reducidas á ser hasta cocineras. Expiación horrenda! (122)

Conquered and annihilated, that kind South fell, despite its errors. Its most beautiful, educated, and opulent women had to live off the labor of their own hands. Some ladies of the best society, from New Orleans, even saw themselves reduced to cooks. Horrendous atonement![30]

Although Mansilla saw herself as a liberal cosmopolitan who was open to the democratizing spirit of the United States, she was still nostalgic for the privileges of the old aristocratic order, as when she bemoans the lack of good servants in the United States as well as in Argentina.[31] Sympathy with southern elite women marks another point of identification between Argentina and the United States, an inter-American alliance that depends on keeping the freed slave barely visible. The tragedy of the post–Civil War era is that erstwhile aristocrats must now do the cooking.

This example of inter-American sympathy—wherein an elite *porteña* sympathizes with elite post-Confederates through the notion of women's work—provides a way for Mansilla to validate Argentine whiteness.[32] "By 1880, Argentina thought of itself as the only great white nation of South America," writes the historian Thomas McGann, "[t]hus the Argentine upper class conceived a splendid isolation, based not only on its wealth but also on the popular doctrine of the superiority of the white race."[33] The fact that Mansilla specifies an upper-class woman from New Orleans illustrates what Kirsten Silva Gruesz has observed, namely how New Orleans signifies as a "liminal zone between the Anglo and the Latin worlds."[34] The "Latinness" of New Orleans makes it a regional point of identification for an elite *porteña*, who sees in the Confederacy's decline the fragility of her own class status in Argentina. Yet the fallen aristocracy of the South offers Mansilla the fantasy not of economic stability but of racial and cultural superiority. The South, she claims, is descended from French nobility (37). In contrast to the artificiality of the New York blondes, southern white women are cast as effortlessly refined. Where the flirt's excess suggests vulgarity, the Confederate woman's opulence is seen as good taste.

Although in the concluding moments of her narrative Mansilla identifies unequivocally with the southern white woman, both types—the flirt and the Confederate—constitute a paradoxical notion of modern Argentine identity. According to Amy Kaminsky, "Argentina projects its desired version of itself outward, hoping to recoup that version when it is reflected back in the eyes—and words and images—from elsewhere."[35] The regional conflict in the United States provided two warring feminine types, the urban northern flirt and the southern belle, both of whom allowed Mansilla to imagine the tensions of Argentine nationhood through the language of paradoxical feminine types.[36] The artificiality of the American flirt de-naturalizes New World nationality, by disclosing the process of its own construction that Mansilla understands in the Argentine context in racial terms as the production of artificial whiteness. She identifies with this figure as echoing the Argentine mimicry of European standards, but it is an identification that she must disavow. She does so in two ways. First, she underscores the vulgarity of the flirt, which she finds both appealing and repulsive, thus producing her own tone of detachment toward this type. Second, Mansilla disavows the flirt's artifice by embracing the Confederate woman and with her a fantasy of racial purity, gentility, and refinement that is reflected back onto the elite *porteña*. If the flirt is a figure of unveiling, then the Confederate woman is the veil; she sustains the illusion of refinement without hair-dyes and perfumes.

Both Vicente Gregorio Quesada and Eduarda Mansilla use travel writing as a way to negotiate Argentina's rising position within the hemisphere and internationally. But where Quesada uses this genre to articulate the necessity of boundaries, to draw limits for U.S. Pan-Americanism and to resist incorporation, Mansilla transgresses these boundaries by importing a Confederate ideal as a model of feminine refinement. Where the American flirt for Quesada is all about playing with the tensions surrounding the limits of not-having, which includes the self-regulating behavior of American men vis-à-vis the flirt, the American flirt for Mansilla is a mark of limitlessness.

Quesada and Mansilla reveal how exceptionalism is constructed through relationality, whether it is the U.S. or the Argentine versions.

For Mansilla, Argentine exceptionalism derives from racial borrowing from southern white womanhood, whereas for Quesada, Argentine exceptionalism is produced out of a refusal to import or borrow from the North. The American flirt creates the discursive space through which these different views of Argentine–U.S. relations are played out. Where Quesada views American flirtation as a distinctly Yankee phenomenon, as an exercise in libidinal restraint that both fascinates and perplexes, Mansilla's relation to the American flirt resonates with the Freudian uncanny. For Mansilla, the flirt is distinctly "other" particularly in terms of her vulgar eating habits that disgust and intrigue. But as a sign of excess, the flirt is also strangely familiar, accentuating the artificiality of femininity, especially in terms of New World mimicry of European manners and styles. Yet for Domingo de Pantoja, the American flirt does not exist; instead, the U.S. woman is an anti-flirt, a commentary on the absence of sociality that also betrays Pantoja's own anxieties about women's expected role of giving men attention without intention. All three narratives use the trope of the flirt in significantly different ways to highlight the challenges, limits, and advantages of inter-American relations. To articulate hemispheric contact through the figure of the flirt suggests how appealing, uncertain, and even potentially dangerous this encounter (and possible non-encounter) can be.

NOTES

Many thanks to Jean Dickson and Laura Taddeo, research librarians at the University at Buffalo, for directing me to invaluable primary sources. Eva Juarros-Daussà kindly reviewed my translations. I am grateful to David Schmid, Ann Colley, and Carolyn Korsmeyer for comments on earlier drafts, and to Prentiss Clark for her research assistance.

1 Rudyard Kipling, *American Notes* (New York: Arno Press, 1974), 126.

2 Mary Louise Pratt, "Modernity and Periphery: Toward a Global and Relational Analysis," in *Beyond Dichotomies: Histories, Identities, Cultures, and the Challenge of Globalization*, ed. Elisabeth Mudimbe-Boyi (Albany: State University of New York Press, 2002), 53.

3 Marx writes that value "does not have its description branded on its forehead; it rather transforms every product of labor into a social hieroglyphic. Later on, one tries to decipher the hieroglyphic." Just as a commodity like a woman's dress, to use Marx's example, appears to be "an extremely obvious, trivial thing," its analysis reveals that it is actually a "very strange thing." Karl Marx, *Capital*, Vol. 1 Trans. Ben Fowkes (London: Penguin, 1976), 167–68.

4 For a discussion of post-exceptionlism, see Donald Pease, "Rethinking American Studies after US Exceptionalism," *American Literary History* 21.1 (Spring 2009): 19–27.

5 Amy Kaplan, "The Tenacious Grasp of American Exceptionalism," *Comparative American Studies* 2.2 (2004): 153–59.

6 See Sandhya Shukla and Heidi Tinsman, "Editor's Introduction," *Radical History Review* 89 (2004): 1–10.

7 Qtd. in *The Argentina Reader: History, Culture, Politics*, ed. Gabriela Nouzeilles and Graciela R. Montaldos (Durham, N.C.: Duke University Press, 2002), 10.

8 "Buenos Aires se contempló a sí mismo como una coqueta que se mira al espejo," in Domingo Faustino Sarmiento, *Educar Al Soberano*, in *Obras de Domingo Faustino Sarmiento*, vol. 47 (Buenos Aires, 1900): 185.

9 David Viñas, *De Sarmiento a Dios. Viajeros argentinos a USA* (Buenos Aires: Sudamericana, 1998), 60. Throughout the nineteenth century, the only way in which one could reach New York City from the southern cone was through Europe, with the two major steamship lines based in Paris and Liverpool. Direct travel from South America to the United States began only in 1906 from Rio de Janeiro to New York City. Through the outspoken persona of Domingo de Pantoja, Vicente Quesada accuses the United States of refusing to establish steamship lines directly between the two countries as a way to control the importation into the U.S. market of Argentine products such as beef and tallow. See Alicia Vidaurreta, "Tres visiones Argentinas de los Estados Unidos," *Revista de Historia de América* 111 (Jan.–June, 1991): 80.

10 Domingo Faustino Sarmiento, *Travels: A Selection*. Trans. Inés Muñoz (Washington: Pan American Union, 1963), 143.

11 Sarmiento 143.

12 Vicente Gregorio Quesada, *Recuerdos de mi vida diplomática: Misión en Estados Unidos, 1885–1892*, Vol. VI (Buenos Aires: J. Menéndez, 1904), 11. Hereafter cited parenthetically.

13 Adam Phillips, *On Flirtation* (London: Faber, 1994), xvii. Georg Simmel, "Flirtation," *Georg Simmel: On Women, Sexuality, and Love*, trans. Guy Oakes (New Haven, Conn.: Yale University Press, 1984), 133–52.

14 David Pletcher, *The Diplomacy of Trade and Investment: American Economic Expansion in the Hemisphere, 1865–1900* (Columbia: University of Missouri Press, 1998).

15 Vidaurreta, "Tres visiones."

16 Vicente Gregorio Quesada [Domingo de Pantoja], *Los Estados Unidos y la América del Sur: Los yankees pintados por sí mismos*, ed. Jacobo Peuser (Buenos Aires: Rosario, 1893), 4. Hereafter cited parenthetically as *EU*.

17 On the concept of "non-encounter," see Carl Good, "A Chronicle of Poetic Non-Encounter in the Americas," *CR: The New Centennial Review* 3.1 (2003): 225–55.

18 Bonnie Frederick, "El viajero y la nómada: los recuerdos de viaje de Eduarda Mansilla y Lucio Mansilla," *Mujeres y cultura en la Argentina del siglo XIX* (Buenos Aires: Feminaria, 1994), 249. Also see María Rosa Lojo, "Eduarda Mansilla:

entre la 'barbarie' *yankee* y la utopia de la mujer profesional," *Gramma* (Sept. 2003): 14–25. www.salvador.edu.ar/gramma/37/05.pdf.

19 Mónica Szurmuk, *Women in Argentina: Early Travel Narratives* (Gainesville: University Press of Florida, 2000).

20 Eduarda Mansilla, *Recuerdos de Viaje*, ed. J. P. Spicer-Escalante (Buenos Aires: Stockcero, 2006), 108. Hereafter cited parenthetically.

21 The 1880s, the period in which Mansilla wrote her travel narrative, was a time of rapid transformation and national consolidation, when Buenos Aires became the capital of the nation and embodied the new Argentina. According to the historian Julia Rodríguez, "the economic boom of the late nineteenth century led to Argentina's stunning transformation from colonial backwater to an urban, industrial society largely based on exploitation of agricultural resources, in particular, cattle and wheat, and aided by foreign investment, mostly British." Although the United States possessed greater absolute wealth, Argentina's rate of expansion surpassed that of the United States in the twenty years before 1914. Julia Rodríguez, *Civilizing Argentina: Science, Medicine, and the Modern State* (Chapel Hill: University of North Carolina Press, 2006), 21.

22 For a discussion of Mansilla's flirtatious description of domestic interiors, see Samuel Monder, "De la seducción y otras miradas. La institución del *flirt* en los recuerdos de viaje de Eduarda Mansilla," *Revista Iberoamericana* 71:210 (enero-marzo 2005): 105–17.

23 Juana Manso writes, "Yo creo que hay un instinto de coquetería, inherente a la mujer, y que no se puede ser mujer sin ser coqueta," *Album de señoritas* (Buenos Aires, 1854), 79.

24 Juana Manso, *Recuerdos de viaje* (1846) quoted from María Velasco y Arias, ed. *Juana Paula Manso: vida y acción*, (Buenos Aires, 1937), accessed on January 15, 2011, from now-defunct website: http://www.juanamanso.org/2010/06/recuerdos-de-viaje.html.

25 *Porteña* is a woman from the city of Buenos Aires.

26 Julia Rodríguez, *Civilizing Argentina*, 4.

27 For more on Mansilla's views on race, see Eva-Lynn Alicia Jagoe, "Familial Triangles: Eduarda Mansilla, Domingo Sarmiento, and Lucio Mansilla," *Revista Canadiense de Estudios Hispánicos* 29.3 Primavera 2005: 507–524; Beatriz Urraca, "Quien a Yankeeland se encamina . . .": The United States and Nineteenth-Century Argentine Imagination," *ciberletras* 1:2 (enero 2000).

28 Enrique Dussel with Fernando Gomez- Herrero, "Ethics Is the Original Philosophy; or, The Barbarian Words Coming from the Third World: An Interview with Enrique Dussel," *Boundary 2* 28.1 (Spring 2001): 19–73.

29 Qtd. in Amy Kaminsky, *Argentina: Stories for a Nation* (Minneapolis: University of Minnesota Press, 2008), 120.

30 Translation from Szurmuk, *Women in Argentina*, 62.

31 Mansilla writes, "El oficio de sirviente, es más complicado de lo que en las Américas se cree, y tanto nosotros como los Yankees, estamos servidos por *aficionados*"

(original emphasis, 77) (The job of the servant is more complex than what is believed in the Americas. We, as much as the Yankees, are being served by *amateurs*) (translated by Szurmuk, 62).

32 Mansilla writes, "Pobre Sud! A pesar de sus faltas, del látigo cruento con que azotaba las espaldas de sus negros, era simpático. Lo compadezco y le dedico aquí un latido de mi corazon feminino" (40) (Poor South! Despite their faults stemming from the cruel whip that was used to beat the backs of the negroes, they are still sympathetic. I feel sorry for them and I here dedicate to them a beat of my feminine heart). For a discussion of the post-Confederate, see Neil Schmitz, "Faulkner and the Post-Confederate," *Faulkner in Cultural Context/Faulkner and Yoknapatawpha, 1995*, eds. Donald M. Kartiganer and Ann J. Abadie (Jackson: University Press of Mississippi, 1997), 241–62.

33 Thomas F. McGann, *Argentina, the United States, and the Inter-American System, 1880–1914* (Cambridge, Mass.: Harvard University Press, 1957), 57.

34 Kirsten Silva Gruesz, "The Gulf of Mexico System and the 'Latinness' of New Orleans." *American Literary History* 18.3 (2006): 469.

35 Kaminsky, *Argentina: Stories for a Nation*, 57.

36 For more on the southern belle as a postbellum construct, see Nina Baym, *Feminism and American Literary Theory: Essays* (New Brunswick, N.J.: Rutgers University Press, 1992), ch. 12.

12

"Hacemos la guerra pacífica"

Cuban Nationalism and Politics in Key West, 1870–1900

GERALD E. POYO

For thirty years, Key West hosted a radical community of Cuban nationalists who first arrived with the outbreak of the Cuban insurgency of 1868 known as the Ten Years War and, in coordination with other communities of exiles, unwaveringly promoted revolution in Cuba.[1] During this era, rapid expansion of a prosperous Cuban cigar industry made Key West one of Florida's largest and most important cities as well as an important tobacco importer from Cuba. It was a gateway for thousands of Cuban and Spanish cigar workers who participated in a circular migration pattern seeking work in Key West, Tampa, New York, New Orleans, and other less prominent cities.

Cubans in Key West carried transnational interests and perspectives into their daily political, socioeconomic, and cultural realities, founding labor organizations throughout Florida, maintaining busy religious lives especially in Protestant churches, pioneering baseball leagues, and always keeping an eye on their homeland. Cuban nationalist leaders in Key West created numerous institutions, including political clubs and newspapers that helped form a highly politicized and patriotic culture. They also encouraged Cubans to obtain citizenship, participate in local politics, and vote their socioeconomic interests. In exchange for their support in local electoral politics, Cubans expected Anglo Americans to tolerate their constant and frequently disruptive activism, which often involved violations of a variety of U.S. laws, producing interesting political coalitions that often resulted in cordial and mutually advantageous relations, but also tensions and conflicts. Most Cubans imagined their participation in Key West politics an integral part of advancing their local economic well-being, but also critical to their ongoing nationalist struggle. Even the ease with which Cubans became U.S. citizens to defend their local social and economic interests betrayed an adamant rejection of Spanish nationality.

Cuban workers and manufacturers commanded considerable economic resources in the community, and these resources solidified their political influence. The cigar industry was the primary source of wealth for virtually everyone in Key West, and Cubans played a critical role in this prosperity. Tobacco workers usually backed the Republican Party, which often supported their labor demands, while manufacturers found Democrats sympathetic to their interests. Although Cuban cigar manufacturers and workers at times found themselves at odds over labor–management issues, they found ways to cooperate around nationalist concerns and presented a united front advancing Cuban independence goals. Political awareness, economic resources, and social importance in Key West ensured Cubans an important role in local politics as U.S. ethnic subjects in support of exile goals.

When Cubans arrived in Key West in the early 1870s, they entered a community enmeshed in post–Civil War Reconstruction politics. The end of the war led to a general disfranchisement of white southerners who had rebelled against the Union. Northern troops occupied the southern states and Republicans took charge of reorganizing government. Republicans controlled local, state, and federal politics but attracted the support of only a minority of southern whites. Courting former slaves and carpetbaggers, black immigrants from the Bahamas, and white and black Cubans, they fashioned electoral majorities. Already highly politicized, Cubans initially engaged local politics on the side of Republicans. Committed to slave abolition in Cuba, they felt more ideologically compatible with "the party of Lincoln" than with white pro-slavery southerners. They took advantage of Florida laws that allowed immigrants to vote after six months of residence if they filed an intention to seek citizenship, which they could acquire after five years according to federal law.

Republican Party leaders cemented their coalition through carefully calculated patronage appointments. In 1870, the Republican governor appointed Alejandro Mendoza as justice of the peace in Key West and Angel Loño as Monroe County judge. The next year, Juan María Reyes became justice of the peace and the most important Cuban Republican political organizer until his untimely death in a shipwreck in January 1877. Poised to lose city council elections in 1875, Republicans nominated for mayor Carlos Manuel de Céspedes, the son of Cuba's insurgent president of the same name. Céspedes won with the Cuban vote while Anglo American Democrats won the majority of the council, thus demonstrating the effectiveness of a Cuban bloc vote. In the mid-1870s, Céspedes and Manuel Govín secured appointments as Customs House inspectors.[2]

Later, in 1883, contenders within the Republican Party vied for Cuban support. State Senator George Allen headed a faction called the Court House Ring, while Customs Collector Frank Wicker led the party's other major wing. Hoping to replace Wicker as customs collector, Allen courted the Cubans heavily, asking them to sign a petition addressed to the secretary of the treasury requesting his appointment as customs collector and forcing Wicker to defend himself in Washington, D.C. After consolidating his position in Washington, Wicker did the same in Key West among Cubans by appointing Ramón Alvarez deputy customs collector and Fernando Figueredo and Manuel Escassi customs inspectors.[3] These appointments were particularly important for an insurrectionary community involved in smuggling arms and munitions to Cuba on vessels departing Key West.

Cubans also engaged the Democratic Party when doing so seemed advantageous. Disgusted at the Grant administration's failure to help the insurgency in Cuba, some Cubans in 1876 formed a Cuban Democratic Club, attracted 200 to 300 followers, and successfully split the Cuban vote, providing Democrats with a victory. Loño lost his job as county judge for switching political loyalties but astutely recognized the emerging Democratic ascendancy in Florida politics.[4] During the 1880 campaign, competing Cuban newspapers entered the fray. José Rafael Estrada, Pedro Someillán, and Loño published *El Localista* to rally support for the Democrats while a labor newspaper, *La Fraternidad*, edited by Ramón Rivero, supported the Republican Party. The Cuban Hancock and English Club of Key West mobilized 150 supporters for the Democratic presidential ticket. Democrats won the municipal election with less than a 200-vote majority and in the November presidential elections even Manuel Escassi, a Cuban Republican candidate for the state assembly, failed to attract Cuban Democrats and lost with the rest of the Republican ticket. After the election, the Executive Council of the Monroe County Democratic Party rewarded Loño with an appointment to its ranks, and several other prominent Cubans also joined the party, including prominent cigar manufacturer Teodoro Pérez and merchant Carlos Recio.[5]

Cubans even experimented with nontraditional parties. In November 1882, Fernando Figueredo stood for Monroe County representative to the Florida Assembly as a member of a dissident Independent Party that challenged Republicans and Democrats. Except for one popular Anglo American Independent Party candidate, who attracted sufficient Democratic votes to win a U.S. Senate seat, Independents, including Figueredo, lost to Democrats but defeated Republican candidates.[6]

Initially many Floridians resented the important role played by Cubans and other immigrants in Key West, county, and state politics. In 1876, for example, the Key of the Gulf declared, "[T]he idea that foreigners, seeking a temporary refuge on our shores from oppression, should be allowed to control our State, is revolting and antagonistic to every feeling of free and popular government." It continued, "We believe in the permanent residents of any country or state dictating its policy."[7] Another newspaper, The Key West Dispatch, followed with a complaint that "there are already far too many people on the island. Everybody is in everybody's way."[8] While the Dispatch rabidly opposed black Bahamian immigrants, its calmer coverage of Cubans reflected a realization of their growing political power. In fact, Florida newspapers learned to be careful how they wrote about Cubans, fearing political repercussions. One newspaper using the phrase "the scum of the contiguous West India Islands" in referring to recent immigrants to Key West felt compelled to explain that it meant only "the ignorant 'Bahama Negroes.'" "The Cubans are not Negroes," it declared despite their obvious racial diversity, "nor [are they] to be confounded with the 'scum' which floats to our shores from the Bahamas group and floats off again according to circumstances."[9]

National Interests and Local Responses

In 1880, Spain finally pacified Cuba and only a handful of small insurgent groups remained active in the countryside, but in Key West, nationalist leaders continued to agitate for revolution and reorganized the community into an even more militant center. In his newspaper *El Yara*, leading nationalist leader José D. Poyo unceasingly encouraged insurrection, and tobacco workers and cigar manufacturers contributed funds for a variety of revolutionary activities. Cuban militants essentially operated with impunity until 1884, when national political realities impinged on local politics in Key West. In late 1883, Carlos Aguero, a veteran of the Ten Years War who had continued guerrilla operations and remained in touch with Key West's revolutionary community, arrived to raise resources and expand his operations. Alerted to Aguero's arrival by their consul, Spanish diplomats in Washington, D.C., immediately submitted an extradition request characterizing him as a common bandit guilty of "rapine, arson, highway robbery and murder."[10] Ordinarily such a request would have caused little stir in Washington, but high-profile government trade negotiations with Spain produced action. Throughout the 1880s, the Republican Party advocated greater U.S. commerce and economic involvement with Latin America, which in 1889 culminated in the first Inter-American Conference. Especially interested in expanding trade with Cuba, during 1883 officials of the Chester A. Arthur administration were in negotiations with Spain to reduce tariffs across the board, including on sugar and tobacco, and the Aguero case threatened to complicate matters.[11] In January 1884, the administration instructed Key West District Attorney George B. Patterson to arrest Aguero and consider the extradition request in the U.S. District Court presided over by Judge James W. Locke.[12] Though Democrats controlled state and local politics, Republican federal officials in Key West faced the ticklish challenge of enforcing the neutrality laws and prosecuting those sponsoring Aguero's activities.

While the revolutionary leader languished in prison, an outraged Cuban community protested Aguero's arrest, mobilized, and flexed its political muscle. Democrats took advantage of the situation to attract Cuban support when in February Senator Wilkinson Call of Florida offered a resolution in the U.S. Senate characterizing the extradition request as politically motivated and demanded the president prevent the delivery of Aguero.[13] Trying to outdo Democratic politicians, Republican District Attorney Patterson cited a lack of evidence proving Aguero a common criminal and on February 21, Republican Judge Locke formally rejected the extradition request and freed the insurgent activist.[14]

A jubilant Cuban community took to the streets. After a special lunch for Aguero hosted by the nationalist leaders at the offices of *El Yara*, a large crowd proceeded to the San Carlos Community Center, where they celebrated the insurgent chief and *Cuba Libre*. Another Cuban nationalist newspaper, *La Voz de Hatuey*, declared that a freed Aguero planned to leave immediately for Cuba to launch a new war against Spanish colonialism and would be joined by the much-admired and better-known military chieftains Generals Máximo Gómez and Antonio Maceo. "Therefore," declared the newspaper, "let's work with fervor, do what we can," and in the future the historical record would gloriously highlight Cuba's Key West émigrés.[15] A representative of the sheriff, a former slave, spoke in support of Cuban freedom and against the "tyrannical Spanish government." Accompanied by the *Libertad* brass band, the crowd then paraded through the streets demonstrating their appreciation to the supportive local politicians. They stopped before the homes of Aguero's defense attorney and Florida Lieutenant Governor Livingston W. Bethel, District Attorney Patterson, and Customs House Collector Frank Wicker, who openly sympathized with the nationalists. Mounting a stage erected on Front Street, Aguero and others spoke, and later at San Carlos several Republican Party officials also offered their sympathetic thoughts about Cuban independence.[16] Throughout the day, the revolutionary committee received funds to send Aguero to Cuba, including $100 from Wicker in flagrant violation of his obligation to detain military expeditions.

Aguero's clandestine departure on April 1 incensed the Spanish consul, who complained to Washington about the complicity of local officials with the revolutionaries, especially implicating Wicker and his Cuban employees Figueredo and Escassi for their lax enforcement of the neutrality laws. Unfortunately for Wicker, President Arthur's interest in negotiating the reciprocity treaty with Spain outweighed his willingness to support the Republican Party's interests in southern Florida, and the treasury secretary sent special agents to Key West to ensure proper coastal enforcement. In late April, the U.S. Senate removed Wicker from office as a warning to local Republican appointees to uphold the nation's laws.[17]

Spanish consular complaints and more warnings from Washington again reluctantly pushed Patterson into action. The district attorney filed neutrality-violation charges against the now-absent Aguero, as well as everyone involved. Emilo Díaz and Bruno Alfonso faced charges for facilitating the departure; Clinton Shavers, who owned the vessel, was arrested and had his ship confiscated; and Poyo, in charge of the overall operation, received notice of his pending arrest.[18] Further actions followed against the Cuban insurrectionists, with arrests of Cubans involved in stocking arms, munitions, and explosives. On June 11, 1884, Wicker's successor orchestrated the arrest of Federico Gil Marrero, who arrived on a steamer from New York with 100 explosive caps, 500 feet of fuse, and "a dangerous substance called mealed powder, which same were not duly packed and marked as required by law." He also possessed 12 glass tubes, four thermometers, mercury, and alcohol for use in manufacturing dynamite. Charged and arraigned on July 2, Marrero posted a $1,000 bond.[19] Poyo was also accused of storing a large cache of weapons, munitions, and dynamite in his home.[20]

The cases came before Judge Locke's U.S. District Court, but the Cuban community's political influence prevailed. On June 16, the judge refused without comment Patterson's request for a warrant against Poyo, clearing him of any further action. Citing his absence from the city, the court dismissed Aguero's case. While the court did arrest and place on trial activists Díaz, Alfono, and Shavers, local juries convicted only Díaz, who received a sentence of eight months in prison and a $500 fine.[21] The prosecution had no better luck in the dynamite cases. The jury found Marrero not guilty, and several days later Judge Locke returned all the seized items.[22] Not very confident of a victory, the court again dropped weapons charges against Poyo. Frustrated at the verdicts and Locke's return of evidence to Marrero, the Spanish consul commented to his superiors that "the court has yet to find anyone guilty of crimes committed against our government."[23] The Key West courts rarely convicted Cuban nationalists.

Despite the pressure from Washington, Cubans, recognizing that local officials had not pursued the cases with much enthusiasm, rewarded them at the polls that fall. Cubans helped elect Democratic Lieutenant Governor Bethel mayor of Key West as well as Republican Judge Locke to the U.S. Congress, but just to ensure that local politicians recognized their continuing electoral importance, Cubans in a bloc vote seated Fernando Figueredo in the State Assembly, the first Cuban elected to the Florida legislature.[24] Among Figueredo's first acts in Tallahassee was

to sponsor a resolution asking the U.S. Congress to defeat the reciprocal trade agreement and protect Florida's tobacco industry, which was
threatened by the contemplated 50 percent reduction in tariffs on cigars.[25] As Tallahassee's *Weekly Floridian* reported, "There is much anxiety in Key West. . . . as the reduction of the duty would tend to break
down the manufacture of cigars, the principal industry in the city and
chief source of prosperity."[26] More to the point, the Cuban nationalist
community stood to lose its most important source of revolutionary
funds. National elections in November 1884 resulted in the presidency
of Democrat Grover Cleveland, who, to the relief of Key West's cigar
industry, promptly tabled the treaty and reduced the pressure on local
federal authorities to monitor their Cuban citizens.

Diverging Local Interests

Throughout the mid-1880s, Anglo American politicians finessed the
complications arising from Aguero's activities and benefited from
Cuban political support, but attitudes and circumstances changed in
the face of new developments. After 1885, immigration from Cuba
increased, bringing to Key West scores of what Anglo Americans, and
some Cubans, considered unsavory nationalist and radical anarchist
labor activists intent on creating mischief. Cubans arriving in the
late 1880s included a significant number of men who operated on
a blurred border between banditry and nationalist-inspired guerrilla
operations. The Ten Years War had left the Cuban countryside devas-
tated, and many lived as common bandits and highwaymen, raiding
and robbing small towns and plantations. When the Spanish authorities countered with increased military pressure that culminated in the
imposition of martial law in the provinces of Havana, Matanzas, Santa
Clara, and Pinar del Rio, many departed for Key West, where they
found jobs in the cigar factories and were politicized in the nationalist
community.

  Key West's traditional nationalist leaders encouraged them to return
to Cuba and use their unconventional skills to raise funds for the independence movement. Key West revolutionary leaders, most prominently Poyo and Juan Fernández Ruz, sponsored one such personality,
Manuel García, who infiltrated Cuba in 1887 and initiated operations

that lasted until his death at the outbreak of the independence war in 1895.[27] Though the Spanish labeled García a bandit for his raids, kidnappings, and ransom demands and issued warrants for his arrest, he sent considerable sums of money to Key West to support nationalist activities. García's followers and supporters in Key West did what they could to raise funds locally and send reinforcements.[28]

Media reports about these activities created a generally negative image of Key West, as did testimonies from visitors and the Spanish consul in Key West. Spanish newspapers in Cuba and some of the English-language press in Florida characterized the Cuban community as infested with criminals. Referring to Key West as a "nido de sabandijas" (nest of vermin), one Spanish observer who visited in 1889 declared that the town was "nothing notable." "On disembarking," he explained, "it appears as if one had entered some of the most reeking neighborhoods in Havana." Cuban Key West offended his sensibilities as he contemplated "the uproar, disorder, and squalid licentiousness of that heterogeneous group of men, women, youngsters, blacks, mulattos, undefined, and whites chattering endlessly at the docks." He completed his comparison of "these low classes of Key West with their similar types in the capital of the island of Cuba," observing that the "groups of unemployed on the corners" and the "bums in the barrooms possessed identical language styles and absolutely similar vices." The only reason this visitor even bothered to disembark at Key West on his return to Havana from New York, he claimed, was to satisfy his curiosity, to see the place so well known in Cuba as a center of bandits and pirates.[29]

Many Anglo American citizens of Key West, or "Conchs" as they called themselves, agreed that bad elements within the Cuban community harmed Key West's reputation and business environment. They thought that nationalist and anarchist radicals provoked the departure of many cigar entrepreneurs to the Tampa Bay area during 1888 and 1889, directly threatening Key West's commercial dominance in the tobacco trade. Though Cuban nationalist and labor activists had different and often competing agendas and frequently fell into bitter disagreements, Anglo Americans did not distinguish, seeing them all as troublemakers. A few Anglo American businessmen, including a few Spaniards and Cubans, resorted to threats of lynching and deportation. Tampa's leadership implemented such tactics with considerable success in early 1887 to rid their community of troublesome Cuban nationalists they considered detrimental, a strategy Key West then adopted.[30]

The Key West Board of Trade (Chamber of Commerce) took action in 1888 after a Spanish cigar manufacturer, Celestino Palacio, complained that Cuban refugees had demanded "loans or donations" from him and other manufacturers for their nationalist activities. The board unanimously adopted a resolution stating that "all such lawless intimidators are hereby informed that they are known by name and character, and that they be warned to immediately cease all such illegal demands and menace," and demanded from the authorities "a most vigorous prosecution" of anyone violating the resolution. Taking their cue from the Board of Trade, local officials took immediate action against those already identified and characterized as "criminals" and threatened to deport them to Cuba. During April and May, the sheriff arrested nationalist activists Emilio Díaz and Emilio García and scheduled them for trial in November. Another well-known activist, Perico Torres, and some of his followers also suffered arrest, but they posted bond. Isidoro Leijas and José Rodríguez left for Nassau before their arrest, while several others left for Tampa and Jacksonville. Spanish authorities actively sought most of these men whose experience with rebel groups in Cuba certainly operated between nationalism and banditry.[31]

Charles B. Pendleton, former state senator and editor of Key West's *Equator Democrat*, took an aggressive stance against the Cubans. Pendleton reprinted a Havana newspaper report that "the bandit Leijas" in Key West had threatened a Havana resident with kidnapping if he did not respond to his demands for money.[32] When nationalist José R. Estrada's Key West newspaper *La Propaganda* protested and condemned the Board of Trade's actions and threats to lynch Cubans, the *Equator Democrat* observed that the newspaper's effort to "borrow sympathy for these men" was unwise and "is treading upon dangerous ground for its own reputation." "We are no advocate of such means, but these scoundrels have gone further than lynching, they have assassinated," referring to murder charges Emilio García and Leijas had faced in Tampa during 1887 of which they were acquitted. All this focus on Leijas led British authorities in Nassau to arrest him at the insistence of authorities in Cuba, but Leijas hanged himself in his cell rather than face Spanish justice.[33] More to the point, Pendleton claimed that the activities of the two and others like them "have also driven from this city men who contributed largely to our growth and development." He blamed nationalist activists for the departure or pending relocation of numerous manufacturers to Tampa, including Ybor, Lozano Pendas & Co., Palacios, and Villamil Pino & Co. Key West did not yet fully recognize Tampa's real economic comparative advantage that provoked the continual relocation of factories, regardless of the activities of the Cuban nationalists.[34]

A general strike in the Key West cigar industry the next year further aggravated the growing discord between Cubans and Anglo Americans. When the strike began and more manufacturers threatened to move to Tampa, the Board of Trade again took action. It sent a message to the most prominent strike leader, Enrique Messonier, demanding that he meet them at the Key West Bank. Known as the "capitán de los linchadores," Peter Knight greeted Messonier at the bank door and "in a violent tone and impertinent manners told him in English . . . to present himself in the department to which he had been called." Knight ushered him into a room where he met with prominent businessmen, including Pendleton, who said they could not vouch for his safety and ordered him to leave town. At first, Messonier resisted and went to City Hall to file a complaint, but in the presence of the mayor and police chief, the city secretary reiterated the order and the local militia escorted him to the dock. Shortly, other members of the strike-organizing committee received similar warnings.[35]

These actions by the Board of Trade represented a shift in the traditionally tolerant attitudes of the local Anglo American political and economic establishment, a shift that many Cubans resented and condemned. Nationalist leaders reacted angrily, including *El Yara*. Even though Poyo disagreed with Messonier's anarchist affiliation, which threatened nationalist ascendancy among workers, he protested the assaults of the business community on the Cubans. "The injustice committed against D. Enrique Messonier by individuals of the Chamber of Commerce of this city not only violates the constitution and the laws of the United States, but establishes a threatening precedent." *El Yara* declared, "From the moment a citizen is left at the mercy of a coterie that arbitrarily pistol-whips the laws, there can be no liberty, security, no recourse in civil society, since arbitrary action against one is arbitrary action against all."[36]

Another Cuban vented his anger in a Havana newspaper, characterizing the "Yankees de Cayo Hueso" as "old southern Confederates, eternal enemies of the Union, and animated with an unchanging and formidable hate of the colored race." They prohibited marriage between whites and blacks, threatening ministers with a loss of privilege to celebrate marriages and a $1,000 fine. The mayor of Key West, he added, enjoyed extraordinary powers to imprison people accused of public drunkenness and put them to work in chains on city streets without even making formal charges or going to court. The "Yankees," he further noted, considered Cuban workers an "inferior race, almost the same as the negroes of Nassau who have been the object of the worst and harshest treatment that can be conceived."[37]

Once again, in light of these conflicts, ethnic resentments filtered into the electoral arena in 1888, and the Cuban community sent a strong message to Anglo Americans. Well-known Cuban nationalist activists stood for election in both parties that year to the Florida House of Representatives. Cigar maker and associate editor of *El Yara* Manuel P. Delgado ran as a Democrat while Dr. Manuel Moreno, who had also prominently backed guerrilla fighter Manuel García, offered his candidacy as a Republican. The November elections resulted in a victory for both Cubans, who defeated their Anglo American opponents in a close contest. An ethnic bloc–vote delivered both seats to the Cuban candidates as well as a caution to Anglo American politicians, rejecting their high-handed approach to resolving concerns about the Cuban community.[38] Cubans again demonstrated their determination to defend exile goals and interests through ethnic activism in the political system.

"Guerra pacífica"

The usually contained tensions between Cubans and Anglo Americans exploded into open conflict with the onset of the national economic downturn of 1893, which ruptured what remained of the coexistence between Anglo American economic interests and Cuban nationalist goals. Since January 1892, the Cuban nationalist movement, now headed by prominent New York activist José Martí, had grown more powerful with the founding in Key West of the Cuban Revolutionary Party (PRC). Poyo headed the party's local council and oversaw the creation of an effective fundraising system in the cigar factories that provided resources for a large military expedition Martí secretly organized. In most factories, workers contributed enthusiastically, and Cuban manufacturers generally went along, but many resented the arrangement. Workers opposed to or ambivalent about nationalist politics also had to contribute in the factories in order to secure employment while many non-Cuban businessmen protested nationalist interference in their enterprises.

Whenever Martí visited Key West's highly politicized factories, manufacturers braced for interruptions in their production. In July 1892, for example, accompanied by local PRC commissions, dozens of workers, and much fanfare, Martí visited numerous factories, delivering speeches and raising money. After his departure, the local correspondent of the trade newspaper *Tobacco Leaf* declared, "Peace reigns at last." "For the first time in three weeks," the correspondent explained, "the work of the cigar makers has been uninterrupted by demonstrations of the Cuban revolutionists."[39]

This increased nationalist activity in the factories combined with difficult economic conditions in 1893 provoked tensions in the community. Problems began when manufacturers facing a rapidly declining demand for cigars imposed a unilateral reduction in wages, provoking a number of strikes. As the year's end approached, La Rosa Española, one of Key West's largest factories owned by German entrepreneur William Seidenberg, tried to reopen after a short strike, but workers refused to return when they learned that the company had recruited thirteen Spanish workers in Havana at lower wages. The PRC expressed solidarity with the workers, viewing the arrival of Spanish labor as a threat to the integrity of the Cuban nationalist community, and called for a reasonable negotiated solution to the general strike. Seidenberg appealed to the Key West Board of Trade, threatening to move operations to Tampa if the board failed to confront striking workers and facilitate the importation of Spanish workers directly from Havana. Fierce competition with Tampa and other Florida cigar communities like Jacksonville and Ocala increased daily, convincing Key West officials of the need to control labor and break the power of the PRC in the factories. Though they expected a strong reaction from the unions and the PRC leadership, they feared greater problems if Seidenberg left Key West.

On January 2, 1894, a special PRC crisis commission composed of Poyo, Figueredo, Manuel P. Delgado, Teodoro Pérez, and Miguel A. Zaldívar joined a multitude including several Protestant ministers and their congregations at the docks, where an armed police contingent awaited the arrival of a steamer from Havana with about one hundred Spanish cigar workers. Also on hand was the Partida La Tranca, a Cuban vigilante group traditionally dedicated to intimidating Spaniards attempting to disembark in Key West, and dozens of Ten Years War veterans.[40] Among the first to disembark was Seidenberg himself and the delegation of the Key West Board of Trade that had traveled to Havana in late December to negotiate directly with the Spanish captain general for permission to recruit workers. The delegation included the mayor, collector of customs, federal and county judges, and prominent religious and business leaders. They wanted only Spanish workers unsympathetic to the Cuban nationalist cause and guaranteed them protection, which the Spanish government applauded and believed would weaken the Cuban nationalist enclave. With Cubans expressing their displeasure, police escorted the Spanish workers to their quarters close to the Seidenberg factory. The day did not end without confrontations and fights that led to arrests of numerous Cubans, including Rosendo García, a well-known nationalist leader of the Partida La Tranca, whom the authorities held without charges, hoping to intimidate the Cuban community.[41]

As the Spanish workers took their jobs, Cuban leaders fully understood that local authorities had violated the country's laws prohibiting foreign contract workers. The crisis commission Poyo headed set out to find a lawyer to challenge the action, but no Key West lawyer dared take the case. Poyo then contacted Martí in New York who arranged for an attorney to travel to Key West. In the meantime, when La Rosa Española resumed work with Spanish workers, the nationalist community called on Cubans to boycott Anglo Americans in every respect. Military veteran of the Ten Years War Serafín Sánchez explained, "Hacemos guerra pacífica," meaning the Cuban community launched a boycott against all American economic establishments: "no Cuban spends a cent on any American." "We don't buy anything," he said. "Cubans stay away from American shops, the butcher can't sell meat, the American carriage driver has no customers, the black domestic does not cook, clear floors, or even wash clothes, and so it goes."⁴² Cuban women took the lead in organizing the boycott, and one well-known activist and orator, Carolina "La Patriota," took up guard at a Cuban monument at the cemetery commemorating Cuban war dead after hearing that someone had attempted to vandalize the symbol of independence. After consulting the spirits, she told the community not to worry, that "time is on our side."⁴³

Within a few days of the confrontations, twenty-four-year-old New York attorney Horatio Rubens arrived in Key West and the PRC crisis commission assigned Manuel P. Delgado to aid him. As a former Monroe County representative in Tallahassee and fluent in English, Delgado knew the local Anglo American politicians well and as a notary prepared the necessary legal documents for the local court. Disturbed at Rubens's presence in Key West and noting his youth, local authorities attempted to intimidate the lawyer. During his first night in Key West, several men entered his hotel room and suggested he leave the city, but the Cuban community kept a close guard on him.⁴⁴ Rubens turned his attention to the contract labor case, quickly concluding that local federal authorities, including the district attorney and district court judge, planned to ignore what was an obvious violation of federal contract labor laws. He filed a complaint with the superintendent of immigration at the U.S. Department of Treasury, who investigated and summoned the contending parties to Washington.⁴⁵ Rubens represented the Cubans while the Key West delegation included the mayor, collector of customs, Seidenberg, and a few others. They met with the superintendent and the secretary of the treasury and finally on January 27 with the attorney general, who ruled that deportation warrants be prepared against the Spanish workers.⁴⁶

On receiving the formal order of deportations, lawyers for the Spanish workers secured orders of *habeas corpus* placing the deportations in abeyance and secured further legal protection by having the Spaniards sign affidavits declaring their intentions to become U.S. citizens. The Treasury Department also ordered Patterson to arrest those responsible for bringing the workers to Key West, but a visiting district judge from New Orleans summarily dismissed the charges and turned the proceedings against the Cuban community. The Cubans, not the Anglo American citizens of Key West, were the lawbreakers, the judge told Patterson in open court. He reprimanded the district attorney for neglecting "his duty in not making charges against General [*sic*] Martí and others who had been raising funds here at various times for the purpose of carrying on a war with a nation with which the United States was at peace and had a treaty." The citizens of Key West did err, he said, in not "taking steps long ago to have prevented such illegal matters."[47] According to Rubens's account, when he objected the judge accused him of interfering in local matters and defending delinquents "who raised funds—and on this matter he was very well informed—to promote revolution in Cuba against Spain." "You should all be in jail," he yelled at Rubens. He immediately sent a cable to the secretary of the treasury and the attorney general, who appealed the case even as relations between Cubans and North Americans further deteriorated.[48] The next day, the Immigration Bureau's agent in Key West arrested ninety-three Spanish workers, and their attorneys requested writs of *habeas corpus* in two test cases. Judge Boarmann again dismissed the cases, citing the lack of evidence and prompting defense attorneys to issue writs for the rest of the laborers. Patterson immediately prepared a case for the appeals court, but workers remained at their jobs and the Cuban community felt betrayed.[49]

The district judge's verbal assault on the members of the PRC highlighted the local authorities' intention to disrupt revolutionary activities, and in this, they were somewhat successful. Threatened with arrest, Poyo and local PRC leaders temporarily ceased their fundraising activities while investigating their legal rights to conspire against Spanish rule in Cuba. Rubens assured Martí and Poyo that nothing in U.S. law prohibited the PRC's activities, at least until they launched an assault on a friendly nation. Given the threats, Martí nevertheless urged Poyo to proceed with prudence and at his own pace, even suggesting that PRC Secretary Gualterio García take the lead initially and Poyo remain less visible.[50]

The conflict became even more complicated as a war of words embroiled the *Equator Democrat, El Yara*, José Martí's *Patria*, and *El Porvenir*, a newspaper in New York. A personal enemy of Martí, *El Porvenir's* editor, Enrique Trujillo, condemned the introduction of contract workers but also opposed revolutionary nationalism and held Martí and the local PRC responsible for the escalating tensions. Martí's nationalist rhetoric and the PRC's militant ethos, Trujillo argued, provoked the violent confrontations. He complained of Martí's inflammatory article

"A Cuba," also reprinted in English in the *Equator Democrat*, which reassured Cubans of the justness of their cause, condemned the Anglo American community, and interpreted these events as further motivation to secure their own country.[51] Trujillo condemned the politicization in the cigar establishments designed to raise funds for revolution as well as the military-like organization on the factory floors that enforced the exclusion of Spaniards. Rather than rejecting and alienating Spanish workers, Trujillo counseled Cuban workers to respect their right to work, tell them of their nationalist aspirations, and win them over.[52]

Cubans debated how best to respond and initially attempted to influence the political parties, but this no longer made sense in this ethnically polarized circumstance. Democratic and Republican party politicians unanimously supported the actions of the local authorities, causing many frustrated Cubans to bolt the parties altogether. On February 6, a group of Cubans formed a new political party, Partido Independiente, whose executive committee included Fernando Figueredo (president), Martín Herrera (first vice president), M. R. Moreno (second vice president), and Manuel P. Delgado (secretary). The first three were Republicans and the last a Democrat, reflecting Cuban disaffection with both parties. Now they had little leverage in the face of the apparent unity of Anglo Americans of both parties.[53] Feeling a deep sense of betrayal and without leverage to influence developments, Cubans decided to abandon the city and relocate to the Tampa Bay area.

During January and February, hundreds of workers departed in search of work, but manufacturers and important Cuban community leaders joined the migration. In early March, a committee of Cubans, strongly supportive of the PRC and associated with the tobacco industry, including E. F. O'Halloran, Teodoro Pérez, Manuel Barranco, Martín Herrera, Severo de Armas, F. Fleitas, and Fernando Figueredo, visited Tampa and soon returned determined to relocate.[54] In Tampa, the Cuban entrepreneurs received inducements to move their factories, including land and buildings, and a new cigar center in Ocala offered further possibilities. In addition to an estimated 1,500 to 2,000 workers, important PRC leaders followed the manufacturers, including Figueredo.[55] *El Yara* announced, "It is resolved: the indecisiveness of the majority of Cubans about leaving to other places is now firmly resolved. The agreement by seven or eight Cuban manufacturers to transfer their factories to West Tampa is definite." "The new Israelites," declared *El Yara*, "depart to plant their tents in less ungrateful lands . . . let us take up the pilgrim's knapsack . . . and prepare to leave."[56]

The PRC experienced a difficult setback during the first half of 1894. The revolutionary community seemed on the verge of collapse after so many years of careful organizing. Threats to arrest its leaders, as well as the mass exodus of manufacturers and workers, left the PRC depleted; the number of revolutionary clubs declined and the contributions in the factories almost ceased. PRC structures in the factories, including the collection committees, disappeared or at least weakened as many manufacturers took advantage of the PRC's lower profile to establish greater control over hiring and managing the factory floors. Equally troubling, events poisoned the careful relationships nationalists had built with local Anglo American supporters who now seemed to be dangerous enemies.

Despite the bleak situation, Poyo remained in Key West, as did Manuel P. Delgado, and many military veterans like General Serafín Sánchez and General Carlos Roloff, who viewed the city as an indispensable location for communicating with insurgent organizers in Cuba and eventually infiltrating the island. Among the major Cuban-owned manufactories only Eduardo Gato remained despite worker pleas to relocate his factory. In a petition to Gato, they denounced recent events and expressed solidarity with the manufacturer. "Mr. Gato," the workers declared, "in search of justice we arrived at these shores . . . there is no justice [here] . . . we must go where it is offered. Let us all depart." Though grateful for the workers' solidarity, Gato made clear he did not intend to be driven from Key West and revealed that he had been offered economic inducements to remain, the first sign of a change of heart by local authorities.[57] Poyo and Delgado still published *El Yara*, including the launching of an English-language version in March hoping to open a conversation between the Cuban and Anglo-American communities. "Animated and brilliant is the first issue in English," observed Martí in *Patria*. "Its soul is José Dolores Poyo, and its language—precise and sharp—belongs to Manuel Delgado."[58]

The road to reconciliation began in earnest when another dramatic event startled the Anglo American community and forced a new attitude. On March 20, a dispute in La Rosa Española factory over layoffs and wages led to a confrontation but this time between the newly imported Spanish workers and the factory management. When conversations broke down, workers stoned the factory, broke windows, and attempted forcibly to enter the building. A contingent of police rushed to the scene and pushed the protesters back, but not before a flying rock struck and severely injured the Spanish foreman who had overseen the importation of the workers. The disturbance outraged Seidenberg, who issued a statement declaring that this incident represented a victory for the Cubans and a humiliation for Anglo Americans. The factory opened again after three days, but in the meantime Seidenberg also made plans to relocate to Tampa.[59]

Key West's Anglo American leadership realized their miscalculation. Importing Spanish strike breakers to undermine Cuban labor unions and the PRC complicated relations with the federal authorities in Washington, D.C., and sparked a wholesale exodus of Cuban workers and manufacturers. Gato's factory, the largest remaining Cuban-owned establishment, stayed, but only because the authorities courted him and provided the kinds of inducements offered in Tampa. Anglo Americans harmed relations with their Cuban neighbors without stemming the movement of factories to the Tampa Bay area, which they learned had more to do with economic competition than labor and nationalist activism. Furthermore, they were sorely disabused of their expectation that contracting anarchist-influenced Spanish laborers in Havana uninterested in Cuban nationalism would resolve their labor–management problems. This unfortunate event and its consequences caused some, including Pendleton's *Equator Democrat*, to rethink their attitude and seek reconciliation, asking Cubans to remain in Key West, where they could more effectively serve the Cuban independence movement.[60] Throughout April tensions declined and both sides worked to bring the conflicts and animosities to an end. In February 1895, Cubans finally launched their uprising against Spain and though federal authorities in Key West remained vigilant, most local Anglo American politicians rallied behind the Cuban cause.

Conclusion

Cubans in Key West participated politically as U.S. ethnic subjects but always with a transnational perspective that advanced Cuban independence. Cordial relations between Cubans and Anglo Americans usually prevailed, but whenever events derailed the political quid pro quo and threatened the nationalist cause, relations quickly deteriorated into disagreement, distrust, and angry ethnic strife. During 1880–95, political pressures external to Key West as well as local Anglo American perceptions that nationalist activism affected the city's prosperity threatened the local political understandings created in the 1870s. The U.S. government's desire to advance a reciprocal trade agreement with Spain first provoked tensions between Cubans and local authorities during 1883 and 1884. Although local federal officials took legal action against leading Cuban nationalists for launching expeditions and accumulating weapons, they did so with little enthusiasm, leading to the acquittal of most. However, when Anglo Americans perceived their local economic interests to be in jeopardy during 1888 and 1889, they took firm action against offending Cubans, including imprisonment, deportations, and threats of lynching. Anglo Americans blamed disruptive Cubans for the departure of cigar factories to Tampa and other locales and determined to control them more effectively. Cubans did not bend to intimidation and continued defending their nationalist activism through local participation as ethnic subjects. José Martí's arrival in Key West injected even more nationalist enthusiasm, which Anglo Americans viewed as a further assault on their economic integrity. In 1894, this resulted in direct and even violent ethnic confrontations between Cubans and Anglo Americans that dissipated only when Key West authorities recognized that the mass exodus of Cubans from Key West represented a greater threat to their interests than refusing to continue satisfying the demands of important non-Cuban cigar manufacturers.

After a tenuous reconciliation, Cubans returned to their nationalist work and Anglo Americans reassured them of their sympathy for Cuban independence, especially after the outbreak of the second war of independence in early 1895. The two groups dealt with each other carefully and avoided direct confrontations. Expeditionary organizing resumed in direct violation of neutrality laws, again complicating U.S. relations with Spain, and while federal authorities guarded the coasts and intercepted numerous expeditions, Anglo Americans in Key West turned a blind eye when they could. After Spain's defeat most Cuban political leaders returned to Cuba, transforming politics in Key West. Exile politics disappeared and Cuban involvement in politics reflected more clearly ethnic interests focused on defending local economic and social concerns rather than nationalist ideals and transnational experiences.

NOTES

1 For background on the Cuban nationalist communities in the United States during the nineteenth century see Gerald E. Poyo, *"With All, and For the Good of All"*: *The Emergence of Popular Nationalism in the Cuban Communities of the United States, 1848–1898* (Durham, N.C.: Duke University Press, 1989).

2 Gerald E. Poyo, "Cuban Revolutionaries and Monroe County Reconstruction Politics, 1868–1876," *Florida Historical Quarterly* (April 1977): 407–18.

3 Consuelo E. Stebbins, *City of Intrigue, Nest of Revolution. A Documentary History of Key West in the Nineteenth Century* (Gainesville: University Press of Florida, 2007), 167–71.

4 Jefferson B. Browne, *Key West. The Old and the New* (Gainesville: University Press of Florida, 1973), 69; Poyo, "Cuban Revolutionaries," 419.

5 *Semi-Weekly Floridian* (Tallahassee), September 17, October 8, 12, 15, November 23, 1880; February 7, 1882, University of Florida Libraries (UFL).

6 *Weekly Floridian* (Tallahassee), November 21, 1882; January 23, April 12, 1883, UFL.

7 *Key of the Gulf* (Key West), July 1, 1876, UFL.

8 *Weekly Floridian* (Tallahassee), August 15, 1876, UFL.

9 *Weekly Floridian* (Tallahassee), November 24, 1874, UFL.

10 Browne, *Key West*, 120–21.

11 Tom Terrill, *The Tariff, Politics, and American Foreign Policy, 1874–1901* (Westport, Conn.: Greenwood Press, 1973), 72, 85.

12 Mr. Frelinghuysen to Mr. Reed, April 30, 1884, in House Executive Documents, 2nd Session, 48th Congress, 1884–1885, I, document 359, in *Papers Relating to the Foreign Relations of the U.S. Transmitted to Congress, With the Annual Message of the President, December 1, 1884.* (Washington: U.S. Government Printing Office, 1885).

13 *Weekly Floridian* (Tallahassee), February 12, 1884, UFL.

14 *Weekly Floridian* (Tallahassee), February 26, 1884, UFL.

15 *La Voz de Hatuey* (Key West), March 1, 1884, H 1868, 1885–1896, Archivo del Ministerio de Asuntos Exteriores. Madrid (AMAE).

16 *El Yara* (Key West), February 23, 1884, Correspondence from Enrique Dupuy de Lome to US Secretary of State, March 17, 1884, Notes from the Spanish Legation in the US to the Department of State, 1790–1906, National Archives and Records Administration.

17 *Weekly Floridian* (Tallahassee), April 22, 29, 1884, UFL; Browne, *Key West*, 120; U.S. Congress, Senate Journal, 48th Congress, 1st Sess., 272; House Journal, 48th Cong., 1st Sess., 531, 635; House Executive Documents, 48th Cong., 2nd Sess., I, 493–95, 502–21.

18 United States vs. Emilio Diaz, case no. 213 (pages 1–8); United States vs. Bruno
    Alfonso, case no. 214 (pages 9–14); United States vs. Clinton Shavers, case no. 221
    (pages 25–35); United States vs. Carlos Aguero, case no. 222 (37–40) in Criminal
    Final Record, July 1884–May 1906; United States vs. José D. Poyo, July 5, 1884,
    Violation of Neutrality Law in General, Minutes, February 1883–April 1888. U.S.
    District Court. Southern District of Florida, Record Group 21. National Archives
    and Records Administration, SE Division, Atlanta, Georgia (NARA, SE)

19 United States vs. Federico Gil Marrero, case no. 220 (pages 18–24), July 1884 in
    Criminal, Final Record, July 1884–May 1906. NARA, SE.

20 Stebbins, City of Intrigue, 138–39.

21 United States vs. Emilio Diaz, case no. 213 (pages 1–8); United States vs. Bruno
    Alfonso, case no. 214 (pages 9–14); United States vs. Clinton Shavers, case no. 221
    (pages 25–35); United States vs. Carlos Aguero, case no. 222 (37–40) in Criminal Final
    Record, July 1884–May 1906; United States vs. José D. Poyo, July 5, 1884, Violation of
    Neutrality Law in General, Minutes, February 1883–April 1888. NARA, SE Division.

22 United States vs. Federico Gil Marrero, case no. 220 (pages 18–24), July 1884 in
    Criminal, Final Record, July 1884–May 1906. NARA, SE Division.

23 Stebbins, City of Intrigue, 138–39.

24 Weekly Floridian (Tallahassee), October 28, December 9, 1884, UFL.

25 Weekly Floridian (Tallahassee), January 27, February 3, 1885, UFL.

26 Weekly Floridian (Tallahassee), December 9, 16, 1884; January 13, February 3, 1885,
    UFL.

27 Joaquin M. Torroja, Consul, Cayo Hueso to Excmo. Señor Ministro de Estado,
    Madrid, August 22, September 14, 1887, AMAE; "Manifiesto," Las Novedades,
    November 8, 1888, "Hispanic American Newspapers, 1808–1980," Readex Digital
    Collections, Newsbank (RDC).

28 For background on the problem of banditry in Cuba during the 1880s, see Rosalie
    Schwartz, Lawless Liberators: Political Banditry and Cuban Independence (Dur-
    ham, N.C.: Duke University Press, 1989).

29 El Bandolerismo en Cuba, 3 vols. (Havana: Establecimiento Tipográfico, 1890), I,
    117–23.

30 Joaquin M. Torroja, Consul, Cayo Hueso to Excmo. Señor Ministro de Estado,
    Madrid, February 8, 11, 1887, AMAE.

31 The Daily Equator Democrat (Key West), May 31, 1888, AMAE.

32 The Daily Equator Democrat (Key West), June 8, 1888, AMAE.

33 The Daily Equator Democrat (Key West), May 31, 1888, AMAE.

34 The Daily Equator Democrat (Key West), June 12, 1888, AMAE.

35 El Productor (Havana), November 3, 1889, Biblioteca Nacional José Martí (BNJM)

36 El Yara (Key West), October 29, 1889, Legajo 721, Caja 54/7986, Fondo 26.1, Grupo
    de Fondo 10, Archivo General de Administración. Alcala de Henares (AGA).

37 El Español (Havana), November 26, 1889," in "Recortes de Periódicos, 23 Noviem-
    bre al 1 de Diciembre de 1889," Legajo 260, no.4, Asuntos Politicos, Archivo
    Nacional de Cuba (ANC).

38 *Weekly Floridian* (Tallahassee), January 1, 1889, UFL; *La Propaganda* (Key West), November 12, 1888, AMAE.

39 *Tobacco Leaf* (New York), July 20, 27, August 3, 1892.

40 Gerardo Castellanos y Garcia, *Motivos de Cayo Hueso* (UCAR, García y Cia., 1935), 287–91.

41 Ibid., 290–91.

42 Serafín Sánchez a Gerardo Castellanos, January 17, 1894, in Castellanos, *Motivos de Cayo Hueso*, 293–94.

43 Castellanos, *Motivos de Cayo Hueso*, 293–94.

44 Horatio S. Rubens (trans. Adolfo G. Castellanos), *Libertad. Cuba y su apostol* (Havana: La Rosa Blanca, 1956), 2–10.

45 Rubens, *Libertad*, 31–36; *Charlotte Observer* (Charlotte, N.C.), January 10, 1894; *The State* (Columbia, S.C.), January 12, 1894, "Early American Newspapers, 1690–1922," RDC.

46 *Charlotte Observer* (Charlotte, N.C.), January 21, 1894; *Savannah Tribune* (Savannah, Ga.), January 27, 1894; *The State* (Columbia, S.C.), January 29, 1894, "Early American Newspapers, 1690–1922," RDC.

47 *Columbus Daily Enquirer* (Columbus, Ga.), February 10, 1894, "Early American Newspapers, 1690–1922," RDC.

48 Rubens, *Libertad*, 33–35.

49 *Columbus Daily Enquirer* (Columbus, Ga.), February 11, 1894, "Early American Newspapers, 1690–1922," RDC.

50 José Martí to Presidente del Cuerpo de Consejo de Cayo Hueso, April 4, 1894; to Gualterio García, April 3, 1894, Luis García Pascual and Enrique Moreno Pla, eds. *José Martí. Epistolario.* 5 vols. (Havana: Editorial Ciencias Sociales, 1993), IV, 96, 101–2.

51 *Patria* (New York), January 27, 1894.

52 *El Porvenir* (New York), January 24, 1894, BNJM.

53 *El Porvenir* (New York), February 14, 21, 1894, BNJM; José Martí to Antonio Maceo, February 1, 1894, García Pascual, ed., *José Marti. Epistolario*, IV: 37–38; Castellanos, *Motivos de Cayo Hueso*, 301.

54 *El Porvenir* (New York), March 14, 1894, BNJM; *Tobacco Leaf* (New York), March 14, 1894.

55 José Martí to Ramón Rivera, [April] 1894, García Pascual, ed., *José Martí. Epistolario*, IV: 125.

56 *Patria* (New York), April 5, 1894.

57 *Patria* (New York), March 16, 1894.

58 Ibid.

59 *The Sun* (Baltimore), March 24, 1894; "Early American Newspapers, 1690–1922," RDC; *Tobacco Leaf* (New York), March 28, April 4, 1894.

60 *Patria* (New York), April 5, 1894.

13

Citizenship and Illegality in the Global California Gold Rush

JUAN POBLETE

But the story as told by the foreign populations is not known
to us. We can see only indirectly, through the furious and
confused reports of the American themselves, how much of
organized and coarse brutality these Mexicans suffered from
the miners' meetings.
—Josiah Royce, *California*

On the stage of this most raucous international fair in human memory, no actor played the part that had been his lot
in his native land. The master became a servant, the lawyer a
freight agent, the physician a long-shoreman. . . .
—Vicente Pérez Rosales, *Times Gone By*

The Immigrant eloquently shows the philosopher that not
just the corner where he was born but the world is man's
homeland.
—Vicente Pérez Rosales[1]

At the time of the Gold Rush, important forms of connection between
California and Chile became readily apparent in both Chile and the
United States. First, there was an oceanic connection and a circuit that
travelers and goods would follow. A Chilean newspaper presented it succinctly in 1848: "It is a true fever of immigration what has taken over a
part of our population; a fever that the Americans will use to speculate.
Their interest is to populate the Californias, give them more commercial
value and create on the Pacific a State capable of balancing or even dom-
inating if possible the mercantile ports on the coast, from Cape Horn to

the Isthmus of Panama."[2] The quote embodies well the dual nature of the California challenge as seen from the southern Americas: It was both a great opportunity for Chilean commerce and people and a direct threat to the Chilean hegemony on the Pacific coast.

Second, as Brian Roberts has shown, those traveling around Cape Horn and through the Panama isthmus participated in processes of racialization that shaped the American perception of Latin American immigrants and residents. Roberts explains: "[T]here is evidence that forty-niners meant this darkness literally, that is, that these deeds had originated with the dark people of the rush, with Mexican bandits, Chilean gamblers, and Latina prostitutes. An examination of forty-niners' contact with Latin America during their voyage to California reveals the social history of these 'dark' deeds."[3] These narratives of deeds by so-called dark people account for a good deal of the power of the Gold Rush over the American imagination, for they presuppose a middle-class northeastern reader for whom such deeds, in their blatant challenge to Victorian values of "repression, refinement and self-control,"[4] would have been particularly egregious and attractive.

These racialized depictions raise important questions about how participants in this migration were affected by and responded to the formation of new social structures. A series of texts produced in Chile and California by Chilean and U.S. writers about the Gold Rush offers early expressions of the tensions between immigration, illegality, and citizenship. In the context of the early Gold Rush, all miners—American, Chilean, Peruvian, Mexican, Californio, Chinese, Australian—were in the words of Josiah Royce "trespassers" and "intruders" because they were all making private claims in what were legally federal lands. However, because land claims necessarily involved claims to citizenship, Gold Rush California could be seen as a kind of political, social, and cultural laboratory for the articulation of land rights and citizenship status for minority groups. My chapter analyzes Chilean author Vicente Pérez Rosales's *Diario de un viaje a California* (1949) and his *Recuerdos del Pasado* (1882) and American philosopher Josiah Royce's *California: From the Conquest in 1846 to the Second Vigilance Committee in San Francisco* (1886) and argues that both authors considered the rights of those from differing racial, ethnic, and national origins who found themselves sharing a particular territory. This form of co-presence created the context within which answers were produced to the questions of who is the subject of rights and what are the legitimate grounds of such claims.

While both Pérez Rosales and Royce were severe critics of the many forms of abuse against racially and ethnically defined immigrants and indigenous peoples during the Gold Rush, they shared a racialized national imaginary that placed the interests of the state above those of the inhabitants of their territories. In turn, they distinguished between those who were considered desirable and undesirable inhabitants of the South of Chile and the U.S. Southwest, respectively. Or, to put it in a more provocative way, this chapter deals with the partially transnational origins of racial and ethnic discrimination in California and the emergence in the state and in Chile of a white social imaginary animating immigration and settlement policies.

Another connection, this time physical, between California and Chile, was described by Benjamin Vicuña Mackenna in his *La Edad del Oro en Chile*. Vicuña Mackenna highlights the close resemblance between the two geographies: ". . . that country which, being in a certain sense our antipode, would seem by its nature, orography, latitude, its productions, climate, geological phenomena only a reproduction of ours or vice versa."[5] Vicuña Mackenna's point was twofold. On the one hand, he insisted, like so many of the Chilean Forty-Niners, on the geographic similarities of the two territories; on the other, he pointed to the natural similarity and complementarity of seasonal agricultural production in Chile and California which, given the multiple needs of the suddenly populated California, made them potential partners in the development of commerce.

Several other forms of connection between Chile and California also emerged during this period, including a textual or more broadly discursive connection formed by a series of texts in California and Chile. To the writings by Royce and Pérez Rosales already mentioned and the countless newspaper articles in both contexts, one could add those of Vicuña Mackenna, Ramón Jil Navarro, and Pedro Ruiz Aldea on the Chilean side, and Richard Henry Dana, Bancroft and his collaborators, and the many analyzed by Roberts and others on the American side. This textual connection is extended and well represented today in books such as Ariel Dorfman's recent novel *Americanos: Los Pasos de Murieta*—concerning twin brothers who upon seeing Joaquín Murieta's head at a bar embark on divergent California-based trajectories. Isabel Allende's *Daughter of Fortune* and *Zorro* are two other recent novels concerned with the early days of California in the form of historically based fictional explorations of the Gold Rush and Spanish and Mexican California. These last three texts share their interest in the foundational moment of California history, banditry, justice and the lack thereof, and their connections to the fate of Californios and Chilean immigrants. They are the latest examples within a constellation of texts exploring the California borderlands as a cultural contact zone. According to Robert McKee Irwin, in such a borderland a series of texts revisits at multiple times the life of a cultural icon from the different cultural and political perspectives of different populations. Contact zone texts are written and rewritten, told and retold, reproduced and changed orally and in various forms of writing by different communities, using their own protocols for historical and cultural interpretation. Studying Mexico's northern borderlands, McKee proposes a transnational approach capable of considering "more than just a summation or fusion of two national cultures"[6] incorporating both local and regional dynamics and other national immigrant aspects. It is in that spirit that I study Pérez Rosales's and Royce's texts, to see how the respective national histories help us understand the regional California one, and how the latter may have marked those national narratives.

California and Chile also share a history of sponsored and spontaneous immigration that has been crucial in their respective histories and developments. While the California context is apparent, immigration has been a constant in Chilean national history from the Germans who populated the South of the country and revolutionized Chilean social institutions in the nineteenth century to the Spaniards, Palestinians, Koreans, and Peruvians who transformed culture, commerce, and cuisines in the twentieth.

The Chilean View

According to Roberto Hernández, the Treaty of Guadalupe Hidalgo had one consequence not usually considered in U.S. or Mexican accounts: It gave the United States a new preponderant place on the Pacific Ocean and in so doing displaced Chile from that position: "At the beginning of

1848, a year full of international events, no other state on the Pacific had the importance of Chile as a maritime power, and no other had as many national ships at its disposal either."[7] These consequences were immediately apparent to the Chilean press at the time. *El Mercurio de Valparaíso* wondered, "What is going to happen with the Chilean fleet, with Chile's maritime future? The occupation of Mexico has already taken Mexican markets away from Chilean commerce. They will become tributaries of the United States. Soon even American flour will come to Peru."[8]

The historian Arnold Bauer confirms that both the Gold Rush in California and a similar rush in Australia a few years later had direct, differential, and long-lasting impact on the Chilean economy and society. Chile had "a natural advantage in supplying the new markets": When ships rounded Cape Horn, the Chilean ports of Concepción and Valparaíso offered the first two welcoming stops. Along with Oregon, Chile was one of the most important producers of wheat on the Pacific. As a result, "the number of ships that called at Chilean ports doubled with the gold rush" and a full industry of wheat and flour to supply them emerged. "By 1855, however, sufficient grain was raised in California to take care of local needs, and except for rare bad harvests, Chilean wheat was not imported again. By the end of the decade California not only became self-sufficient but quickly ended the near monopoly that Chilean growers enjoyed in the Pacific. From 1858 on, Chile faced stiff competition from West Coast grains throughout the Pacific, and California flour was even offered for sale in Valparaíso."[9]

Benjamín Vicuña Mackenna, who visited San Francisco in 1853, had already anticipated much of this: "The development of this land[,] peopled by a youthful and energetic race, is bound to be swift and sure. (. . .) In terms of production it will be, beyond dispute, a formidable rival for Chile, which lies in a comparable southern latitude and produces the same things."[10] The Australian Gold Rush had a similarly contradictory trajectory for Chileans. While it prolonged the boom of the wheat and flour market well into the 1850s, it also showed Chile's loss of a competitive edge in providing imports for Australia. This confirmed what California meant for Chile in the longer run: "Even under fortunate circumstances Chile was able to supply less than half of Australia's imports in the peak year of 1855. After 1857, Australian export was effectively finished for Chilean producers: not because the market 'closed' but because of Californian competition."[11]

The plight of compatriots in California itself had other resonances too. When the Chilean Argonauts were mistreated and expelled from their placers in California, a Chilean in San Francisco wrote demanding action from the Chilean state in a letter published in *El Progreso* in Santiago in March 1850: "Chileans need protection for their lives, their honor, and their interests. . . . They need protection in order to work as freely as an American without being coerced, insulted, and summarily executed by the outlaws of North America. Every day an abuse or an atrocity is perpetrated at the placers against the Chileans and there is nobody to protect these defenseless people."[12] An 1849 editorial in *El Comercio de Valparaiso* stated: "The exploration of the golden sands of the American river has been forbidden to Chileans, including under this patronymic all of the foreigners. This decision was not made by any established authority but by the same Yankee citizens who have been thus able to cheat their most prepared competitors."[13]

What was emerging was a certain form of actively produced illegality or para-legality: the category of the foreign miner, whose rights to work the mines and rivers were increasingly questioned and then flatly violated and often denied. To be Chilean came to mean being a racialized, second- or third-class inhabitant whose only right or, even more, whose natural destiny was to work servicing American citizens. To be called "Chilean" in this context—not unlike being called "Mexican" in the United States today—became an index of a longstanding racialized dialectic between (white) Americans and their Latino others.

The National Productivity of the California Gold Rush I

Josiah Royce's *California from the Conquest in 1846 to the Second Vigilance Committee in San Francisco: A Study of American Character* was published in Boston in 1886. It was a commissioned work that afforded the author a chance to test, against the historical particularities of his native California,[14] some of his more general philosophical ideas explored in books such as *The Religious Aspect of Philosophy* (1885).[15] *California*'s main focus was dual: "This book is meant to help the reader toward an understanding of two things: namely, the modern American state of California, and our national character as displayed in that land."[16] Royce's method is to pay significant attention to historical specificities without simultaneously losing track of the grander design being drawn, logically governing the multiplication of individual and local stories to philosophically fit them into one big picture. For what must be seen in reading *California*, Royce states, is that "We Americans therefore showed in early California new failings and new strength."[17] Among the former, he counted "a novel degree of carelessness, [. . .] a previously unknown indifference to our social duties, and an indifference to the rights of foreigners, whereof we cannot be proud."[18] On the new strengths Royce concluded: "[W]e also showed our best national traits—traits that went far to atone for our faults."[19]

In the "process whereby a new and great community first came to a true consciousness of itself,"[20] there were forces of order and forces of disorder. Royce was explicitly writing against an already prevalent romanticization of frontier justice and of jolly and drunk American miners that miraculously came together to form a prosperous society. For the Harvard philosopher, the excesses of the Gold Rush marked the low point of an emerging state of California and its society. For him, the disruptions were not produced by an external agent and were not simply the result of the accumulation of too many young and ambitious men in one place, but instead "the symptom of an inner social disease."[21] The disease, according to Royce, was forgetting that the individual is to serve the social order and not despise or use it for his own shortsighted gain. The crimes were circumstantially connected to "this hatred of foreigners, this blind nativism"[22] but more crucially a reflection of a broader social ailment: "If we leave out the unprovoked violence frequently offered to foreigners, we may then say that well-known crises and tragedies of violent popular justice during the struggle for order were frequently. . . . simply the outwards symptoms in each case of the past popular crimes of disloyalty to the social order."[23]

The cure against that disease may have cost a few "greasers" (Royce's word) their lives, like that of the infamous pregnant "young woman of Spanish American race" subjected to lynch law and hanged by a mob in 1851, an event that Royce laments. But this violence resulted in the end, in Royce's view, in a transformation and rebirth that should make any

American proud: "[T]he moral elasticity of our people is so great, their social vitality so marvelous, that a community of Americans could sin as fearfully as, in the early years, the mining community did sin, and could yet live to purify itself within so short a time, not by a revolution, but by a simple progress from social foolishness to social steadfastness."[24] This we could call the philosophical productivity of the story. While Royce's expressed desire was to write against easy celebrations of American frontier spirit and acknowledge the many abuses and crimes committed, especially against those who were deemed foreign and illegitimate, his conclusion is still a redemptive narrative of a self-organizing state and citizenry. This narrative in the end explains away or elides the constitutive role of a racialized social and economic regime that underpinned the state's organization. This was philosophy working for the State.

Bayard Taylor, one of the few American Argonauts who preferred writing to mining in Gold Rush California, put it more succinctly in his *El Dorado: Adventures on the Path of Empire*: "Hundreds of instances might be adduced to show that the worst passions of our nature were speedily developed in the air of California, but the one grand lesson of the settlement and organization of the country is of a character that ennobles the race."[25]

Looking at the issue from the viewpoint of the Californios and their foundational role in the history of Mexican Americans in California, Leonard Pitt, on the other hand, sees the history of the Gold Rush as producing long-lasting but different results. In *The Decline of the Californios*, he gives us a brief indication of how transformative the Gold Rush may have been for Californios: "After a century of slow population growth, during which the arrival of twenty five cholos or fifty Americans seemed a momentous occasion, suddenly California faced one of the swiftest, largest, and most varied folk migrations of all time. . . . Briefly told, the story of the Californians in the gold rush is their encounter with 100,000 newcomers in the single year of 1849—80,000 Yankees, 8000 Mexicans, 5000 South Americans, and several thousand miscellaneous Europeans—and with numbers that swelled to a quarter million by 1852."[26]

But in addition to shocking the Californios, the Gold Rush—with its sizable population migrations and its history of displacement, conflicting claims over property and civil rights, and the ensuing development of frontier justice—had other effects that Pitt highlights. In a negative contrast of self and other, all people of Latin American origin, including old-time Californios, were seen as belonging to the same despised people: "[A]ngry Yankees simply refused to recognize any real distinctions between Latin Americans. . . . all the Spanish-speaking were lumped together as 'interlopers' and 'greasers.'"[27]

There was still another related consequence. While the influx of new immigrants from Mexico, Peru, and Chile generated a white hate of Hispanics, those factors also acted as catalysts that both geographically and symbolically forced those Latin American Forty-Niners who stayed, after being displaced from their claims, to fuse with the old Californios in: "the established old communities of California. . . . This tended to break down the old and somewhat artificial distinction between 'Native Californians' and 'Mexicans.' The fusion went on continuously thereafter."[28]

This we could call the double racial and ethnic productivity of the story. If the California Gold Rush allowed for the constitution of the new state, that process of self-formation was marked not only by the remarkable upward social mobility of many American miners and merchants full of Western frontier spirit but also by the corresponding disenfranchisement of Californios, the disdain for foreign nationals of color, and by the formation of groups of racially and ethnically marked second- and third-class citizens or noncitizens who were often henceforth violently dispossessed of their rights and properties.

For many Americans in California this violence was made much more acceptable and often even legitimate once the "true nature" of these darker people was considered. The authors of the *Annals of San Francisco*, "the primary historical source for the period" and also "a delightful narrative for general readers" according to the facsimile reissue of 1999, were in 1855 clear in this regard: "[A]ll the Mexicans and Chilians[,] [*sic*] like the people of negro descent, were only of the commonest description. The women of all these various races were nearly all of the vilest character, and openly practice the most shameful commerce."[29]

While acknowledging different degrees of education and literacy between Chileans and Mexicans and other people of Hispanic descent, there were some general traits that not only could be highlighted but would in fact explain some of the violence descended upon them:

The Hispano-Americans, as a class, rank far beneath the French and German. They are ignorant and lazy, and are consequently poor. . . . Both peoples [Mexican and Chileans], when roused by jealousy or revenge, as they often are, will readily commit the most horrid crimes. . . . The Hispano-Americans fill many low and servile employments, and in general engage only in such occupations as do not very severely tax either mind or body. They show no ambition. . . . They seem to have no wish to become naturalized citizens of the Union, and are morally incapable of comprehending the spirit and tendencies of our institutions.[30]

What emerges thus is not simply a picture of isolated or even generalized racism but a much more complex set of connected propositions that create what we could call a form of structural racism tied to a highly productive political economy. In it, certain subjects are always below the radar of deserving citizenship, inclined to the most menial jobs, lacking in ambition and initiative, victims of "destiny, dirt, ignorance, and sloth."[31] In other words, radically un-American, or perfect fodder for what Mae Ngai has called, in a different context, "impossible subjects." Studying the racialized restrictions on Third World immigrants to the United States from 1924 to 1965, Ngai has outlined the emergence of the illegal alien as a racialized and discriminated-against actual presence that cannot turn itself into a full person. This specific form of limited belonging, this "inclusion in the nation [that] was simultaneously a social reality and a legal impossibility,"[32] forms the basis of what Nicholas de Genova has called the economically highly productive *deportability* of the undocumented worker. My contention, then, is that the case of racialized foreign others in the California Gold Rush was already a manifestation of this later logic of the production of exploitable subjects.

In a passage full of irony, Royce correctly identifies this xenophobic racism but goes on to attribute it to "a social disease" eventually overcome in what he calls "The Attainment of Order": "Therefore the life of a Spanish American in the mines in the early days, if frequently profitable, was apt to be a little disagreeable. It served him right, of course. He had no business, as an alien, to come to the land that God had given us. And if he was a native Californian, a born 'greaser,' then so much the worse for him. He was so much the more our born foe; we hated his whole degenerate, thieving, landowning, lazy, and discontented race."[33]

Rather than being overcome by "the attainment of order," as Royce would have it, I maintain that this racism against so-called foreigners and alleged barbarians became a permanent feature of California society, regulating relations among racial and class groups and affecting access to rights, property, and labor. Moreover, as in the late twentieth century—during which a significant increase in Latin American–origin migration since 1965 has had the effect of re-racializing the native born Chicano population—in the middle of the nineteenth century a massive migration of Latin Americans also played a crucial role in reshaping the ethnic and racial status of native Hispanics, which, in turn, planted the seeds for the eventual emergence of pan- or transnational forms of Hispanicity or Latinidad.

The National Productivity of the California Gold Rush II

In his *Recuerdos del pasado*, published in 1882, Vicente Pérez Rosales begins the section on California with a rich but ambiguous paragraph, setting the stage for his extended memoir as a Forty-Niner: "Twenty nine years have passed since foreign immigration, with its usual accompaniment of enterprise, energy and progress, began to reach the lonely and remote regions that today make up the flourishing State of California. . . . [dormant under Spanish rule for centuries] Another more enterprising and more daring race had to come."[34] The passage is ambiguous because it is unclear who the foreign immigrants were and whether that category included the Forty-Niners from other parts of the United States. Both a celebration of the progressive role of immigration and of American industriousness, the passage manages to suggest that foreign and American workers and miners operated under a single conceptual umbrella: immigration, and foreign immigration at that.

At the moment of writing his *Recuerdos*, decades after his travails in California, Pérez Rosales was in a rare historical position. Having been one of those racialized Hispanic American darker immigrants in the Gold Rush (although he often could or would try to pass as French), and having suffered the consequences of that status, he had gone on to become the officer in charge of promoting and implementing German immigration to Chile. Thus a former immigrant to the United States in charge of thousands of European immigrants to Chile confirmed the connection between these two stages of his life. A few pages later, Pérez Rosales clarifies his thoughts: "I repeat, however, that it would be a great error, as well as an injustice, to attribute the phenomenon of this transformation [of California] solely to the influence of the Anglo-Saxon race. It is also the product of the individual contributions of the most daring and enterprising elements of the superior strata of every other human race."[35]

Along with their immigrant status in this newly acquired California, white U.S. Forty-Niners and white Chileans shared two additional traits at the time of the Gold Rush. They considered themselves particularly civilized and enterprising, and they had a low opinion of Mexican miners and an even lower one of Native Americans. Praising what he deemed California pioneer J. A. Sutter's effective treatment of the natives, Pérez Rosales declares: "At the outset, then Sutter was cruel, . . . attending by turns to the sword and the plow, he fought, won, worked the land, forced the conquered to labor on it; and only when the treacherous and fickle tribes were fully persuaded that they had to choose between death and submission did our pioneer begin to set in motion all those civilizing ideas that do him honor."[36] Barely six pages later, however, the line separating civilization from barbarism is much less clear. Here Pérez Rosales, posing as French and invoking Lafayette, arrives just in time to save a Chilean compatriot about to be hanged in Gold Rush California: "The cause of this act of hasty and barbaric justice was our scatter-brained countryman's meddlesome character. . . . since a shovel had gone astray and the only likely suspect was that scion of Africans, which is what the Yankees called the Chileans and the Spaniards, the theft was attributed to him, and without further ado those savages set themselves up as a jury and were about to do with Alvarez what was often done everywhere with known thieves."[37]

Thus begins an account that would include equal amounts strong denunciation of the arbitrariness and racism of Americans, as well as tributes to their civilizing might. The foreign miners, but especially the racialized ones—including thousands of Mexicans, Peruvians, Chileans, and Chinese—quickly became the victims of discriminatory and arbitrary legal and paralegal activities. Those included summary trials and executions, forced displacement from their placers, and a racially enforced law taxing foreign miners $20 a month for access to the gold fields.[38] Pérez Rosales's narrative combines strong support for the beneficial aspects of immigration on the development of the nation, a clear view of the need to eliminate or subjugate Native Americans, as well as critiques of the blatant and, in Pérez Rosales's view, mistaken racialization of and violence against those immigrants. His perspective is that of the residing immigrant that he could have become in California, but it is also a nineteenth-century white national immigrant view. His critiques of illegitimate violence and arbitrariness are shaped by his immigrant experience, but also by a class, race, and nationality-inflected worldview of the salutary effects of white European foreign immigration in the Americas.

California first appears to Pérez Rosales, who came for gold along with "four brothers, a brother-in-law, and two trusted servants," as a land of great opportunity and radical democratization, a new social space open to all kinds of progressive developments. Just arrived in San Francisco and even before they reached land, they were welcomed by an account that "the stories being told in Chile couldn't hold a candle to reality. . . . that we had reached the land of equality, and that the noble and the plebeian walked shoulder to shoulder in California."[39] This radical leveling of the social field seemed, at least at first, capable of erasing or neutralizing other more recalcitrant forms of social distinction such as race and nationality. But then, as we know, the Golden State turns bad for Pérez Rosales and other nonwhite immigrants. Expelled like many of his compatriots from his placers, he would move from gold-seeking in mining to a rediscovery of the more sober economic and social potential of commerce and industry. He first lamented his crew's own blindness to real estate (at one point offered at low or no cost and then, just a year later, highly valued in the emergent urban centers of California) as a way of finding a fortune. Summarizing his trajectory, he wrote: "What had we done since the joyful day that had seen us arrive in California? For a while we had been in the freight business, we had been miners, and things had gone badly for us in the mines. . . . [We] had been merchants. . . . [W]e had become Frenchmen, drowned, been poisoned. . . . What was there left for us to be? . . . the idea of setting up a hotel."[40]

It is clearly not an accident that the name of the restaurant-hotel Pérez Rosales and his group founded after their hasty and forced exit from their mining efforts was "Restaurant de los Ciudadanos." What was being claimed was not simply one of the few kinds of activity left open to foreign immigrants, but also their final and perhaps desperate affirmation of a certain claim to rights in their new polis. Using biblical language, Pérez Rosales hints at the true racializing nature of the process that had turned them from immigrants into pariahs. Victims of spontaneous and coordinated legal and illegal violence, the displaced Chileans began retreating. He writes, "While this was going on, Sacramento kept filling up with Chileans, who, driven from the placers by the lack of security, came grumbling and dispirited to seek refuge there; and as though the new laws and Yankee hostility were not enough to destroy the accursed race, the weather decided also to take a hand in the matter."[41]

He closes his California account with a melancholic thought: "We went for wool and, like so many others, we came back shorn, but satisfied because we had steadfastly stood our ground till we had fired our last shot."[42] Writing three decades after his California adventure and having had significant experience promoting German immigration to the South of Chile, Pérez Rosales was in a position to extract what he then saw as the true moral of his experience in the United States. He lamented his own blindness, as an adventurous and ambitious immigrant to the Golden State, to the sober benefits of real estate investment, commerce, agriculture, and industry. Because in the end he realized that "to judge from what I have seen up to now, gold will some day be the least of California's riches. . . . because the industrious Yankees will wisely prefer the inexhaustible sources of agricultural and manufacturing wealth."[43]

This conclusion was as much a result of his own travails in California as it was a reflection of his ideas about the true contribution that the right kind of immigrant could make to a country. Those "right" immigrants excluded the proletarian and the adventurers and included the capitalist, the artisan, and the farmer. Their capacity to become a force of progress in their adopted country depended on access to property, religious and civic tolerance, and the right kinds of laws and policies. One example of the last of these was the 1845 law on immigration in Chile that, according to Pérez Rosales, put immigrants "in a better position than the nationals."[44] By far, however, the most crucially important aspect of a good immigration policy was access to citizenship: "Much more than unlimited religious freedom, easy access to citizenship influences the spirit of those who migrate. The migrants give up citizenship when abandoning their home countries, and this causes a deep vacuum in their souls that can only be filled in the adopted country, erasing with nationalism the title of foreigner from their foreheads."[45]

After California, Pérez Rosales had a second chance to show what foreign immigrants, treated the right way and given full access to citizenship, could do for a country, and yet he also confirmed that this process was frequently connected to multiple forms of racism and sometimes involved preferential treatment for white immigrants and the displacement of less-favored populations. White immigrants and Native Americans continued to perform different roles within the national political imagination. This we could call the southern hemisphere form of national political productivity of the experience of immigration in the Gold Rush.

The Other Half of the Story

After his difficult and complex experience in Gold Rush California from 1849 to 1850, Vicente Pérez Rosales returned to Chile and, in the same year, was named colonization agent for the southern Valdivia region. There he would help settle the first wave of German immigrants, followed later by other numerous groups of Germans. Pérez Rosales—who eventually published a series of texts extolling the virtues of the Valdivia region, the German immigrants, and the beneficial aspects of an immigration and colonization policy—was also sent to Europe for four years as Chilean colonization agent and consul general, first to Hamburg and then to Denmark, Prussia, and Hannover.[46] In Europe he wrote in French and published in Germany an *Essai sur le Chili* (1857, soon translated as *Ensayo sobre Chile* and published in Santiago in 1859). The book was both a practical answer to the many questions about Chile that Pérez Rosales regularly received from scientists and potential immigrants, and part of his state-mandated task of celebrating the virtues of the country to interested European immigration agents and immigrants.

Comparing his life in California with his new location in the South of Chile, and perhaps using all the wisdom acquired as a struggling but ultimately proud immigrant, Pérez Rosales states his vision of the role of foreigners in the advancement of the nation:

The spirit of progress was only dormant, not dead. . . . and so much so that the presence of a foreign element, even on a very small scale, has sufficed. . . . to awaken the province of Valdivia from the stupor in which neglect had sunk it. . . . [Valdivia] lacked the stimulus that only foreign immigration can supply to a society stupefied by inertia. . . . A country like ours absolutely requires the active collaboration of the foreign element, a powerful factor that, as it tries to enrich itself, enriches the country offering it shelter.[47]

However, showing the limitations of a national white imaginary, he reflected on Sutter's treatment of Native Americans in California and compared it to the Spanish and Mexican way of the missions as well as the effort in Chile "to win over and civilize our Araucanians." He wrote, "[B]ecause the wild Indian, stubborn or dominated by his bad instincts, will accept peace, work, and respect for the property of others only once he is persuaded that as soon as he comes within rifle range, if he comes with hostile intentions, he will die or be enchained."[48]

Pérez Rosales thus actively participated in the implementation of an immigration policy that was generous and proactive toward European white immigrants at the same time that it was racist and ethnocentric against natives and *mestizos*. Lamenting state budget priorities that still funded an army presence but not enough enticements for German immigrants, Pérez Rosales complained, "[O]nce again, foreign immigration[,] which alone could incorporate the natives into society without exterminating them, was passed over."[49] In what one could call vigilante-style civilization, however, he clarified exactly what such a new policy would entail. Recommending that the nation instead of the army bring 2,000 European families and give them "modern arms," Pérez Rosales concluded, "So substantial a group of foreigners would not flinch before the natives. No matter how bold and brave he may be the Indian is not likely to get in the way of a rifle that would wound or kill him as soon as he comes within range, even if he has lost some of his former fear of firearms."[50]

Such was the civilizational knowledge Vicente Pérez Rosales drew from the combination of his immigration-related experiences in California and the South of Chile. Three decades later, the Chilean state (and Chilean public opinion) would justify the annexation of significant portions of Peruvian and Bolivian territories, using California and Manifest Destiny–style racialized arguments against "inferior races." What Ericka Beckman has called "the creolization of imperial reason"[51] ended up ideologically positing a distinctive white identity for the Chilean nation, confirmed immediately after the War of the Pacific by a campaign against the same Mapuche Indians Pérez Rosales had dealt with.

Back in the United States, Josiah Royce would, in turn, correctly analyze many of the real issues that had been at stake in Gold Rush California: the corrupting effect on the social and political community from an absence of formal institutions for the administration of justice and the institutionalization of discrimination against community members. Both had led to an abundance of selfishness and violence. However, Royce himself ended *California* by covering up the problem he had correctly detected. Yes, there was an extended wild period in the Gold Rush; yes, abuses were committed and rights violated; but once the dust settled, the story that emerged was, for Royce, a civilizational and moral one. Order prevailed and the interests of the community were correctly placed above those of the selfish individual. What Pérez Rosales and Royce shared was their inclination to see the nation-state as the evidence of moral progress and community growth. They both excused or even justified the constitutive violence (created by the policies and practices they celebrated) against Hispanics, Native Americans, and other undesirables. Decentering the national, a comparative and transnational approach makes evident the ugly continuity of this form of organized racism in the state-making history of the continent.

The Productivity of the Racialized Immigrant for California

After the war with Mexico, coexistence in Gold Rush California marks the second extended white U.S. engagement with people of Hispanic origin (what we would more generally call Latinos today). The racialized interactions among people from different areas ended up generating a caste system, a form of discriminating and legitimized practice of para and legal racism that would regulate the co-presence within the national territory of people of color and whites. What arises then, instead of the purely teleological narrative of California's self-constitution, is not a different tale marked by a sin of youthful hurriedness but constituted by the para-legally sanctioned practices of discrimination and racism that have since regulated the contact between racially and ethnically marked populations. What emerged was a racial formation characteristic of the Southwest, different from the black and white formation dominant in the rest of the United States, and one in which the actual and perceived Latino foreigner played a constitutive role. Tomás Almaguer, studying "the historical origins of white supremacy in California," has spoken of a basic racializing system structuring relations of inequality and based on social closures that prevent competitors deemed as outsiders from entering into competition with insiders for social and economic rewards: "The particular success of European-American men in securing a privileged social status was typically exacted through contentious, racialized struggles with Mexicans, native Americans, and Asian immigrants over land ownership or labor-market position."[52]

The blatant racism of the early Gold Rush that Pérez Rosales and Royce wrote against cannot be excused or bracketed as an anomaly. Instead, it has to be recognized as a long-lasting trait of California's relations with nonwhite immigrants and non-immigrant populations. Studying what he calls the "critical legacy of the Gold Rush era,"[53] Stephen J. Pitti analyzes the crucial role of racism in the disenfranchisement and dispossession of old Californios and newly arrived Mexican and Chilean miners in his *The Devil in Silicon Valley* (the devil is of course racism itself). According to Pitti, the San José area became the destination of thousands of Mexican and Chilean miners displaced from their claims by the combined effect of the Foreign Miners Tax and Anglo racism. Two thousand of them landed in what is now known as the Silicon Valley, and many worked in the New Almaden mercury mine in what Pitti calls "the largest Latino immigrant population in the United States"[54] and "the first Latino industrial workers in the United States."[55] In the company-segregated Spanishtown, these Mexicans and Chileans experienced a newly racialized regime of social relations and labor— that, according to Pitti, has continued to keep "many Latino residents confined to menial occupations in ways long dictated by ideologies of race"[56]—and, partly as a result of this shared experience of white racism, developed in the next two decades a strong transnational (Mexican and Chilean) culture of labor organization and activism.[57]

According to Bonnie Honig's *Democracy and the Foreigner*,[58] in the American political tradition foreign immigrants have often been a catalyst of at least two discourses that, in trying to answer the questions "How should we solve the problem of *foreignness*" and "What should we do about them [foreigners]," have become crucial for the U.S. political imaginary. On the one hand, they force social scientists to ask if the alleged equilibrium between social integration (homogeneity) and democratic system has been altered or could be threatened by the presence of foreign elements such as immigrants, who supposedly would not share the cultural principles that sustain the nation. On the other hand, the immigrant is central to that national imaginary insofar as immigrants choose freely and actively to belong to that community of citizens and thus, they confirm for the native-born the many advantages of their belonging. Such imaginary also considers the country as the land of freedom and opportunity for anybody who, regardless of class, origin, or religion, is willing to work and save to reach success. If the doors are closed for the immigrants, internal coherence is, at least hypothetically, reinforced even while a central value to American self-perception is sacrificed. On the other hand, if the doors are opened, the alleged identity of the *we* is questioned by its pluralization and widening.

While Honig's reading of the politico-philosophical role of the foreigner in American history has been justly celebrated as a radical and pioneering effort, I would like to add the question of the foreigner's politico-economic yield. Here there is less a contradictory relation to the foreigner and more a high political and economic productivity that empowers dominant white sectors of the American population while it disempowers immigrants and people of color. The heuristic value of the foreigner, allowing a more complex understanding of the American, does not just stem from their simple provisional exclusion (affecting historically both European and non-European immigrants) on their way to assimilation but is instead part of a wider but also more specific phenomenon: the integral role of racism against people of color in American history.

In addition to generating a socioeconomic structure based on and regulating racism against perceived "foreigners," the California Gold Rush could be seen as providing one of the origins of the category of the illegal alien that would have such a long, constitutive, and productive history in the state to this day. During the Gold Rush, many Latinos would quickly move from the category of foreign miners to that of illegal and undeserving foreigners. Racism limited claims to rights by placing the actor claiming rights in a special category of sub-subjects, intrinsically incapable of such good behavior or with a natural tendency to conflict with it. In those years, too, the seeds of the future legal codification of the connections and disconnections between race and citizenship were planted in ways that would then and later affect not just Latinos but also other national immigrant groups, including Chinese, Japanese, and Filipinos.[59] Racialized foreigners of color, both documented and undocumented, have thus been working and been made to work politically, ethnically, and philosophically for the state of California in ways that not only must be added to their significant economic contribution but have, in fact, created the conditions under which those economic contributions have been most profitable for the dominant white population. Those conditions include what we could call the racialization, permanent stain, and suspicion of foreignness extended to most U.S.-born ethnic communities of color. This chapter has sought to excavate some of the regional, national, and transnational origins of such a configuration.

NOTES

1 Josiah Royce, *California from the Conquest in 1846 to the Second Vigilance Committee in San Francisco* (Santa Barbara and Salt Lake City: Peregrine Publishers, 1970), 286; Vicente Pérez Rosales, *Times Gone By: Memoirs of a Man of Action*, trans. John H. R. Polt (Oxford: Oxford University Press, 2003), 270; Pérez Rosales, *Memoria*, 27.

2 Quoted in Roberto Hernández, *Los Chilenos en San Francisco de California* (Valparaiso: Imprenta San Rafael, Vol. 1.I, 1930), 39. Unless otherwise noted, all translations from Spanish in this chapter are mine.

3 Brian Roberts, "'The Greatest and Most Perverted Paradise.' The Forty-Niners in Latin America," in *Riches for All: The California Gold Rush and the World*, ed. Kenneth N. Owens (Lincoln: University of Nebraska Press, 2002), 73.

4 Ibid., 72.

5 Benjamín Vicuña Mackenna, *La Edad del Oro en Chile* (Santiago: Editorial Francisco de Aguirre, 1969), 238.

6 Robert McKee Irwin, *Bandits, Captives, Heroines, and Saints: Cultural Icons of Mexico's Northwest Borderlands* (Minneapolis: University of Minnesota Press, 2007), xvi.

7 Hernández, *Los Chilenos*, 13.

8 Quoted in Hernández, *Los Chilenos*, 14.

9 Arnold Bauer, *Chilean Rural Society: From the Spanish Conquest to 1930* (Cambridge: Cambridge University Press, 1975), 63.

10 Quoted in Edwin A. Beilharz and Carlos U. López, eds., *We Were 49ers! Chilean Accounts of the California Gold Rush* (Pasadena: Ward Ritchie Press, 1976), 206. I have slightly modified the translation. Original in *Viajes*, 9.

11 Bauer, *Chilean Rural Society*, 63.

12 Quoted in Hernández, *Los Chilenos*, 187.

13 Ibid., 131.

14 His mother, Sarah Royce, wrote at his request a full account of her California memories that was fundamental to Royce in his writing and may account for some of the emphasis on the role of religion and families or lack thereof in that history. Sarah's text was later published as a book, under the title *A Frontier Lady*.

15 John Clendenning, *The Life and Thought of Josiah Royce* (Madison: University of Wisconsin Press, 1985), 144–56.

16 Royce, *California*, 3.

17 Ibid.

18 Ibid., 3–4.

19 Ibid., 4.

20 Ibid., xvii.

21 Ibid., 296.

22 Ibid., 219.

23 Ibid.

24 Ibid., 296.

25 Bayard Taylor, *El Dorado: Adventures on the Path of Empire* (Santa Clara: Santa Clara University/Heyday Books [1850], 2000), 249. For Taylor, the "race" here was, of course, that of white Americans in California.

26 Leonard Pitt, *The Decline of the Californios: A Social History of the Spanish-Speaking Californios, 1846–1890* (Berkeley: University of California Press, 1971), 52.

27 Ibid., 53.

28 Ibid., 68.

29 Frank Soulé, John H Gihon, and James Nisbet. *Annals of San Francisco* (Berkeley: Berkeley Hills Books [1855], 1999), 412.

30 Ibid., 472.

31 Ibid.

32 Mae Ngai, *Impossible Subjects: Illegal Aliens and the Making of Modern America* (Princeton, N.J.: Princeton University Press, 2004), 4.

33 Royce, *California*, 286–87.

34 Vicente Pérez Rosales, *Recuerdos del Pasado. 1814–1860* (Santiago: Imprenta Gutenberg, third edition, 1886), 207–8.

35 Ibid., 211.

36 Ibid., 214.

37 Ibid., 221. For a detailed account of Anglo abuses against Chileans and their responses to such violence in Gold Rush California, see Fernando Purcell,

"Becoming Dark: The Chilean Experience in California. 1848–1870" in *How the United States Racializes Latinos: White Hegemony and Its Consequences*, ed. José A. Cobas, Jorge Duany, and Joe R. Feagin (Boulder: Paradigm Publishers, 2009).

38 Kevin Starr, *California: A History* (New York: The Modern Library, 2007), 86.

39 Pérez Rosales, *Recuerdos del Pasado*, 226.

40 Ibid., 299.

41 Ibid., 280.

42 Ibid., 294.

43 Ibid., 255.

44 Pérez Rosales, *Times Gone By*, 45.

45 Ibid., 50.

46 Rolando Mellafe, "Introducción," in *Ensayo sobre Chile*, ByVicente Pérez Rosales (Santiago: Ediciones de la Universidad de Chile, 1986), 21–22.

47 Pérez Rosales, *Ensayo sobre Chile* 300–1.

48 Ibid., 214.

49 Ibid., 352.

50 Ibid.

51 Ericka Beckman, "The Creolization of Imperial Reason. Chilean State Racism in the War of the Pacific," *Journal of Latin American Cultural Studies* 18, no. 1 (2009): 74–75.

52 Tomás Almaguer, *Racial Fault Lines. The Historical Origins of White Supremacy in California* (Berkeley: University of California Press, 1994), 3.

53 Stephen J. Pitti, *The Devil in Silicon Valley: Northern California, Race, and Mexican Americans* (Princeton, N.J.: Princeton University Press, 2004), 76.

54 Ibid., 41.

55 Ibid., 51.

56 Ibid., 4.

57 Racially based but economically productive violence could also be even more direct. Mike Davis in *No One Is Illegal: Fighting Racism and State Violence on the US-Mexico Border* (Chicago: Haymarket Books, 2006) proposes to consider vigilantism (i.e., "ethno-racial and class violence [or threat of violence]"): "a distinctive system of locally sanctioned violence throughout the former Western frontier states. . . . Vigilantism—often extolled from the pulpit or editorial page—policed the boundaries of 'whiteness' and 'Americanism'" (17). This we could call the long-lasting political productivity of the story of the Gold Rush as it relates to the presence and perception of people conceptualized as racially othered foreigners. Thus, in studying the history of lynching in the West, Ken Gonzales-Day can state, "One of the fundamental goals of this book is to allow the nation. . . . to finally acknowledge that when taken collectively, the lynching of American Indians, blacks, Chinese, and Latinos constituted the majority of cases of lynching and extrajudicial executions in California [between 1830–1935]." (*Lynching in the West. 1850–1935* (Durham, N.C.: Duke University Press, 2006), 14.

Historical understandings of popular justice including lynching in the West have managed to obscure this fact, idealizing frontier justice as a manifestation of direct democracy and community self-organizing when it was in fact one extreme manifestation of the above-mentioned xenophobic and racialized inter-group logic.

58 Bonnie Honig, *Democracy and the Foreigner* (Princeton, N.J.: Princeton University Press, 2003).

59 Ngai, *Impossible Subjects* (Princeton, N.J.: Princeton University Press, 2004).

14

"El negro es tan capaz como el blanco"

José Martí, "Pachín" Marín, Lucy Parsons, and the Politics
of Late-Nineteenth-Century Latinidad

LAURA LOMAS

I wear an iron ring, and I have to do iron deeds. . . . No suffering as the black men in my country.
—José Martí

Y los negros? ¿Quién que ha visto azotar a un negro no se
considera para siempre su deudor? Yo lo vi, lo vi cuando
era niño y todavía no se me ha apagado en las mejillas la
vergüenza.
—José Martí[1]

Scribbling in the margins of his copy of the Scottish economist John
Rae's *Contemporary Socialism*, New York–resident Cuban poet and revolutionary José Martí introduces the issue of racism and racial equality as
a factor flagrantly missing from Rae's volume and from the work of the
major figures of socialist thought whom Rae treats therein: Ferdinand
Lasalle, Karl Marx, Henry George, and a range of Russian anarchists
and Christian socialists.[2] While it sounds pedantic today, Martí's anno-
tation that "el negro es tan capaz como el blanco" (the black man is just
as capable as the white) in 1887 (the date of the edition in which Martí's
comments appear) suggests that Martí's claim that all people belong to a
single human race may best be read as a proactive critique of entrenched
and growing white supremacist terror in the United States rather than as
a misguided belief that the effects of racism no longer merited attention
and redress. Both this subtle critique of European and North American
socialism's blindness to white racism and Martí's subsequent critique of

his own independence movement suggest that anti-racism became an ethos of organized, self-conscious Hispanic Caribbean migrant communities.[3] The critique of class and race relations in the late nineteenth century influenced the definition of *Latinidad* and set the stage for ongoing struggles for racial and class justice.

In 1887, the year historians locate as the fulcrum of Martí's radicalization, large audiences congealed around the Afro-Tejana anarchist leader Lucy Eldine González Parsons and Afro-Puertorriqueño poet and revolutionary Francisco Gonzálo "Pachín" Marín Shaw, who became active in the pursuit of racial, decolonial, and class justice. I suggest that the speeches, writings, and courageous examples of Marín and Parsons form part of the historical context that transformed Martí and the politics of *Latinidad*. While a full treatment of Afro–North American and Afro-Latin@ immigrant relations far exceeds the scope of this chapter, this argument puts pressure on the definition and borders of the term *Latin@* by reading across national, racial, gender, and language borders to consider three key nineteenth-century Latin@s—Martí (Cuban), Marín (Puerto Rican), and Parsons (Texan)—as contributing to the definition of *Latinidad*.

Afro-Latin@s played a role in making nineteenth-century Latin@s aware of themselves as people of color committed to revolutionary change.[4] While decolonizing nationalist movements and black self-emancipation from slavery have been intertwined in the Americas since the Haitian revolution ending in 1804, the U.S. War of Independence and the Spanish American revolutions of the early nineteenth century implemented notoriously unequal versions of independence, where freedom from colonialism did not spell freedom for the people bound by racial slavery or address the entrenched inequalities that slavery forged. As Martí commented, the resulting form of self-government in the United States "*bambolea sobre los hombros de una raza esclava*" (wobbles on the backs of an enslaved race).[5] Leaders of creole revolutions—including some erstwhile slavemasters—signed idealistic proclamations that excluded or devalued the racialized working masses.[6] White racism thus aimed to divide and has often prevented unity among a multiracial working class by granting access to citizenship only to those who conformed to the dominant racial operations. The longstanding Eurocentrism inherited from centuries of Spanish colonialism makes Latin@

immigrants' interrogation of the dominant U.S. racial system an unlikely, difficult, yet urgent response. At the same time, Hispanic Caribbean migrants of African descent on the islands and inside the various
territories of the new U.S. empire experienced racialized violence at the
hands of the police, the Guardia Civil, and other state or vigilante forces.
The critical response to a racist and classist application of state violence
shapes the consciousness of Latin@ migrants from the islands to the
mainland in the late nineteenth century. As racial terror and imperial
expansion increased in the United States, light- and dark-skinned working class Spanish-speakers on the islands and in the diaspora experienced common, brutalizing processes of racialization.

"De gente latina": Multiracial and Anti-Racist Latinidad

In the late nineteenth century, revolutionary militancy in the overlapping struggle to end colonialism and slavery became a defining
characteristic of the Hispanic Caribbean migrants of various shades who
supported Cuban and Puerto Rican independence and became identified as a distinct social formation under the emergent appellation "gente
latina" (Latina/o people), a term that appears in Martí's correspondence
in 1885: "De siete artículos que escribí para un periódico de esta ciudad,
pero de gente latina, hallé que tres eran de cosas mexicanas" (Of seven
essays that I wrote for a newspaper of this city, but for Latinas/os, I found
but three were on Mexican topics).[7] Thus Martí tells Manuel Mercado,
his friend and editor in Mexico, of a print community of Latin American
origin based in the city in which he was living—New York. The reference
marks a space of educational (and implicitly light-skinned) privilege but
also refers to a minority group in an Anglocentric America. Moreover,
the group interpolated by the term Latina/o expands beyond limited circles of reading and writing with the practice of tobacco workers (many
of whom were of African descent) paying a portion of their wages to
a "lector" (reader) to perform readings of Spanish-language news and
literature of their choosing while rolling cigars, the occupation of most
of the Hispanic Caribbean immigrants, as Bernardo Vega suggests.
Related terms appeared in English, as the "Latin portion of North America," or in Spanish as "Hispanoamericano"—set often in opposition to
"Saxon," "Anglo," "United States," or "Norteamericano"—and circulated

in English- and Spanish-language periodicals such as *La América, The North American Review, La Nación,* or *Patria*—to refer to differences of dress, style, values, cultural practices, and political allegiances in articles that circulated in the United States and internationally.[8]

The Spanish-speaking migrant communities in the New York metropolitan area and beyond formed cross-class and cross-race alliances in the nineteenth century's last two decades despite pressures to fall into the patterns of color segregation. The Cuban and Puerto Rican anticolonial, anti-racist social movement refused to abide by customary and eventually official legal public segregation laws, which raised eyebrows in New York as the color line was wending its way around the world to become "the problem of the twentieth-century" in W. E. B. Du Bois's phrase from *The Souls of Black Folk.* Bernardo Vega's recollections of his fictional Uncle Antonio's experiences in late-nineteenth-century New York evoke a Puerto Rican immigrant family's refusal to accommodate the pressure to engage in segregation. Uncle Antonio recounts how their German and Irish neighbors near 88th Street and Lexington Avenue came to complain that the Vegas "frequently have Negroes coming to [their] house" and ordered them to "be more careful" about whom they invited over.[9]

In the late-nineteenth-century United States, structures of exclusion and state or police abuse positioned recently emancipated U.S. and Caribbean migrants of African descent alongside formerly indentured Asian laborers, annexed native Americans and Mexicans, and immigrant workers.[10] State-condoned disenfranchisement in the post-Reconstruction United States—from mob lynching to capital punishment administered through politicized juridical procedures such as the Chicago anarchists' trial (to which I turn below)—shaped the emergence of an anti-racist Latina/o self-consciousness opposed to, rather than invested in, white supremacy, Anglo expansion, and the concomitant economic hierarchies among classes and nations. Lived experience in the United States led some of Latin American and Caribbean origin in New York who could and did pass as white to begin to conceive of themselves as different from a privileged white group, because they underwent "metropolitan racialization," a term Yolanda Martínez San Miguel coins to describe Afro-Caribbean citizens Frantz Fanon and Piri

Thomas's mid-twentieth-century experiences of marginalization as minorities in Paris and New York, respectively. Both Fanon and Thomas find that their status as "legal citizens" does not enable them to escape the second-class status of colonial and ethnoracial subjects.[11] I endow Martínez San Miguel's phrase with a longer history extending back to the nineteenth century and stretch it to encompass the complex range of skin tones of *Latinidad*.

In the late nineteenth century, *metropolitan racialization* refers to the process by which multiracial Hispanic Caribbean migrants in New York realized that their linguistic difference and national origin excluded them from white privilege insofar as they refused to participate in negrophobia or did not disavow national origins, their home language, and anticolonial politics. Just as Frantz Fanon describes becoming black for the first time under the destructive weight of the white Parisian gaze upon his arrival in Paris from Martinique, late-nineteenth-century Latin@ self-consciousness emerges in response to experiences of racialization in North America.

Vindicating *Latinidad*

The vindication of *Latinidad* calls for an end to a quotidian experience of discrimination, disdain, and exclusion on the basis of non-native pronunciation in English, bias against a "swarthy" or "half-breed" appearance, or stereotypes about how Latin American countries and their peoples should relate to the country and people of the United States.[12] Martí's English-language letter to the editor of *The New York Evening Post*, entitled "A Vindication of Cuba," attacks stereotypes of Cubans, black and white, as "supine" or "pitifully ineffective" because of a supposed lack of manly force or self-respect. Martí's indignant letter responds to an anonymous writer in *The Manufacturer* who speculated on the danger of incorporating Cuba's 1 million blacks into the United States in the event of annexation, particularly insofar as all Cubans spoke an Africanized Spanish tongue that would create "dire confusion" for governmental bodies overseeing the annexed territory.[13] Martí defends Cubans against the implication that Africanized Cuban Spanish would necessarily be problematic while simultaneously denouncing the proposal of annexation.[14] In impeccable English, Martí's letter argues against annexation in part because of the reigning racial views of the United States, in which "[the Cuban's] ability is denied, his morality insulted, and his character despised."[15] To refute the stereotypes circulating in the U.S. press, Martí offers a catalogue of achievements of Cubans on the island and in exile, in Key West, Philadelphia, New York, Latin America, and in Europe and defends the Cuban war of independence as key to abolishing slavery, and successful in keeping at bay the crumbling empire of Spain "with a loss to him [Spain] of 200,000 men, at the hands of a small army of patriots, with no help but nature."[16]

This public defense of Cubans in the diaspora and on the island alludes to an emergent transnational formation of *Latinidad* in his complaint about derogatory stereotypes of Cubans lumped "in a mass with other countries of Spanish America."[17] The letter to the editor denounces the dual vulnerability of Cuban migrants and islanders to invasion and annexation by the emerging U.S. empire, which proposed to render the blood of all those who died fighting for independence "but the fertilizers of the soil for the benefit of a foreign plant, or the occasion for a sneer from the *Manufacturer* of Philadelphia."[18] Late-nineteenth-century vindications of Hispanic Caribbean people or an emerging formation of Latin@s undermines discourses that attribute qualities of unruliness, indolence, empty talk, and an incapacity for self-governance to the "hybrid" racial and cultural mixtures of African and indigenous-descended peoples of Latin America, the Caribbean, and their diasporas.

Despite his professional status and light skin color as a child of Spanish immigrants to Cuba, Martí's anger at the stereotypes circulating in the U.S. press was not unrelated to his individual encounters with racial disdain, or reactions to his status as a dark-haired, Spanish-dominant speaker of accented English. As Martí notes in his 1887 chronicle "Great Cattle Exposition," the U.S. environment reduced him to the status of a domesticated herd animal, "*acorralado de todas partes por la lengua inglesa*" (corralled on all sides by the English language).[19] Martí's personal notebooks and fragmentary writings underscore the violence of an Anglocentric milieu. For example, Martí recalls the disdain with which he was received by a hotel employee in Murray Hill in New York City, upon inquiring after his Latin American colleagues, diplomats who were guests at the hotel:

—"Conoce V. a un caballero sudamericano, muy alto, que come aquí
desde hace un mes?"
—"No sé. Entran y salen. El no se ha hecho conocer de mí." ("He has not
made himself known to me.") ¡Y la mirada de desprecio, y el gesto
de ¡deje en paz al Emperador! con que acompañaba la repuesta! Vive
uno en los Estados Unidos como boxeado. Habla esta gente, y parece
que le está metiendo a uno el puño debajo de los ojos.

[—"Do you know a South American gentleman, very tall, who has been
eating here for the past month?"
—"I do not know. They come and they go. He has not become known
to me." ("He has not made himself known to me" [in English in the
original].) And the gaze of disdain! And the gesture of "Leave the
Emperor in peace!" that accompanied his response! One lives in the
United States as if subject to blows. These people speak and it seems
like they are waving a fist in front of one's eyes.][20]

In light of his being snubbed by this hotel employee in what he perceives to be an imperious linguistic environment, it is not surprising that
Martí elsewhere identifies a hotel for Spanish-speakers, Hotel América,
and recommends it to Spanish-speakers he recruited to the cause of
Cuban independence. Galician Mambí Félix de los Ríos recalls meeting
with Martí in the welcoming space of this hotel's lobby, a part of which
was "only for Latinos [my translation, lowercase *L* in Spanish origi-
nal] although there was no difference in the service on each floor and
one elevator served all floors."[21] The existence of such Hispanophone
spaces, which Spanish-speakers embraced and promoted, suggests that
the group welcomed the protection of an enclave where it was possible
to enact a distinct subculture.

Los compontes of 1887, "Pachín" Marín's Poetry, and the Radicalization of Afro-Latin@s in the Diaspora

The failure of states to guarantee even a semblance of racial equality in
post-slavery Puerto Rico, Cuba, and the United States convinced Afro-
Cubans and Afro–Puerto Ricans to support the revolutionary movement
that adopted an officially anti-racist position. If we consider factors that

led Puerto Rican migrants to seek exile in New York in the late nineteenth century, it is possible to see continuities between the abuse of
state power in Spain's colonies and in the United States, a complaint
which Martí paraphrased in 1887 in an emphatic standalone paragraph
in his chronicle on the mostly German anarchist martyrs: "America,
then, is the same as Europe!"[22] In the United States and in Europe's colonies, we learn, migrants have in their recent memory direct experiences
of racialized and class-marked violence.

In the colonial Puerto Rican context in particular, violent repri-
sals against the founders and members of the Autonomist Party—
which upheld liberal ideals of racial equality—led to the exile of key
Afro–Puerto Ricans who played a foundational role in the struggle
for Cuba's and Puerto Rico's independence and in disseminating radical politics among Latin@ immigrant communities in New York.[23] A
notable poet, chronicler, newspaper editor, and revolutionary of African descent through both of his grandmothers, a beloved member
the class of "*artesanos*" (artisans) who worked as a typesetter, "Pachín"
Marín was forced out of Puerto Rico because of his egalitarian political
views. Marín published his second chapbook of poetry, *Mi óbolo*, in
1887 after participating in the assembly at which the Autonomist Party
was founded, which was also the ignominious year of the *compontes*, a
term that refers to the violent "ordering" of society carried out by the
Guardía Civil under General Romualdo Palacios in 1887.[24] The historian Jesse Hoffnung-Garskof notes that during the *compontes*, Puerto
Ricans of African descent disproportionately suffered gross abuses and
torture: "Guard members hung Victor Honoré, a mulato stonemason
from Mayagüez, by his arms and legs for days and beat him with sticks
across his torso. They broke the fingers of Gil Bones, a mulato [*sic*]
tailor from Ponce. They hung a cobbler in Guayanilla by his feet from
a telegraph post. Other men of low status, including some common
laborers, were hung by their testicles or dunked head first into latrines.
By one contemporary account, 197 pardo and moreno artisans were
arrested, 130 of whom were tortured."[25] Hoffnung-Garskof notes that
this personal experience had a "profound effect on the evolving politics
of both [Sotero] Figueroa and [Pachín] Marín."[26] Already artisans had
condemned the presence of racism in 1874. An anonymous letter to *El
Artesano* of Mayagüez calls the attention of its readers to Puerto Rican

society's persistent complicity with racist views: "Still flourishing in our society is that system of privilege which recognizes one race's supremacy over another."[27] Upon the arrival of Figueroa and Marín to the shores of New York, both became involved in meetings that led to the founding of the Cuban Revolutionary Party; they were active in labor movements and *sociedades de color*; and they helped found a political club to promote Puerto Rican independence.[28] In other words, one effect of the repression in Puerto Rico was the radicalization of Latin@ communities in New York.

In the case of "Pachín" Marín, who was called "a Black Lord Byron," the threat of torture or death during the *compontes* prompted him to abandon the island for a period of five years of nomadic political and creative activity.[29] During this time he lived and continued to expand his revolutionary, poetic, and journalistic activities in the Dominican Republic, Venezuela, Haiti, Martinique, and New York. In 1887, Marín first fled to the Dominican Republic. Although his literary prowess initially gained him favor from General Ulises Heureaux ("Lilí"), the Dominican dictator forced Marín to march through the city in chains and very nearly ordered his assassination after Marín published a critical editorial.[30] Deported first to Curaçao for six days, and then to Venezuela in 1889, Marín worked in South America as a typesetter by day and performed his poetry by night. His fellow typesetter and fellow-traveler, the self-declared socialist Afro-Colombiano Juan Coronel, likened their low-budget lives to scenes from Henri Murger's *La Vie bohéme* (1851).[31] Marín, his daughter Quisqueya, Juan Coronel, Felix Matos Bernier, and Luis Caballer—the last two exiled Puertorriqueños who also contributed to *La Sombra* (*The Shadow*), a leftist newspaper in Venezuela—were all imprisoned and then deported in August 1890 to Martinique, because of their public critique of Venezuela's Liberal Party president, Raimundo Andueza Palacio.[32] Marín's Caribbean migrations took him to St. Thomas and Jamaica before he returned to Ponce, where he rejoined protests and demonstrations led by his cousin Américo Marín. Forced into a second exile in a matter of months in 1891, Marín migrated to New York. In 1893, Marín returned to the Caribbean to establish in Haiti a hotel named *El Internacional*, where he corresponded with combatants and generals in the midst of the war in Cuba, but his last entrepreneurial initiative burned to the ground and within two years he returned again to New York, where he resided only a short time before departing for the battlefront in Cuba.

Inspired by the deaths of his brother, *tabaquero* and militant Wenceslao Marín; by Maceo's assistant, the young Afro-Cuban Francisco Gómez; and by the greatest strategist of Cuba's wars of independence, the Bronze Titan, Antonio Maceo, Marín joined the revolutionary forces in 1897. He perished in the Cuban Manigua, alone in his hammock, shaking with yellow fever. Before his departure, he became a beloved bard and shining star of New York's late-nineteenth-century Latin@ community.[33]

According to Bernardo Vega, Marín—"a young mulatto with sparkling eyes"—was the first one to greet Martí as he stepped down from the podium after he returned from his first visit to the *tabaqueros* in Key West and Tampa, and an enthusiastic audience called for him to speak.[34] Pachín often shared the podium with Martí, who described Marín's oratory in *Patria* as "elegant and ardent eloquence" (*eloquencia elegante y ardiente*) or as "sizzling improvisation (*calurosa improvisación*)."[35] An accomplished guitar player, Marín lent his often-improvised musical and oratorical talents to Rafael Serra's La Liga, a night school created by and for Puerto Ricans and Cubans of African descent, and he worked as a correspondent for Serra's *La Doctrina de Martí*. Marín formed part of the interracial Liga Antillana and Liga de Artesanos, both of which were "bulwarks of the Partido Revolucionario Cubano."[36] Together with Arturo Schomburg, Marín was a founding member of the Cuban Revolutionary Party and secretary of the Club Borinqueño. Marín is credited with designing the Puerto Rican flag.[37]

Marín's poetry and prose affirm his dark skin, which disobeys the dominant pressure to "improve the race" or to silence race by disavowing, bleaching, or disappearing blackness through *enblancamiento*. Marín denounces the exclusion and disdain with which the United States and other American or Caribbean societies treat black people, and especially poets of African descent, like Marín himself. He alluded to himself as a "*bardo oscuro*" (dark bard) and famously attacked the Dominican dictator General Ulises Heureaux for disdaining Marín's and his own blackness: "Tirano, entre tú y yo hay una gran diferencia: ambos llevamos sangre africana en las venas: pero tú te avergüenzas de ella y yo no" (Tyrant, between you and me there is a significant difference: African blood flows in both of our veins, but you are ashamed of it, whereas I am not).[38] This refusal to deny or see his blackness with shame suggests that Marín resists the rhetoric of "pardoism," which emphasizes mixture with whiteness or *"mejorando la raza"* (improving the race) by valuing brown over black.

While Marín's poetry extols liberty as the greatest consolation available on Earth and associates freedom with taking up arms against Spain, he acknowledges that Enlightenment ideals did not often extend to the *"raza perseguida"* (persecuted race). In *Emilia*, a narrative poem about a love affair across color lines, the father of the light-skinned lover responds to the couple's love affair with a *"¡no!"* (*E* 151) so strong that this *"sílaba que mata"* (syllable that kills) initiates the path of the girl to her grave and of her dark-skinned lover to madness. Opening with an epigraph from the Buddha affirming "Todos los hombres son iguales" (All men are equal), Marín's controversial narrative poem suggests that skin color sadly may also determine whether a creative artist will enter the canon of cultural memory.

Marín writes furiously, right up until his death, against his oblivion or erasure as an Afro-Latin@ poet. In his poem "Un Puerto," Marín's poetic persona accuses his interlocutor (the beloved Filena) of drawing negative conclusions about him based on his skin color:

> ¡Acaso piensas que en mi tez de cobre
> se anubla la expresión de la mirada
> y ves que está mi cabellera pobre
> por el sol de los trópicos quemada!
> ¡Acaso antes tus ojos mi alma es muda
> e ignoras niña, en tu razón secreta
> que bajo el bosque de mi crencha ruda
> la inspiración se oculta del Poeta! (*E* 54)

> (Have you considered before my copper skin
> clouds the expression of the gaze
> and you only see my poor hair
> is burned by the tropical sun!
> Before your eyes my soul is mute

and in your secret reason, girl, you haven't noticed
that beneath the rude forest of my parted curls
lurks the hidden inspiration of a Poet!)

This poem, which alludes in a coded fashion to the poetic speaker's island origins in the title "Un Puerto" and in the first stanza's reference to "*mi riqueño cielo*" (my Rican sky) (*E* 52), also exposes Filena's racist inability to perceive the poet's soulful self-expression. The poem's second stanza develops this meditation on the effects of centuries of pejorative coding of appearance: "sobre la frente/ llevo escrita la historia de mi pena" (on my forehead/ is written the history of my pain) (*E* 53). Because the very creole nationalism to which Marín had committed himself denied racial difference as a way of distinguishing and distributing value among a supposedly equal citizenry—when in fact Puerto Ricans of African descent did not enjoy equal access to rights—it is all the more remarkable that the poem returns to a coded discussion of blackness. The third stanza repeats the word *negro* as an adjective to modify the poet's heavy burden of pain: "*Como el negro pesar que me devora/ negra es también tu hermosa cabellera*" (As the black burden that devours me/ black too is your beautiful hair) (*E* 53). This adjectival description of a burden as "black" invites the reader to deconstruct the association of blackness or Africanity with pain or stupidity. As the speaker notes, his beloved Filena too has black hair and black eyes, but ironically her vision remains cloudy and in her eyes his soul is "mute." Marín's blackness, like his vocation as a poet, renders him "agorero/ pájaro de la noche tenebrosa" (ominous bird of the gloomy night) within a world where reason has become delirious, where the poet who would know himself lives without a country, beckoned to sleep or to drunkenness.[39]

From *Los compontes* to Chicago Haymarket Hangings

The emergence of a discourse of *Latinidad* in the writings of Martí and of his interlocutors, as a Hispanophone print community, but moreover, as an explicitly nondominant and politicized working class–identified formation, responds to a specific historical conjuncture. In 1887, Martí revised his initial position aligned with mainstream views critical of the Chicago Haymarket anarchists to sympathize with the "Eight-hour day movement" leaders as heroic victims of a biased judicial system. Some of Martí's untranslated writings on the Chicago anarchists, and on Lucy Parsons in particular in Mexico's *El Partido Liberal*, furthermore condemn the disproportionate abuse of politically radical, working class, non-native protesters and affirm the need to address the structural causes of the misery that the anarchists and working class leaders had mobilized hundreds of thousands to denounce. The mass marches during the eight-hour-day movement suggest a generalized understanding of the need for sweeping structural change to which Martí and his circle too became sympathetic, in part because they felt in the metropolis the violence of racialization and their exploitation as workers.

Both Pachín Marín and Lucy Parsons pushed Martí to interrogate his own presuppositions about structural privilege, because as African-descended Spanish-speakers they experienced firsthand the multiple discourses of domination that led to their "triple-consciousness" as American, black, and Latin@.[40] A Spanish-speaking woman of color, Lucy González Parsons was born Lucy Ella Waller in Waco, Texas, in the same year as Martí (1853) to a black mother and a Mexican father. Founder of the Working Women's Union in Chicago in 1879, she had become a nationally notorious public figure when she spoke at Clarendon Hall on October 16, 1887, in New York. Shelly Streeby re-centers Lucy Parsons as a bilingual, anti-racist, class-conscious, and globally beloved figure who makes it possible to see connections between Haymarket in 1887 and the Mexican Revolution, which is to say, between anarchists, socialists, Wobblies, and Magonistas.[41] Victor Valle and Rodolfo D. Torres have noted Parson's influence on Martí in encouraging him to imagine Latina leadership and engage fearlessly in revolutionary change.[42] With the "atrevida claridad de mundo nuevo" (daring clarity of a new world), Parsons jolts Martí because she speaks from her condition of African and indigenous descent, in Spanish and English, in arguments that defend a working class majority and defend Spanish-speakers' historic native connections to America.[43] Martí's encounter with Parsons brings about a crisis regarding his own masculine, white, and class privilege. Martí's Parsons, every bit as "implacable e inteligente" (implacable and intelligent) as her husband, "habla con feroz energía en las juntas publicas" (speaks with ferocious energy in public meetings) and marches at the head of 40,000 to 80,000 workers, inspiring a revelatory and sympathetic portrait of a Latina anarchist's persuasive power.[44] Parsons, like other Afro-Latin@s directly radicalized by the non-universality of Enlightenment ideals and liberal rights, pushes Martí toward his role in founding a revolutionary mass movement in which a majority of workers of African descent expected to enjoy equal rights, and in which blacks and whites ideally would be considered equally capable.

Martí's superlatives in his chronicle of November 7, 1886, in Mexico's *El Partido Liberal*, reveal the effect of Lucy Parsons' speaking tour in New York on the Cuban leader. She exemplified the dramatic and *"curiosísima"* (extremely curious) prominence of women in the public life of North America. As Parsons outlines in a letter to fellow labor leader Joseph Labadie, the purpose of this speaking tour, including Cincinnati, Louisville, Cleveland, New York, and Pittsburgh, was to counteract the misinformation about the eight anarchist labor leaders, including her husband, Albert Parsons, who were being tried for a bombing in Haymarket Square that took place at a protest against police brutality in Chicago in May 1886, and to raise funds for their legal defense. She singles out mainstream reporting of the case by a "lying monopolistic press" as the reason so many had initially presumed the anarchists guilty.[45] Part of what makes her unusual is that Parsons uses the speaking engagement in Clarendon Hall not to beg for clemency for her husband, slated to be hanged, nor to portray herself as a victim, but rather to denounce the root causes of the desperation of a group of working people to which she herself belonged. In a "Letter to the Editor" in the *Columbus Sunday Capital*, Parsons recounted how in Columbus, Ohio, she was beaten and jailed in a filthy basement cell upon speaking out about the shutting down of the venue where she had been invited to speak. In an essay from this period, "What Anarchy Means," she denounces the wage system that "creates famine in the midst of abundance, and makes slaves of nine-tenths of the human family."[46] In her New York speech, she teaches about the anarchists' vision of a new order, without child labor, and criticizes the excessive consumption of elite women, whom she depicts as impinging on the children of the working class majority. In his review of Parsons' oratory, Martí represents anarchy, unlike the mainstream U.S. press, not as anathema, but as a necessary call for justice. He legitimizes Lucy Parsons' response to the unjust legal process, one that did eventually hang her husband:

He aquí como ella misma describe [la anarquía], con sus proprias palabras: "Pedimos la descentralización del poder en grupos o clases. . . .
No se abochorna de confesar sus hábitos llanos: "Fischer," dice, "estaba
entonces tomando cerveza conmigo en un salón cercano." ¿Quién ha di-
cho en el proceso que vio tirar la bomba, a ninguno de los condenados?
¿Acaso los que van a matar llevan a ver el crimen, como llevó mi marido,
a su mujer y a sus hijos?" "¡Ah, la prensa, las clases ricas, el miedo a este
levantamiento formidable de nuestra justicia ha falseado la verdad en ese
proceso ridículo e inicuo!"[47]

Here is how she herself describes [anarchy] in her own words: "We seek
the decentralization of power among groups or classes. . . . She is not em-
barrassed to confess her free habits: "Fischer," she says "was at that time
drinking a beer with me in a bar nearby." "Who has said in this trial that
they saw any of the condemned throw the bomb? Is it likely that those
who go to kill would take their wife and children to see the crime, as my
husband took us?" "Oh, the press, the wealthy classes, the fear of this formidable uprising for our justice have falsified the truth in this ridiculous
and iniquitous trial!"

Economic elites had corrupted the press's ability to offer an impartial
representation of the trial. Martí's reporting counteracts this process by
citing Lucy Parsons' testimony about where the accused were during the
incident, and why it is unlikely that her husband would have engaged in
throwing a bomb at that time.

Parsons' commentary, as transcribed by Martí, also makes visible the
failure of modernity, and industrialization in particular, to bring about
the promised liberation of the masses of people, in particular women
and children. Parsons gives convincing eyewitness reports of the ways
the factories increased the misery of those who walked long distances to
labor in them. The juxtaposition of these working class experiences with
those of wealthy women suggests that Parsons' understanding of class
injustice inexorably informs her feminist critique:

Cuando habla de la miseria de los obreros halla frases como esta: "Oigo
vibrar y palpitar las fábricas inmensas; pero sé que hay mujeres que tienen
que andar quince millas al día para ganar una miserable pitanza." "Decid

que no es verdad, a los que os dicen que aquí se adelanta. Cuando a mis propios ojos andaban en Chicago descalzos diez mil hijos de obreros, en Washington se presentaba en un baile una señora con todo el vestido lleno de diamantes, que valían $850,000: y otra llevaba en el pelo $75,000, y el pelo después de todo no era suyo!¡No! no es bueno que los ojos de vuestros hijos pierdan su luz puliendo esos diamantes."[48]

When she speaks of the misery of the workers she uses phrases such as this: "I hear vibrate and palpitate the immense factories; but I know that there are women who have to walk fifteen miles a day to earn a miserable pittance." "Say that it is not true, to those who tell you that here there is progress. When before my own eyes ten thousand workers' children walked barefoot, in Washington a lady attended a ball dressed in a gown full of diamonds that was worth $850,000: and another wore $75,000 in her hair, and the hair after all wasn't even hers! No! It is not just that the eyes of your children lose their brilliance in order to polish those diamonds."

Parsons speaks with special sympathy for working class women and laboring children, whose living conditions relate to the extreme concentration of wealth among the political and economic elite. Thousands of working class children had to labor in factories at a wage so low they could not afford shoes, yet their labor produces the excess wealth that the politician's wife in Washington, D.C., conspicuously loaded upon her gown or her wig. Parsons predicts an imminent revolt in the face of these contradictions, so that factories propelled by children's labor could become schools.

In Martí's chronicle, Lucy Parsons shines as a compelling spokesperson, with the ability of the greatest orators to command the attention of her audience. With the crowd outside pushing to enter, everyone in the room jumped to their feet. Martí acknowledges Parsons' power to move men, women, and children to tears and to action:

¿Por qué no ha de decirse? Esa mujer habló ayer con todo el brío de los grandes oradores. . . . Cuando acabó de hablar esta mestiza de mexicano e indio, todas las cabezas estaban inclinadas, como cuando se ora, sobre los bancos de la iglesia, y parecía la sala henchida; un campo de espigas encorvadas por el viento.[49]

Why not say it? This woman spoke yesterday with all the force of the great orators . . . When this Mexican and Indian *mestiza* finished speaking, all the heads were bent, as if in prayer over the benches of a church, and the room seemed full; a field of wheat bending in the wind.

By acknowledging Parsons' oratorical skill, by depicting men whose tears covered their beards after hearing her speak, and by describing little girls shouting "hurra" while atop their fathers' shoulders, Martí's reportage sketches men in awe of this woman who was enacting new protagonistic roles for Latinas, roles that challenge the traditional ideal of women as receptacles designed to satiate men's physical or emotional needs and/or as fulfilling their duty to the nation strictly through reproduction.[50] The description of the room as people bowing to pray, or as a field of wheat bending before the power of the wind, attribute both divine and natural powers of this *mestiza*, Mexican and indigenous, and of African descent, as Martí and the mainstream press elsewhere underscore. The rhetorical question—"Why should it not be said?"—suggests Martí's anticipation of the way his chronicle would ruffle the feathers of his readers, just as she had shaken him, but he does not for this reason deter his account of her inspired voice, which flowed from her "*labios llenos*" (full lips) like "*globos de fuego*" (globes of fire), as if her speech were the lava of a volcano.[51]

Between May 15, 1886, the date Martí affixed to his first essay on the trial of the seven anarchists of Chicago, and fall and winter of 1886, when Martí addresses a range of social questions ranging from class conflict, the concentration of wealth among a small elite, and the increasingly numerous and organized working class movement, Martí's experiences in the city provoke a dramatic shift to acknowledge the anarchists' claims that a radical transformation needed to occur.[52] In numerous essays that originally appeared in the *Partido Liberal*, and many of which were not included in Martí's *Obras Completas* until 2003, Martí wonders whether educational reform can bring about change, whether freedom of the press really exists in the United States, and whether immigrant, working class people of color can obtain fair representation in U.S.-style democracy. Martí notes, perhaps reluctantly, the need for a shift in women's roles, and for an organized movement to respond to class injustice, racial terror, and state-sponsored violence. The shock and novelty of Lucy Parsons' masterful oratory awakens Martí—like tens of thousands of others—to move beyond reflection and resentment toward radical action. For Martí, the encounter with Parsons suggests a shock of recognizing a peer, a fellow Spanish-speaker, and a teacher.

The official end of racial slavery and the emergence of working class, anti-imperialist, and anti-racist movements constitute enduring legacies of the nineteenth century. The multiracial formation of late-nineteenth-century *Latinidad* defines itself against monolingualism, imperialism, and U.S.-style racism. The Spanish-speaking feminist of color Lucy Parsons and the Afro-Puertorriqueño "Pachín" Marín did not hesi-tate to speak out against the violence they faced, as people of color, as workers, and as colonial subjects. The contributions of these dynamic wordsmiths, fearless orators, and indefatigable organizers push Martí to address his own blind spots, especially concerning race and gender, to inscribe a multiracial Latina/o social movement into the margins, as a critical supplement to the socialist and revolutionary projects that emerged in the late nineteenth century.

NOTES

In Memoriam Michael Brown, Eric Garner, Tameer Rice, Akai Gurley, Trayvon Martin, Andy López, Anthony Rosario, Anthony Baez, Israel Hernández Llach, Reefa Henández, Islan Nettles, Oscar Grant, Kenneth Chamberlaine Sr., Sean Bell, Amadou Diallo, Abner Louima, David Perez, and many thousands of other black and Latin@ victims of police or vigilante abuse and of an unjust legal system. I am grateful to José Aranda, who organized "Global Hispanisms" at Rice University in 2014; Carmen Lamas, who organized a panel at the Latina/o Studies Association in 2014; and Silvio Torres Saillant, who organized "Prensa, Latinidad y Legado: Spanish-Language Press and Print Culture" at Syracuse University in 2014, where I was able to present earlier versions and receive invaluable feedback on this chapter.

1 José Martí, Fragment 184, *Obras Completas* 22, 108 (in English in the original); Fragment 286, *Obras* 22, 189.

2 José Ballón's indispensable archival research documents Martí's marginal manu-scripts on his personal copy of Scottish economist John Rae's treatise *Contem-porary Socialism* (New York: Charles Scribner's Sons, 1887; f.p. 1883), available in

the Archivo de Asuntos Históricos del Consejo de Estado de Cuba. See Ballón's detailed documentation of all legible annotations in *Lecturas norteamericanas de José Martí: Emerson y el socialismo contemporaneo (1880–1887)* (México: Centro Coordinador y Difusor de Estudios Latinoamericanos, Universidad Nacional Autónoma de México, 1995), 36–58.

3 Martí, *"Mi Raza"* (My Race), admonishes racism in the Independence movement, in an article that simultaneously addresses blacks and whites.

4 This argument responds to the review of my book *Translating Empire* by Manuel Tellechea, in which he identifies the notion of Martí's learning from his colleagues of African descent as "the most offensive reference to Martí in *Translating Empire*." "Part II, Review of Laura Lomas *Translating Empire*." (http://www.josemarti-blog.blogspot.com, accessed on September 11, 2014).

5 Martí delivered his speech, "Madre América," in New York to Latin American leaders on December 19, 1889. See *Obras* 6: 135.

6 See, for example, Martí's critique of the weakness and divisions that Spain has exacerbated by "taking advantage of our preoccupations of the former master [*antiguo señor*], to divorce us from those who, because they have suffered in slavery like us, should and could be always our natural allies" ("A Ricardo Rodríguez Otero" 16 May 1886); *Obras* 1:194. The referent for the collective pronoun *us* seems to be white creoles, but to claim that whites experienced enslavement just as Afro-Cubans is highly problematic.

7 This term appears in Martí's correspondence to Manuel Mercado, his Mexican friend and editor, for whom he wrote his serialized novel *Amistad funesta*, which appeared in New York in *El Latino Americano*. See Martí, "A Manuel Mercado, April 12, 1885," in Martí, *Epistolario*1: 299.

8 In "The Truth about the United States," Martí discusses the supposed differences between "Latins" and "Saxons" but concludes they are nil. See Lomas, *Translating Empire*, xii, 92, 217, 232–35, 272–75, 285n6, 335n1.

9 Even when these "white" neighbors made their lives unbearable by throwing feces at their door and disrupting their employment, the Vegas continued their patterns of socializing until, eventually, they had to move. See *Memoirs of Bernardo Vega*, trans. Juan Flores (New York: Monthly Review Press, 1984), 85.

10 See *crónicas* that represent a critical reading of racial terror in the section on the "Asesinato de chinos" (*La Nación*, September 19, 1885) and "El problema industrial en los Estados Unidos" (*La Nación*, October 23, 1885); rpt. *En los Estados Unidos: periodismo de 1881–1892*, ed. Roberto Fernández Retamar and Pedro Pablo Rodríguez (Havana: Casa de las Américas, 2003), 540–44; "A Town Sets a Black Man on Fire," in Martí, *Selected Writings*, ed. and trans. Esther Allen (New York: Penguin, 2002).

11 Yolanda Martínez-San Miguel, *Coloniality of Diasporas* (New York: Palgrave Macmillan, 2014), 101.

12 See Martí, *Selected Writings*, 296, 264.

13 This phrase, which acknowledges the ways in which African culture had always already marked Cuban culture (and Caribbean culture more generally), appears in an excerpt from *The Manufacturer*, reprinted in Martí, *Selected Writings*, 262.

14 The pro-annexationist Cuban travel writer Ricardo Rodríguez Otero falsely attributed his views of autonomy to Martí. For discussion, see *Translating Empire*, 210–12.

15 Martí, "A Vindication," *Selected Writings* 263.

16 Ibid., 267.

17 Ibid., 264.

18 Ibid., 267.

19 Martí, "Gran exposición de ganado" (May 24, 1887, La Nación July 2, 1887) in *En los Estados Unidos*, 872–79. Cf. Lomas, "Imperialism, Modernization and Commodification of Identity," 201.

20 Obras 21:399; *Selected Writings*, 287.

21 Ríos, "El tren de Martí," 152–53.

22 Martí, "Class War in Chicago: A Terrible Drama," *Selected Writings*, 200.

23 Bernardo Vega makes the case to recognize Puerto Rico's fundamental contribution in his chapter entitled, "With the help of Puerto Ricans like Sotero Figueroa and Pachín Marín, the Partido Revolucionario Cubano is founded," in his *Memoirs*, 63–71.

24 Francisco Gonzálo Marín, *Mi óbolo, Mis dos cultos, A la asamblea, Al sol* (Ponce: Tipografía El Vapor, 1887). As I have noted in "Migration and Decolonial Politics in Two Afro-Latino Poets: 'Pachín' Marín and 'Tato' Laviera" *Review* 47.2 (2014): 157, the word *componte* derives from the Spanish use of torture to *componer* (put in order) and refers specifically to repression of rebellious free black artisans in Cuba during La Escalera several decades earlier in 1844.

25 Jesse Hoffnung-Garskof, "'To Abolish the Law of Castes: Merit, Manhood and the Problem of Colour in the Puerto Rican Liberal Movement, 1887–1892," *Social History* 36.3 (2011): 332–33.

26 Hoffnung-Garskof, "To Abolish the Law of Castes," 333.

27 See "Letter from an Artisan to His Newspaper," in *Workers' Struggle in Puerto Rico: A Documentary History*, ed. Angel Quintero Rivera, trans. Cedric Belfrage (New York: Monthly Review Press, 1976), 186.

28 See Hoffnung-Garskof, "To Abolish the Law of Castes," 314.

29 See Vega, *Memoirs*, 128.

30 After seeing a production of Marín's play *27 de Febrero* (1888), Lilí appointed Marín director of a school in Santiago de los Caballeros, but Marín was forced to flee shortly thereafter. Victor Coll y Cuchí describes the "macabre spectacle that this sublime sweaty, exhausted and enchained pilgrim presented" (qtd. Figueroa de Cifredo 44–46).

31 See Juan Coronel, *Un peregrino*. Pre-Biblión de Aníbal Esquivia Vasquez (Cartagena: Dirección de Educación Pública de Bolívar, Extensión Cultural, Imprenta Departamental, 1944), 302. In this remarkable document, Coronel reprints articles

from *El Obrero* to which Marín contributed, and in the chapter on socialism in his memoir he notes "de hecho me declaré socialista" (in fact, I declared myself a socialist) (324). See Lawrence E. Prescott, "A Colombian Pilgrim in the Caribbean: Juan Coronel, alias *Un Peregrino*," *Crítica Hispánica* 22.1 (2000), 135–47.

32 See Marín's further denunciation in his poem entitled "Andueza Palacio," *En la arena: Poesías* (Manzanillo, Cuba: Editorial el Arte, 1944), 102; hereafter cited parenthetically as *E*. Jorge Quintana has located archival evidence to show that the cause of Marín's deportation from Venezuela was an article criticizing Andueza Palacio, not the critique of Lilí, in "La expulsión de Venezuela de Francisco Gonzálo Marín," *Revista 37* (October 10, 1967), 27–32.

33 According to his biographer, Patria Figueroa de Cifredo, a manuscript eulogizing two African-descended warriors fallen in the struggle—Antonio Maceo and Francisco Gómez—was found on Marín's corpse. See Figueroa de Cifredo, *Pachín Marín: Héroe y Poeta* (San Juan: Instituto de Cultura Puertorriqueña), 1967.

34 Vega, *Memoirs*, 67.

35 José Martí, "Los Clubs: Rifleros de la Habana," *Patria* (28 de mayo 1892); rpt. *Obras completas* 1:471; and "El Club 'Mercedes Varona,'" *Patria* (1 de noviembre 1892); rpt. *Obras completas* 2: 178. See also José Ramón Freyre, *El Machete*, 2 de mayo de 1909; qtd. Figueroa de Cifredo 70.

36 Vega, *Memoirs*, 66.

37 See Figueroa de Cifredo, *Pachín Marín*, 71–73, where she cites correspondence with personal testimony from Domingo Collazo and J. de H. Terreforte crediting a letter from Marín, then in Jamaica, for the design of the Puerto Rican flag.

38 Marín, "Victor Hugo," *En la Arena*, 60; Marín, Preface to "Emilia," qtd. in Carlos N. Carreras, "El heroismo de Gonzalo Marín en la época de los compontes," *Puerto Rico Ilustrado* 27.1441 (23 oct 1937): 61; qtd. in Figuroa de Cifredo, *Pachín Marín*, 46.

39 Marín, "Las Botas," *En la Arena*, 108.

40 See Juan Flores and Miriam Jiménez Román's use of this term in their Introduction to their edited volume *The Afro-Latin@ Reader: History and Culture in the United States* (Durham, N.C.: Duke University Press, 2010), 1–15. Roberto Zurbano also uses the term *triple consciousness*, but in his case to refer to a concept elucidated by Frantz Fanon in *Black Skin White Masks*, to refer to the overlapping categories of blackness, nationality, and "a decolonizing consciousness." See Roberto Zurbano, "Cuba: Doce dificultades para enfrentar al (neo) racismo o doce razones para abrir el (otro) debate," *Universidad de la Habana* 273 (Enero-Febrero 2012), 273.

41 Shelly Streeby, *Radical Sensations: World Movements, Violence and Visual Culture* (Durham, N.C.: Duke University Press, 2013).

42 Victor Valle and Rodolfo D. Torres, "After *Latino Metropolis*: Cultural Political Economy and Alternative Futures," in *Latino Urbanism: The Politics of Planning, Policy and Redevelopment*, ed. David R. Dias and Rodolfo D. Torres (New York: New York University Press, 2012), 181–201.

43 Martí, "Grandes motines de obreros," *En los Estados Unidos*, 627.

44 Martí, *En los Estados Unidos*, 726; "Grandes motines de obreros," 632.

45 Parsons, "Challenging the Lying Monopolistic Press: A letter to Joseph Labadie," in *Freedom, Equality and Solidarity: Writings and Speeches 1878–1937* (Chicago: Charles H. Kerr Publishing Company, 2004), 56–67.

46 Parsons, "What Anarchy Means," *The Advance and Labor Leaf* (March 12, 1887); rpt. *Freedom, Equality and Solidarity: Writings and Speeches 1878–1937*, 57–61.

47 Martí, "La mujer norteamericana," *El Partido Liberal* (November 7, 1886); rpt. *En los Estados Unidos*, 738–40.

48 Ibid., 740.

49 Ibid., 739.

50 Ibid., 740.

51 Ibid., 739.

52 On the key role of anarchists in the Cuban Independence movement, after Martí persuaded them that the nationalists and anarchists had common interests, see Gerald Poyo, "*With All, and for the Good of All*" (Durham, N.C.: Duke University Press, 1989) and Frank Fernández, *Cuban Anarchism: The History of a Movement*, Trans. Charles Bufe (Tucson: See Sharp Press, 2001).

15

Sotero Figueroa

Writing Afro-Caribbeans into History in the Late
Nineteenth Century

NICOLÁS KANELLOS

African American scholarship is replete with references and homages
to Arthur A. Schomburg, né Arturo Alfonso Schomburg (1874–1938),
the Afro–Puerto Rican who became the archivist and bibliographer for
the Harlem Renaissance and who assembled the most extensive collection of African diaspora writings of his time. Quite often, Schomburg
is treated as unique in having transitioned from his Spanish-language,
Afro-Hispanic background in Puerto Rico to American Negro culture, to use the term in vogue during his lifetime. But Schomburg was
hardly unique, considering the number of Afro–Puerto Ricans and
Afro-Cubans who settled in African American neighborhoods, inter-
married within those communities, and adopted the language and ways
they encountered there,[1] while never truly giving up their Hispanic-
Caribbean identity. What is unique about Schomburg, however, is that
as a lay historian and archivist/bibliographer he contributed so much
to establishing a history and awareness of the African diaspora. This
chapter purports not to review that well-traveled ground[2] but to study
instead a friend and antecedent of Schomburg, another Gramscian
organic intellectual who sought to document his people's story from
the intersecting margins of both the Spanish and U.S. empires. Both
intellectuals coincided in building their histories by recovering the lost
biographies of Afro-Caribbeans and establishing an alternative archive.
Schomburg and Sotero Figueroa had grown up in Puerto Rico as disadvantaged children of mixed racial heritage, often called *mulatos* or
pardos because of skin color. Both were largely self-educated and learned
crafts, especially typesetting, on the island; both migrated to the United

States prior to the U.S. war with Spain; and both became associated with José Martí as they engaged in revolutionary activity to free Spain's Caribbean colonies. And, finally, both became subjects of the United States following this growing empire's victory over Spain.

Sotero Figueroa (1851–1923) somewhat antedates Schomburg both chronologically and in his dedication to research and the writing of history, including the history of Puerto Rico's chapter of the African diaspora. Born to free parents of color in Ponce, Puerto Rico, Figueroa may have had some elementary education in San Juan from Rafael Cordero y Molina (1790–1868), a famed black teacher who instructed children of all backgrounds for free;[3] as I indicate below, Figueroa wrote passionately about Cordero in his book of biographies, *Ensayo biográfico de los que más han contribuído al progreso de Puerto Rico* (1888). Not having the financial resources for higher, private education, Figueroa became apprenticed to a printer and learned the trade during the time when typographer-printers in Puerto Rico formed an intelligentsia among the working classes, akin to the leadership that the *lectores* in Cuban tobacco factories maintained. The vast majority of printers at that time were men of color. With access to the liberal writings he printed, Figueroa became an autodidact who studied historical documents, edited and published newspapers, and wrote and published poetry and plays. In 1873, he was a member of a literary society, Club Artístico y Literario Borinqueño, for which he became the secretary.[4] Through his printing and because of his literary interests, he became an important link to the working classes for white liberals seeking autonomy from Spain.[5] Figueroa was arrested twice for his participation in the Autonomist cause. In 1880, he founded his own print shop and began publishing newspapers, notably *El Eco de Ponce* and *La Avispa*; both enterprises eventually failed. He would continue to write for various periodicals and, in 1886, once again failed at publishing his own newspaper, *El Imparcial*, which lasted a little less than two years.[6]

Before making the transition to the United States and becoming involved in the independence movement led by José Martí, as did Schomburg, Figueroa began to delve into Puerto Rican history in general and to consider in his writings and publications the history of Africans and their condition on the island, although he did so often in a somewhat veiled and indirect manner, cloaking his aspirations for his people within general liberal causes. As Jesse Hoffnung-Garskof has shown, Figueroa and his printer-poet, later revolutionary comrade Francisco "Pachín" Marín,

> sought to insert a radical politics of social equality into liberal projects, arguing that the abandonment of prejudice of rank and caste in favour of a system of reward based on merit should be at the centre of colonial reform. They sought to enshrine particular notions of social and racial equality as fundamental elements of a liberal Puerto Rican 'regional' identity, and of modern, civilized, society. . . . [They] argued that prejudices of caste and rank, which they attributed to conservatives and Spanish officials, were a form of obscurantism.[7]

In much of his periodical writing and in his compilation of historical biographies, Figueroa argued for progress and civilization, often weaving in the leitmotivs of eliminating the disadvantages of race and class and taking pains to include the names and biographies of Afro–Puerto Ricans he considered worthy of respect by the nation. In his fervor for researching and writing biographies, he antedates Schomburg's similar obsession. Figueroa continued to recognize African-heritage heroes in his later periodical writing as part of the independence movement in New York City. Figueroa's well-documented volume *Ensayo biográfico*, which he dedicated to some of the most radical leaders of the Autonomist movement, was written for a contest on biography, which the Afro–Puerto Rican autodidact won.

It is obvious from the outset that biography was for Figueroa a lens through which to explore Puerto Rican history. Throughout the text, Figueroa makes use of the historian's tools, recovering and citing documents from the archive, citing newspaper stories and letters to the editor as well as testimonies and accounts of witnesses contemporary to the biographical subjects. Along the way he demonstrates his erudition, citing classical works, intellectual sources, and even the poetry of Luís de Camoens.[8] He refers to the words of educated historians and writers, such as Alejandro Tapia y Rivera and Salvador Brau, and offers alternative interpretations that conflict with their conclusions. He also corrects inaccuracies published in periodicals. In all, he assumes the role of historian with remarkable confidence and, at times, remarkable audacity by criticizing Spanish historical and contemporary authority and rule while Puerto Rico was still a colony of Spain.

Figueroa begins his collection of biographies with sketches of missionaries and colonizers but dwells more extensively on the lives of personages of the nineteenth century. Despite his excellent documentation, Figueroa extends his biographies to include paragraphs on varied subjects as well as his own editorials on social life and conditions. The *Ensayo biográfico* can be read in a number of ways because of Figueroa's criteria for selection and the leitmotivs that run through many of the thirty entries. Figueroa, ever aware of his unprivileged place in colonial society and his being deprived of a formal education, throughout the document traces what education was available on the island and for whom, and the lengths that many of his biographical subjects went to in making up for their lack of schooling. His interwoven history of education ties in neatly with his repeatedly developed liberal ideas about the march toward civilization and progress on the island, despite the disregard of Spain for the welfare of its colonial subjects (*EB* 61). Along the way, Figueroa also traces the history of slavery and its eventual abolition on the island; for him, slavery and its sociopolitical aftermath were the most serious barriers to enlightenment and civilization in Puerto Rican society—and the world. And the greatest heroes in Figueroa's pantheon are those who pulled themselves up from poverty and disadvantage in that society and participated in bringing progress to Puerto Rican culture; many of these were of African heritage. They were, Figueroa insists, self-made and without assistance from the white hierarchy; this, too, is a theme that will be repeated and expanded upon by Schomburg.

Notably, the second biography is that of the mulatto rococo painter José Campeche (1752–1809), who also served as a beacon for Schomburg in his gallery of race heroes. Besides the obvious renown of the painter, Figueroa chose Campeche because his life's story offered the latter-day artisan the opportunity to editorialize on the lack of opportunity and privilege for people like him. He states that the painter would have been able to cross the Atlantic, see the works of antiquity, and learn from the court painters of his time and thus increase his fame (*EB* 14) had he been born into a family privileged by the purity of Spanish blood and access to the financial resources to purchase an education. Figueroa states that his example teaches us, "lo que puede la fuerza creadora del genio, aún no auxiliada por la educación" (*EB* 15) (what the creative power of genius can do, even without the help of education).

Among the heroes who furthered education, Figueroa included Fray Benigno Carrión (1798–1871), Nicolás Aguayo y Aldea (1808–78), and Manuel Sicardó y Osuna. The entry on Sicardó y Osuna gave the author the opportunity to comment on the lack of opportunities on the Island: ". . . como tantos hijos de este país á quienes faltan alas de oro para volar á otras regiones donde saciar el ansia de saber, que es tanto más vehemente cuanto mayores son los obstáculos que se oponen a ello . . ." (*EB* 114) (. . . like so many sons of this country who do not have golden wings to fly to other regions to satisfy their hunger for learning, which is that much more stronger as greater are the obstacles that oppose it. . . .).

This theme of being deprived of access to education because of lack of the financial resources to travel where there are schools and universities will be repeated numerous times in the *Ensayo biográfico*. It is, however, the biographical entry dedicated to the self-taught teacher Cordero y Molina, known in some circles as the "Father of Public Education in Puerto Rico," that is one of the longest entries. Figueroa details at length this Afro–Puerto Rican tobacco worker's selfless contribution to teaching children of all backgrounds for free, perhaps even Figueroa himself at some point. He calls Cordero a "pobre hijo del pueblo, marcado con el sello de la degradación" (que así se decía en épocas de lamentable atraso del que tenía la piel negra) (*EB* 141) [poor child of the people, branded with the stamp of degradation (that is what black skin was called in epochs of lamentable backwardness)]. Cordero serves as a fundamental example for Figueroa's lobbying for public education, but also as an example of another self-taught intellectual like himself: "que se levanta del nivel común, sobrepuja en consideración de sus paisanos, *y por su propio y exclusivo esfuerzo* [my italics] escribe su nombre en el templo inmortal de nuestros benefactores" (*EB* 141) (who rises up from the common folk, overcompensates in favor of his countrymen, and by his *own and exclusive effort* writes his name in the immortal temple of those who have benefited us). Figueroa speculates on the great tenacity it would have taken Cordero[9] to overcome the barriers presented by the racist society of his day, when *negros* were not allowed to attend the one school that existed in San Juan.

In the chapter on Cordero, Figueroa lambastes the institution of slavery and its deleterious effects on society, especially in terms of depriving that society of the genius and contributions that people of African heritage could have made to the nation had they just been offered the opportunity of an education. He affirms in many different ways that the color of one's skin has nothing to do with intelligence and talent, and societies that discriminate in this way cannot be considered civilized. It is in this chapter as well that Figueroa brings up one of his greatest race heroes, the same one praised later by Schomburg: Toussaint L'Ouverture. Figueroa's choice is especially daring given how most whites detested L'Ouverture, especially the whites in Figueroa's homeland of southern Puerto Rico, where many refugees of the Haitian revolution settled. But he sees in L'Ouverture the proof that people of African blood have rights and can be great men. He ends his discussion with a call to philanthropists, even if they think their blood is superior, to educate black people: "¡Perfeccionad al negro, filántropos que os creeis de raza privilegiada!" (*EB* 142). He notes that even white Europe arose from a barbarian past and goes on to cite legal documents dating to as late as 1848 that allowed summary execution and maiming of slaves in Puerto Rico (*EB* 143–44). In effect, Figueroa was turning the tables, asking who was the barbarian, the so-called *savage* African or the *civilized* white (*EB* 145)?

Among the heroes who forwarded the abolitionist cause, Figueroa praises Ramón Power y Giral, Fray Benigno Carrión, the above-mentioned Nicolás Aguayo y Aldea, Luis Padial y Vizcarrondo, and various others, but he reserves his greatest praise and the longest entry in his book for Segundo Ruiz Belvis (1824–67). Belvis, explains Figueroa, tirelessly and through self-sacrifice worked to free the slaves in Puerto Rico, a deed that was finally accomplished in 1873, six years after Belvis drafted the key document for abolition that was made law six years after his death in exile. Figueroa quotes extensively from Belvis's co-written document known simply as the "*Informe*" (Report) and took the opportunity to depict slavery in the longest editorial of his book. Slavery, he stated, just fifteen years after its abolition,[10] was "la iniquidad de los siglos" (*AB* 131) (the iniquity of the centuries); he pictured the subjects of this iniquity as dehumanized ". . . máquinas de carne que se movían continuamente en el fondo de las plantaciones y establecimientos agrícolas, accelerando la fatigosa faena al sentir el chasquido del látigo sobre su extenuado cuerpo" (*EB* 131) (. . . machines made of flesh that continually worked their way through plantations and agricultural fields, the lash of the whip accelerating the pace of their fatigued and exhausted bodies). Contrasted with this horrible depiction, Figueroa followed with a poetic description of some 30,000 slaves receiving the news of their liberation: "¡Libres! ¡Con cuánta emoción no lanzarían los esclavos por primera vez esta palabra! Es decir, que ya amparados por la ley, eran *hombres* y no *cosas*. Ya podían andar los lazos de la familia, sin pensar en que sus hijos fueran arrancados del seno materno, y vendidos para otras poblaciones. . . . Ya podían ilustrar su razón, tener creencias, fundar familias sin temor á que las brutas caricias del *capataz* ó del *amo* violaran, con su dignidad, la honra de sus esposas, la inocencia de sus hijas" (*EB* 136–37) (Free! How great would they have expressed their emotion when they first heard that word! That is, finally supported by law, they were now *people* and not *things*. They now could maintain family ties, without the fear that their children would be torn from maternal breasts and sold to other regions. . . . Now they could manifest their reasoning, have beliefs, start families without the fear that the brutal embraces of the foreman or of the owner, with their dignity intact, would violate the honor of their wives, the innocence of their daughters).

Last in the *Ensayo biográfico*, Figueroa memorialized artisans like himself, such as Juan González y Chaves (1810–65) and Pascasio P. Sancerrit (1833–76), among others. González y Chaves advanced Puerto Rican culture by being among the first to publish books on the island and even a newspaper, *Fomento* (Development). Figueroa classed him a *laborioso obrero* (122) (hard-working laborer), thus emphasizing that the working classes could produce intellectuals, even if they are self-made, implying that civilization could be advanced in Puerto Rico only by offering such people opportunities and supporting them. On the other hand, Figueroa makes clear that Sancerrit was of African heritage and became a distinguished typographer, poet, and newspaper publisher despite his lack of formal education, that he accomplished so much all by himself (*EB* 172), "como un ejemplo admirable de lo que puede la voluntad auxiliada por la inteligencia" (173) (an admirable example of what will power aided by intelligence can accomplish). Figueroa also paid homage to Félix Padial y Vizacarrondo (1838–80) and José Pablo Morales (1828–82), who, although not of the artisan class, distinguished themselves as journalists. Padial took in Figueroa as an apprentice and initiated the young aspirant in not only literary pursuits, but also to work on Padial's own newspaper, *El Progreso*; Padial also introduced Figueroa to political liberalism. Morales, insisted Figueroa, was self-taught, *se formó solo* (*EB* 229), and his success was due to his powerful intelligence and perseverance at a time when island culture was utterly backward and offered no training. Morales's biography gave Figueroa the opportunity to editorialize that withholding educational opportunities and keeping Puerto Ricans backward and ignorant were purposeful strategies of Spain to keep the population docile and governable (*EB* 230).

Thus, it seems, unlike in traditional biographies and accounts of great men of the past—no women, of course, unfortunately—Figueroa's criteria for the most part did not include politicians and many men of wealth and renown but favored those who worked to free the slaves and advance education on the island. His particular selection of biographical subjects, as we have seen, was replete with artisans and men of African or Afro-European heritage, those who despite discrimination and lack of opportunity for them as free blacks or the children of manumission succeeded in intellectual or artistic endeavors *on their own*, that is, *self-made*.

Shortly after publishing his *Ensayo biográfico*, in 1889 Figueroa left the island with his own printing press and equipment for New York,[11] where he joined up with the leaders of the independence movement, as did Schomburg in 1891. Both became aligned with the Cuban Revolutionary Party and associated with its leader, José Martí. Figueroa established a print shop, named América, where he published newspapers and books, among other types of documents. He was also the editor, from 1890 to 1892, of the renowned cultural magazine *Revista Ilustrada de Nueva York*. On the presses of Imprenta América, Figueroa issued the Revolutionary Party's newspaper, *Patria*, which he edited when Martí was traveling. Among the qualities that drew Figueroa to José Martí and later to apotheosize him after Martí's death on the battlefield in Cuba was precisely the patriarch's well-known stance on doing away with all racial distinctions in the independent Cuba they were fighting to establish; just as important was Martí's success in uniting the Afro-Cuban revolutionary forces with the traditionally white liberal ones and extending leadership to men of color, such as Figueroa and his printer-publisher colleague from Ponce, Francisco "Pachín" Marín, as well as Arturo Alfonso Schomburg, all three Afro–Puerto Rican autodidact artisans.

In his periodical writing from within the revolutionary movement, Figueroa continued his leitmotivs of Afro-Caribbean contributions and the self-education of those from disadvantaged backgrounds, especially those of African lineage. For instance, he included Toussaint L'Ouverture alongside Simón Bolívar, Miguel Hidalgo, and other famed liberators of the Americas in his article "Meeting de Proclamación," in which he explains that "Toussaint, que surge de las lobregueces de la esclavitud y derrota las mejores huestes de la Francia napoleónica; su amor para los infelices subyugados, su magnaminidad para los vencidos . . ." (Toussaint, who arises from the darkness of slavery and demolishes the best of France's Napoleonic armies; his love for the unhappy oppressed, his magnanimity for the vanquished . . .).[12] In this same article, he compares the fallen Martí to Jesus Christ and repeats his recurrent gloss on Martí's vision: "no reconoce categorías ni colores, sino hermanos en la patria y la libertad" (he does not recognize class distinctions or skin color, only brothers in the fatherland and liberty). But more strikingly he repeats numerous times in editorials that the revolution would bring about equality of people, irrespective of their skin color: ". . . será igualmente justa la revolución en que han caído, sin mirarse los colores, todos los cubanos . . . (donde no) se distinguiera un hombre de otro por el calor del corazón ó por el fuego de la frente" [the revolution in which they have fallen will be just if all Cubans pay no attention to color . . . (where) a man would only be distinct from another because of the warmth of his heart or the fire on his brow].[13] It is noteworthy that Figueroa actually interprets the actions of Martí as similar to those of Christ regarding class distinctions: ". . . dar la vida por la redención de su pueblo, se lanza pobre y oscuro, solo é indefenso, a través de la Judea, a levantar en los corazones el imperio de la justicia, abolir la ley de casta, predicando el dogma iluminador de las conciencias y dignificador de la humanidad, que se encierra en estas tres sublimes palabras: Libertad, Igualdad, Fraternidad" (. . . to sacrifice one's life for the redemption of his people, he emerges poor, dark,[14] alone and defenseless across Judea to raise up in hearts the empire of justice, to abolish the law of castes, preaching the dogma enlightening the conscience and dignifying humanity, which can be summarized in three sublime words: Liberty, Fraternity, Equality).[15] Figueroa continues the essay, warning that those who maintain social discrimination will not participate in the benefits of the victorious revolution: ". . . los que se excluyan de la revolución por arrogancia de señorío ó por reparos sociales . . . ." He continues in the same article to speak of the social justice and equality that must be enforced upon the success of the revolution, in which color and class discrimination must be abjured. In a front-page editorial on October 2, 1894, he emphasizes that one of the reasons for the independence movement was to abolish slavery, that "Los dominadores de la colonia . . . apenas si se detenían a pensar que el esclavo podía ser libre, y que el criollo debía administrar sus propios intereses" (The colonial dominators . . . hardly ever paused to think that the slave could be free and that the creole could take care of his own business), thus proffering the analogy that abolition was to slavery as independence was to the creoles.

Beyond these recurrent themes, Figueroa assumes the confident stance of a true historian in many of the speeches and periodical articles he penned and published in New York. For instance, in his series of seven articles entitled "La verdad de la historia" (The Truth of the History), which ran in *Patria* from March 19 to July 2, 1892, he traces the history of the independence movement in Puerto Rico, from its origins to the Grito de Lares (Shout at Lares) insurrection in 1896, correcting various published versions about the shout while foregrounding the role of Afro–Puerto Rican patriot Ramón Emeterio Betances, who receives from Figueroa reverence similar to that he showed for José Martí. Another example is his published speech on the anniversary of Martí's death, "Primer Aniversario" (February 29, 1896), in which he announces the names of the meritorious fallen in the pages of history. In the speech, he summarizes the independence movement and war, taking pains to enumerate the heroic fallen. And this, once again, gives him the opportunity to specifically name Afro-Caribbean heroes in his pantheon: Victoriano Garzón (1847–95), Francisco Adolfo Crombet Tejera (1851–95), Alfonso Goulet (?–1895), and the famed carpenter who became a general, José Guillermo Moncada (1841–95). What is interesting is that they all died in battle the same year as Martí, and in Figueroa's shorthand they merit the same respect as their white comrades.

Noteworthy in the same speech, he returns to the need for education of the poor, now seen as an outcome of the revolution: Revolutionary man will educate "la clase obrera para que marche concientemente a la conquista de sus derechos" (the working class so that it can consciously march forward to conquer its rights); and, maintaining the humility of the working classes, he emphasizes again: "el hombre modesto, que se prodiga sin ostentación" (modest man who will give of himself without ostentation).

Soon after Martí's death, Figueroa was marginalized by the white liberals[16] in the movement in New York, which led him to leave *Patria*. Hoffnung-Garskof attests that "After Martí left for Cuba in 1895, the leadership of the party increasingly excluded men like Serra and Figueroa from decision-making and from editorial input in *Patria*."[17] Figueroa then proceeded to establish his own newspaper, *La Doctrina de Martí*, which he published from 1896 to 1898 with the help of other Afro–Puerto Ricans, including Francisco "Pachín" Marín and Rafael Serra. *La Doctrina de Martí* sought to continue what Figueroa interpreted as Martí's "socially and racially progressive view of the revolutionary cause,"[18] thus challenging the conservatism of *Patria*. Among his diverse writings in his newspaper, Figueroa began a series of seven articles, from September 16, 1896, to March 2, 1897, defining what for him was the discipline of history and the role of historian, while he attacked and deconstructed Cuban newspaper publisher Enrique Trujillo's recently issued book, *Apuntes históricos* (Historical Notes).

After the war with Spain was concluded and the United States obtained its Caribbean colonies, Figueroa in 1899 migrated to Cuba, intending once again to transport his printing press and set up shop to print and publish for the new nation; his plans were frustrated, however, when the same conservatives who pushed him out of *Patria*, notably Tomás Estrada Palma, intercepted the importation of his Imprenta América.[19] In Havana, he nevertheless continued to participate in political life and write Afro-Caribbeans into history through articles in such newspapers as *La Discusión* and others. In 1900, he became a founding member of a political group, Asociación de Emigrados Revolucionarios Cubanos, and by 1900 he would become a founding member of the revived Partido Revolucionario Cubano, which aspired to maintain the values of the independence movement; Figueroa became the editor of the party's newspaper, *Independencia*.[20] In 1902, when Cuba became an independent republic—although under U.S. interventionist clauses in its constitution—he was named director of the republic's official organ, *La gaceta oficial*. In 1904, Figueroa wrote a column for the *El Mundo* newspaper entitled "Nuestros héroes," in which along with well-known creole revolutionary figures he made a point of including biographies of Afro-Cuban heroes, such as Antonio Maceo, José Maceo, Néstor Aranguren, and Vidal Ducasse. Figueroa's mission as journalist and historian, as well as protector of the Afro-Caribbean legacy, was continually frustrated to the point of his living his later years in penury. The conservative forces led by U.S.-supported President Tomás Estrada Palma prevailed in suppressing Afro-Cuban movements for equal rights, and a disillusioned Figueroa retired from public life while having to sue for his pension as a veteran of the war for independence.[21]

In a trajectory to the United States comparable to Figueroa's, Alfonso Arturo Schomburg relocated in 1891 to New York, where he became actively involved in the Cuban and Puerto Rican independence movements. Like Figueroa, he soon became a member of revolutionary clubs, such as Club Borinquen and Las Dos Antillas, and became associated with José Martí and with Figueroa, in whose home club members occasionally met.[22] Schomburg was born to an unwed launderette or midwife of free African heritage and a father of German or *mestizo* heritage who seems to have abandoned his wife and son.[23] Although Schomburg himself made references to having had some education of one sort or another while growing up in Puerto Rico, there is really no evidence that he received any type of formal education,[24] especially because there were practically no free public schools on the island during the nineteenth century and his impoverished mother certainly could not afford private tutelage.[25] This lack of formalized study and degrees or certificates bothered Schomburg throughout his life and was an obstacle to his pursuing education and a law degree in the United States.[26] It also was evident to his university-educated American Negro brethren, such as W. E. B. Du Bois and Carter Woodson, as they willingly received his documentary research but slighted his insight and understanding, even his accented speech and poor writing style that needed extensive editing.[27] And when he was a candidate to be hired to curate the collection he had sold to the

New York Public Library, it was Du Bois and his followers who opposed him because of his lack of formal preparation. Despite his references to some type of schooling, Schomburg proudly referred to himself as self-made.[28] It would strain credulity to think that a bibliophile such as Schomburg did not read Figueroa's *Ensayo bibliográfico* or that the two comrades did not exchange ideas, especially those about the struggle for racial equality and Afro-Caribbean history. Both activists were essential in articulating the struggle for racial equality as part of the movement for independence from Spain.

During this early period in New York, Schomburg sent articles and letters in Spanish to periodicals in support of the revolution. He also had occasion to visit independence chapters in New Orleans and travel in the South, where he observed the condition of African Americans.[29] Unlike Figueroa, however, Schomburg stayed in the United States after the war, when Puerto Rico became a colony of the United States. He and his fellow Afro-Caribbeans also set up a bilingual freemasonry lodge, El Sol de Cuba, which in 1911 changed its name to the Prince Hall Lodge and accommodated a growing African American membership; Hoffnung-Garskof calls attention to the lodge's reinforcement of Schomburg's constant preoccupation: "The brothers in the Prince Hall lodges glorified the image of the 'self-made man,' a message that appealed to Schomburg, the humble artisan, whose humiliation before the New York State Board of Regents was replayed multiple times at the hands of elite black intellectuals."[30] Despite racism among white Masons, Schomburg eventually became general secretary of the Grand Lodge of the State of New York, becoming in this sense self-made; it was an intellectual distinction that he was unable to duplicate in his work life as a humble bank mailroom clerk and messenger. After the United States took possession of Cuba and Puerto Rico, among the last colonies of Spain, Schomburg directed his intellectual energies toward studying the worldwide African diaspora and constituting its documentary history. It was also in 1911 that Schomburg and four others founded what eventually would be known as the Negro Society for Historical Research, and, in 1914, he was elected a member of the American Negro Academy, whose membership was made up mostly of formally educated African Americans.[31] Schomburg was now in full gear in his historical research and providing the documentary basis for Pan-Africanism, or what we might today call black nationalism.

It is in Schomburg's twentieth-century cultural work that his decolonizing archival work and writings strive to revise the white man's history
to create a space for African heritage and even at times to document
African and Afro-Hispanic antecedence in developing "civilization." As
he wrote in "The Negro Digs Up His Past," "History must restore what
slavery took away, for it is the social damage of slavery that the present
generation must repair and offset."[32] And where Martí may have tipped
his hat to creating a multiracial society[33] in Latin America, Schomburg
on the other hand placed the African presence in the center of Latin
American history[34]—in this he departed somewhat from Figueroa,
who unflaggingly praised Martí's ideas on racial integration. And like
Figueroa in preserving the heroic role of Toussaint L'Ouverture, Schomburg went a step further and proposed that one of the greatest gifts to
the Americas was black Haiti's blazing the path to independence from
Europe.[35] Thus recurring throughout his collecting and his essays and
speeches, Schomburg took pains to recover from the past African "firsts"
in order to correct the historical record.

For Schomburg, biography became a mainstay in his research and
writing methodology. Much like Figueroa's, many of Schomburg's articles rescue the contributions of African heritage figures to the development of the Americas. He filled the pages he wrote with biographies of
philosophers, poets, politicians, artists, educators—all types of accomplished individuals of African heritage who blazed paths in Europe and
the Americas. Writing in "The Economic Contribution by the Negro to
America" about Africans forcefully brought to the New World, Schomburg stated, "They were not the untutored savages we are expected to
believe from modern histories."[36] Thus, like Figueroa as well, Schomburg here and in most of his works was motivated to challenge and correct official history. The latter is obvious in his closing remarks in this
essay: "Suffice it to say that the position which the Negro and his mixed
progeny of European or Indian blood had won in South America, they
have also earned, if even they have not as yet received, due recognition
therefore in North America."

Schomburg relied on biography as a means to rewrite Western history by bringing to light historical figures of African heritage and, thus,
challenge ideas of African inferiority and combat stereotypes that were
widely held even among the educated classes. Among the historical fig-

ures Schomburg rescues are the colonial Mexican poet Juan Cortez; "the first Negro librarian," Manuel Socorro Rodríguez; the Cuban poet Plácido; and numerous others.[37] He coincided with Figueroa in drafting essays on such heroes of the independence movement as Antonio Maceo and José Martí, but the notable recovery was his biographical exaltation of the same Puerto Rican painter whom Figueroa had researched before him: José Campeche. Thabiti Asukile asserts that in his lifetime and even today, Schomburg's contributions as a writer and scholar were not and are not valued, largely because he did not have the sanctioned training or use the accepted scholarly methodology.[38]

Aside from the biographical methodology employed by the autodidact Schomburg, his writings reveal a similar leitmotiv to Figueroa's: the value of self-education for Afro-Caribbeans, and others, who despite tremendous barriers have made impressive contributions to civilization.[39] And his famous declaration on the need for "Negro" history reveals that concern for knowledge produced by non-academic as well as academic sources: "We need in the coming dawn the man who will give us the background of our future; it matters not whether he comes from the cloister of the university or the rank and file of the fields."[40] Schomburg, more than Figueroa, most certainly faced this quandary of producing scholarship without the academic credentials that his rivals, such as Du Bois and Alain Locke, had and held over him. And he defensively asserted the value of being self-taught and experienced rather than just formally educated, as affirmed in his 1913 Masonic speech: "The university graduate is wont to overestimate his ability, fresh from the machinery that endows him with a parchment and crowns him with knowledge, he steps out into the world to meet the practical men with years of experience and mother wit."[41] Jossiana Arroyo has also noted the role that Masonic thought played in reaffirming Schomburg's confidence in being self-made: "During his life, Schomburg would intertwine his definition of the Masonic workshop with his own story as a self-made man, which included his interaction with other Masons who were also free-born slaves who became leaders and mentors of other African Americans (such as John Bruce), and his work as a bibliographer and historian of the African diaspora."[42] While Hoffnung-Garskof acknowledges that the Prince Hall Masons offered Schomburg continuity with the African-heritage societies that he and other self-taught Afro-

338 | NICOLÁS KANELLOS

Hispanic intellectuals joined, he does not, nor does Arroyo, highlight how this self-making was a common theme among the accomplished but unschooled African-heritage organic intellectuals in the Caribbean, and no one has identified Sotero Figueroa as his antecedent and probable discussant on this and other issues, such as history and biography. The renowned collector/historian Schomburg was carrying out a decolonizing project that had its roots in the Puerto Rican and Cuban independence movements, and some of his expressed approaches and concepts were preceded by his elder and associate Sotero Figueroa. Before Schomburg, Figueroa had inserted Afro-Caribbeans into history as part of his decolonizing mission and had used biography as a means of expanding and correcting official history. The archive Figueroa created in his book, his articles, and speeches was just as much a counter-archive as Schomburg's. Cognizant of the educational deprivation of slaves and their descendants, Figueroa also anticipated Schomburg in emphasizing the meritorious role that self-education, drive, and native intelligence played and should play in the making of the independent, freed man who would construct his people's identity with pride in the racial past that he was/should be committed to bring forth from the shadows.

NOTES

1 See Jesse Hoffnung-Garskof, "The World of Arturo Alfonso Schomburg," In *The Afro-Latin@ Reader* (Durham, N.C.: Duke University Press), 70–91.

2 Within the last ten years a scholarly debate has developed regarding Schomburg's contribution to African American studies and culture as well as to the sources and influences, whether they were Puerto Rican, Afro-Caribbean, Masonic, or even matrilineal. See, among other articles, Agustín Laó-Montes' "Afro-Latinidades and the Diasporic Imaginary," *Iberoamericana* 5:17 (Marzo 2005): 117–30.

3 Jesse Hoffnung-Garskof, "To Abolish the Law of Castes: Merit, Manhood and the Problem of Colour in the Puerto Rican Liberal Movement, 1873–92," *Social History* 36:3 (2011): 323.

4 Josefina Toledo, *Sotero Figueroa, Editor de Patria* (Havana: Editorial Letras Cubanas, 1985), 23.

5 Hoffnung-Garskof, "Law of Castes," 323.

6 Toledo, *Sotero Figueroa*, 30.

7 Hoffnung-Garskof, "Law of Castes," 314.

8 Sotero Figueroa, *Ensayo biográfico de los que más han contribuído al progreso de Puerto Rico* (San Juan: Editorial Coquí, 1973), 139; hereafter cited parenthetically as *EB*.

9 It is interesting to note that, among the numerous paintings of aristocrats and landed gentry affected by José Campeche, there is a painting of a very dark Cordero, teaching students of various hues of skin color.

10 The "former" slaves were actually required to work three years more and could not participate in the political process for five years. The reaction among plantation owners was to round up the abolitionists, including Belvis and the mulatto lawyer-abolitionist Ramón Emeterio Betances, and send them into exile in Spain.

11 There is no documented evidence that Figueroa was persecuted or sent into exile because of his criticism of Spanish rule in Puerto Rico, but one can imagine that it would have been uncomfortable for him to remain on the island as his biography became circulated and commented upon. It is known that he went into hiding in 1887, when Spanish authorities pursued political dissidents without quarter, so much so that it became known as "the terrible year" that resulted in many patriots' going into exile; it is thought that while hiding in 1887, Figueroa was able to write his *Ensayo biográfico* (Toledo: Sotero Figueroa, 34).

12 *Patria*, July 20, 1895, 1–2.

13 *Patria*, March 14, 1892, 7.

14 This ambiguous use of *oscuro* or *dark* may mean that Jesus emerged from obscurity or, even more interesting, that Jesus was dark-complected.

15 See "Discursos en la confirmación de la proclamación del Partido Revolucionario Cubano" http://www.wwnorton.com/college/english/latino-literature/pdfs/2_Annexations/Figueroa_Discursos.pdf.

16 For details, see Toledo, *Sotero Figueroa*, 69–70.

17 Hoffnung-Garskof, "The World of Arturo Alfonso Schomburg," 81.

18 Jesse Hoffnung-Garskof, "The Migrations of Arturo Schomburg: On Being Antillano, Negro, and Puerto Rican in New York 1891–1938." *Journal of American Ethnic History*. 21:1 (Fall 2001): 17.

19 Toledo, *Sotero Figueroa*, 91.

20 Ibid., 98–99.

21 Ibid., 110–11.

22 Flor Piñero de Rivera, ed., *Arturo Schomburg: Un puertorriqueño descubre el legado histórico del negro, sus escritos anotados y apéndices* (San Juan: Centro de Estudios de Puerto Rico y el Caribe, 1989), 178–79.

23 Elinor Des Verney Sinnette, *Arthur Alfonso Schomburg: Black Bibliophile and Collector: A Biography* (Detroit: New York Public Library and Wayne State University Press, 1989), 8.

24 Flor Piñero de Rivera constructs a complete educational history through college in the Virgin Islands, based on a 1977 report, "'The Spirit that Moves Us': A Profile of Arthur A. Schomburg." *Schomburg Center Journal* 1:2 (1977), 19. But many of Schomburg's biographical references have been contradictory and given little credence by scholars.

25 Sinnette, *Schomburg*, 9.

26 Ibid., 35.

27 Ibid., 41, 52, 55.

28 His friend Bernardo Vega in his memoir attests to Schomburg's self-education, although he possibly attended some primary education classes and learned somewhat from the equally self-educated tobacco workers, who were among the most enlightened of the working classes. See *Memoirs of Bernardo Vega: A Contribution to the History of the Puerto Rican Community in New York*, ed. César Andreu Iglesias (New York: Monthly Review Press, 1984), 195.

29 Sinnette, *Schomburg*, 22.

30 Hoffnung-Garscof, "Migrations," 34.

31 Sinnette, *Schomburg*, 38.

32 Schomburg, "The Negro Digs Up His Past" in *The Norton Anthology of Latino Literature*, ed. Ilan Stavans (New York: Norton, 2011), 372.

33 Hoffnung-Garskof clarifies that "Martí's idea of a Cuba with no Blacks or Whites could also hide persistent racism and racial inequality behind a mask of race blindness." See "The World of Arturo Alfonso Schomburg" in *The Afro-Latin@ Reader*, ed. Miriam Jiménez-Román and Juan Flores (Durham, N.C.: Duke University Press, 2010), 79.

34 Kevin Meehan, "Martí, Schomburg y la cuestión racial en las Américas." *Afro-Hispanic Review* 25:2 (Fall 2006): 78.

35 Schomburg, "The Economic Contribution by the Negro to America." *Papers of the American Negro Academy*. Nos. 18–19, p. 6. http://www.gutenberg.org/files/35352/35352-0.txt.

36 Schomburg, "Economic Contribution," 18.

37 Meehan's is an in-depth study comparing Schomburg's and Martí's ideas on race in the Americas in which he concludes that Martí's pronouncements of African heritage were largely impressionistic, if not paternalistic, while Schomburg was intent on transforming the image of Afro-Latins from passive to powerful and, in the process, de-colonizing them intellectually. See p. 78, for instance.

38 Thabiti Asukile, "Arthur Alfonso Schomburg (1874–1938): Embracing the Black Motherhood Experience in Love of Black People." *Afro-Americans in New York Life and History* 30:2 (July 2006): 79.

39 Asukile sees this as a mainstay contribution of African descent people to the Americas: "a long tradition of non-academic intellectuals who were committed to the life of the mind" (70).

40 Schomburg, "Racial Integrity," in *The Afro-Latin@ Reader*, 69.

41 Quoted in Hoffnung-Garskof, "Migrations," 34.

42 Jossianna Arroyo, "Technologies: Transculturations of Race, Gender & Ethnicity in Arturo A. Schomburg's Masonic Writings." *Centro Journal*. 12:1 (Spring 2005): 12.

Response

From Criollo/a to Latino/a: The Latino Nineteenth Century in a Hemispheric Context

RALPH BAUER

The chapters assembled here call our attention to a very rich and heterogeneous archive that has all too long been ignored by an Anglocentric tradition of literary history in the United States. As such, this volume makes an important contribution to the ongoing "recovery" project of the rich U.S. Hispanic Literary Heritage in the United States launched by Arte Público Press in 1992. Equal in significance to its project of archival recovery, however, is this volume's critical intervention in forcing us to think beyond some of the conceptual vocabulary that has conventionally informed Latino studies, a subdiscipline that emerged with a primary focus on an archive produced in the wake of the civil rights movement in the United States. As such, the chapters gathered here splendidly respond to Lazo's challenge to "open research into writing and textual production that may move us in unexpected directions and new archival sites," thereby illuminating the "material conditions, spatial trajectories, hemispheric movements, and forms of colonization and war that contribute what we can perceive in the texts that remain" of the nineteenth-century Latino archive.

One important difference, Lazo notes, between the archival encounter of Latino/a writing in the nineteenth century and that of more recent times is with regard to the issue of language. Whereas the Latino literature written since the 1960s has been published primarily in English, much of nineteenth-century Latino writing is preserved in Spanish. This may be one of the reasons, as Raúl Coronado points out, for the continued marginalization of this archive in American literary criticism, which has by and large followed an "English only" language policy, despite embracing multiculturalism and historicism in recent decades. Latino literature, in this critical tradition, belonged to U.S. literature only when it was written in English, but to Latin American literature when it was written in Spanish. Thus, as Carmen Lamas points out in her chapter, "it is only by way of accessing the Latin American archive . . . that we gain new insight into the Latina/o experience of the nineteenth century." Indeed, only recently have some widely distributed literary anthologies, such as *The Multilingual Anthology of American Literature*, edited by Werner Sollors and Marc Shell, begun to reflect the impact of seminal critical works about the Spanish-language literature of the United States, including the works of many of the authors gathered in this volume. From this point of view, *The Latino Nineteenth Century* contributes to a new understanding not only of the *longue durée* of the Latino literary heritage but also of the nineteenth-century literary landscape of the United States.

But language aside, there are other reasons why *The Latino Nineteenth Century* challenges conventional paradigms guiding our archival encounters. While some of the texts and authors considered here manifest the beginnings of what we might call a "minority discourse" that speaks back to Anglo American hegemony and racism already alive and well in the nineteenth-century United States, the overall picture that emerges from this collection is that of a diverse set of Latino subject-positions, some of which point not forward to twentieth-century power relations in the United States but rather backward to those of late colonial and early national Latin America. As José Aranda observes in his contribution, "the 'coloniality of power'" that resides in these texts is often "double-edged, fighting off an Anglo-American colonial presence, only to hide, make natural, or complicate older Spanish-Mexican colonial narratives." Indeed, as Aranda goes on to argue, many nineteenth-century Latinos such as María Ruiz de Burton were no "subalterns." Thus, Ruiz de Burton was the "daughter of the Enlightenment and a colonialist," and, like many post-1848 writers of Mexican descent in the United States, she appears "as both colonizer and colonized, as beneficiary and victim of settler colonialism, as white and non-white, and as gendered, and therefore disciplined, in accordance to a European patriarchal system." For this reason, Aranda concludes, the conceptual paradigms that grew out of the "counter-nationalist, Marxist leaning, activist archive of the Chicana/o Movement" of the twentieth-century United States have limited value for understanding the world of nineteenth-century Latinas/os such as Ruiz de Burton, who belonged to "other times and other politics." This is what Aranda calls (borrowing from the Argentine Mexican theorist Enrique Dussel) the "transmodernity" of the Latino nineteenth century, a modernity that bridges and hybridizes Latin American and U.S. modernities that emerged from their respective histories of conquest and colonialism in the Americas.

This is an important point that is reinforced by Robert McKee Irwin's notion of the "almost Latino" of more recent days. Insofar as the authors and agents discussed in this volume can be seen as representative of the Latino nineteenth century, Irwin's notion challenges us to ask who was *not* included among the migrants and settlers whose stories we learn about in these chapters and to raise "questions about the relationship between a US-based identity category and its Latin American beginnings." What the chapters in this volume thus collectively underscore is the need for a hemispheric and transnational perspective on the Latino nineteenth century, one that would consider Latinos in the context not only of the United States but also of colonial and postcolonial Latin American history and literature. Indeed, while the term *Latino* has come to distinguish an ethnic minority from an ethnic "Anglo" majority (as well as other ethnic minorities) in the United States, in the (post-) colonial Latin American context the identity category referencing a subject's Latinidad has had very different social implications. In Latin America, the word *ladino* is generally used to distinguish *mestizos* and Indians who use or have adopted the Spanish language and culture (including dress, diet, agriculture, and so on) from "*indios*" or "*indígenas*" on the one hand and, on the other, from Spanish-descended and American-born creoles (*criollos*) as well as Spanish-born Spaniards (*peninsulares*). *Latinidad*, in other words, evokes not social and cultural marginalization but rather the assimilation to the culture of the (post-) colonial elite in the social order that had emerged from the European conquest by those who could not themselves lay claim to belonging.

Keeping in mind the (post-) colonial Latin American social context of Latinidad brings into focus the fact that most of the authors and subjects under consideration in this collection—the exception being the Afro-Puertorriqueño activists Francisco Gonzálo "Pachín" Marín Shaw

(discussed by Laura Lomas) and Sotero Figueroa and Arturo Schomburg (discussed by Nicolás Kanellos)—belonged to the social class of
"creoles" (*criollos*), the American-born descendants of European conquerors or immigrants. Although in the sociopolitical order of the
Spanish American viceroyalties creoles were frequently discriminated
against in the allocation of imperial offices, the colonial *casta* system
made no distinction between American-born and European-born *españoles*. Regardless of the place of birth, the social prestige, wealth, and
power of the caste of *españoles* were largely based on the exploitation of
the labor and land of socially abject *indios* who had been turned into
neo-feudal peasants in the colonial *encomienda* system, which conferred
on the Euro American subject the right to the tribute and labor of an
allotted number of Indians. By the nineteenth century, this system had
been replaced by the *hacienda*, the great plantation estates that were now
privately held by the creoles and on which the Indians were obliged to
work—now no longer by imperial law but rather by economic necessity,
after having lost most of the fertile lands to the *haciendas* or *fincas*. In
the Spanish Caribbean, where the Indian *encomienda* had collapsed as
a result of the demographic catastrophe resulting from disease and conquest, the rise of a plantocracy had depended mainly on African slave
labor as early as the sixteenth century.

The interconnections between African slavery, the politics of its abolition, and national independence therefore loomed largest in those regions of Latin America, such as Cuba and Brazil, which depended most
heavily on African slave labor, rather than on that of Indian peasants.
In those Latin American territories that had gained political independence by the third decade of the nineteenth century, slavery never had
the same economic significance as it had had in the Caribbean, Brazil, or
the South of the United States, as Indians in *encomienda* had not legally
been slaves. Nevertheless, throughout colonial Latin America a sort
of neo-feudal aristocracy had formed that disproportionally benefited
from a (neo-) colonial economy and social hierarchy that circumscribed
the evolution of the sort of "liberal" revolutionary ideologies facilitated
by the Native American holocaust in the northern and western areas
of the nineteenth-century United States. The aristocratic pretentions of
the creole elite were frequently mocked by the Old World aristocracy,
for their class included many family lineages of humble background in

Europe who had been able to elevate their social status in the colonial order of the viceregal Americas.

But despite these important historical variations, the distinction that the title of María Amparo Ruiz de Burton's novel *The Squatter and the Don* (1885) initially appears to draw between legitimate Spanish American "dons" and illegitimate Anglo American "squatters" obscures an uncanny historical resemblance between the descendants of two groups of Euro American conquerors whose economic privilege had similarly been founded on stolen Native American land and whose social privilege in the colonial order had been rationalized by a new conception of "race"—not in its traditional (Old World) sense of noble family lineage or pedigree but rather in the modern (New World) sense of belonging to a certain phenotype, namely that of being "white." Although this modern idea of race did not fully form in Latin America until the nineteenth century, the fiction of a Euro American aristocracy (Latin American "dons" and U.S. southern aristocrats) pretending to hold legitimate title to American land has a long tradition in colonial American writing. There, it reaches back perhaps as far as the letters of Hernando Cortés to Charles V in the 1520s, in which the Spanish conqueror attempted to argue that the Spaniards, not the Mexica elite, were the legitimate and "natural" lords of Mexico, the fulfillers of ancient American prophecies and national destinies. If, as Marissa López shows, Ruiz de Burton's novel ultimately resolves the conflict between Latino aristocrats and gringo squatters with which it begins by imagining a "western" or "local" solidarity in opposition to the railroad tycoons and tyrannical Federal policies, Ruiz de Burton builds on (and synthesizes) long colonial literary and political traditions of local creole patriotism in both colonial Latin and British American writing, in which the "first" conquerors register their indignation about and resistance against the alleged injustices of the "second" conquest by the advancing imperial state.

Keeping in mind this sociopolitical background of many of the authors and actors who appear in this volume helps shed light on the ambiguity of their subject-positions, as they transform from (neo-) colonial Latin American *criollos* to become U.S. American Latinos. Thus, Juan Poblete argues (following Ericka Beckman) that the Chilean Forty-Niner Vicente Pérez Rosales, in his *Diario de un viaje a California* and *Recuerdos del Pasado*, engages in the "creolization of imperial reason" by actively participating in the "implementation of an immigration policy that was generous and proactive towards European white immigrants at the same time that it was racist and ethnocentric against natives and mestizos." Indeed, his strategy of countering the Anglo racism he faced in California is in part predicated on a particular kind of historical vision that would still inspire hemispheric American historiography in the early twentieth century, most prominently represented by that of Herbert Eugene Bolton—the idea that the history of the Americas can be understood in terms of a parallel or analogous scheme of progress resulting from the European conquest and (post-) colonial presence. Thus, Poblete argues, Pérez Rosales's narrative combines "strong support for the beneficial aspects of immigration on the development of the nation, a clear view of the need to eliminate or subjugate Native Americans, as well as critiques of the blatant and, in Pérez Rosales['s] view, mistaken racialization of and violence against those immigrants." While his perspective is in part inflected by his immigrant and minority experience, Poblete argues, "it is also a nineteenth-century white national immigrant view" that celebrates the "salutary effects of white European foreign immigration in the Americas."

Indeed, the antipodal and exceptionalist New World logic of Pérez Rosales's hemispheric vision—Chile is South America's "California" and vice-versa—has a long history of entanglement with proto-racist explanations of the origins of Americas' indigenous populations rationalizing enslavement, exploitation, and genocide, reaching back to Amerigo Vespucci's pronouncement, in the early sixteenth century, that America was a "New World," unknown by the Ancients and never mentioned in the Book of Genesis. If the logical conclusion—hinted at here and there already in the sixteenth century—was that of polygenesis, its heretical implications had prevented it from finding overt scientific support throughout the early modern period. However, once religion lost its grip on science during the nineteenth century, polygenesis prominently reared its ugly head in nineteenth-century anthropology, providing the ideology of white settler colonialism and creole nationalism with a scientific underwriting throughout the Americas. Thus, creoles throughout the Americas argued that "progress" had been encumbered not by the natural environment—as eighteenth-century French and German philosophers had argued—but rather by the sloth and inferiority of its indigenous races.

But despite Pérez Rosales's attempt to place European settler colonialism in a hemispheric perspective, his Latino subjectivity formed partially, Poblete also shows, in response to Anglo prejudice, injustice, and even racism against non-Anglo immigrants and especially again immigrants from Latin America. Thus, Poblete underscores the solidarity that formed during the California Gold Rush between Latino native-born Californios and Latin American, especially Mexican, immigrants in the face of Anglo racism. Similarly, John Alba Cutler suggests that while Latin American identities are largely constructed along lines of national divisions that would militate against any sort of common identity (drawing distinctions, for example, between what it means to be Mexican, Chilean, or Argentine), a Latino identity as it emerged in the nineteenth-century United States is predicated on "communities, unrestricted by particular nationalities," communities united by the common idiom of the Spanish language and by being the common target of Anglo American racism, which made no distinctions of national origin.

Thus, in the context of the nineteenth-century United States, the category of the Latino emerged as a fifth racial category that had never appeared in any of the neoclassical eighteenth-century racial taxonomies and theories of Carl Linnaeus, Johann Friedrich Blumenbach, and others postulating the existence of four races (black, white, yellow, red). Late-nineteenth-century Latinos such as José Martí were acutely aware of this emergent racial formation, as Laura Lomas shows in her chapter. While some of the early Latin American creole revolutionaries had courted the support of the various racialized *castas* for their political and military cause, many—having themselves been slavemasters—also "explicitly or implicitly excluded or devalued the racialized working masses." In the context of the nineteenth-century United States, however, even socially privileged "white" Latinos such as Martí, who found themselves to be the objects of Anglo racism against all Latinos (regardless of skin color), came to an acutely critical understanding of the racial logic that had undergirded socioeconomic relations throughout the Americas. In a process that Lomas calls (borrowing from Yolanda Martínez San Miguel) "metropolitan racialization," some U.S. Latinos of various races "came to realize that their linguistic difference and national origin excluded them from white privilege" and therefore formed multiracial alliances (in Martí's case with Afro-Puertorriqueño Francisco Gonzálo "Pachín" Marín Shaw and Afro-Tejana anarchist leader Lucy Eldine González Parsons). In the process, they utterly "transformed the politics of *latinidad*."

The fact that racial prejudices against Latinos are often ventriloquized by non-Anglo subjects—as they are in Alba Cutler's example of Carlos Galán's *costumbrista* short fiction by "white" Irish immigrants (rather than Anglo Americans)—underscores that the notion of a Latino formed in the United States not in isolation from a broader transnational context that saw the rise of the ideas not only of "Latin America" but also of a Global South as geocultural entities. This formation of a fifth ethnic and racial category distinctive to the United States takes place in the context of a larger shift during the nineteenth century from a hemispheric discourse of European settler colonialism in the Americas predicated on a spatial "east–west" network of colonial exploitation in *both* Latin and Anglo America since the sixteenth century to a hemispheric discourse predicated on a global "north–south" network of neocolonial power relationships.

The third salient aspect of Latin subjectivity emphasized by the chapters in this collection is its trans-American dimension, as subjects move and act across national borders and defy being classified as either Latin American or U.S. American (and hereby, of course, the presumption that U.S. American equals Anglo American). On the one hand, the vast majority of Latinos such as Ruiz de Burton "entered" the United States with the Treaty of Guadalupe Hidalgo (1849), which ended the U.S.–Mexico War and formalized the annexation by the United States of vast territories and populations formerly belonging to Mexico. On the other hand, the volume also highlights the importance of "hemispheric mobilities." Thus, many Latinos entered the United States "errantly" (as Kirsten Silva Gruesz puts it)—as travelers, migrants, and exiles—in the context and aftermath of the Latin American independence movements, which would open up opportunities to citizens of the newly independent Latin American nation-states for travel across the old imperial lines or even obliged many Latin American revolutionaries from not yet independent Spanish imperial territories (such as Cuba) to take up refuge in the United States. Thus, U.S. cities and locations such as Philadelphia, Key West, and Tampa became "peripheral centers" (as Emily García writes) in the Latin American independence movements.

A fascinating case in point is that of the Cavada brothers, discussed by Jesse Alemán in his contribution. Living in Pennsylvania, the Cavadas joined the Union Army in the American Civil War before returning to their native Cuba to fight for independence in the Ten Years War. Significantly, the Cavada brothers saw Cuba's struggle for independence as an analogue not to the Confederacy's secession but rather to the American Revolution, especially with regard to the all-important issue of slavery. Unlike the Confederacy's secession, the Cuban bid for independence was not fought to protect the Peculiar Institution. At the same time, like patriots of the American Revolution, the champions of the Ten Years War in Cuba could not afford to alienate the powerful interests invested in slavery—in the Cuban case, the powerful interests of the sugar planters on the western parts of the island. It was, like the American Revolution, a pragmatic compromise between the emancipatory ideals of the Enlightenment and its darker side of economic liberalism as it had emerged since the seventeenth century in the Atlantic world—the "liberty" to hold humans as property.

Frederic Cavada's "touristic" account of Cuba's Bellamar Cave in *Harper's New Monthly Magazine* invites a comparison with another nineteenth-century account of Cuba's sublime subterranean world—in Gertrudis Gómez de Avellaneda y Arteaga's description of the Caverns of Cubitas in her novel *Sab* (1841). But while Gómez de Avellaneda y Arteaga similarly extolls Cuba's sublime nature as an emblem of impassioned (Latin American) creole patriotism, her female personification of the Cuban nation, Carlotta, is seduced by the villainous gringo Enrique Otway, while her true and heroic lover, the black slave Sab, is driven to his death. Gómez de Avellaneda's novel foreshadows both José Martí's vision of an oppositional relationship between "Our" (Latin) America and the "Other" (U.S.) America, a hemispheric opposition that would find numerous iterations in Latin America during the twentieth century, such as José Enrique Rodó's seminal essay *Ariel* (1900), which distinguished the "aristocratic" ("Arielesque") spirit of Latin America from Anglo America's "Calibanesque" spirit of crass capitalism, liberalism, materialism, and pragmatism. But unlike

Rodó, Martí, or Gómez de Avellandeda y Arteaga, whose articulation of a "Latin American" identity was shaped by an engagement with the emergent North American giant, Cavada's "trans-American" Latino subjectivity bridges U.S. and Latin America: "both Americas are his," and he has a "voice in both worlds." Thus, Alemán concludes, the Cavada brothers must properly be considered as trans-American hemispheric subjects who complicate José Martí's famous distinction between "Our [i.e., Latin] America" and that America (i.e., the United States) "which is not ours." This trans-American hemispheric subjectivity is key to understanding Latino political activism in the nineteenth century, as Gerald Poyo shows in his discussion of how the Cuban exile community in Key West deftly imprinted its political weight through ethnic activism onto the Florida political landscape with a trans-American perspective that advanced Cuban independence. But it inflects not only political activism but also literary form, as John Alba Cutler shows in his discussion of Carlos F. Galán's California *costumbrismo* short fiction. While the *modernismo* short story developed in Latin America, under the sway of intellectuals such as Martí and Rodó, with "an attitude of resistance toward the encroachments of U.S. imperialism and the crassness of U.S. materialism," Galán's sketches reject the bifurcation of our/other America and instead "anticipate modern Latino/a communities, unrestricted by particular nationalities."

As a whole, *The Latino Nineteenth Century* thus challenges several conventional assumptions about "Latino" literature, nineteenth-century "American" literature, and Latin American studies. As such, perhaps the most prominent theme that emerges from this collection is the multiplicity of Latino writing in the nineteenth century—a "multiplicity of the uncommon," as Lazo aptly writes in his Introduction. On the one hand, many of the writers discussed here find themselves in a subject-position distinct from that of many of their Anglo (American) counterparts with regard to the dominance of Protestant liberalism in the Anglo American literary tradition, the rise of U.S. imperialism in the nineteenth century, and transforming nineteenth-century ideas about race and attitudes toward racial mixture. On the other hand, many of the Latino writers we encounter here share with their Anglo American contemporaries the ambiguities of creole patriotism, its colonial past, and its postcolonial legacies. While one of the effects of U.S. imperialism in the nineteenth century seems overall to have been an "inward" turn toward the national—disavowing the cosmopolitanism of many of the eighteenth- and early-nineteenth-century writers such as Thomas Jefferson or Alexander von Humboldt—this collection shows that many nineteenth-century Latino writers remained thoroughly committed to a transnational (and especially "trans-American") perspective. And while many prominent nineteenth-century Latin American intellectuals—from Andrés Bello to José Enrique Rodó—turned toward Europe in order to counter the increasingly dominant hegemony of the United States in the hemisphere, this collection powerfully demonstrates how Latino writers of the nineteenth century bridged the gulf between "Our" American and the "Other" America. Hemispheric subjects, their America was both.

ABOUT THE CONTRIBUTORS

Jesse Alemán is Professor of English at the University of New Mexico, where he teaches courses on the American gothic, southwestern literature and film, and theories of the novel. He has published more than a dozen articles on nineteenth-century American literature and Latino/a literary histories. He edited Loreta Janeta Velazquez's 1876 autobiography *The Woman in Battle* (2003) and is co-editor of *Empire and the Literature of Sensation* (2007). Alemán has won numerous teaching awards at New Mexico and is working on a book titled *Wars of Rebellion*, which considers Hispanic writing about the U.S. Civil War in relation to contemporaneous civil wars in Cuba and Mexico.

José Aranda is Professor of Chicano/a and American Literature at Rice University and author of numerous articles on early U.S. criticism, nineteenth-century Mexican American literature, and the future of Chicano/a studies. Aranda is the author of *When We Arrive: A New Literary History of Mexican America* (2003). He is also co-editor of *Recovering the U.S. Hispanic Literary Heritage Project*, Vol. IV (2002). Aranda is working on a book titled *The Places of Modernity in Mexican American Literature, 1848–1960*.

Ralph Bauer is Associate Professor of English and Comparative Literature at the University of Maryland, College Park, where he teaches courses on the literatures of the Americas, including Anglo, Spanish, and Native American literatures. His publications include *The Cultural Geography of Colonial American Literatures: Empire, Travel, Modernity* (2003); *An Inca Account of the Conquest of Peru* (2005); and (co-edited with José Antonio Mazzotti) *Creole Subjects in the Colonial Americas: Empires, Texts, Identities* (2009). He is currently completing a monograph titled *The Alchemy of Conquest: Prophecy, Discovery, and the Secrets of the New World*.

Carrie Tirado Bramen is the author of *The Uses of Variety: Modern Americanism and the Quest for National Distinctiveness* (2000), which was co-winner of the Thomas J. Wilson Prize by the Board of Syndics at Harvard University Press for best first book. She has published on a range of topics, including essays on Leslie Fiedler, Henry James, and Gayl Jones. She is currently completing a book entitled *American Niceness: A Cultural History*.

Raúl Coronado is Associate Professor of Ethnic Studies at the University of California, Berkeley. His book *A World Not to Come: A History of Latino Writing and Print Culture* (2013) has received nine prizes, including the 2013 Modern Language Association Prize for best first book, the 2014 American Studies Association Prize for best book in American studies, the 2015 National Association for Chicana/o Studies best book prize, and the 2014 Texas State Historical Association Prize for historical research. His other publications include translations and contributions to the *Heath Anthology of American Literature*, short stories, and essays in queer and feminist studies, literary history, and Marxist cultural studies.

John Alba Cutler is Associate Professor of English and Latina/o Studies at Northwestern University. He is the author of *Ends of Assimilation: The Formation of Chicano Literature* (2015) as well as of many essays on Latina/o literature and culture.

Emily García is Associate Professor of English and Coordinator of Latina/o and Latin American Studies at Northeastern Illinois University in Chicago, where she teaches courses in American literature, Latina/o studies, and women's and gender studies. She has published in *Literature in the Early American Republic* and the forthcoming *Cambridge History of Latin@ Literature*, among other venues. Her current book project "*Novel Diplomacies: Literary and Cultural Interdependence Across the Americas*" examines writing by Latin American and U.S. authors in the eighteenth and nineteenth centuries.

Kirsten Silva Gruesz is Professor of Literature at the University of California, Santa Cruz, where she teaches the comparative literatures of the

Americas, especially Latino/a writing in historical perspective. She is the author of *Ambassadors of Culture: The Transamerican Origins of Latino Writing* (2002) and more than two dozen essays. Her forthcoming book *Cotton Mather's Spanish Lessons: Language, Race, and American Memory* locates contemporary debates about language politics in the deep context of colonialism in the hemisphere.

Robert McKee Irwin is Chair of the Graduate Group in Cultural Studies and Professor in the Department of Spanish and Portuguese at the University of California, Davis. He is co–principal investigator of UC Davis's Mellon Initiative in Comparative Border Studies (http://borderstudies.ucdavis.edu/) and directs the Sexualidades Campesinas digital storytelling project (http://sexualidadescampesinas.ucdavis.edu/en/about-the-project/).

Nicolás Kanellos is Brown Foundation Professor of Hispanic Studies at the University of Houston and Director of Arte Público Press and the Recovering the U.S. Hispanic Literary Heritage Project. The founding publisher of the literary journal *The Americas Review*, Kanellos is the principal editor of *Herencia: The Anthology of Hispanic Literature of the United States.* His books include the award-winning *History of Hispanic Theater in the United States, Origins to 1940* (1990) and *Hispanic Immigrant Literature: El sueño del retorno* (2011), which won the PEN Southwest Award for nonfiction. His distinctions include an American Book Award in the publisher/editor category and a Hispanic Heritage Award for Literature presented by the White House.

Carmen E. Lamas is Assistant Professor of English and American Studies at the University of Virginia. She has published numerous articles on Cuban culture and nineteenth-century Latina/o literature. Lamas is working on a book titled *Latina/o Continuum: Rethinking American and Latin American Studies."*

Rodrigo Lazo is Associate Professor of English and an affiliate of the Chicano/Latino Studies Department at the University of California, Irvine, where he is Director of the Humanities Core, an interdisciplinary year-long course for first-year students. He is author of *Writing to Cuba:*

Filibustering and Cuban Exiles in the United States (2005) and more than a dozen articles on nineteenth-century U.S. literature, hemispheric studies, Herman Melville, and archive theory. He is working on a book titled *Letters from Filadelfia*.

Laura Lomas teaches Latina/o and U.S. literature in the English Department at Rutgers University–Newark, where she is affiliated with the Graduate Program in American Studies and Women's and Gender Studies. Her book *Translating Empire: José Martí, Migrant Latino Subjects and American Modernities* (2008) won the MLA Prize for Latina/o and Chicana/o literature and an honorable mention from LASA's Latina/o Section. Co-editor of the forthcoming *Cambridge History of Latin@ Literature*, Lomas is working on a new book titled *In-Between States: Lourdes Casal and the Poetics of the New York Borderlands*. She co-directs the Latin@ Studies Working Group at Rutgers University–Newark.

Marissa K. López is Associate Professor of English at the University of California, Los Angeles. She is author of *Chicano Nations: The Hemispheric Origins of Mexican American Literature* (NYU Press, 2011). López has published articles on Ana Castillo, Alurista, early Chicano historiography, and pedagogy, among other topics. Her research interests include literature and visual culture of the West, particularly California.

Juan Poblete is Professor of Latin/o American Literature and Cultural Studies at the University of California, Santa Cruz. He is author of *Literatura chilena del siglo XIX: entre públicos lectores y figuras autoriales* (2003) and editor of *Critical Latin American and Latino Studies* (2003). Among books he has co-edited are *Redrawing the Nation: National Identities in Latin/o American Comics* (with Héctor Fernández-L'Hoeste, 2009); *Desdén al infortunio: Sujeto,comunicación y público en la narrativa de Pedro Lemebel* (with Fernando Blanco, Santiago, 2010); and *Sports and Nationalism in Latin America* (with Héctor Fernández L'Hoeste and Robert McKee Irwin, 2015). Poblete is at work on a book titled *Angel Rama y la Critica Cultural Latinoamericana*.

Gerald E. Poyo is Professor and Chair of the History Department at St. Mary's University, San Antonio, Texas. His research has focused on U.S.

Latino history, especially Cuban exile communities in the United States. He is the author and editor of six books, including *"With All, and for the Good of All": The Emergence of Popular Nationalism in the Cuban Communities of the United States, 1848–1898* (1989); *Cuban Catholics in the United States, 1960–1988: Exile and Integration* (2007); and *Exile and Revolution: Jose D. Poyo, Key West, and Cuban Independence* (2014).

Alberto Varon is Assistant Professor of English and Latino Studies at Indiana University, Bloomington, where he is also affiliated with the departments of American Studies and of Gender Studies. He teaches in American literature of the late nineteenth and early twentieth centuries and in Latina/o literatures and cultures. He is currently at work on a book that examines the intersection of gender and citizenship in U.S. Latino cultural life before the Chicano movement.

INDEX